Civil Forfeiture of Criminal Property

Civil Forfeiture of Criminal Property

Legal Measures for Targeting the Proceeds of Crime

Edited by

Simon N.M. Young

Associate Professor and Director, Centre for Comparative and Public Law, Faculty of Law, University of Hong Kong

Edward Elgar

Cheltenham, UK • Northampton, MA, USA

Published by
Edward Elgar Publishing Limited
The Lypiatts
15 Lansdown Road
Cheltenham
Glos GL50 2JA
UK

Edward Elgar Publishing, Inc.
William Pratt House
9 Dewey Court
Northampton
Massachusetts 01060
USA

A catalogue record for this book
is available from the British Library

Library of Congress Control Number: 2008939749

PEFC
PEFC/16-33-111
CATG-PEFC-052
www.pefc.org

ISBN 978 1 84720 826 2

Typeset by Cambrian Typesetters, Camberley, Surrey
Printed and bound in Great Britain by MPG Books Ltd, Bodmin, Cornwall

Contents

PART III FORFEITURE OF CRIMINAL PROPERTY IN CHINESE SOCIETIES: PROSPECTS FOR MODERN FORFEITURE LAWS

Contributors

Stefan D. Cassella is the former Deputy Chief for Legal Policy of the Asset Forfeiture and Money Laundering Section of the United States Department of Justice, and is now a Special Assistant United States Attorney in the Eastern District of Virginia. He is an instructor at the National Advocacy Center at the University of South Carolina – the training facility for all federal prosecutors in the United States – and the author of the treatise, *Asset Forfeiture Law in the United States*.

Sara Dayman is a partner in BDO Stoy Hayward LLP. For over 15 years she has been involved in asset forfeiture, being appointed as court receiver in the majority of the leading UK cases. She has assisted the United Nations, Commonwealth Secretariat and the US Department of Justice in the provision of training to overseas governments.

Kate Egan is a member of the Irish bar and former Senior Research Assistant in the Centre for Comparative and Public Law, Faculty of Law, University of Hong Kong.

Jorge A.F. Godinho is Assistant Professor in the Faculty of Law of the University of Macau. He is a graduate of the Faculty of Law of the University of Lisbon and has obtained a LLM degree in the University of Macau and a PhD in the European University Institute, Florence. He previously worked as a legal adviser in the Monetary Authority of Macau and as a lawyer.

Sylvia Grono is Senior Assistant Director in the Brisbane office of the Commonwealth Director of Public Prosecutions, Australia.

Raylene Keightley is Director of the Centre for Applied Legal Studies at the University of the Witwatersrand in Johannesburg, South Africa. She is also an advocate and a practising member of the Johannesburg Bar. She was previously Regional Head of the Asset Forfeiture Unit in Johannesburg.

Kung Shun Fong is currently a trainee solicitor at Simmons & Simmons, a BCL graduate of Oxford University, a graduate of the Faculty of Law, University of Hong Kong and was formerly a research assistant in the Centre for Comparative and Public Law.

Lawrence L.C. Lee is Associate Professor and Director, Department of Financial and Economic Law, Asia University; S.J.D., Wisconsin University School of Law. Lawrence is an international editor of an international financial crime journal. He worked as a research fellow at Columbia University from 1998 to 2000 and was a visiting scholar at New York University School of Law from 2001 to 2004 and from 2007 to 2008.

Angela V.M. Leong is a Consultant to the European Commission AGIS Programme; an Associate Research Fellow at the Institute of Advanced Legal Studies, University of London; a Member of the Executive Editorial Board of *The Company Lawyer*; and an Associate Fellow of the Centre for Criminology at the University of Hong Kong. Prior to her current post, she worked in the Operations Division of the Assets Recovery Agency and was an Accredited Financial Investigator in the UK.

James McKeachie is Senior Counsel in the Civil Remedies for Illicit Activities Office, Ministry of the Attorney General, Toronto, Ontario, Canada.

Felix J. McKenna served as Chief Bureau Officer of the Criminal Assets Bureau in Ireland until his retirement in 2006.

Jeffrey Simser is the Legal Director of the Civil Remedies for Illicit Activities Office, Ministry of the Attorney General, Toronto, Ontario, Canada.

Xing Fei is an Asociate Human Rights Officer at the United Nations Office of the High Commissioner for Human Rights and was formerly Assistant Research Officer in the Centre for Comparative and Public Law, Faculty of Law, University of Hong Kong.

Simon N.M. Young is Associate Professor and Director of the Centre for Comparative and Public Law in the Faculty of Law, University of Hong Kong. He is also a member of the Hong Kong and Ontario (Canada) bar.

Preface

In 2000 when I was still working for the Ontario government I witnessed the political process of how civil forfeiture laws were proposed, deliberated upon, marketed to the public and introduced into the provincial legislature. It was a cornerstone of the then Conservative government's get tough on crime platform. The government's political resolve to pass the law notwithstanding real constitutional concerns over provincial authority to enact such a law was impressive. The proposed law was also controversial from a rights perspective and a lively public debate both inside and outside the legislature ensued.

When I left Canada for Hong Kong in 2001, about a year before the Ontario law was passed, I was hoping to find a similar debate in this new jurisdiction. Not only was such a debate non-existent but many had not heard of civil forfeiture. Over the next few years the introduction of civil forfeiture in the United Kingdom and Australia did little to stimulate public discussion of the topic in Hong Kong. Thus in 2005–2006, I applied for and was successful in obtaining a research grant to study the topic in a new government initiative to promote better public policy research. This was an opportunity not only to research what would be best for Hong Kong (in terms of both the need and manner of reform) but also to stimulate interest and discussion in the community.

The project, which became known as the Hong Kong Civil Forfeiture Project, was housed in the Centre for Comparative and Public Law (CCPL) in the Faculty of Law, University of Hong Kong. The project invited leading practitioner experts from Ireland, Canada, Australia, New Zealand, United Kingdom, Macau and Taiwan to visit CCPL in 2006. Each expert spoke in a public seminar and also in a private meeting where they engaged with a specially established local focus group of experts. The aim of the private meetings was for key local stakeholders to gain a full and candid understanding of not only the laws and practices in the foreign jurisdiction but also in the international expert's estimation of how well those processes worked in practice. The papers presented by the experts were revised after the visit and all except one have become chapters in this book. As explained in the Introduction, the paper on New Zealand could not be finalized before the manuscript deadline due to uncertainties in the legislative progress of their civil forfeiture bill. With the assistance of Jeffrey Simser, for which we are most grateful, we were fortunate to obtain chapter contributions from leading experts from the United States and South Africa, two very important civil forfeiture jurisdictions.

I need to thank a number of people who contributed to both the project and the book. First, there are the international experts and members of the local focus group. Secondly, there are the CCPL researchers and staff who provided invaluable research and other assistance. Thanks to Jennifer Stone, Cheng Yulin, Kung Shun Fong, Kate Egan, Xing Fei, Jonathan Ah-weng and Flora Leung. Finally, I thank my family for their patience during the time I had to spend away from them.

I hope this book will help to stimulate more international debate and study on the global proliferation of civil asset forfeiture systems.

Simon N.M. Young
University of Hong Kong
August 2008

Acknowledgements

The project that made this book possible was fully supported by a grant from the Central Policy Unit of the Government of the Hong Kong Special Administrative Region and the Research Grants Council of the Hong Kong Special Administrative Region, China (Project No. HKU 7023-PPR-20051).

Some of the writing in Chapters 2 and 3 was based on previously published works which are duly acknowledged below:

Stefan D. Cassella (2006), *Asset Forfeiture Law in the United States*, Huntington, NY, US: Juris Publishing, chapters 1 and 2.

Stefan D. Cassella (2003), 'The Development of Asset Forfeiture Law in the United States', *Acta Juridica* (University of Cape Town, South Africa) 314.

Stefan D. Cassella (2004), 'Overview of Asset Forfeiture Law in the United States', *South African J. Crim. Justice*, **17**, 347.

Fachtna Murphy and Barry Galvin, 'Targeting the financial wealth of criminals in Ireland: the law and practice' in J. P. McCutcheon and D. Walsh (eds) (1999), *The Confiscation of Criminal Assets: Law and Procedure*, Dublin, Ireland: Round Hall Sweet & Maxwell, pp. 9–35.

Cases

Hong Kong

European Court of Human Rights

Legislation

Introduction

Simon N.M. Young

The expression 'civil forfeiture of criminal property' can evoke a number of different responses. First there is the common response of 'what the hell is it?'. This is sometimes followed by the question, 'does it have something to do with terrorism?'. It is not easy to answer the first question simply, and as for the second question civil forfeiture includes and goes beyond the forfeiture of property used to finance terrorism. Most countries which now have a regime of civil forfeiture had either adopted or decided to adopt the regime well before the tragic events of 11 September 2001. These regimes are a response to domestic and international organized crime generally. They primarily target the profits and proceeds of serious and organized criminal activities as a means to eliminate such activities.

The aged and wise may wonder why we are still discussing forfeiture of property when 'it was abolished many years ago and is no longer legitimate'. While it is true that common law jurisdictions abolished the old punishment of general forfeiture for committing treason or a felony, this does not mean that modern forfeiture laws are illegitimate.[1] General forfeiture which deprived a traitor or felon of all of his personal property (and sometimes his real property as well) was clearly disproportionate punishment on the offender and his family members. Such punishment also denied victims the opportunity to obtain money damages from the wrongdoer. General forfeiture in today's world is also inconsistent with the goals of rehabilitating offenders and reintegrating them back into society.

Modern forfeiture laws are concerned not so much with punishing individuals for their past wrongs but with achieving specific criminal justice objectives including disgorging offenders of their ill-gotten gains, disabling the financial capacity of criminal organizations, and compensating victims of crime. These laws respond to the increasing sophistication of profit-motivated crime that transcends borders and uses every innovative means to

---

[1] See Forfeitures for Treason and Felony Act 1870 (UK); Criminal Law Act (Northern Ireland) 1967, s. 7(7); Criminal Procedure Ordinance (Cap. 221), s. 69 (HK). See generally Arie Freiberg and Richard Fox (2000), 'Fighting Crime with Forfeiture: Lessons from History', *Australian Journal of Legal History*, **6**, 1.

obfuscate the trail of criminal income. In modern societies such laws will typically have procedural and substantive safeguards that protect due process interests and legitimate property rights of individuals.

A common law lawyer may wonder whether the 'civil' in 'civil forfeiture' refers to the civil law legal system that exists in continental Europe and other places. The answer is no. As Jorge Godinho remarks in Chapter 11, civil forfeiture is 'so unfamiliar to lawyers trained in the civil law tradition that most probably have never heard of it'. Modern civil forfeiture originated in the United States in the 1970s and 1980s and has since proliferated in predominantly common law jurisdictions. Québec, a civil law jurisdiction within Canada, is undergoing an interesting experiment. As Ontario lawyers, James McKeachie and Jeffrey Simser, observe in Chapter 6, Québec's 2007 law 'attempts to wed common law ideas somewhat anchored in admiralty concepts to a different civil system'.

The lack of universality of civil forfeiture explains the ambivalence of international treaties on drug trafficking, organized crime and corruption in mandating civil forfeiture of criminal property.[2] While these treaties impose obligations on states parties to have laws that allow for the restraint and confiscation of proceeds of crime and other criminal property, they stop short of specifying what form such laws should take. Parties are left a margin of discretion to determine whether they wish to implement such obligations within their existing criminal justice system or by other means including the adoption of a civil forfeiture regime.

If 'civil' refers to the distinction between civil and criminal law, the common law lawyer may still remark that civil forfeiture is rather a strange animal when compared to a typical civil lawsuit as between private persons. The hallmark of civil forfeiture is its *in rem* character at all stages of the process, from application to enforcement. It is also a branch of public law because invariably it is the state seeking to have private property forfeited pursuant to legislation with high public policy content. The proceeding is brought against property and not property owners. While notice is usually given to persons with an interest in the targeted property, a significant amount of civil forfeiture proceeds uncontested, either because no one has come forward to contest the government's claim or a settlement has been reached with all the relevant parties.[3]

---

[2]   See the development of this point in Chapters 11 and 10 of this book.

[3]   Stefan Cassella notes in Chapter 2 that about 80% of the United States forfeiture cases in drug matters are uncontested and resolved by way of administrative forfeiture. Federal prosecutors follow a policy that civil forfeiture settlements are not to be made for the purpose of obtaining an advantage in a criminal case. Prosecutors should not agree to release forfeitable property to coerce a guilty plea or agree to dismiss

Criminal lawyers may not be any more familiar with civil forfeiture than civil practitioners. While civil forfeiture bears a resemblance to its sibling, criminal forfeiture, it instinctively resists any attempt to classify it as general criminal law or procedure. When countries began enacting modern forfeiture laws, it was generally done first within the confines of the criminal justice system. Forfeiture was part of a sentence which a convicted person received. Forfeiture could be *in rem*, against the offender's property, or *in personam*, in the form of a confiscation or penalty order, or a combination of both to most effectively make the offender account for all of his ill-gotten gains.

The experience of criminal forfeiture in many jurisdictions revealed its inherent limitations to achieving its objectives. The sentencing process was an unsatisfactory forum to confiscate *all* of the proceeds that may have been generated from the commission of the offence. Achieving such an outcome would usually require that a person of sufficiently high rank in the criminal organization be convicted of a scheduled offence and sufficient evidence be adduced to connect the property to the offender or the offences for which he was convicted. Adding a financial dimension to already complex criminal investigations and prosecutions was an added burden to law enforcement and prosecutorial agencies. A new breed of financial investigators and asset forfeiture prosecutors had to be cultivated and trained, a process which was bound to be slow at the beginning and impeded unless sufficient resources were dedicated to this new dimension of law enforcement.

Civil forfeiture emerges in response to the shortcomings of the criminal forfeiture model. It is the second generation of modern forfeiture laws. The *in rem* character of civil forfeiture which avoids the need to prove a person's guilt beyond a reasonable doubt has obvious appeal to policy makers. Some countries such as Ireland and South Africa were driven to enact civil forfeiture laws given the very visible face of organized crime in those societies at the time. Other jurisdictions such as the United Kingdom, Commonwealth Australia and Canada adopted a civil forfeiture regime after a careful review of domestic laws and processes and a consideration of overseas experience. But even where there is a political will to adopt civil forfeiture, the process of enactment is not always easy or expeditious. A case in point is New Zealand where in March 2004 the Minister of Justice was given the green light by Cabinet to develop a detailed policy proposal to introduce civil forfeiture. The first bill was tabled in June 2005, but did not receive a first reading that year as the result of pressure on House time before a general election. A replacement bill was introduced and read for the first time in

---

charges to coerce a forfeiture settlement. See The US Department of Justice, *United States Attorneys' Manual*, paras 9–113.100 and 9–113.106, March 2001.

March 2007, but as of August 2008 had only passed a review by a parliamentary select committee.[4]

Inevitably the question is asked whether civil forfeiture is really 'criminal forfeiture dressed up in sheep's clothing'? A common criticism is that civil forfeiture achieves the same objectives as criminal forfeiture but without the procedural safeguards and human rights protections that apply to criminal proceedings. International human rights treaties and constitutional bills of rights do not often provide a clear indication of what procedural and substantive norms should apply to civil forfeiture. These instruments bifurcate the world of adjudication into criminal and non-criminal proceedings, with the former given superior rights protections and the latter only minimal ones. In this bifurcated world, civil forfeiture sits well in neither of the two realms. Strained arguments to bring civil forfeiture within the criminal realm have been made in courts around the world but have generally failed.

Civil forfeiture has managed to survive human rights challenges mostly because of the foresight of policy makers and legislators who included an abundance of discretion in the laws to enable courts to do justice in individual cases. A good example of this is in several of the Canadian provincial laws that provided a power in the court to refuse to order forfeiture if it was not in the 'interests of justice'.[5] Courts have also had to step in to ensure that human rights principles guide the application of the law. For example, as Raylene Keightley notes in Chapter 4, South African courts have adopted a proportionality analysis to the forfeiture of instruments of crime, although the judges there have not always agreed on how the safeguard should be applied. In Australia, where there is no constitutional bill of rights, it was held that by virtue of statutory implication and common law principles derivative use of information obtained by an examination order under the Proceeds of Crime Act 2002 was not allowed.[6] Similarly, in Ireland and Hong Kong, courts have insisted that discovery processes and production orders be limited by undertakings or conditions that protect an individual's right of silence.[7] In addition

---

[4]   See the Criminal Proceeds (Recovery) Bill, No. 81-1. New Zealand was originally meant to be covered in a chapter in this book but unfortunately due to uncertainties about aspects of the proposed recovery scheme in the bill it could not be included.

[5]   For more details, see Chapter 6 of this book and particularly the laws in Ontario, Nova Scotia, Manitoba, Saskatchewan and British Columbia. A similar safeguard appears in the laws of Ireland, and in Australia courts retain the power to stay proceedings if it is in the interests of justice; see Chapters 3 and 5 respectively in this book.

[6]   See *DPP (Cth) v. Hatfield* [2006] NSWSC 195, mentioned by Sylvia Grono in Chapter 5 of this book.

[7]   See Chapters 3 (Ireland) and 10 (Hong Kong) of this book.

to legislative and judicial safeguards, law enforcement agencies have had to adopt special processes and barriers to ensure high standards of fairness and an impermeable separation between the criminal and civil routes of proceeding.

At the end of all these questions, the cynical observer will ask whether civil forfeiture is 'really worth it', in other words, 'does it work?'. There is no doubt that civil forfeiture substantially increases government revenue (whether general revenue or in the form of a special fund), but this does not necessarily mean that it is achieving its objectives, a matter that is much more difficult to measure. Civil forfeiture laws are not a panacea. Criminal forfeiture continues to exist, and the two regimes must work together to co-ordinate efforts. Deficiencies in either regime or in effective co-ordination and co-operation will inevitably impair the overall impact of forfeiture laws. Impact largely depends on how well the laws are being enforced, and effective enforcement depends on having sufficient government resources.

It is misleading to measure impact or performance by a simple calculus of cost based on the total amount of dedicated resources and benefit based on the total amount forfeited. The United Kingdom's Assets Recovery Agency attracted criticism based on this kind of thinking after its first five years of operation.[8] But actual impact in disrupting and deterring criminal enterprises may require a longer time frame to measure. Less easily quantifiable benefits that come from having safer cities, fewer victims of crime, increased utilization of property to produce lawful income, etc, must be taken into account in the balance of costs and benefits. The authors of many of the chapters in this book tend to see their civil forfeiture regime as having achieved on balance some measure of the regime's objectives. But for some of these jurisdictions the full impact of civil forfeiture has yet to be realized.

Academic writing on civil forfeiture is growing in volume but is still very much in its early days. Legal practice in this area remains a specialty, especially in jurisdictions outside the US. Those who are most knowledgeable and experienced are usually government prosecutors and policy researchers who work in the area but have limited time to publish academic writing on the topic.

This book which grew out of a project to study the need for civil forfeiture in Hong Kong has become something more. It attempts to capture the development of the major international civil forfeiture regimes in the past 10 to 15 years. These chapters are written by the leading practitioners (both government and non-government) working in each of the respective jurisdictions.

---

[8]   See Chapters 7 and 8 of this book, and also Richard Girling, 'The battle to break Britain's crime lords', *The Sunday Times*, 17 February 2008.

The book is also forward looking with an awareness of the serious problems with money laundering in Asia. With reform in mind, the book examines the practice of asset confiscation in Chinese societies where the rate of wealth accumulation (both legitimate and illegitimate sources) is unlike anywhere else in the world. There is no single answer to the likely prospect of introducing civil forfeiture in the four Chinese societies. Each has a unique response to this issue given their fundamentally different political and legal systems.

The book begins with an introductory chapter by Jeffrey Simser who answers the initial question of 'what the hell is it?' in a clear and concise overview piece entitled 'Perspectives on civil forfeiture'. Simser reminds us of the historical origins of civil forfeiture in the law of admiralty and in protecting US territory from piracy. He traces the development of US civil forfeiture law and highlights its influence and inspiration for jurisdictions around the world.

Part II of this book, entitled 'Global Proliferation of Civil Forfeiture Laws', contains the core chapters that describe and analyse the civil forfeiture regimes in major jurisdictions including the US, Ireland, South Africa, Australia, Canada and the United Kingdom (UK). The chapters are arranged in this order to try to present an historical picture of the development and spread of these laws; however, the introduction of civil forfeiture in the last three jurisdictions occurred around the same time in 2002. Part II is essential reading for policy makers and legislators around the world in jurisdictions that are contemplating and researching the possible adoption of a civil forfeiture law.

Chapter 2, 'An overview of asset forfeiture in the United States', is written by one of the foremost experts, both academic and in practice, on the US asset forfeiture system. Stefan Cassella has written 'the book' on US asset forfeiture law and from his text he has contributed this chapter which provides a lucid outline of the current federal law. His discussion of notable cases demonstrates the power and extent of civil forfeiture, particularly in respect of the forfeiture of facilitating property. In his discussion of the objectives of forfeiture, Cassella admits that forfeiture can constitute 'a form of punishment or retribution exacted by the criminal justice system'. The passing of the 2000 Civil Asset Forfeiture Reform Act reminds us of the need for safeguards in a civil forfeiture regime especially in respect of administrative forfeitures. A highlight of the chapter is his review of the practical advantages and disadvantages of civil forfeiture, noting that with civil forfeiture there is no net saving of efforts to be expended and that possible interference with criminal proceedings is real.

Chapter 3 turns to Ireland where civil forfeiture laws were enacted in 1996 in record speed following two shocking murders committed by organized crime gangs. Felix McKenna and Kate Egan provide a comprehensive review of the legal regime, the abundant amount of case law that has resulted, and the workings of the Criminal Asset Bureau (CAB), of which McKenna was bureau chief until his retirement in 2006. As the title of the chapter indicates, the CAB practises a multi-agency approach to forfeiture which has proven to have significant advantages over traditional single-agency approaches. The authors highlight the use of the taxing power to attack criminal wealth which is a controversial measure but has been demonstrated to be an effective instrument in Ireland. The chapter contains a useful summary of the valuable human rights jurisprudence on civil forfeiture that has developed in that jurisdiction.

Poor implementation of criminal forfeiture legislation prompted South Africa to adopt civil forfeiture to curtail the rising levels of organized crime in that jurisdiction. But, as Raylene Keightley notes in Chapter 4, it was not only the new law that was essential but also the establishment of a specialist agency, the Asset Forfeiture Unit (AFU), 'to ensure that the innovations introduced by POCA 1998 were implemented'. Keightley details the ups and downs of the AFU in litigating the new legislation over the past decade. South Africa has had some interesting battles over the forfeiture of instrumentalities. The chapter concludes noting that while some of the fundamental constitutional issues have been settled, the courts have not always provided a clear majority view on the law and many other issues have yet to be raised and considered.

In Chapter 5, Sylvia Grono helps us to understand and see clearly the complex Proceeds of Crime Act 2002 which now applies in Commonwealth Australia. Like the US, Australia has different civil forfeiture regimes at both the federal and state levels. One of the reasons for the complexity of the federal law is its comprehensive nature, providing multiple means for law enforcement to recover ill-gotten gains as fully as possible. Unlike other regimes, the Australian law allows for both *in rem* and *in personam* orders in both the conviction and non-conviction streams. Grono believes that the civil forfeiture provisions which came into effect on 1 January 2003 has made a difference as it has allowed for earlier restraint orders, quicker interdiction of proceeds of foreign offences, and the possibility for action where the criminal cannot be located or is residing in a place from which extradition is not possible.

Canada might have had civil forfeiture legislation earlier than 2002 if it was not for uncertainty as to which level of government could and should enact such legislation. Under the Canadian Constitution, the federal Parliament has legislative authority over criminal law and procedure in criminal matters, while provinces have an exclusive power to legislate on property and civil rights. James McKeachie and Jeffrey Simser describe in Chapter 6 how the daring move by Ontario in 2001 to introduce civil forfeiture triggered a chain reaction across provinces to introduce their own civil forfeiture legislation. The Supreme Court of Canada will hear a case in late 2008 to determine whether all these pieces of legislation are constitutional. Charter of Rights and Freedoms issues have also been raised, but as McKeachie and Simser note, so far the schemes have been found to be Charter compliant.

Chapters 7 and 8 provide different and contrasting perspectives on the UK's Proceeds of Crime Act 2002. Angela Leong, a former investigator with the Assets Recovery Agency (ARA) and now a notable scholar in this area, provides a comprehensive and critical overview of the new scheme. There are many lessons to be learned from the early years of the UK regime. Leong notes three factors that have hindered the progress in these early years: litigation arising in several court challenges; lack of understanding and experience among law enforcement agencies and interim receivers; and the lack of international powers. She also expresses concerns about whether the merger of the ARA into the Serious Organised Crime Agency (effective 1 April 2008) will give rise to new problems of administration and enforcement.

Sara Dayman provides us with a unique glimpse of the operations of the UK regime from the perspective not of a lawyer but of an accountant serving as a highly experienced management receiver. The UK regime relies upon independent receivers to play an active role in the preservation and investigation of assets pending recovery. Dayman counters the criticisms that have been made against the ARA by noting that the public agency was under funded, had unrealistic targets and was given insufficient time to meet its objectives. She highlights the importance of the work of the interim receiver in the UK system, particularly in the ability of receivers to seize assets in foreign jurisdictions (something which the ARA cannot do given the lack of international powers) and in assisting the court with its independent report. Her experience confirms the short-sightedness of the regime's initial policy, which was later changed, to deny access to restrained property in order to pay reasonable legal expenses, as such policy had delayed proceedings unnecessarily and affected the completeness of the receiver's report.

Part III of this book provides a different dimension to the topic. It examines the asset forfeiture laws in major Chinese jurisdictions in Asia with a view to determining if civil forfeiture already exists and, if not, the prospects of introducing such laws. Chapter 9, by Xing Fei and Kung Shun Fong, looks at the confiscation system in Mainland China. As one sees from the chapter, China is in a state of transition. The state's powers to confiscate both criminal property and property as punishment are wide and historically entrenched. However, with increased economic wealth and power in international trade, the country has moved towards greater protection of private property rights. It also strives to be an international partner in both anti-corruption and anti-terrorism measures. The authors argue that modern civil forfeiture laws have yet to be adopted even though there exists a power in the civil court to order confiscation in disputes between private parties. Despite mostly academic criticism of the overbreadth of existing confiscation laws (which are reminiscent of the old common law general forfeiture power) the authors conclude that the reform of these laws does not appear to be on the government's agenda.

Hong Kong, on the other hand, is in a more realistic position to reform its laws which are still based on the old English criminal confiscation model. Chapter 10 reviews the history of asset confiscation before making out a case for reforming the law and enforcement processes. With profit-motivated crime rates still high and a poor performance record in interdicting proceeds of crime, I argue that the case for reform is a strong one, although there is some uncertainty in the government and legislature's will and resolve to adopt such laws.

Whereas Hong Kong is the common law face of China, Macau represents the continental civil law jurisdiction of China. Jorge Godinho begins Chapter 11 with the point made earlier that civil forfeiture is generally unknown to civil law jurisdictions. He explains that in Macau there exists two main confiscation powers: one for proceeds of crime but requires proof of unlawful activity beyond a reasonable doubt, and the other for instrumentalities which does not require proof of unlawful activity. There is also an unjustified wealth provision that requires civil servants to justify the lawful origins of any wealth they possess beyond their declared assets, or else they stand to have any unjustified wealth confiscated. In critiquing this latter provision on the basis that it interferes with an accused's presumption of innocence, Godinho has broader concerns about whether a civil forfeiture regime would be consistent with fundamental human rights norms in Macau.

Taiwan is the last Chinese society to be discussed and an important one given the strong economic and human ties with mainland China, Hong Kong and Macau. Lawrence Lee in Chapter 12 observes that while criminal and administrative confiscation exists for breaches of criminal laws and administrative regulations, civil forfeiture has yet to be adopted. His chapter highlights anomalies in the existing law and administrative difficulties in the pre-forfeiture management of assets. He argues for a wholesale review of the status quo and reform along the lines of the US model. With the new Kuomintang President elected in 2008, President Ma Ying-jeou, who has a doctorate from Harvard Law School, more US influence on Taiwanese law is foreseeable.

In the coming years there is little doubt that the world will see even more civil forfeiture laws. There is no indication at all that the jurisdictions that have adopted it thus far are likely to backtrack. Countries with entrenched crime problems including vulnerability to money laundering will find civil forfeiture an appealing measure to supplement (rather than replace) existing measures for dealing with profit-motivated crime. However, any measure that potentially increases 'public' finances is vulnerable to abuse by governments. In adopting the laws and procedures of other jurisdictions, governments must also adopt the human rights safeguards that exist in those jurisdictions, particularly the safeguard that places the confiscatory power in the authority of the judiciary and not purely in the hands of the executive.

It awaits to be seen whether civil law jurisdictions will be able to reconcile civil forfeiture with their own domestic human rights norms and traditions. But if common law experience is any indication, civil forfeiture is destined to spread to civil law jurisdictions, though with modifications necessary to suit their unique circumstances. For some countries, such as mainland China, it is hoped that the question of adopting civil forfeiture will become part of a broader reform exercise that sees the reduction if not repeal of indiscriminate forfeiture as punishment for criminal and administrative offences.

Another development to watch for in the coming decade is whether new international and regional treaties or declarations on crime will make specific mention of civil forfeiture as a means to interdict criminal property. If a consensus emerges on the effectiveness of civil forfeiture it may well develop into an international standard. Related to this question is whether and when international tribunals will include powers of civil forfeiture in their constitutive document. For example, the Rome Statute of the International Criminal Court only provides at present for forfeiture after a person has been convicted of a crime in the statute.[9]

When seen from a broader historical timeline, this book provides foundational reading on civil forfeiture in its early years. It tackles the questions of what it is, why and how it spread across the common law world, and what basic jurisprudential and operational issues it faced in its first 10–15 years. As these existing regimes continue to evolve and develop, one hopes that a body of critical and in-depth academic scholarship will accompany their evolution and development.

---

[9]   See Article 77(2)(b) of the Rome Statute of the International Criminal Court.

PART I

An introduction to civil forfeiture

1. Perspectives on civil forfeiture

Jeffrey Simser*

Civil asset forfeiture is a remedial statutory device designed to recover the proceeds of unlawful activity, as well as property used to facilitate unlawful activity. Generally, the state brings a proceeding against property (*in rem*) rather than against individuals. In the case of proceeds of unlawful activity, the court is invited to inquire into the origin of the property. If the provenance of the title lies in unlawful activity, and the state proves this to the satisfaction of the court, then the court is empowered to transfer title to the state. Property law abhors a void in title, and forfeiture ensures no *lacuna* by passing title to the state. In the case of property used to facilitate unlawful activity, the court is asked to inquire into the property's usage. Should this property be forfeited to prevent further facilitation of unlawful activity?

In general, there are two policy rationales for civil forfeiture. First, gains from unlawful activity ought not to accrue and accumulate in the hands of those who commit unlawful activity. Those individuals ought not to be accorded the rights and privileges normally attendant to civil property law. In cases of fraud and theft, the proceeds ought to be disgorged and distributed back to victims. Secondly, the state as a matter of policy wants to suppress the conditions that lead to unlawful activities. Drug profits also represent capital for more drug transactions, which can bring further harm to society. Leaving property that facilitates unlawful activity in an individual's hands creates a risk that he or she will continue to use that property to commit unlawful activity. In South Africa, the courts have accepted a policy rationale based on the fact that it is often impossible to bring the leaders of organized crime to book, in view of the fact that they invariably ensure that they are far removed from the overt criminal activity involved.[1] An effective organized crime operation ensures that only the eminently replaceable foot soldiers are brought to book.

---

*   The views expressed in this chapter are mine alone, and do not represent the views of the Government of Ontario. I am grateful for the comments of colleagues and friends, including Stefan Cassella, James McKeachie, Elizabeth Cowie and an anonymous colleague from Europe; all errors are mine alone.
[1]   See *NDPP v. Mohamed No and others* (2002) 4 SA 843 (CC) at 853; see also (2003) 4 SA 1 (CC). See further Chapter 4 of this book.

Civil forfeiture bypasses this problem by allowing the gains of an unlawful enterprise to be brought to justice.

There are a number of legal and linguistic terms applied to civil forfeiture depending on the jurisdiction being studied.[2] This chapter refers to civil forfeiture, which in other places can be civil asset forfeiture, non-conviction based forfeiture, asset forfeiture, civil recovery or confiscation. The standard of proof is civil, usually on the balance of probabilities or preponderance of the evidence. Generally, proceedings are brought *in rem*, or against the thing, something made clear by the American style of cause (see *US v. One Assortment of 89 Firearms*,[3] for example). By way of contrast, criminal asset forfeiture is *in personam*, against the person; following conviction, forfeiture is part of the sentencing process.

Most legislative schemes start with a proceeds provision, and the underlying definition can be relatively narrow[4] or broad.[5] Under Part II of Ontario's Civil Remedies Act 2001, for example, the Attorney General may commence an *in rem* proceeding against a proceed of unlawful activity. A proceed is any property 'acquired directly or indirectly, in whole or in part, as a result of unlawful activity ...'. The statute makes specific provision to protect legitimate owners. It permits an interlocutory preservation order, which allows assets to be frozen and held for litigation. In the forfeiture proceeding itself, where the court finds that the property is a proceed of unlawful activity, it shall be forfeited except where it would clearly not be in the interests of justice to do so. Furthermore, the statute has retrospective application. The *in rem* nature of the proceeding offers a viable device to attack difficult problems, particularly for issues such as corruption in the developing world. If the looted money is in Ontario, as long as the corruption (or fraud or outright theft) would have been an offence in Ontario, the courts can take jurisdiction over the property (notwithstanding that the unlawful activity occurred in another country).[6]

---

2   See A. Kennedy (2006), 'Designing a Civil Forfeiture System: An Issues List for Policymakers and Legislators', *Journal of Financial Crime*, **13**(2), 132.

3   (1984) 465 US 354: this case happens to canvass some interesting issues respecting collateral estoppels. For further references, see Chapter 2 of this book.

4   Civil forfeiture is available only if there is money laundering under Antigua and Barbados' Money Laundering (Prevention) Act 1996, s. 20; in the UK, it is property obtained by or in return for unlawful conduct: see Proceeds of Crime Act 2002, s. 242.

5   See, for example, Ireland's Proceeds of Crime Act 1996, s. 1, or South Africa's Prevention of Organised Crime Act 1998, s. 1. For more on these jurisdictions, see Chapter 3 (Ireland) and Chapter 4 (South Africa) of this book.

6   See Ontario's Civil Remedies Act 2001 (hereinafter Civil Remedies Act), ss. 2, 4 and 17. For further references, see Chapter 6 of this book.

Many jurisdictions permit proceedings to be brought against property used to engage in unlawful activity; such property might be referred to as instruments, instrumentalities or facilitating property. Under Part III of the Civil Remedies Act 2001, a proceeding may be brought against an instrument, which is property that is 'likely to be used to engage in unlawful activity that, in turn, would be likely or is intended to result in the acquisition of other property or in serious bodily harm …'. Provision is made to protect responsible property users. The statute creates a presumption in that proof of past use is indicative of future use. To date, the courts have held that a property used to process and package marijuana was an instrument.[7] The process, preservation and forfeiture, is similar to that for proceeds described in the previous paragraph.[8]

Conviction-based forfeiture is an important element of our criminal justice system, as it is part of the sentencing process. Civil forfeiture laws, by contrast, do not create offences, nor do they prohibit any conduct or impose any penalty, fine or imprisonment on an individual. Civil forfeiture has nothing to do with the identification, search, arrest, detention, charging, prosecution or conviction of any person. Rather it responds to the policy challenge of ensuring that wrongful proprietary gains are disgorged. The state has an interest in ensuring that victims can be effectively compensated; civil forfeiture can meet that policy goal. The state also has an interest in suppressing the conditions likely to favour the commission of crime; removing the instruments and the capital used to commit unlawful activity meets this objective. The *in rem* provisions achieve these goals by focusing on a specific property that is traced, as a proceed or instrument, of unlawful activity.

The ancient roots of forfeiture can be traced into the word 'felony'. The Saxon words 'fee', or landholding, and 'lon', or price, combine to define an act or omission that could result in the loss of property.[9] The concept of forfeiture reaches far back into the ancient history of Saxon and Scandinavian legal thought, survived the Norman invasion of 1066 and played a role in the legal system of feudal England. A man convicted of treason against the King would forfeit not only his life, but also his interest in land and chattels, as well as his ability to pass title to his heirs. Lords with treason on their minds, no doubt on advice from the family lawyer, attempted to circumvent the rules by passing their estate to their heirs prior to being caught. To defeat this, the courts developed a 'relation-back' theory, which is still important in US law. Under that

---

[7]   See *Ontario (Attorney General) v. Jinarern* [2005] OJ No. 6008 (SCJ).

[8]   See Civil Remedies Act, s. 7; on the conviction-based side in Canada, the Criminal Code 1985, s. 2 refers to 'offence-related property'.

[9]   See A. Mitchell, S. Taylor and K. Talbot (eds) (1997), *Confiscation and the Proceeds of Crime*, London, UK: Sweet & Maxwell, at p. 1.

theory, the forfeiture relates back to the time of the offence and defeats or knocks out any intervening property interests (for example, the heirs of the treasonous lord). Over time, a distinct but related forfeiture concept was developed.

In rem proceedings were particularly important in admiralty law. In a pre-globalized era, once a ship left the harbour, it could forever remove itself from the jurisdiction of the courts by simply sailing to another country. There was no practical way, outside of an *in rem* order, for domestic courts to follow that ship. The *in rem* order makes the thing, the ship in this case, the defendant. As the great American jurist, Oliver Wendell Holmes, once noted wryly to his students at Harvard, a 'ship is the most living of inanimate things'.[10]

In the US, a form of civil asset forfeiture was passed into law by the first US Congress in 1789. Until the 16th Amendment granted the power in 1913 to levy income taxes, forfeiture was a critical tool to protect the fiscal position of the US, which relied heavily on the imposition of tariff duties.[11] Civil forfeiture was also an important tool used to protect US shores from piracy. One of the seminal US Supreme Court decisions was rendered in 1827: a ship chartered by the King of Spain, the *Palmyra*, was captured as a pirateering vessel. The ship's captain argued that, as the king was not culpable, his ship ought not to be forfeited. The court ruled that the *in rem* proceeding was brought against the thing, the ship, and the culpability of the owner was not relevant. The ship, worth US$10 228 in 1827, was forfeited.[12]

Following the advent of income tax, forfeiture was little used in the US until the 1970s and 1980s, although there were some interesting prohibition cases.[13] In 1970, the US Congress focused on organized crime with the passage of the well-known Racketeer Influenced Corrupt Organization Act; a lesser known statute was passed at the same time, being the Continuing Criminal Enterprise Act. However, it was not until 1984, with the passage of the Comprehensive Crime Control Act, that civil forfeiture began to be used

---

[10]   See Oliver Holmes (1880), *The Common Law*, Boston, US: Little, Brown and Co., at pp. 24–25.

[11]   'In 1902, for example, nearly 75 percent of total federal revenues – $479 million out of a total of $653 million was raised from taxes on liquor, customs and tobacco.' Forfeiture was used to ensure those income flows kept coming: see *US v. James Daniel Good Real Property* (1993) 510 US 43, at p. 60, per Kennedy J. See further references in Chapter 2 of this book.

[12]   See *The Palymra* (1827), 12 Wheat 1 (USSC). See further Chapter 2 of this book.

[13]   See *JW Goldsmith, Jr-Grant Co v. US* (1921) 254 US 505; *Van Oster v Kansas* (1926) 272 US 465. See also Chapter 2 of this book; S. Cassella (2007), *Asset Forfeiture Law in the United States*, Huntington, NY, US: JurisNet (hereinafter *Asset Forfeiture Law in US*), chapters 2 and 3.

extensively across the US. Forfeiture attracts the 8th Amendment protection which constitutionally prohibits excessive fines.[14] In 2000, this and a number of other issues were addressed by the Civil Asset Forfeiture Reform Act 2000. In the federal system alone, US$1.2 billion was recovered in 2006 and the estimate for 2007 is US$1.6 billion. Only one-third of that money will be recovered through conviction-based forfeiture. The balance will be recovered through civil asset forfeiture cases.[15]

Civil forfeiture has spread across the common law world. Australian developments can be traced to their customs law, which in 1977 addressed drug money through an *in rem* forfeiture, and a working group of Attorneys General who in the mid-1980s were concerned with drug trafficking. A series of conviction-based laws were developed between 1985 and 1993. In 1990, New South Wales significantly reformed their law to add civil forfeiture.[16] A report of the Australian Law Reform Commission looked closely at the New South Wales law and subsequently the Commonwealth of Australia introduced comprehensive civil forfeiture legislation, with several states then either upgrading their own civil forfeiture legislation or introducing such legislation for the first time. New Zealand has for some time had legislation before their legislative assembly.

The Republic of Ireland has become one of Europe's leading jurisdictions in this field. Their non-conviction based forfeiture scheme developed out of a tragic series of events. In 1995, a campaigning reporter, Veronica Guerin, began to compile a story on a local crime figure, John Gilligan. She went to his house and interviewed him; he attacked her violently, punching her in the

---

[14] See *US v. Bajakajian* (1998), 524 US 321 (found that a forfeiture would be punitive and violate the 8th Amendment if it was grossly disproportional to the gravity of the offence it was designed to punish. Section 2(g) of the Civil Asset Forfeiture Reform Act codifies the procedure requiring a claimant to bear the burden of showing that forfeiture is grossly disproportional). See further Chapter 2 of this book.

[15] 38 per cent were uncontested civil cases and 29 per cent were contested civil cases. These numbers only represent Department of Justice agency forfeitures; Treasury and Homeland Security forfeitures typically forfeit 50 per cent of Department of Justice agency forfeitures. So, the numbers are considerably higher. See S. Cassella, 'The Case for Civil Forfeiture: why *In Rem* Proceedings are an Essential Tool for Recovering the Proceeds of Crime', Cambridge, UK: Cambridge International Symposium on Economic Crime, 7 September 2007, available online at http://works.bepress.com/cgi/viewcontent.cgi?article=1019&context=stefan_cassella, accessed 25 December 2007.

[16] See the Australian Law Reform Commission (1999), *Report No. 87, Confiscation That Counts: A Review of the Proceeds of Crime Act, 1987*, Canberra, Sydney, Australia: Australian Government Publishing Services: online version available at http://www.alrc.gov.au/media/1999/mb0616.htm, accessed 20 September 2007. See further references in Chapter 5 of this book.

head and body, and threatened to kill her. A complaint was launched and an assault prosecution commenced. On 26 June 1996, a day after the prosecution had been adjourned, Guerin was shot dead in her car as she drove back to Dublin from County Kildare where she had contested a traffic ticket. There was a tremendous outpouring of grief and anger across Ireland. This was compounded by the fact that, weeks earlier, an IRA gang had shot dead a policeman, Jerry McCabe, and wounded his partner during a botched robbery. The government reacted quickly, using portions of a private member's bill lowering the standard of proof for forfeiture and addressing a long-standing tension between the police and customs by introducing the Proceeds of Crime Act 1996 and by creating a new agency, the Criminal Assets Bureau (CAB).[17] The work of CAB attracted the interest of officials in the United Kingdom (UK).[18]

The UK Home Office developed a working group that produced some groundbreaking ideas by late 1998.[19] Ultimately, the Cabinet Office produced an influential report on the proceeds of crime in 2000.[20] The report, endorsed by the British Prime Minister of the day, Tony Blair, stated that most crime is motivated by profit. Pursuing and recovering the proceeds of crime would send out a message that crime does not pay; prevent criminals from finding further criminality; remove negative role models in communities; and decrease the risk of instability in financial markets. Following consultation,[21] legislation was introduced that became the Proceeds of Crime Act 2002. That legislation has been influential in a number of jurisdictions, including Jamaica.

Meanwhile, the American approach was influential in a number of countries. South Africa, for example, drew many concepts from American law. Statutory concepts, like the 'innocent owner defence', were brought into the Prevention of Organized Crime Act 1998. The courts continue to apply

---

[17]   See P. Williams (2006), *The Untouchables*, Dublin, Ireland: Merlin Publishing, at pp. 37–51. The Criminal Assets Bureau was created by the Criminal Assets Bureau Act 1996. See further references in Chapter 3 of this book.

[18]   See R.E. Bell (1999), 'Prosecuting the Money Launderers Who Act for Organized Crime', 2 *Journal of Money Laundering Control* **104**, 110.

[19]   See Home Office (November 1998), *Working Group on Confiscation Third Report: Criminal Assets*, London, UK: Home Office (Organised and International Crime Directorate).

[20]   See Cabinet Office (June 2000), *Recovering the Proceeds of Crime*, London, UK: Cabinet Office (Performance and Innovation Unit); see further references in Chapter 7 of this book.

[21]   See for example Home Office (March 2001), *Proceeds of Crime: Consultation on Draft Legislation,* London, UK: Home Office.

American jurisprudence as they interpret the statute.[22] South Africa is, in turn, likely to influence other countries. The American influence was also imported into the non-conviction based forfeiture legislation in the Philippines, although Canada had some influence in the finishing details.[23]

In Canada, we had the benefit of the experience in the US, although as noted above, American law developed over time through an array of statutory provisions.[24] We had the opportunity to address matters comprehensively. We also had the benefit of the Australian, Irish and South African experiences, all of which influenced portions of Ontario's statute. We also had a sense of the burgeoning developments in the UK. As Ontario's statute developed, important jurisprudence supporting civil forfeiture, including cases in Ireland, came in a series of court decisions. Foremost among them was *Gilligan v. Criminal Assets Bureau*;[25] in Europe, non-conviction based forfeiture had been considered under a European Court of Human Rights challenge, *M. v. Italy*.[26] The Australian case of *DPP v. Toro-Martinez*[27] considered the constitutionality of the federal Proceeds of Crime Act 1987. Other Canadian jurisdictions have, to some degree, been influenced by the Ontario experience.

Civil forfeiture can address a variety of problems, including corruption, which is particularly challenging for developing countries that can ill-afford to have their treasuries looted. Vladimiro Montesinos, the former head of the Peruvian National Intelligence Service, fled Peru in September 2000. Within two weeks, Swiss prosecutors began freezing US$113.6 million in corruption-related proceeds. The government of Nigeria has received back, through civil forfeiture, US$1 billion of the US$5 billion looted by late dictator Abacha, who took bribes and stole directly from the Central Bank. The Philippines have received an estimated US$2 billion of the US$5 billion (some estimates are US$10 billion) stolen by Ferdinand Marcos. Civil asset forfeiture can be an important tool to disgorge the proceeds of corruption wherever they are located.[28] Traditional criminal justice mechanisms, from bringing a dictator

---

22   See for example *Mohunram and Another v. National Director of Public Prosecutions* [2007] ZACC 4 (26 March 2007), CCT 19/06 (South Africa Constitutional Court). See further references in Chapter 4 of this book.
23   See J. Simser (2006), 'The Significance of Money Laundering: the Example of the Philippines', 9 *Journal of Money Laundering Control* **293**.
24   See *Asset Forfeiture Law in US, supra*.
25   [1998] IR 185; for Canadian practice in general, see Chapter 6 of this book.
26   [15 April 1991] ECHR Application No. 12386/ 86.
27   (1993) 119 ALR 517 (NSW CA).
28   See the U4 Anti-Corruption Resource Centre (a non-governmental organization under the auspices of Transparency International), 'Recovery of Corruption-Related Assets', available at www.u4.no/helpdesk/helpdesk/queries/query4.cfm, accessed 20 December 2007; see also United Nations Convention Against Corruption,

to trial, convicting him to forfeiting his assets in a sentencing hearing, will often not be a viable method of proceeding.

Civil forfeiture is an important remedial tool which is a particularly precise device. An *in rem* proceeding requires the state to adduce evidence that shows the property's provenance lies in unlawful activity. Unlawful activity conducted for profit, whether it be drugs, weapons or people smuggling, still needs to be addressed by traditional criminal justice methods of arrest, prosecution and incarceration. Civil forfeiture creates an option to ensure that wrongful proprietary gains do not remain in the hands of a wrongdoer. It further ensures that the capital needed for further unlawful activity is removed, preventing further harm to society. In the case of acquisitive unlawful activity, such as fraud or theft, civil forfeiture allows the state to stand in the shoes of a victim, to disgorge the illicit profits of a wrongdoer, and to see that money is returned to the victim. Finally, where organized crime insulates itself from culpability through the use of foot soldiers, civil forfeiture can still effectively get at the lifeblood of the organization – its money.

---

arts 31, 54 and 55; see also A. Maria Costa, 'Striking Back at Kleptocrats', *International Herald Tribune*, 12 September 2007. Civil recovery can be instituted at the behest of a state, see *AG of Zambia v. Meer Care and Desai and Ors* [2007] EWHC 952 (Ch).

PART II

Global proliferation of civil forfeiture laws

2. An overview of asset forfeiture in the United States

Stefan D. Cassella*

INTRODUCTION

Asset forfeiture came into prominence as a law enforcement tool in the United States during the 1990s. At the beginning of that decade, the Department of Justice – the principal federal law enforcement agency – was forfeiting approximately US$200 million per year in criminal assets, mostly from drug cases. By the end of the decade, it was forfeiting more than US$600 million per year in assets involved in an enormous variety of serious crimes.[1]

In short, in the last decade, asset forfeiture became institutionalized as an essential weapon in the arsenal that the federal law enforcement agencies in the United States could bring to bear on the perpetrators of crime. But the statutes, procedures and policies that govern the application of the forfeiture laws did not spring full grown from a single Act of Congress. Nor were the various statutes that were enacted piecemeal over many years accepted by the courts without scepticism or controversy. To the contrary, laws and concepts that developed slowly throughout the 19th and 20th centuries were greatly expanded in the last 20 years, applied in new contexts and subjected to close scrutiny by a sceptical judiciary. Only now, after more than a dozen constitutional challenges in the Supreme Court of the United States and the enactment

---

* The chapter consists of extracts from chapters 1 and 2 of Stefan D. Cassella (2006), *Asset Forfeiture Law in the United States*, Huntington, NY, US: Juris Publishing (hereinafter *Asset Forfeiture Law in US*) which were based on earlier published work found in Stefan D. Cassella (2003), 'The Development of Asset Forfeiture Law in the United States', *Acta Juridica* (University of Cape Town, South Africa) 314 and Stefan D. Cassella (2004), 'Overview of Asset Forfeiture Law in the United States', *South African J. Crim. Justice*, **17**, 347.

[1] Statistics provided by the Asset Forfeiture Management Staff of the US Department of Justice. As a result of amendments made by the Civil Asset Forfeiture Reform Act of 2000 (hereinafter CAFRA), Pub. L. 106–85, 114 Stat. 202, the US now has criminal and civil forfeiture authority for well over 250 federal, state and foreign crimes.

of comprehensive reform legislation, can it be said that most of the major issues have been settled. Many issues remain, but to a large extent when the practitioners of forfeiture law go to federal court today, they are litigating over the details.

This chapter traces the evolution of the asset forfeiture laws in the United States to see how concepts at first perceived as foreign or even antithetical to well-settled norms of legal practice came to be accepted as integral to the fabric of federal criminal law. It goes on to outline the current legal regime governing the forfeiture of criminally tainted property in the federal system.

THE FIRST FORFEITURE STATUTES: WHAT DOES IT MEAN TO FILE AN ACTION *IN REM*?

Asset forfeiture has an ancient tradition in the United States dating back to the English common law.[2] The First Congress, in 1789, enacted statutes authorizing the seizure and forfeiture of ships and cargos involved in customs offences, and later statutes authorized the forfeiture of ships engaged in piracy and slave trafficking.[3] The Act of 3 March 1819, which authorized the forfeiture of any vessel from which any 'piratical aggression' was attempted or perpetrated, was typical.[4]

All of these early statutes allowed the government to forfeit the property by filing a civil lawsuit against the property itself, rather than by filing an action, civil or criminal, against the property owner. In other words, the government could proceed against the property without having to wait until the owner was identified, apprehended and convicted. The notion was that the property itself was the offender and could be named as the defendant *in rem* in a civil case.[5]

---

[2]   See *Austin v. United States,* 509 U.S. 602 (hereinafter *Austin*), at pp. 611–13 (1993) (tracing the asset forfeitures laws back to the enforcement of English statutes and common law by the colonies before the adoption of the US Constitution, and tracing the common law concept of forfeiture, in turn, back to Biblical times); *Calero-Toledo v. Pearson Yacht Leasing Co.,* 416 U.S. 663 (hereinafter *Calero-Toledo*), at pp. 680–83 (1974) (same).

[3]   See *United States v. Bajakajian,* 524 U.S. 321 (hereinafter *Bajakajian*), at pp. 340–41 (1998) (citing the early statutes); see also *ibid.* at pp. 345–46 (Kennedy J, dissenting) (same); see also *United States v. Ursery,* 518 U.S. 267 (hereinafter *Ursery*), at p. 274 (1996) (same); see also *United States v. A Parcel of Land . . . 92 Buena Vista Ave.,* 507 U.S. 111 (hereinafter *92 Buena Vista*), at pp. 119–20 (1993) (same); see also *Austin,* at pp. 613–14 (same); *Calero-Toledo,* at p. 683 (same).

[4]   *The Palmyra,* 25 U.S. (12 Wheat.) 1 (hereinafter *The Palmyra*), at p. 8 (1827).

[5]   See *The Palmyra,* at p. 14 ('The thing is here primarily considered as the offender, or rather the offense is attached primarily to the thing. . . . [Thus,] the

This was a matter of convenience and necessity. Frequently, in cases involving smuggling, piracy and slave trafficking, the ship or its cargo might be found within the jurisdiction of the United States, but the property owner either remained abroad or could not be found at all.[6] Only by styling the action as a proceeding *in rem* against the property could the government hope to prevent the property from being used again to commit another offence, or in the case of a customs offence only by bringing an *in rem* action could the government hope to recover the duties that were owed on the imported goods.[7]

Styling the case as an action against the property, however, meant that the role of the owner in the commission of the offence was irrelevant. Not only was it unnecessary to convict the owner of the underlying crime before a court could assert jurisdiction over the property, but because the property itself was the offender, it was unnecessary to show that *the owner* had any role in the offence at all.[8] For example, in *Harmony v. United States*,[9] a pirate case involving the Act of 3 March 1819, the Supreme Court said, '[T]he vessel which commits the aggression is treated as the offender, as the guilty instrument or thing to which the forfeiture attaches, without any reference whatsoever to the character or conduct of the owner.'[10] It was enough to show that *someone* had committed the crime and used the defendant property to commit it.

---

proceeding *in rem* stands independent of, and wholly unaffected by any criminal proceeding *in personam*.'); see also *Bennis v. Michigan,* 516 U.S. 442 (hereinafter *Bennis*), at p. 447 (1996) (citing *The Palmyra* as the earliest decision in *in rem* actions); see also *Calero-Toledo,* at p. 684 (same).

[6]   See *Austin,* at p. 615 n. 9 ('The fictions of *in rem* forfeiture were developed primarily to expand the reach of the courts, which, particularly in admiralty proceedings, might have lacked *in personam* jurisdiction over the owner of the property.') (citations omitted); see also *Bennis,* at p. 472 (Kennedy J, dissenting) (*in rem* forfeiture evolved 'from the necessity of finding some source of compensation for injuries done by a vessel whose responsible owners were often half a world away and beyond the practical reach of the law and its processes.')

[7]   See *Bennis,* at p. 461 n. 5 (Stevens J, dissenting); see also *Harmony v. United States,* 43 U.S. (2 How.) 210 (hereinafter *Harmony*), at p. 238 (1844) (treating the property as the offender, without regard to the owner's conduct, seen 'as the only adequate means of suppressing the offense or wrong'); see also *Bajakajian,* at pp. 340, 344 n. 17 (noting that *in rem* forfeiture of smuggled goods served to 'vindicate the government's underlying property right in customs duties'); see also *United States v. 1,960 Bags of Coffee,* 12 U.S. (8 Cranch) 398, at p. 405 (1814) (forfeiting cargo transferred in violation of the Non-Intercourse Act of 1809), cited in *Calero-Toledo,* at p. 684 n. 24.

[8]   See *The Palmyra.*

[9]   43 U.S. (2 How.) at pp. 233–34.

[10]   Quoted in *Bennis,* at p. 461 n. 5 (Stevens J, dissenting); see *United States v. United States Coin and Currency,* 401 U.S. 715 (hereinafter *United States Coin and Currency*), at pp. 719–20 (1971) (discussing the early cases); see also *The Brig. Ann,* 13 U.S. (9 Cranch) 289 (1815).

The notion that the property itself could be considered guilty of the offence sounds strange to the modern ear. Today we would say that the property is subject to forfeiture not because the property itself did something wrong, but because it was the 'instrumentality' of the offence, but that term did not come into common usage in forfeiture cases for a surprisingly long time.[11]

IN REM FORFEITURE IN THE 20TH CENTURY: FORFEITING THE INSTRUMENTS OF CRIME

The concept of *in rem* forfeiture continued to evolve throughout the 19th and early 20th centuries, with the focus increasingly on property used to commit violations of the laws relating to taxation on alcohol and distilled spirits.[12] In a series of cases between the 1870s and 1920s, the Supreme Court consistently upheld the notion that such property could be forfeited without regard to the role of the property owner in the commission of the offence.

For example, in *Dobbins's Distillery v. United States*,[13] the court upheld the forfeiture of land and buildings used in connection with the operation of a tax-delinquent distillery, even though the property was in the control of a lessee when the offence occurred.[14] And in *J.W. Goldsmith, Jr.-Grant Co. v. United States*,[15] and *Van Oster v. Kansas*,[16] the court upheld the forfeiture of auto-

---

[11]   As noted in the text, the term 'guilty instrument' appeared in *Harmony* as long ago as 1844. In that case, the court also observed, '[I]t is true that inanimate matter can commit no offense. But this body is animated and put in action by the crew, who are guided by the master': see *Harmony*, at p. 234. But the Supreme Court nevertheless considers the term 'instrumentality' to be of recent vintage. See *Bajakajian,* at p. 333 n. 8 (noting that the term 'instrumentality' relates back only to Scalia J's concurring opinion in *Austin,* at pp. 627–28 (Scalia J, concurring in part and concurring in judgment))

[12]   In the early 20th century, the federal government in the US relied on taxes on liquor, customs and tobacco for as much as 75 per cent of its total revenue. See *United States v. James Daniel Good Real Property,* 510 U.S. 43 (hereinafter *James Daniel Good*), at p. 60 (1993).

[13]   96 U.S. 395 (1878) (hereinafter *Dobbins's Distillery*).

[14]   See *James Daniel Good,* at pp. 60 and 75 (Rehnquist CJ, dissenting); see also *Austin,* at p. 624 (Scalia J concurring); see also *Bennis,* at p. 447; see also *Calero-Toledo,* at p. 685; see also *92 Buena Vista,* at p. 120 n. 14; see also *United States v. Stowell,* 133 U.S. 1 (1890) (forfeiture of land and buildings in connection with the operation of an illegal brewery). Nearly a century later, the government was still using civil forfeiture to recover property from a person who failed to pay taxes. See *United States Coin and Currency,* at pp. 719–20 (civil forfeiture action against money used in violation of internal revenue statute requiring gamblers to register and pay taxes).

[15]   254 U.S. 505 (1921) (hereinafter *J.W. Goldsmith, Jr.-Grant Co.*).

[16]   272 U.S. 465 (1926).

mobiles used to transport bootleg whiskey or other illegal spirits by persons other than the vehicles' owners.[17] To be sure, the court continued to rely on the legal fiction that the property itself was the wrongdoer,[18] but in these cases it was increasingly clear that the property was subject to forfeiture because it was the instrument by which the offence was committed, and that it was necessary to confiscate such property to remove it from circulation or to recover taxes or other payments to which the government was entitled.[19]

THE LATE 20TH CENTURY: EXPANDING FORFEITURE FOR DRUG OFFENCES

By the middle of the 20th century, the US Congress had enacted statutes authorizing the forfeiture of property involved in a much wider variety of crimes including counterfeiting, gambling, alien smuggling and drug trafficking.[20] Initially, these forfeiture statutes closely paralleled the early statutes used to enforce the customs, piracy and revenue laws, in that they were limited to the instrumentalities of the crime.[21] But a dramatic expansion of the forfeiture laws occurred in 1978 and 1984 when Congress amended the drug forfeiture statutes, first to allow the forfeiture of the *proceeds* of the offence, and then to permit the forfeiture of property used to *facilitate* it.[22]

---

[17] See *Bennis*, at pp. 998–99; see also *Calero-Toledo*, at p. 686; see also *United States v. One Ford Coupe Automobile,* 272 U.S. 321, at pp. 329–30 (1926) (using a vehicle to evade tax on liquor during the Prohibition subjected the vehicle to forfeiture).

[18] See for example, *Dobbins's Distillery,* at p. 400 (quoting *The Palmyra*).

[19] See *Austin*, at p. 615 (describing the dual rationale for the forfeitures in such cases as *Dobbins's Distillery* and *J.W. Goldsmith, Jr.-Grant Co.*); see also *Calero-Toledo*, at pp. 686–87 (listing the purposes served by the forfeiture of instrumentalities); see also *Bajakajian*, at p. 333 n. 8 (noting that although the term 'instrumentality' is of 'recent vintage', 'it fairly characterizes property that historically was subject to forfeiture because it was the actual means by which an offense was committed'), citing *J.W. Goldsmith, Jr.-Grant Co.*

[20] See for example, *United States Coin and Currency.*

[21] See *92 Buena Vista*, at pp. 121–22 (noting that the drug forfeiture statutes were initially limited to 'the instruments by which [the drugs] were manufactured and distributed,' but then were expanded to include proceeds and property 'used in the commission' of the offence).

[22] See 21 U.S.C. § 881(a)(6) (enacted 1978) (authorizing forfeiture of the proceeds of a drug offence) and 21 U.S.C. § 881(a)(7) (enacted 1984) (authorizing forfeiture of real property used or intended to be used to commit or to facilitate the commission of a drug offence); see also *James Daniel Good*, at p. 53 (noting addition of authority to forfeit real property to the drug forfeiture statute in 1984).

The idea of forfeiting the proceeds of crime was entirely new, and forfeiting facilitating property meant that the government could confiscate not only the instrument actually used to commit the offence, like an automobile used to transport bootleg whiskey, but also any property that made the crime easier to commit or harder to detect.[23] For example, the government could use the facilitation theory to forfeit the *location* where an offence took place: for example, the building where the drugs were stored, where laundered money was counted or where gambling bets were tallied, even though the location was not the *instrument* by which the offence was committed. Accordingly, courts today more frequently talk in terms of the forfeiture of 'facilitating property' instead of 'instrumentalities', though the broader term fairly encompasses the narrower one as well.

By the 1990s, civil forfeiture authority had not only been expanded to cover proceeds and facilitating property, but had also been extended to most federal crimes. Today, there is still no single over-arching statute authorizing forfeiture in all federal cases, but there is forfeiture authority for virtually all serious offences, including money laundering, car-jacking, espionage, child pornography, bank fraud and most other 'white collar' crimes. Thus, the ancient practice of *in rem* forfeiture that was originally used to confiscate pirate ships and whiskey stills in rare cases, came to be used thousands of times a year to forfeit houses, farms, businesses and bank accounts in the most commonly occurring cases.

Along the way, the legal fiction that the property itself had done something wrong, or even that it was the instrument by which the crime was committed, had given way to more modern notions of *in rem* forfeiture. Today, it is understood that proceedings *in rem* are simply structures that allow the government to quiet title to criminally tainted property in a single proceeding in which all interested persons are required to file claims contesting the forfeiture at one time.[24] As it has always been, the civil forfeiture is entirely independent of and wholly unaffected by any criminal proceeding, and the role of the property owner in the commission of the offence is irrelevant.[25] It is only necessary that

---

[23]   See *United States v. Schifferli*, 895 F.2d 987 (hereinafter *Schifferli*), at p. 990 (4th Cir. 1990) (facilitating property is anything that makes the offence easier to commit or harder to detect).

[24]   See *Ursery*, at pp. 295–96 (Kennedy J, concurring).

[25]   See *United States v. One Assortment of 89 Firearms*, 465 U.S. 354 (hereinafter *One Assortment of 89 Firearms*), at p. 366 (1984) (acquittal on gun violation under § 922 does not bar civil forfeiture); see also *One Lot Emerald Cut Stones v. United States*, 409 U.S. 232 (hereinafter *One Lot Emerald Cut Stones*), at p. 237 (1972) (acquittal on criminal smuggling charge does not bar later civil forfeiture); see also *United States v. One 'Piper' Aztec 'F' Deluxe Model 250 PA 23 Aircraft*, 321 F.3d 355 (hereinafter *Model 250 PA 23 Aircraft*), at p. 360 (3d Cir. 2003) (that claimant's crim-

the government prove, by a preponderance of the evidence, that the property was derived from, used to commit or used to facilitate the commission of a criminal offence.[26]

Though the rationale, the scope and the application of the civil forfeiture statutes all have changed, *in rem* forfeiture continues to serve a vital purpose in allowing the government to take criminally tainted property out of circulation, abate nuisances, discourage certain types of unregulated commerce and encourage property owners to take care in managing their property.[27] It is also the only means of confiscating forfeitable property when the owner cannot be identified, is deceased or beyond the reach of the court, or when the owner either negligently or purposefully allowed another to use his property to commit a criminal offence.[28]

---

inal conviction for alien smuggling was overturned has no effect on civil forfeiture); see also *United States v. $734,578.82 in U.S. Currency*, 286 F.3d 641 (hereinafter *$734,578.82 in U.S. Currency*), at p. 657 (3d Cir. 2002) (civil forfeiture is an *in rem* action against the property itself; the forfeiture is 'not conditioned on the culpability of the owner of the defendant property'); see also *United States v. 1988 Oldsmobile Cutlass Supreme*, 983 F.2d 670 (hereinafter *1988 Oldsmobile Cutlass Supreme*), at p. 675 (5th Cir. 1993) (acquittal of claimant does not undermine finding of forfeitability in civil forfeiture case).

[26]   There is also a subset of civil forfeiture statutes that do not require proof of any nexus to the crime at all but rather allow the civil forfeiture of 'the value' of the property involved in the criminal offence: see for example, 18 U.S.C. § 545; see *United States v. Ahmad*, 213 F.3d 805 (hereinafter *Ahmad*), at p. 809. These statutes represent an exception to the traditional view of *in rem* forfeiture as requiring a nexus to the offence and not permitting forfeiture of substitute assets.

[27]   See *Ursery,* 518 U.S. at pp. 290–91 (listing the benefits of civil forfeiture).

[28]   The adaptation of ancient forms to modern purposes was described eloquently by Justice Oliver Wendell Holmes in *The Common Law* 5 (1881), quoted in *Calero-Toledo* at p. 681:

> The customs, beliefs, or needs of a primitive time establish a rule or a formula. In the course of centuries the custom, belief, or necessity disappears, but the rule remains. The reason which gave rise to the rule has been forgotten, and ingenious minds set themselves to inquire how it is to be accounted for. Some ground of policy is thought of, which seems to explain it and to reconcile it with the present state of things; and then the rule adapts itself to the new reasons which have been found for it, and enters on a new career. The old form receives a new content, and in time even the form modifies itself to fit the meaning which it has received.

There are cases, of course, that directly parallel the 19th Century scenario in which the pirate ship was in the jurisdiction of the federal court but the owner was not, for example, an airplane seized in Tennessee with a cargo of cocaine belonging to a South American drug lord, or a bank account in New York belonging to a Brazilian money launderer.

At the same time, by the 1990s, Congress had resurrected and began to apply the old English common law notion of criminal forfeiture to a wide variety of crimes.[29] In so doing, it gave the government the option of seeking forfeiture of the proceeds and other property involved in a criminal offence from the property owner himself if he was named as the defendant in a criminal case, or of pursuing the property directly in a civil case when the circumstances warranted that approach.[30]

As the Supreme Court noted, these changes 'marked an important expansion of government power'[31] and led directly to a series of challenges to the forfeiture statutes on a variety of constitutional grounds. Whereas the forfeiture of pirate ships and other instruments of crime in an *in rem* proceeding had survived constitutional challenge for 200 years, the forfeiture of vehicles, houses, businesses and bank accounts as property used to facilitate an offence, and as property representing criminal proceeds, subjected the ancient practice to new scrutiny and led the Supreme Court to devote significant attention to this area of criminal law in a relatively short period of time. Issues of constitutional dimension that had been percolating in the courts for years, or that had lain moribund for decades, were suddenly at the cutting edge of the most vibrant and rapidly changing area of criminal law.[32]

THE CURRENT STATE OF ASSET FORFEITURE LAW IN THE UNITED STATES

Asset forfeiture is an integral part of federal criminal law enforcement in the United States. This brief introduction to federal forfeiture law attempts to answer three questions: first, why asset forfeiture is important to law enforcement; secondly, in what circumstances and what types of property are subject to forfeiture; and thirdly, how forfeiture is accomplished.

---

[29]   See *Bajakajian*, 524 U.S. at p. 332 n. 7 (noting that Congress 'resurrected' the English common law of criminal forfeiture in 1970 as part of the Racketeer Influenced and Corrupt Organizations Act (hereinafter RICO)).

[30]   In 2000, Congress completed a 30-year expansion of criminal forfeiture authority by providing that the government may seek criminal forfeiture as part of the prosecution for any offence for which civil forfeiture is authorized: see 28 U.S.C. § 2461(c).

[31]   See *92 Buena Vista*, 507 U.S., at p. 121.

[32]   See *Asset Forfeiture Law in US*, *supra* at ch. 2 for a detailed consideration of the US Supreme Court authorities on asset forfeiture law.

Why Do Forfeiture?

There are many reasons to include the forfeiture of assets as part of a criminal case. First, law enforcement agents and prosecutors want not only to arrest the wrongdoer and put him in jail for some period of time, but also to remove the tools of the crime from circulation so they cannot be used again, either by the wrongdoer himself once he gains his release or by members of his organization. Thus, law enforcement would want to seize and forfeit the guns, the airplanes and the cars with concealed compartments that are used for drug smuggling; or to take the computers, printers and other electronic devices used in child pornography, counterfeiting and identification fraud cases; and to shut down the 'crack house' where drugs are distributed to children on their way to school, to confiscate the farm used for the marijuana growing operation and to close down the business used to commit insurance fraud, telemarketing fraud or to run a Ponzi scheme. In this sense, asset forfeiture is a form of incapacitation.

Secondly, in any case where the crime involves innocent victims, such as property offences and fraud, asset forfeiture turns out to be the most effective means of recovering property that may be used to compensate the victims. Indeed, restoration of property to victims in white collar cases is the first priority of law enforcement when it comes to disbursing forfeited property,[33] and much time and effort is expended in such cases to ensure that the wrongdoer's assets are preserved pending trial so that they remain available for this purpose once the case is over.

Thirdly, asset forfeiture takes the profit out of the crime. Obviously, there is an element of simple justice in ensuring that a wrongdoer is deprived of the fruits of his illegal acts. But there is also an element of general deterrence as well. Surely the incentive to engage in economic crime is diminished if people contemplating such activity understand that there is a high likelihood that they will not be allowed to retain any profits that might flow from their temporary success. Conversely, convicting the defendant but leaving him in possession of the riches of wrongdoing gives others the impression that a life of crime is worth the risk.

There is also the matter of the message that is sent to the community of law-abiding citizens when a notorious gangster or fraud artist is stripped of the trappings of what may have appeared to be an enviable lifestyle. Criminals typically spend their spoils on the expensive homes, airplanes, electronic

---

[33]   See 18 U.S.C. § 981(e)(6) (authorizing the government to use forfeited property to pay restitution, in civil forfeiture cases, to the victims of the underlying crime); see also 21 U.S.C. § 853(i) (same for criminal forfeiture).

goods and other toys that everyone else wishes he had the resources to acquire. Taking the criminal's toys away, as law enforcement agents typically put it, not only ensures that the criminal enterprise is deprived of its economic resources, and not only makes funds available for restitution to the victims, it also sends a signal to the community that the benefits of a life of crime are illusory and temporary at best.[34]

Finally, asset forfeiture constitutes a form of punishment. While taking the instrumentalities of crime out of circulation, obtaining funds for restitution, taking the profit out of crime and achieving some measure of deterrence all constitute remedial aspects of forfeiture, it cannot be denied that depriving a wrongdoer of the accouterments of an expensive lifestyle, or the items that gave him the leverage, prestige or wherewithal to commit a criminal act, can serve, in some cases, as a form of punishment or retribution exacted by the criminal justice system. Forfeiture, in other words, gives the criminal his just desserts.

What Can the Government Forfeit?

In most countries, the asset forfeiture laws are written in generic terms. A typical statute will authorize a court to order the forfeiture of 'all proceeds of any crime' (often including foreign crimes) and any property 'used to commit, or to facilitate the commission' of any such crime. However, as the asset forfeiture laws in the United States developed piecemeal over a long period of time, they were not written in generic terms at all. There is neither a common law of forfeiture nor a single provision authorizing forfeiture in all cases. To the contrary, Congress enacted different forfeiture provisions at different times for different offences, with the result that what can be forfeited varies greatly from one offence to another. Indeed, the first task of a federal prosecutor is always to check the statute for the crime under investigation to see what, if any, asset forfeiture options might be available.

The process has almost no rhyme or reason. For some crimes, Congress has not authorized any forfeiture authority at all; for others, law enforcement can

---

[34]   This rationale for asset forfeiture has been cited, as well, by the courts in other countries that have recently enacted forfeiture laws. For example, in turning back the first challenge to the civil forfeiture statute enacted in the United Kingdom in 2002, the court said the following: '[T]he purpose of the legislation is essentially preventative in that it seeks to reduce crime by removing from circulation property which can be shown to have been obtained by unlawful conduct thereby diminishing the productive efficiency of such conduct and rendering less attractive the "untouchable image" of those who have resorted to it for the purpose of accumulating wealth and status.' See *In the Matter of the Director of the Assets Recovery Agency and in the Matter of Cecil Stephen Walsh*, 2004 NIQB 21, High Court of Justice in Northern Ireland, 1 April 2004.

confiscate only the proceeds of the offence itself,[35] or only the instrumentalities used to commit the offence.[36] Other statutes are broader, permitting the forfeiture of any property 'involved' in the offence,[37] or property that provides a criminal with economic power over a criminal organization, whether that property was involved in the offence or not.[38] Finally, one statute permits law enforcement to confiscate virtually everything the wrongdoer owns.[39]

The following is a brief survey of some of the better-known forfeiture provisions in federal law.

(a) Proceeds

The closest Congress has come to enacting an all powerful forfeiture statute is 18 U.S.C. § 981(a)(1)(C), which authorizes the forfeiture of the *proceeds* of more than 200 different state and federal crimes.[40] The federal crimes include all of the common ones, like fraud, bribery, embezzlement and theft, and scores of more obscure ones as well. The state crimes include murder, kidnapping, gambling, arson, robbery, bribery, extortion, obscenity and state drug trafficking.[41]

Many other statutes also provide for the forfeiture of the 'proceeds' or 'gross proceeds' of a particular offence. Indeed, statutes authorizing the forfeiture of proceeds in one form or another are scattered throughout the federal criminal code.[42]

Proceeds are defined in the case law by a 'but for' test: the proceeds of an offence comprise any property, real or personal, tangible or intangible, that the

---

[35] See 18 U.S.C. § 981(a)(1)(C) (authorizing the forfeiture of the proceeds – but only the proceeds – of a long list of federal criminal offences).

[36] See 16 U.S.C. § 470gg (authorizing forfeiture of tools and equipment used to steal archaeological treasures, but not the proceeds of such offence).

[37] See 18 U.S.C. § 981(a)(1)(A) and 982(a)(1) (authorizing civil and criminal forfeiture, respectively, of all property involved in a money laundering offence).

[38] See 18 U.S.C. § 1963(a)(2) (authorizing forfeiture of any property giving a defendant a source of influence over an racketeering enterprise).

[39] See 18 U.S.C. § 981(a)(1)(G) (authorizing forfeiture of all assets of a person engaged in terrorism).

[40] See *United States v. All Funds Distributed to Weiss*, 345 F.3d 49, at p. 56 n. 8 (2nd Cir. 2003) (as amended by CAFRA, § 981(a)(1)(C) permits the forfeiture of all proceeds of an 'specified unlawful activity'; it is no longer necessary for the government to use the money laundering statute to forfeit such proceeds).

[41] The crimes for which forfeiture is authorized in § 981(a)(1)(C) are listed in 18 U.S.C. § 1956(c)(7).

[42] Some examples include 18 U.S.C. § 982(a)(5) (forfeiture of the gross proceeds of trafficking in stolen automobiles), *ibid.* § 982(a)(7) (forfeiture of the proceeds of a federal health care offence) and *ibid.* § 794(d) (forfeiture of proceeds of espionage).

wrongdoer would not have obtained or retained but for the crime.[43] Moreover, the forfeiture of proceeds is not limited to depriving a criminal of his net profits. Someone who invests $10 000 in start up costs for a fraud scheme and then bilks a victim of only $10 000, makes no profit at all. Forfeiting the net profit in that case would simply leave the criminal where he was when he started. For forfeiture law to achieve its various public policy purposes, it must allow the government to recover the gross proceeds of the offence without reduction for overhead expenses or start-up costs.[44] Thus, a criminal who engages in illegal activity will know from the outset that he risks both his initial investment as well as any potential profits.

The proceeds of an offence also include property derived indirectly from the offence, such as the appreciation in the value of property purchased with criminal proceeds,[45] or payments received on an insurance policy when the property acquired with the criminal proceeds is lost or destroyed.

While statutes authorizing the forfeiture of proceeds of the crime are powerful and necessary law enforcement tools, they are limited in scope. Because only the proceeds of the crime (or property traceable to it) are forfeitable under such statutes, the government may be required to separate the tainted proceeds and return the untainted portion to the wrongdoer.[46] This contrasts with the scope of forfeiture under the money laundering statutes and others discussed below.[47]

---

[43]   See *Asset Forfeiture Law in US, supra* at ch. 25.

[44]   *Ibid.*

[45]   See *United States v. Real Property Located at 22 Santa Barbara Dr.*, 264 F.3d 860 (9th Cir. 2001) (property traceable to criminal proceeds is forfeitable in its entirety even if it has appreciated in value); *United States v. Hawkey*, 148 F.3d 920 (8th Cir. 1998) (hereinafter *Hawkey*) (if property is subject to forfeiture as property traceable to the offence, it is forfeitable in full, including any appreciation in value since the time the property became subject to forfeiture); *United States v. Hill*, 46 Fed. Appx. 838 (6th Cir. 2002) (Table) (following *Hawkey*; stock that appreciates in value is forfeitable as property traceable to the originally forfeitable shares); *United States v. Young*, 2001 WL 1644658 at *2 n. 3 (M.D. Ga. 2001) (defendant, whose residence was forfeited upon his conviction, cannot complain that in the year between the conviction and the time the order of forfeiture became final he continued to make repairs to the residence).

[46]   See *United States v. One 1980 Rolls Royce*, 905 F.2d 89, at p. 90 (5th Cir. 1990) (claimant could avoid forfeiture to the extent that he could prove what portions of the property were purchased with legitimate funds); *United States v. One Parcel Known as 352 Northup St.*, 40 F. Supp. 2d 74 (D.R.I. 1999) (in proceeds cases, forfeiture limited to portion of property purchased with drug money; portion traceable to subsequent investment of legitimate funds *not* forfeitable; property apportioned after sale).

[47]   The forfeiture of criminal proceeds is discussed in detail in *Asset Forfeiture Law in US, supra* at ch. 25.

(b) Drug cases

The statutes pertaining to drug offences authorize the forfeiture of more than just the proceeds of the offence. Under 21 U.S.C. §§ 853(a) and 881(a) (criminal and civil forfeiture respectively), a court may order the forfeiture of both the drug proceeds themselves and any real or personal property used to commit or to facilitate the commission of the drug offence. These are the statutes that a federal law enforcement agency or federal prosecutor would use to take a car, boat, gun, airplane or farm away from a drug dealer.

Facilitating property is defined in the case law to mean any property that 'makes the prohibited conduct less difficult or more or less free from obstruction or hindrance'.[48] The drug cases provide a plethora of examples of cases where houses, businesses, and even medical licences have been forfeited as facilitating property.[49]

(c) Other crimes for which facilitating property may be forfeited

Drug cases are, however, not the only ones in which law enforcement can forfeit more than just the proceeds of the offence. Many other statutes authorize the forfeiture of 'facilitating property' as well. Indeed, many older forfeiture statutes authorize the forfeiture of instrumentalities or facilitating property *but not* the proceeds of the offence.

Some typical facilitating property statutes include 8 U.S.C. § 1324(b) and 18 U.S.C. § 982(a)(6) regarding civil and criminal forfeiture of property used by alien smugglers respectively; 18 U.S.C. § 981(a)(1)(B) for forfeiture of the proceeds and property used to facilitate certain foreign crimes, for example drug trafficking, crimes of violence and public corruption; and 18 U.S.C. §§ 2253 and 2254 authorizing criminal and civil forfeiture of property used to commit a child pornography offence respectively.[50]

(d) Money laundering

One of the most powerful and most popular forfeiture statutes is the one that permits the forfeiture of all property *involved in* a money laundering offence. If someone launders the proceeds of a drug offence or a corruption offence by commingling the money with clean money from another source, or by investing it in land or in a business, it is often possible for the government to forfeit

---

[48] See *Schifferli*, at p. 990 ('Facilitation occurs when the property makes the prohibited conduct less difficult or more or less free from obstruction or hindrance'); *United States v. Bornfield*, 145 F.3d 1123 (hereinafter *Bornfield*), at p. 1135 (10th Cir. 1998) (citing *Schifferli*); *United States v. Puche*, 350 F.3d 1137, at p. 1153 (11th Cir. 2003) (citing *Bornfield*).

[49] See *Asset Forfeiture Law in US, supra* at ch. 26.

[50] *Ibid.* for detailed discussion on the forfeiture of facilitating property.

all of the property involved in the offence, not just the proceeds being laundered, under 18 U.S.C. §§ 981(a)(1)(A) (civil forfeiture) and 982(a)(1) (criminal forfeiture).[51]

Accordingly, prosecutors like to use the money laundering forfeiture statute because it eliminates the need, in most cases, to distinguish between the portion of the property traceable to the underlying offence and the portion derived from other sources.[52]

(e) Racketeer Influenced and Corrupt Organizations Act and terrorism

Finally, the most powerful federal forfeiture statutes are the ones that apply to racketeering and terrorism. Under Racketeer Influenced and Corrupt Organizations Act, 18 U.S.C. § 1963(a) (hereinafter RICO), the government can forfeit any property acquired or maintained through the racketeering activity and any interest that the defendant has in the racketeering enterprise itself. So if someone runs his chain of restaurants or convenience stores as a RICO enterprise, a court can order the forfeiture of the defendant's interest in the entire business, whether a given asset or portion of the business was directly involved in the illegal operation of the enterprise or not.[53]

The forfeiture statute for terrorism, 18 U.S.C. § 981(a)(1)(G), is even more powerful. The statute states that if someone is engaged in planning or perpetrating acts of domestic or international terrorism, the government may seize and forfeit *all* of his assets, foreign or domestic, whether the property was involved in the terrorism activity or not. This statute is designed to incapacitate the terrorist completely by leaving him with no assets whatsoever to perpetrate further acts of violence against governments, their citizens or their property.[54]

---

51   *Ibid.* ch. 27.
52   See also Stefan D. Cassella (2004), 'The Forfeiture of Property Involved in Money Laundering Offenses', *Buff. Crim. L. Rev.*, **7**, 583.
53   See *United States v. Angiulo*, 897 F.2d 1169, at p. 1211 (1st Cir. 1990) ('any interests *in* an enterprise, including the enterprise itself, are subject to forfeiture in their entirety, regardless of whether some portion of the enterprise is not tainted by the racketeering activity'); see also *United States v. Busher*, 817 F.2d 1409, at p. 1413 (9th Cir.1987) ('forfeiture is not limited to those assets of a RICO enterprise that are tainted by use in connection with racketeering activity, but rather extends to the convicted person's entire interest in the enterprise'); see also *United States v. Anderson*, 782 F.2d 908, at p. 918 (11th Cir. 1986) ('[a] defendant's conviction under [RICO] subjects all his interests in the enterprise to forfeiture regardless of whether those assets were themselves "tainted" by use in connection with the racketeering activity') (quoting *United States v. Cauble*, 706 F.2d 1322, at p. 1359 (5th Cir.1983)).
54   See Stefan D. Cassella (2002), 'Forfeiture of Terrorist Assets Under the USA Patriot Act of 2001', *Law & Pol'y Int'l Bus.*, **34**, 7.

The Three Kinds of Forfeiture under Federal Law

So far, we have discussed the reasons to include asset forfeiture as part of a criminal investigation and have taken a brief look at the kinds of property that might be forfeited in particular cases. Finally, we will briefly discuss the procedural devices that law enforcement agents and prosecutors in the United States may use to accomplish the forfeiture.

Federal law gives the government three procedural options: administrative forfeiture, civil forfeiture and criminal forfeiture. The first applies only to uncontested cases and can, as the name implies, be undertaken by a federal law enforcement agency as an administrative or 'non-judicial' matter without the involvement of either a prosecutor or a court. In contrast, both civil forfeiture and criminal forfeiture are judicial matters, requiring the commencement of a formal action in a federal court, and concluding, if the government is success-ful, with the entry of a court order directing the transfer of title to the property in question to the United States.

(a)   Administrative forfeiture

The vast majority of all federal forfeitures are administrative forfeitures, for the simple reason that the vast majority of all forfeiture proceedings are uncontested.[55] Basically, an administrative forfeiture begins when a federal law enforcement agency with statutory authority in a given area (eg the Drug Enforcement Administration (DEA) in a drug case, the Federal Bureau of Investigation (FBI) in a fraud case, the Bureau of Alcohol, Tobacco, Firearms and Explosives (ATF) in a firearms case) seizes property discovered in the course of an investigation. The seizure must be based on probable cause to believe that the property is subject to forfeiture and generally must be pursuant to a judicial warrant,[56] but there are numerous exceptions authorizing warrant-less seizures, such as when property is seized in the course of an arrest, or when the property is mobile, making the delay involved in obtaining a warrant impractical.[57]

---

[55]   Prior to the enactment of CAFRA the Drug Enforcement Administration (hereinafter DEA) estimated that 85 per cent of forfeitures in drug cases were uncon-tested. Since CAFRA, which made it easier to contest a forfeiture action, the number of uncontested DEA cases has dropped to 80 per cent. Other seizing agencies report similar figures.

[56]   See 18 U.S.C. § 981(b).

[57]   See *Florida v. White*, 526 U.S. 559 (1999) (warrantless seizure of automobile did not violate the 4th Amendment where there was probable cause to believe the auto-mobile was subject to forfeiture and it was found in a public place); see further *Asset Forfeiture Law in US, supra* at ch. 3.

Once the property has been seized, the agency commences the administrative forfeiture proceeding by sending notice of its intent to forfeit the property to anyone with a potential interest in contesting that action and by publishing a notice in the newspaper.[58] In essence, the agency says to the world, 'we have seized this property and intend to forfeit it to the United States. Anyone wishing to object must speak now or forever hold his peace'. If no one contests the forfeiture by filing a claim within the prescribed period of time, the agency concludes the matter by entering a declaration of forfeiture that has the same force and effect as a judicial order.

An administrative forfeiture is not really a proceeding at all in the judicial sense. It is more like an abandonment. But in 2000, Congress substantially revised the rules governing administrative forfeitures to ensure that property owners are afforded due process.[59] Under the Civil Asset Forfeiture Reform Act of 2000 (CAFRA), the seizing agency must begin the forfeiture proceeding within a fixed period of time and must give the property owner ample time to file a claim. Then, if someone does file a claim, the agency has another fixed period of time in which to refer the matter to a prosecutor for the commencement of a judicial forfeiture action or to simply return the property.[60]

Most types of property may be seized and forfeited administratively. The most important exceptions are real property and personal property (other than cash or monetary instruments) having a value in excess of $500 000. Such property must always be forfeited judicially.[61]

---

[58]   For a summary of the pre-CAFRA administrative forfeiture procedure, see *United States v. Gonzalez-Gonzalez*, 257 F.3d 31 (1st Cir. 2001); see also *United States v. $57,960.00 in U.S. Currency*, 58 F. Supp. 2d 660 (D.S.C. 1999); see also *United States v. $50,200 in U.S. Currency*, 76 F. Supp. 2d 1247 (D. Wyo. 1999); see also *United States v. Derenak*, 27 F. Supp. 2d 1300 (M.D. Fla. 1998); see also *Concepcion v. United States*, 938 F. Supp. 134 (E.D.N.Y. 1996). For a summary of post-CAFRA administrative forfeiture procedure, see *United States v. Weimer*, 2006 WL 562554, *3 n. 1 (E.D. Pa. 2006); see also in general Stefan D. Cassella (2001), 'The Civil Asset Forfeiture Reform Act of 2000', 27 *Notre Dame J. Legis.* 97 (hereinafter The CAFRA Article).

[59]   The procedural statutes governing administrative forfeiture procedure are 18 U.S.C. §§ 983(a)(1) and (2) (enacted by CAFRA), and 19 U.S.C. § 1602 *et seq.* See *United States v. $557,933.89, More or Less, in U.S. Funds*, 287 F.3d 66, at p. 77 n. 7 (2d Cir. 2002) (procedures set forth in 19 U.S.C. § 1602 *et seq.* are superseded by CAFRA where inconsistent).

[60]   Administrative forfeiture procedure is discussed in detail in *Asset Forfeiture Law in US, supra* at chs 4 and 5; see also The CAFRA Article.

[61]   See 19 U.S.C. § 1607 (setting maximum dollar value on administrative forfeiture of personal property); see also 18 U.S.C. § 985(a) (real property may never be forfeited administratively).

If someone does file a claim contesting the administrative forfeiture, the government has two options, being civil forfeiture or criminal forfeiture.[62]

(b) Criminal forfeiture

Criminal forfeiture is part of the sentence in a criminal case.[63] Thus, it is often said that criminal forfeiture is an *in personam* action against the defendant, not an *in rem* action against the property involved in the offence.[64] This is true, and the *in personam* nature of the forfeiture has important consequences. For example, the court in a criminal forfeiture case can order the defendant to pay a money judgment or to forfeit substitute assets if the directly forfeitable property has been dissipated or cannot be found.[65] As discussed below, that could not happen in a civil forfeiture case with an *in rem* action against specific property. Accordingly, in this regard, criminal forfeiture is considered a broader and more powerful tool of law enforcement than is civil forfeiture.

It is also said, however, that the *in personam* nature of a criminal forfeiture means that only property belonging to the defendant can be forfeited in a criminal case.[66] That is not strictly true. Any property described in the applicable forfeiture statute, for example the proceeds of the offence or property used to facilitate it, may be included in the order of forfeiture, if the government establishes the connection between the property and the offence by a preponderance of the evidence.[67] At the time the order of forfeiture is entered, the defendant's ownership of the property is irrelevant.[68] Indeed, there are many cases in which property is forfeited even though the defendant had no legal interest in

---

[62]   See 18 U.S.C. § 983(a)(3).

[63]   See *Libretti v. United States*, 516 U.S. 29, at pp. 39–41 (1995).

[64]   See *United States v. Vampire Nation*, 451 F.3d 189 (3d Cir. 2006) (a criminal forfeiture order is a judgment *in personam* against the defendant; this distinguishes the forfeiture judgment in a criminal case from the *in rem* judgment in a civil forfeiture case); see also *Asset Forfeiture Law in US, supra* at ch. 15.

[65]   This is further explained in *Asset Forfeiture Law US, ibid.* chs 19 and 22.

[66]   See *United States v. Nava*, 404 F.3d 1119, at p. 1124 (9th Cir. 2005) (explaining the difference between civil and criminal forfeiture; because criminal forfeiture is *in personam*, only the defendant's property can be forfeited); see also *United States v. Gilbert*, 244 F.3d 888, at p. 919 (11th Cir. 2001) ('because it seeks to penalize the defendant for his illegal activities, *in personam* forfeiture reaches only that property, or portion thereof, owned by the defendant').

[67]   See *De Almeida v. United States*, 459 F.3d 377, 2006 WL 2106603 (2nd Cir. July 28, 2006) (criminal forfeiture is not limited to property owned by the defendant; 'it reaches *any* property that is involved in the offense' but the ancillary proceeding serves to ensure that property belonging to third parties who have been excluded from the criminal proceeding is not inadvertently forfeited).

[68]   *Ibid.* See also Rule 32.2(b)(2), Federal Rules of Criminal Procedure (providing that the preliminary order of forfeiture must direct the forfeiture of specific property 'without regard to any third party's interest in all or part of it').

the property at all. Stolen property, contraband, the proceeds of a drug sale and money laundered by the defendant for a third party are a few of the most common examples. However, because third parties are excluded from participating in a criminal trial, it would violate the due process rights of a third party to forfeit property that belonged *to him* in the criminal case.[69] Therefore, to protect the property rights of third parties, there must be a procedure for ensuring that the property subject to forfeiture in a criminal case does not belong to a third party. That procedure is called the 'ancillary proceeding' and is conducted by the court after the criminal trial is concluded.[70]

Again discussed below, the inability of the court to order the forfeiture of third party property in criminal forfeiture cases contrasts dramatically with civil forfeiture cases where the *in rem* nature of the proceeding allows the court to order the forfeiture of *any* property involved in the offence, subject only to the statutory innocent owner defence. Thus, in this regard, criminal forfeiture is a much more *limited* tool of law enforcement than is civil forfeiture.

Various statutes and Rule 32.2 of the Federal Rules of Criminal Procedure govern the criminal forfeiture process. To initiate a criminal forfeiture action, a prosecutor must give the defendant notice of the government's intent to forfeit his property by including a forfeiture allegation in the indictment.[71] The case then proceeds to trial in the normal fashion for any criminal case, except that if the property is not already in government custody, the government may apply for a pre-trial restraining order preserving the property pending the conclusion of the criminal trial.[72]

At trial, no mention is made of the forfeiture until and unless the defendant is convicted. In other words, the trial is bifurcated. Once the defendant is convicted, however, the court (or the jury, if a party so requests) hears additional evidence, argument and instructions on the forfeiture and returns a special verdict finding, by a preponderance of the evidence, that the government has established the requisite nexus between the property and the crime.[73] That is, the court (or jury) must determine that the property in question was in fact the proceeds of the offence, constituted facilitating property or property

---

[69]   See *United States v. Totaro*, 345 F.3d 989, at p. 993 (8th Cir. 2003) (because criminal forfeiture is *in personam,* property of third parties cannot be forfeited; if a third party's interest could be forfeited, the forfeiture would become an *in rem* action in which the third party would have the right to contest the forfeiture on more than ownership grounds).

[70]   See *Asset Forfeiture Law in US, supra* at ch. 23.

[71]   See Federal Rules of Criminal Procedure (hereinafter Criminal Procedure), Rule 32.2(a).

[72]   See 21 U.S.C. § 853(e).

[73]   See Criminal Procedure, Rule 32.2(b).

'involved' in the offence, or had whatever other relationship to the offence that the applicable forfeiture statute requires. Once that finding is made, the court enters a preliminary order of forfeiture that is made final and included in the judgment of the court at sentencing.[74] As noted earlier, neither the court nor the jury is concerned with the ownership of the property at this stage of the case; that issue is not litigated until and unless some third party contests the forfeiture on ownership grounds in the post-trial ancillary proceeding.[75]

Criminal forfeiture procedure is a complex topic on which the case law is developing at a tremendous pace.[76]

(c)   Civil forfeiture

Civil forfeiture is *not* part of a criminal case. In a civil forfeiture case, the government files a separate civil action *in rem* against the property itself, and then proves by a preponderance of the evidence that the property was derived from or was used to commit a crime. Because a civil forfeiture does not depend on a criminal conviction, the forfeiture action may be filed before indictment, after indictment or if there is no indictment at all.[77]

It is because civil forfeiture actions are brought against the property directly that federal civil forfeiture cases have what appear to the outsider to be very peculiar names, such as *United States v. Ninety-Three (93) Firearms,*[78] or *United States v. One 1992 Ford Mustang GT,*[79] or *United States v. $557,933.89, More or Less, in U.S. Funds.*[80]

---

[74]   *Ibid.*

[75]   *Ibid.* Rule 32.2(b) and (c).

[76]   This topic is discussed more fully in *Asset Forfeiture Law in US, supra* at chs 15–23.

[77]   See *United States v. One-Sixth Share,* 326 F.3d 36, at p. 40 (1st Cir. 2003) ('Because civil forfeiture is an *in rem* proceeding, the property subject to forfeiture is the defendant. Thus, defenses against the forfeiture can be brought only by third parties, who must intervene'); see also *United States v. Cherry,* 330 F.3d 658, at p. 666 n. 16 (4th Cir. 2003) ('The most notable distinction between civil and criminal forfeiture is that civil forfeiture proceedings are brought against property, not against the property owner; the owner's culpability is irrelevant in deciding whether property should be forfeited'); see also *United States v. All Funds in Account Nos. 747.034/278 (Banco Espanol de Credito),* 295 F.3d 23, at p. 25 (D.C. Cir. 2002) ('Civil forfeiture actions are brought against property, not people. The owner of the property may intervene to protect his interest.'); see also *$734,578.82 in U.S. Currency,* at p. 657 (civil forfeiture is an *in rem* action against the property itself; the forfeiture is 'not conditioned on the culpability of the owner of the defendant property').

[78]   330 F.3d 414 (6th Cir. 2003).

[79]   73 F. Supp. 2d 1131 (C.D. Cal. 1999).

[80]   287 F.3d 66 (2d Cir. 2002).

At one time it was said that civil forfeiture was based on the legal fiction that the property itself was guilty of the offence. That is no longer so. It is true that the property is named as the defendant in the civil forfeiture case, but not because the property itself did anything wrong. Things do not commit crimes; people commit crimes using or obtaining things that consequently become forfeitable to the State. The *in rem* structure of civil forfeiture is simply a procedural convenience. It is a way for the government to identify the thing that is subject to forfeiture and the grounds therefore, and to give anyone and everyone with an interest in that property the opportunity to come into court at one time and contest the forfeiture action.[81] The alternative, being a separate civil action against every person or entity with a potential legal interest in the property, would be administratively impossible.

Essentially then, when the government commences an *in rem* forfeiture action it is saying, 'this property was derived from or was used to commit a criminal offence. For a variety of public policy and law enforcement reasons, it should be confiscated. Anyone who has a legal interest in property and who wishes to contest the forfeiture may now do so.'

Procedurally, civil forfeiture actions are much like other civil cases.[82] The government, as plaintiff, files a verified complaint alleging that the property in question is subject to forfeiture in terms of the applicable forfeiture statute, and claimants are required to file claims to the property and to answer the forfeiture complaint within a certain period of time.[83] Thereafter, the case moves forward through civil discovery, motions practice (for example, motions to dismiss on the pleadings, motion for judgment for the government for lack of standing on the part of the claimant and motion for summary judgment on the merits) and trial. A trial by jury is guaranteed by the 7th Amendment if the claimant has standing and asserts the right to a jury at trial.[84] The government bears the burden of establishing the forfeitability of the property by a preponderance of the evidence.[85]

Even if the government succeeds in establishing the nexus between the property and an offence, the case is not over. To protect the interests of truly innocent property owners who were unaware that their property was being used for an illegal purpose, or who took all reasonable steps under the circum-

---

[81]   See *Ursery*, 518 U.S. at p. 297 (Kennedy J, concurring).

[82]   This topic is discussed more fully in *Asset Forfeiture Law in US, supra* at chs 6–11.

[83]   Civil forfeiture procedure is governed by 18 U.S.C. § 983 and by Supplemental Rule G of the Federal Rules of Civil Procedure.

[84]   See *United States v. One Lincoln Navigator 1998,* 328 F.3d 1011, at p. 1014 n. 2 (8th Cir. 2003) (claimant has a 7th Amendment right to a jury trial on her innocent owner defense).

[85]   See 18 U.S.C. § 983(c).

stances to stop it, Congress has enacted a 'uniform innocent owner defense'.[86] Under that statute, a person contesting the forfeiture must establish his owner-ship interests and his innocence by a preponderance of the evidence.[87]

Ultimately, if the government establishes the forfeitability of the property, and no claimant succeeds in proving the elements of an innocent owner defence, the court will enter judgment for the government and title to the prop-erty will pass to the United States.

For a variety of reasons, in certain cases, civil forfeiture can be a much more powerful tool of law enforcement than criminal forfeiture. As discussed below, it is the option of choice in numerous instances when criminal forfei-ture is unavailable or provides an inadequate remedy. But civil forfeiture has an important limitation of its own: because the forfeiture is limited to the specific property involved in the crime, the government can only forfeit the actual property derived from or used to commit the offence.[88] There are no money judgments and no forfeitures of substitute assets if the property directly traceable to the crime turns out to be missing or has been dissipated or spent.[89]

Tactical Choices: Civil Versus Criminal Forfeiture

The best way to appreciate the differences between civil and criminal forfei-ture under federal law in the United States may be to run through the check-list of tactical considerations that a federal prosecutor takes into account when deciding whether to pursue the forfeiture civilly or criminally. It is entirely appropriate (and commonplace) for the prosecutor to commence parallel civil and criminal cases in order to keep all options open.[90]

What are the advantages of doing the case civilly versus criminally?

---

[86] See 18 U.S.C. § 983(d).

[87] See *Asset Forfeiture Law in US, supra* at ch. 12; see also Stefan D. Cassella (2001), 'The Uniform Innocent Owner Defense to Civil Asset Forfeiture', *Kentucky L.J.*, **89**, 653.

[88] See *United States v. $8,221,877.16 in U.S. Currency*, 330 F.3d 141, at p. 158 (3rd Cir. 2003) (in civil forfeiture cases, the government is required to trace the seized property directly to the offence giving rise to the forfeiture).

[89] There are exceptions to this general rule: several civil forfeiture statutes, for example 18 U.S.C. § 545, permit the forfeiture of the 'value' of the property involved in the offence, see *Ahmad*, at p. 809 (4th Cir. 2000); and 18 U.S.C. § 984 relaxes the tracing requirement for fungible property in certain circumstances. See also 18 U.S.C. § 981(k) (no tracing requirement when the defendant property is funds in the corre-spondent bank account of a foreign bank).

[90] See *United States v. One Parcel... Lot 41, Berryhill Farm*, 128 F.3d 1386, at p. 1391 (10th Cir. 1997) (civil case stayed pending criminal trial; once stay was lifted, court granted motion to civilly forfeit property that was also forfeited in the criminal case).

(a) The advantages of civil forfeiture[91]

1. The lower burden of proof In a civil case, the government is only required to prove the forfeitability of the property by a preponderance of the evidence. That applies both to the proof that the crime was committed and to the proof that the property was derived from or was used to commit the crime. In contrast, in criminal cases, the government must prove beyond a reasonable doubt that the crime was committed and that the defendant committed the crime. Only the nexus between the property and the offence giving rise to the forfeiture can be shown by the preponderance standard.

2. There is no need for a criminal conviction Because the civil forfeiture is a separate civil proceeding against the property *in rem*, neither the property owner, nor anyone else for that matter, need be convicted of the crime giving rise to the forfeiture.[92] Thus, civil forfeiture is an essential tool when the government seeks to forfeit the property of fugitives or of defendants who have died,[93] or where it can prove that the property was involved in a crime but cannot prove who the wrongdoer was. A typical example of the latter situation is when law enforcement officers find a stash of currency bearing all of the indicia of money derived from a drug deal (drug residue on large quantities of small denomination bills, bundled in rubber bands and wrapped in plastic or brown paper) but have no idea who the drug dealer was who assembled the currency.[94]

Civil forfeiture is also available as a means of recovering property for the benefit of victims and for imposing a sanction on the wrongdoer, when the

---

[91]   See also Stefan D. Cassella (2008), 'The Case for Civil Forfeiture: Why in rem proceedings are an essential tool for recovering the proceeds of crime', *Journal of Money Laundering Control*, **11**, 8.

[92]   See *Ursery*, at pp. 267–68 (pursuing civil and criminal forfeiture based on the same underlying offence is not a violation of 5th Amendment Double Jeopardy Clause because *in rem* civil proceedings are not neither punishment nor criminal); see also *One Assortment of 89 Firearms*, at p. 366 (1984) (acquittal on gun violation under § 922 does not bar civil forfeiture under § 982(d)); see also *One Lot Emerald Cut*, at p. 237 (*per curiam*) (acquittal on criminal smuggling charge does not bar later civil forfeiture); see also *Model 250 PA 23 Aircraft*, at p. 360 (overturning claimant's criminal conviction for alien smuggling has no effect on civil forfeiture under § 1324(b)); see also *1988 Oldsmobile Cutlass Supreme*, at p. 675 (5th Cir. 1993) (acquittal of claimant does not create material issue of fact to avoid summary judgment in civil forfeiture case); see also *United States v. Dunn*, 802 F.2d 646, at p. 647 (2d Cir. 1986) (same).

[93]   See *United States v. Real Property at 40 Clark Road*, 52 F. Supp. 2d 254, at p. 265 (D. Mass. 1999) (defendant died while criminal forfeiture was pending, making civil forfeiture necessary).

[94]   See *Asset Forfeiture Law in US, supra* § 25-5.

crime is a relatively minor offence and the interests of justice do not require bringing to bear the full force of the federal criminal justice apparatus against the accused. For example, teenagers who use their home computers to produce counterfeit $20 bills are more likely to have the computer confiscated in a civil forfeiture case than to be prosecuted and sent to prison for the offence.

3.   The forfeiture is not limited to property related to a particular transaction
As already mentioned, because criminal forfeiture is part of sentencing, the forfeiture order imposed by a court in a criminal case is limited to the property involved in the particular offence for which the defendant was convicted. In contrast, civil forfeiture actions *in rem* may be brought against any property derived from either a specific offence or from a course of conduct. For example, criminal forfeiture in a drug case might be limited to the proceeds of the specific transaction charged in the indictment, but a civil forfeiture could reach all proceeds of someone's long-running career as a drug dealer.[95]

4.   Forfeiting the property of third parties   Because third parties are excluded from participating in the criminal case (until the ancillary proceeding), property belonging to third parties is not subject to criminal forfeiture. On the other hand, anyone with an interest in the property can contest a civil forfeiture. Therefore, if the government establishes the required nexus between the property and the offence in a civil forfeiture case, and it has given proper notice of the forfeiture to all interested parties, it is able to obtain a judgment of forfeiture against the property regardless of who the owner of the property might be. Accordingly, a prosecutor will elect to use civil forfeiture when a criminal uses someone else's property to commit a crime, and the third party is not an innocent owner.

5.   There is less work for the criminal prosecutor   Criminal prosecutors like to point out that asset forfeiture law is a bit of a specialty in the United States, and that specialties are best handled by specialists. Thus, in some jurisdictions, policy makers have decided that it is preferable to have a forfeiture specialist handle the forfeiture in a separate civil case, rather than have the overburdened criminal prosecutor go through the trouble of learning forfeiture law so that the forfeiture can be made part of the criminal prosecution and sentence.

---

[95]   See *United States v. Two Parcels in Russell County*, 92 F.3d 1123, at p. 1128 (11th Cir. 1996) (when probable cause is based on evidence that the participants are generally engaged in the drug business, have no other source of income, and bought the properties with drug proceeds, it is not necessary to identify specific drug transactions in the complaint); *United States v. 5443 Suffield Terrace*, 209 F. Supp. 2d 919, at p. 923 (N.D. Ill. 2002) (forfeiture complaint does not have to detail specific transactions supporting government's theory of forfeiture).

(b)   The disadvantages of civil forfeiture

1.   There is more work for everyone else   The flip side of the last point, of course, is that the effort saved by the criminal prosecutor is offset by the additional work that must be done by everyone else when handling a forfeiture separately as a civil matter instead of as part of a pending criminal case. A civil forfeiture requires the filing of a separate action and relitigating all of the issues that were litigated in the criminal case, making work for a civil specialist, his or her support staff and the court.

2.   Filing deadlines   If property is initially seized for the purpose of civil forfeiture, the government must file its complaint against the property within 90 days of the filing of any claim contesting an administrative forfeiture proceeding. If the government fails to comply with this deadline, and no exceptions apply, civil forfeiture of the property in connection with the offence for which it was seized is forever barred.[96] In contrast, criminal forfeiture actions are not subject to any statutory deadlines.

3.   Unless stayed by the court, a parallel civil case can interfere with a criminal investigation or trial   Once a civil forfeiture action is commenced, both sides have the option of requesting the other side to produce evidence in support of its case through the process of civil discovery. Claimants who are also defendants in parallel criminal matters often seek to use this procedure to gain access to the government's witnesses and evidence in ways that would not be allowed in the criminal case. For example, the claimant may seek to get a preview of the government's criminal case by noticing the deposition of the government's case agent or confidential informant. In reality, however, this is rarely a serious problem, as the government's reciprocal right to notice the deposition of the defendant himself usually persuades both sides that it would be preferable for the court to order the stay of the civil case until the parallel criminal matter is resolved.[97]

4.   The forfeiture is limited to property traceable to the offence   The most serious limitation of civil forfeiture is that, as an *in rem* action, the government must prove that the defendant property is directly traceable to the underlying criminal offence. The court may not, in other words, order the forfeiture of a money judgment or substitute assets. This is a particular problem in cases involving cash proceeds of, say, a drug deal or a fraud offence, where the

---

[96]   See *Asset Forfeiture Law in US*, *supra* at ch. 7; see also 18 U.S.C. § 983(a)(3).
[97]   See *Asset Forfeiture Law in US*, *ibid.* § 8-3; see also 18 U.S.C. § 981(g) (providing for the stay of a civil forfeiture case at the request of either side).

money actually involved in or derived from the crime has been commingled with other funds or dissipated. The only salvation for the government in such matters – and for the victims on whose behalf the government may be seeking to recover the property – is that cash and electronic funds are considered fungible for one year after the offence is committed.[98] In cases where that statute applies, it is unnecessary for the government to comply with the strict tracing requirements that otherwise govern civil forfeiture cases.[99]

5. A successful claimant is entitled to attorneys fees The 'American Rule' is that parties to civil cases pay their own costs and attorney's fees. But Congress has provided that a claimant who prevails in a civil forfeiture case is entitled to have the government pay his attorney's fees and other litigation expenses.[100] That is so regardless of how meritorious the government's case might have been. In contrast, in criminal forfeiture cases, third parties are entitled to attorney's fees only in the relatively rare case in which the government's case was not 'substantially justified'.[101]

(c)   The advantages of criminal forfeiture

1. A single proceeding takes care of the forfeiture of the defendant's interest A civil forfeiture is a separate proceeding that can takes years to process through a federal district court. If there is a parallel criminal case, filing a separate civil case means relitigating many if not all of the issues that the government already established in the criminal trial. In contrast, criminal forfeiture permits the court to dispose of the forfeiture as part of the sentencing phase of the criminal trial or guilty plea, saving substantial time and resources.

---

[98]   See *Asset Forfeiture Law in US, ibid.* § 11-3; see also 18 U.S.C. § 984; see also *United States v. U.S. Currency Deposited in Account No. 1115000763247 For Active Trade Company*, 176 F.3d 941, at pp. 946–47 (7th Cir. 1999) (once the government has established probable cause to believe that the amount of money laundered through a bank account in the past year exceeds the balance in the account at the time of seizure, the entire balance is subject to forfeiture under § 984).

[99]   See *Marine Midland Bank, N.A. v. United States*, 11 F.3d 1119, at p. 1126 (2d Cir. 1993) (§ 984 eliminates tracing requirement); See also 18 U.S.C. § 981(k) (eliminating the tracing requirement in cases involving correspondent accounts of foreign banks).

[100]   See 28 U.S.C. § 2465(b).

[101]   See *United States v. Douglas*, 55 F.3d 584, at pp. 587–88 (11th Cir. 1995) (the government's position in obtaining preliminary order of forfeiture not substantially justified where the government failed to take notice that property had been awarded to third party in action enforcing civil judgment).

2.   The court can order the forfeiture of a money judgment and/or substitute assets   The claim to fame for criminal forfeiture is that it allows the court to order a defendant to pay a money judgment in an amount equal to the value of the proceeds the defendant realized from the crime. Thus, a defendant who defrauded his victims of $10 million may be ordered to pay a $10 million judgment to the government, even if the actual money derived from the crime has disappeared.[102] Moreover, the court can order the forfeiture of some unrelated, untainted asset of equal value to satisfy the money judgment.[103] In contrast, civil forfeitures, as they are *in rem* proceedings, are limited to property directly traceable to the underlying offence. The court could no more order the forfeiture of a substitute asset for a missing *in rem* defendant in a civil forfeiture case than it could order the conviction and sentence of a substitute individual for a missing human defendant in a criminal case.[104]

3.   There are no statutory time limits on filing an indictment following seizure of the property   If property is seized in the first instance for civil forfeiture, and someone files a claim, the government must commence judicial forfeiture proceedings within 90 days.[105] But if the property is seized in the first instance for criminal forfeiture, as would generally be the case if the property were seized pursuant to a criminal seizure warrant,[106] the time limits for instituting judicial forfeiture proceedings do not come into play. The trade off is that, in that instance, the government probably must forego the option of disposing of the case as an uncontested administrative forfeiture matter. Generally, the government would prefer to start every case as an administrative forfeiture case so that uncontested matters can be disposed of quickly.

4.   Third parties have no right to recover attorneys' fees   The right to attorneys' fees in 28 U.S.C. § 2465(b) applies only to civil forfeiture cases. It does not apply to any part of a criminal forfeiture case, including the ancillary proceeding in which third party rights are litigated.

---

[102]   See *Asset Forfeiture Law in US, supra* § 19-4.
[103]   See *Asset Forfeiture Law in US, ibid.* ch. 22; see also *United States v. Carroll*, 346 F.3d 744 (7th Cir. 2003) (defendant may be ordered to forfeit 'every last penny' he owns as substitute assets to satisfy a money judgment).
[104]   *But* see 18 U.S.C. § 545 (allowing value-based civil forfeiture orders in smuggling cases); 18 U.S.C. § 984 (treating certain property as fungible for one year after the offence).
[105]   See 18 U.S.C. § 983(a)(3).
[106]   See 21 U.S.C. § 853(f).

(d) The disadvantages of criminal forfeiture

1. Property of third parties cannot be forfeited in a criminal case As already mentioned, because third parties are excluded from participating or intervening in a criminal case, property belonging to a third party cannot be forfeited criminally. Any person who establishes that he or she was the true owner of the property at the time the crime was committed, or that he acquired it later as a bona fide purchaser for value, is entitled to have the forfeiture declared void in a post-trial ancillary proceeding.[107] Most important, a third party challenging a criminal forfeiture on the ground that the property belonged to him, not to the defendant, when the crime occurred does not have to be innocent. He or she must establish *superior* ownership, not *innocent* ownership.[108] Thus, in criminal cases, non-innocent spouses and unindicted co-conspirators who had an interest in the property at the time the crime occurred can recover the forfeited property in the ancillary proceeding. To forfeit the interests of such persons, the government must resort to civil forfeiture and rebut the claimant's attempt to establish an innocent owner defense.

2. Bifurcation of trial and additional jury instructions and special verdicts add to the length of the criminal trial Most criminal forfeiture proceedings are short in duration. Nevertheless, it is undeniable that even the most straightforward criminal forfeiture proceeding will add to the length of what may already have been a protracted criminal proceeding. Often all parties, including the judge and the jury, will be exhausted at the end of the criminal case and will prefer to abort the criminal forfeiture in favor of a separate civil proceeding at another time.

3. Criminal forfeiture requires a criminal conviction Because criminal forfeiture is part of the defendant's sentence, there can be no forfeiture without a conviction.[109] This eliminates criminal forfeiture as an option in cases where the defendant is a fugitive or is dead, or where, in the interests of justice, the government has decided not to prosecute the owner of the property, such as a spouse who played a minor role in the commission of the offence. It also means that if the defendant pleads guilty to just one count of a multi-count indictment, the forfeiture may be limited to the property involved in that single count.[110] To forfeit the property involved in the remaining counts, or in

---

[107] See *Asset Forfeiture Law in US, supra* at ch. 23; see also 21 U.S.C. § 853(n).
[108] *Ibid.*
[109] *Ibid.* § 15-3.
[110] See *United States v. Adams,* 189 Fed. Appx. 600, 2006 WL 1876863 (9th Cir. June 29, 2006) (following *United States v. Garcia-Guizar,* 160 F.3d 511 (9th Cir. Oct

offences that were never charged in the criminal case at all, the government must use civil forfeiture.

4.   Delay in disposing of property   If property is forfeited in a criminal case, it cannot be disposed of until the criminal case is over and all potential third parties have had their chance to contest the forfeiture. This may be years after the property was seized at the outset of the case. In contrast, if the property is forfeited administratively, and no one files a claim, the forfeiture can be concluded within a few weeks of the seizure. Therefore, the government generally prefers to start a forfeiture administratively, even if there is going to be a criminal prosecution, to see if the forfeiture is going to be uncontested.

RETROSPECTIVE ON THE EVOLUTION OF FORFEITURE LAW

The evolution of asset forfeiture law in the United States is a tale of constant expansion and adaptation. Like a rare species of plant that has been plucked from the biological niche where it first evolved, adapted to new uses and new environments, and disseminated across the globe to serve new purposes that humans find useful, the practice of asset forfeiture, has been lifted from the remote corner of admiralty and customs law where it was conceived, applied to an ever-growing set of new crimes and circumstances, and has become a powerful tool of law enforcement routinely applied in tens of thousands of criminal cases. But just as a plant or animal can thrive in a new environment only if, in the course of biological evolution, it is able to adapt its parts to new uses for which they were never intended, it was necessary to adapt, modify and interpret the legal concepts underlying asset forfeiture in new ways so that the ancient practice could serve its new functions.

Sometimes, that process of adaption has gone smoothly, and sometimes it has not. Forfeiting an airplane used to smuggle drugs in the 21st century is not terribly different in either concept or application from forfeiting a vessel used to smuggle pirate booty in 1789. But forfeiting the residence of a drug dealer and his family, or the retirement plan of a corrupt physician, or the bank account of a charitable enterprise accused of financing terrorism is very different indeed. As the old concept designed to collect customs revenue and confiscate pirate ships was applied to these new situations, it was inevitable that it would be modified and subjected to limitations and constraints.

23,1998)); if defendant pleads guilty to a fraud conspiracy beginning 'no later than' 2001, proceeds derived from fraud occurring in 1999 were not related to the crime of conviction and could not be forfeited in the criminal case).

The Supreme Court of the United States has been engaged for a very long time in the process of determining how the protections afforded to individual liberty and property by the Bill of Rights limit the application of the asset forfeiture laws. That process accelerated dramatically in the 1990s: as the forfeiture laws matured and began to realise their full potential as instruments of the state in the battle against crime, the understanding of the constitutional limits of forfeiture practice had to develop and mature. The evolution of forfeiture law has not ended and will likely never end, but from the perspective of the first decade of the 21st century, we are able to look back and see how, in the seminal period just ended, the Constitutional guarantees of due process, proportionality and the right to a fair trial were applied to the process of forfeiting the proceeds and instruments of crime. The courts will be fussing over the details for a long time, but the framework is now set: the basic rules of the game are known.

3. Ireland: a multi-disciplinary approach to proceeds of crime

Felix J. McKenna and Kate Egan*

> Macavity, Macavity, there's no one like Macavity,
> There never was a cat of such deceitfulness and suavity.
> He always has an alibi, and one or two to spare:
> At whatever time the deed took place –
> MACAVITY WASN'T THERE!
>
> T. S. Elliot[1]

INTRODUCTION

Civil forfeiture was introduced to Ireland in the Proceeds of Crime Act 1996 (hereinafter 1996 Act), as part of the infamous 'Summer Crime Package' of that year. The drug problem, from a Garda Síochána (police) perspective,[2] can be traced back to the 1960s when the misuse of amphetamines became widespread, particularly in Dublin.[3] By the 1990s, organized criminal gangs involved in drug trafficking had started to engage in 'gangland murders' to protect their trade. Public alarm at the apparent rise in serious crime reached

---

* Substantial parts of this chapter were published previously in Fachtna Murphy and Barry Galvin, 'Targeting the financial wealth of criminals in Ireland: the law and practice' in J. P. McCutcheon and D. Walsh (eds) (1999), *The Confiscation of Criminal Assets: Law and Procedure*, Dublin, Ireland: Round Hall Sweet & Maxwell, pp. 9–35, and are reproduced here with the permission of the authors of that piece.

1 From 'Macavity – the Mystery Cat', a poem by T. S. Elliot, quoted by O'Higgins J in *Murphy v. GM PB PC Ltd. and GH*, unreported, High Court, 4 June 1999; aff'd [2001] 4 IR 113 (SC) (hereinafter *Murphy*).

2 Meaning literally 'guards of the peace'. Uniformed police do not carry firearms in Ireland.

3 By 1970 the range of drugs in use had extended to barbiturates, tranquillizers, LSD and cannabis. By and large the problem was confined to the greater Dublin area, however, in the late 1970s, recognizable patterns of abuse started to emerge in the provinces too. Heroin first appeared in Dublin in 1979 and was followed by ecstasy in 1991. The latter has spread at an alarming rate throughout the country.

fever pitch in the wake of two high profile murders: those of well-known journalist Veronica Guerin, and Detective Garda Gerry McCabe, just three weeks apart in June 1996.[4]

Inevitably, these developments fuelled a public demand for the law to 'get tough' on organized crime. It proved difficult, however, to secure convictions against those controlling the sophisticated criminal gangs involved. The traditional focus of law enforcement in Ireland had been on arresting and prosecuting offenders. The major perpetrators, however, remained vigilant to ensure that no material evidence could be found to link them with their offences and intimidation of witnesses became widespread.

In this climate, the then Minister for Justice Nora Owen introduced extensive criminal justice reforms in the summer of 1996, including the Criminal Assets Bureau Act, the Proceeds of Crime Act and the Drug Trafficking Act. The last piece of legislation will not be discussed at any length in this chapter, suffice it to say that it expanded the powers of law enforcement agents by allowing suspects to be held for seven days without charge,[5] by vesting authority in senior Garda officers to issue search warrants in cases of suspected drug trafficking,[6] by facilitating the attendance of customs officers in court during the questioning of suspects and by allowing inferences to be drawn from the silence in response to such questioning.[7] The three Acts were pushed through the legislative process in five weeks – remarkably speedily by the standards of the usually thorough Irish legislature – so speedily, in fact, that it has been argued that the haste by which the new crime package passed into law should affect the presumption of constitutionality usually enjoyed by new legislation.[8] Furthermore, 1996 saw for the first time the sanctioning of the exchange of information between An Garda Síochána (Ireland's National Police Service) and the Revenue Commissioners, with the advent of the Disclosure of Certain Information for Taxation and Other Purposes Act 1996.

This chapter examines the current Irish laws and strategies against the proceeds of crime, discusses the case law generated from the 1996 legislation, and describes the functions and operations of the Criminal Assets Bureau.

---

[4]   Ms Guerin is thought to have been killed to silence her investigative reporting into organized crime, while Garda McCabe was shot dead by subversives in the course of a paramilitary style armed robbery.

[5]   See Drug Trafficking Act 1996, s. 2.

[6]   *Ibid.* s. 8.

[7]   *Ibid.* s. 7.

[8]   In *Murphy* this argument was ultimately rejected, see HC transcript, p. 22, para. 1.

OVERVIEW OF IRELAND'S UNIQUE CIVIL FORFEITURE REGIME

Many writers have traced the influence of the United States (US) forfeiture regime on its younger Irish counterpart. However, there already existed an important domestic template for confiscation in Irish counter-subversion legislation, the significance of which should not be underestimated.[9] The US model emerged from the Racketeer Influence and Corrupt Organizations Act 1970 (hereinafter RICO),[10] which was amended to allow confiscation of the proceeds of corporate crime, as well as any instruments involved therein; racketeering; drug trafficking and money laundering.[11] Prior to this, RICO had required a conviction before asset forfeiture could proceed; however, the comprehensive Drug Abuse Prevention and Control Act 1970 made it possible for property to be forfeited in a civil court, without a criminal conviction.[12]

RICO provides for both civil and criminal forfeiture, the latter being minded primarily towards retribution and, as such, dependent on conviction.[13] The actual owner of the property must be convicted before these particular confiscation powers come into effect. The 'sting in the tail' of RICO is that if the crime tainted assets disappear or become unavailable, the State can actually forfeit legitimate assets held by the defendant in their place. The civil forfeiture powers, however, do not depend on conviction and such procedures operate against the property rather than the person. Such forfeiture on the lower civil standard of proof is considered justifiable as it is not thought to constitute punishment. Furthermore, an administrative rather than judicial procedure is available where the property is worth less than $500 000. The US legislation has found itself subject to several challenges and the resulting case law is instructive for the Irish courts.

---

[9] The Offences Against the State (Amendment) Act 1985 (hereinafter 1985 Act), s. 2 of which allowed the freezing and forfeiture of moneys thought to be held by illegal organizations. The significance of this legislation was highlighted by Liz Campbell in a recent article analysing the criminological theory underpinning the Irish forfeiture regime, see Liz Campbell (2007), 'Theorising Asset Forfeiture in Ireland', *Journal of Criminal Law*, **71**, 441 (hereinafter Theorising Asset Forfeiture).

[10] See The Racketeer Influenced and Corrupt Organizations Statute, Title IX to the Organized Crime Control Act 1970, 18 USC S S 1961 *et seq*. For more on the US system, see Chapter 2 of this book.

[11] The history of civil forfeiture in the US is documented in *Calero-Toledo v. Peason Yacht Leasing Co*, 416 U.S. 663 (hereinafter *Calero-Toledo*), at p. 680 (1974). See also Chapter 2 of this book.

[12] See Drug Abuse Prevention and Control Act 1970, 21 USC S 848.

[13] McCutcheon and Walsh think this approach would 'raise a few eyebrows' in Ireland: see J. P. McCutcheon and D. Walsh (eds) (1999), *The Confiscation of Criminal Assets: Law and Procedure*, Dublin, Ireland: Round Hall Sweet & Maxwell (hereinafter *Confiscation of Criminal Assets*), at p. 7, para. 2.

There is still some debate as to whether the Irish forfeiture provisions are truly civil in nature, or whether in fact they create criminal offences.[14] However, a claim that the 1996 Act represents no more than 'ersatz civil law' was dismissed by the High Court in *Murphy*.[15] The court reasoned, *inter alia*, that forfeiture proceedings operate *in rem* (rather than *in personam*); there is (supposedly) no moral opprobrium attached to offences under the statute; no one is put on trial as such; no *mens rea* is required for consummation of the offence; and there is no threat of imprisonment on conviction.[16] Further support for this conclusion can be found in *Goodman v. Hamilton (No. 1)* (hereinafter *Goodman*), where it was held, regarding inquiries by civil tribunals, that since there is no requirement in the Irish Constitution that charges *must* be brought where proscribed acts are alleged, it follows that the criminal trial is not the only legitimate means of investigating such acts.[17] Moreover, and more directly on the subject of forfeiture, it was held by the Supreme Court in *Gilligan* that there is no bar to the determining of matters which may constitute elements of a criminal offence without actually *trying* such offence, and accordingly the Irish constitutional requirement of trial 'in due course of law' does not apply in the course of civil or other proceedings which do not amount to a full scale trial.[18] It was further held in *Goodman* that the establishment of tribunals of enquiry, which are conducted without all the trappings of a criminal trial, is consistent with the European Convention on Human Rights (hereinafter ECHR).[19]

As mentioned, the forfeiture of goods is nothing new to Irish law. However, as McCutcheon and Walsh point out, the 1996 legislation marked a definite change in the approach of the Irish legislature: forfeiture went from a reactive side-effect to convictions for breaches of specific prohibitions, to being deployed as a pro-active crime control strategy in itself.[20] This new Irish strategy reflects the English common-law position, as summarised in *Attorney General v. Blake*.[21] In that case, the Court of Appeal upheld a freezing order placed on profits raised by a book published in breach of official secrets legislation, which was imposed absent any prosecution or conviction. The court reasoned that the fact that no

---

14   See for example, Liz Campbell in *Theorising Asset Forfeiture*, *supra* who argues that based on tests enunciated by the US Supreme Court in *United States v. Ward* (1980) 448 US 242 and *Kennedy v. Mendoza* (1963) 372 US 144 at pp. 168–9, the Irish forfeiture regime is in fact criminal in nature.

15   *Murphy* (HC), transcript, p. 27, para. 4.

16   See *Murphy* (HC), transcript, p. 29, para. 4. The forfeiture order was distinguished from a *Mareva* order, which acts *in personam*.

17   See *Goodman v. Hamilton (No. 1)*, [1992] 2 IR 542.

18   *Gilligan v. Criminal Assets Bureau* [1998] 3 IR 185 (HC), aff'd [2001] T.I.T.R. 383 (SC) (hereinafter *Gilligan*).

19   See *Goodman*.

20   See *Confiscation of Criminal Assets*, *supra* at p. 5, para. 2.

21   See *Attorney General v. Blake*, [1998] 1 All ER 833 (hereinafter *Blake*).

prosecution could be brought did not detract from the Attorney General's right, as guardian of the public interest, to enforce public policy in the civil courts, such policy being that those breaking the criminal law should not be permitted to benefit from their misadventures.[22] The court also went on to hold that said forfeiture powers were compliant with the ECHR. A similar approach was taken by the Irish High Court in *M. v. D.*, where Moriarty J held that in assessing justification for the interference to personal rights caused by forfeiture, it was legitimate to take account of the international phenomenon of organized crime and the characteristic ability of those in the higher echelons of criminal organizations to evade the arm of the law.[23]

The immediate distinction between this old Irish framework and the current regime outlined below is that previously, forfeiture could only flow from conviction of a specific offence. This is no longer necessary, with a new civil forfeiture framework now complementing existing criminal confiscation powers. The latter, of course, takes precedence and is preferred over the former, where conviction is possible. Furthermore, where both civil and criminal proceedings have been instituted, the criminal confiscation overrides any civil freezing order already in place. However, once conviction is entered, the standard of proving that certain property derives from crime and is thus eligible for confiscation is on the balance of probabilities. This reduced standard of proof was thought to be justified by the fact that, in the sphere of organized crime, it is notoriously difficult to institute prosecution let alone secure convictions and existing powers available only on the higher criminal standard had proven wholly inadequate when organized crime came to dominate law enforcement policy in 1990s.

The far-reaching powers contained in the 1996 legislation have received a mixed reception, with some hailing them as a model for the rest of Europe[24] and predicting that civil forfeiture will take centre stage in future crime control strategies,[25] some dismissing them as the product of political hysteria and 'moral panic',[26] and counsel in *Gilligan* going so far as to brand them 'Kafkaesque'.[27] McCutcheon and Walsh have even predicted that the US would look to the novel

---

[22]   *Ibid.*
[23]   See *M. v. D.* [1998] 3 IR 175 (High Court) (hereinafter *M. v. D.*), per Moriarty J at p. 178.
[24]   See *Confiscation of Criminal Assets, supra* at p. 5, para. 3.
[25]   *Ibid.* at p. 6, para. 1.
[26]   See J. Meade (2000), 'Organized Crime, Moral Panic and Law Reform: the Irish Adoption of Civil Forfeiture', *Irish Criminal Law Journal*, **10** (1), 11. For similar readings of the 1996 'Summer Crime Package', see G. Carey (1999), 'The Performative Character of Media Presentation of Crime', *Irish Criminal Law Journal*, **9**, 47; see also I. O'Donnell and E. O'Sullivan (eds) (2001), *Crime Control in Ireland: the Politics of Intolerance*, Cork, Ireland: Cork University Press.
[27]   See *Gilligan*, para. 22.

features of the Irish civil forfeiture regime as a possible approach for overcoming the internal dissent which has plagued their own regime.[28] A 2005 report compiled under the auspices of the Council of Europe by the Group of States Against Corruption (also known as 'GRECO') spoke very positively about the new Irish regime, concluding that 'the efficiency of the civil forfeiture scheme is particularly impressive'.[29]

The problem under previous regimes was that even where convictions were secured, the punishments available were insufficient to remove the financial incentive for committing such crimes in the first place. Generally, a person who had profited from criminal activity could be discommoded only by the imposition of a fine or a term of imprisonment on conviction, unless convicted under one of a few specific statutory regimes. For example, where a person stood convicted of an offence under the Misuse of Drugs Act 1977, the court could order forfeiture or destruction of anything which was shown to its satisfaction to be related to the commission of the impugned offence.[30] In practice, many items of personal property, mostly such things as cars and cash, have been forfeited under this provision. The courts can also order an offender to pay compensation to the victim. While there are some disparate provisions enabling the court to take this action in certain circumstances, they have been infrequently applied.

The Offences Against the State (Amendment) Act 1985 (hereinafter 1985 Act), however, was enacted in haste to respond to the circumstances of one particular case,[31] provides another framework. It permits the Minister for Justice, when of the opinion that moneys held by a bank are the property of an unlawful organization, to require such bank to pay the moneys in question into the High Court.[32] There is also provision enabling the Minister for Justice to apply to the High Court *ex parte*, following a period of at least six months, for an order directing that the moneys be paid to the Minister for Justice or into such account at such bank as the Minister may specify.[33] The provision is significant in that it does not depend on any prior conviction for an offence relating to the moneys.

---

[28]   See *Confiscation of Criminal Assets, supra* at p. 7, para. 3.

[29]   Council of Europe, 'Second Evaluation Round: Evaluation Report on Ireland' (2005). English version available at http://www.coe.int/t/dg1/greco/evaluations/round2/GrecoEval2(2005)9_Ireland_EN.pdf (last accessed 14 October 2007). The group is currently in its third evaluation round, which started in January 2007, the second having taken place between 2003 and 2006.

[30]   See Misuse of Drugs Act 1977, s. 30.

[31]   On the day following its enactment, the Minister for Justice directed the Bank of Ireland to pay into the High Court the sum of £1 750 816.27 held at that time in the joint account of two persons. A challenge to the constitutionality of the statute failed in the High Court; see *Clancy & Anon v. Ireland* [1988] IR 326 (hereinafter *Clancy*).

[32]   See 1985 Act, s. 2(1).

[33]   *Ibid.* s. 2(2).

The problem was that, with the possible exception of charges brought under the 1985 Act, there was little the authorities could do with financial information emerging in the course of a criminal investigation save deploying it in proof of commission of the alleged crime. There was no question of the state recovering the illegitimate profits involved. Generally there was no concept of evaluating the amount by which the person had profited from the criminal activity with a view to depriving him of that profit. This approach shifted in 1994, with the initial catalyst coming from response to Ireland's obligations under European and international law.

PREVIOUS FORFEITURE REGIMES

The Common Law and Regulatory Legislation

For many years, forfeiture has been available both in the common law remedy of restitution[34] and under various statutory regimes, for example under legislation regulating Revenue and Customs. As Shane Murphy observes, it is a long-standing policy of the Irish common law, as well as the English,[35] that those committing crimes do not have the right to enjoy any benefits obtained through such activities, and that neither the offender nor even an innocent third party can gain good title to property which derives from crime.[36] On the extent to which third party title is tainted by the illicit origin of such property, Ashe and Reid have suggested, for example, that a bridal gift from a perpetual tax evader to his daughter might now find itself on the responding end of an order from the Criminal Assets Bureau (hereinafter CAB).[37] At common law, conviction of possessing contraband items could be punished by, *inter alia*, seizure of the prohibited items.[38] Similarly,

---

[34]   See, for example, R. Goff and G. Jones (eds) (1993), *The Law of Restitution*, London, UK: Sweet & Maxwell, at p. 703.

[35]   See *Cleaver v. Mutual Reserve Fund Life Association* [1892] 1 QB 147 at p. 156, per Fry LJ.

[36]   See Shane Murphy (1999), 'Tracing the Proceeds of Crime: Legal and Constitutional Implications', *Irish Criminal Law Journal*, **9** (2), 160 at p. 163 (hereinafter Tracing the Proceeds of Crime).

[37]   See M. Ashe and P. Reid (eds) (2000), *Money Laundering: Risks and Liabilities*, Dublin, Ireland: Round Hall Sweet & Maxwell (hereinafter *Money Laundering*), at p. 205.

[38]   See, for example: Firearms Act 1925, s. 23; Censorship of Publications Act 1929, s. 10; Firearms and Offensive Weapons Act 1990, s. 13; Misuse of Drugs Act 1970, s. 30.

the 1985 Act[39] allowed for the freezing of bank accounts thought to be held on behalf of illegal organizations.[40]

Most of the Irish legislation prior to 1996 had come about as a result of external initiatives. The 1970s and 1980s saw a change in the focus of international law enforcement. Increasing emphasis was placed on international co-operation and awareness grew of the crucial role of financial institutions in facilitating crime. At an international level, promulgation of the United Nations drug trafficking convention,[41] publication of the Basle Statement of Principles[42] and the founding of the Financial Action Task Force[43] all proved hugely influential on Ireland domestically.

---

[39] As amended.

[40] The constitutionality of forfeiting monies to the Exchequer under the 1985 Act was upheld in *Clancy* (HC).

[41] See United Nations (1988), *United Nations Convention Against Illicit Traffic in Narcotic Drugs and Psychotropic Substances*, available at http://www.incb.org/ pdf/e/conv/convention_1988_en.pdf (accessed 11 January 2008). The primary aim of this Convention is to prohibit the laundering of the proceeds of drug-trafficking and to provide for the confiscation of such proceeds. In addition, it provides for, *inter alia*, extradition between countries party to this Convention for relevant offences, mutual legal assistance between the Convention parties, transfer of criminal prosecutions from one signatory state to another, the abrogation of traditional confidentiality between banks and customers during certain criminal investigations, and the adoption of appropriate measures by states to facilitate the confiscation of assets representing the proceeds of money laundering. It was signed in Vienna on 20 December 1988.

[42] The Basle Statement of Principles 1988, drafted by the Basle Committee (now known as the Committee on Banking Regulations and Supervisory Practices), which was composed of representatives from the Central Banks of the G10 nations, at a meeting in the Bank for International Settlements in Basle. These Principles are aimed at preventing use of the banking system for the purpose of money laundering. To this end, they include provision for greater co-operation between banks and law enforcement authorities and a requirement that customers be clearly identified.

[43] The Financial Action Task Force on Money Laundering (hereinafter FATF) was established in July 1989 following the 15th Economic Summit of the G7 nations in Paris to assess the results of the co-operation which had already commenced between them in order to prevent their banking systems from being used, unwittingly or otherwise, as part of money laundering operations. The first report of FATF was published in June 1990 and is regarded as particularly influential since it contains no fewer than 40 recommendations designed to improve the laws against money laundering including adoption and ratification of the Vienna Convention for all G7 countries, curtailment of bank secrecy, criminalization of money laundering by national laws extending not only to proceeds deriving from drug trafficking but also to proceeds derived from other crimes, registration of all cash transactions over certain levels and the reporting of all suspicious transactions, the training of bank employees to recognize suspicious transactions, and strengthening of international co-operation particularly in the extradition of persons suspected of involvement in money laundering schemes.

At the European level, action was also taken under Title VI[44] of the Maastricht Treaty, the so-called 'Third Pillar' of the European Union which governs Police and Judicial Co-operation in Criminal Matters,[45] through the proliferation of legislation aimed at tackling organized crime.[46] In 1998, for example, the Council of Europe adopted a Joint Action on 'identification, tracing and confiscation of instrumentalities and the proceeds from crime' in order to increase effective co-operation between member states and generally to counter organized criminal activity.[47] Similarly, the Strasbourg Convention on money laundering[48] was signed in November 1990. Probably the greatest source of influence, however, were the two European Directives on money laundering of 1991 (hereinafter 1991 Directive)[49] and 2001 (hereinafter 2001 Directive),[50] which sought to

---

44   See European Union (2002), *Treaty on European Union (consolidated text)*, OJ C 325 of 24 December 2002, arts 29 to 42: available at http://europa.eu.int/eur-lex/lex/en/treaties/index.htm (accessed 14 December 2007). The provisions on co-opera-tion in criminal matters were clarified by European Union (1997), *Treaty of Amsterdam Amending the Treaty of the European Union, the Treaties establishing the European Communities and Related Acts*, OJ C 340 of 10 November 1997 (see website, *ibid.* for online version), art. 1, which strengthened inter-governmental co-operation: see C. O'Mara (1998), 'European Social Policy after Amsterdam', CLP, **5** (2), 42.

45   Previously titled 'Justice and Home Affairs'.

46   For a deeper understanding of European Union initiatives in this area, see P. Craig and G. De Burca (eds) (2002), *European Union Law: Text, Cases and Materials*, Oxford, UK: Oxford University Press; see also S. Peers (2002), 'The European Union and Criminal Law: an Overview', *Irish Criminal Law Journal*, **12** (4), 2.

47   See Joint Action 98/699 dated 3 December 1998: Council of European Union (1998), www.eur-lex.europa.eu/LexUriServ/LexUriServ.do?uri=CELEX:31998 F0699 :EN:HTML (accessed 14 December 2007), adopted by the Justice and Home Affairs Council in December 1998 while implementing the 1990 Convention on Laundering, Search, Seizure and Confiscation of the Proceeds of Crime (hereinafter the Strasbourg Convention).

48   The Strasbourg Convention, *ibid.* requires signatory states to make interna-tional money laundering a criminal offence under domestic law and to prohibit banks from refusing to co-operate with relevant investigating authorities on grounds of confi-dentiality. It also promotes international co-operation by, for example, obliging signa-tories to introduce powers to take provisional measures on the freezing or seizing of assets in one country in respect of criminal proceedings taken in another signatory country. It is worth noting that the Strasbourg Convention is only one of a number of Conventions emanating from the Council of Europe. The European Convention on Mutual Assistance, for example, provides for co-operation between the relevant national authorities in obtaining evidence in one state for the purpose of criminal proceedings or investigations in another signatory state.

49   See EC Council Directive 91/308/EEC of 10 June 1991 adopted under arts 57(2) and 100a of the Treaty of Rome of 10 June 1991, on the prevention of the use of the financial system for the purpose of money laundering. A number of countries which are not member states of the Council of Europe, such as Australia, Canada and the USA, participated in the deliberations leading up to the adoption of the Convention.

50   See Council Directive 2001/97/EC of 4 December 2001.

compel banks to carry on business in a transparent fashion to facilitate investigation into money laundering operations where the need arose.

The concept of the single banking licence, which would enable a bank to operate throughout the European Union, was promulgated for the first time in the Banking Directive[51] of 1989, rendering the need to preserve the integrity of the domestic banking regime more pressing. Thus the 1991 Directive set down detailed definitions of 'money laundering', broadening its remit to include non drug-related offences. The Directive was implemented into Irish law by the Criminal Justice Act 1994 (hereinafter 1994 Act). The preamble to the 1991 Directive sets out the concern of the drafters that if financial institutions are used for money laundering, the soundness and stability of banks will be seriously jeopardized, as well as general confidence in the financial markets, resulting in a consequential loss of public trust. Taking action at the European Community level helped to prevent any single member state from becoming a haven for the proceeds of money laundering, which would have threatened the achievement of the single market for financial services. The 1991 Directive thus required financial institutions to introduce measures to check the identity of their customers and to keep adequate records of suspicious transactions, which would then be made available to relevant investigating authorities.

Materials used to identify customers and documents relating to relevant transactions must be retained for a period of at least five years. The 2001 Directive extended the provisions of its 1991 predecessor from a limited application to drug crime to applying to the proceeds of all criminal activity, and it created more indirect offences and obligations to notify authorities. The Directive was implemented into municipal law in the Criminal Justice (Theft and Fraud Offences) Act 2001 (hereinafter 2001 Act), which amended the 1994 Act, adding some indirect offences and notification obligations. Thus under section 21 of the 2001 Act (amending section 31 of the 1994 Act), the general obligation to refrain from money laundering is retained, while adding that someone who 'acquires, possesses or uses' property *knowing or believing* that such property derives from criminal activity is now also guilty of money laundering. It was held in *DPP v. McHugh*[52] that a guilty mind was not sufficient *per se* for conviction, so it seems necessary that the property actually be derived from crime. Under the legislation itself, however, it is not necessary for such property actually to be derived from crime, as it is in the corresponding English provision.[53]

---

51   See Council Directive 89/646/EEC of 15 December 1989 (the second Banking Directive).

52   See *DPP v. McHugh,* [2002] IR 352, Court of Criminal Appeal, Fennelly J.

53   Under the Criminal Justice Act 1988 (UK), the magistrate's court may only issue an order where the defendant has been convicted before it of one of the offences contained in Sch. 4 to the legislation.

Nonetheless, the provisions of the 1991 Directive and 2001 Directive were to be superseded on the effective entry into force of the new, third anti-money laundering Directive (hereinafter 2005 Directive),[54] which was approved by the Council of Europe on 5 May 2005. It was scheduled to be implemented in Ireland in December 2007, and applies to financial and other key services sectors, covering all providers of goods where payments exceeding 15 000 cash are involved.[55] It requires those involved in the provision of financial services to take conscientious measures to establish customers' identities and to monitor relations with the customer,[56] report any suspicions and set up preventive systems within their organizations, such as training and proper compliance procedures. The new 2005 Directive incorporates into community law the June 2003 revision of the Financial Action Task Force's 40 recommendations.[57] As well as banks, it also applies to lawyers, notaries, accountants, real estate agents, casinos, and trust and company service providers.[58] 'Serious crimes' have been defined for the first time[59] and the concept of a 'beneficial owner' has been introduced, in the hope of stopping one person from acting as a façade for another. Finally, member states are required to establish a financial intelligence unit (FIU), where they have not already done so under the previous Directives.[60]

THE CRIMINAL JUSTICE ACT 1994

Ireland gave effect to the 1991 Directive with the enactment of the 1994 Act.[61]

---

[54] See Directive 2005/60/EC of the European Parliament and of the Council of 26 October 2005 on the prevention of the use of the financial system for the purposes of money laundering and terrorist financing (hereinafter 2005 Directive). It was overseen by the Internal Market and Services Commissioner, Charles McCreevy, who happens to be Irish.

[55] The Directive has still not been implemented. According to The Department of Justice, Equality and Law Reform, this is due to necessary amendments to various criminal law statutes and the time required to complete a public consultation process. The Department stated that implementation is a priority and maintains that it will be implemented before the end of 2008, see http://www.justice.ie/en/JELR/print/EU_directives (last accessed 14 July 2008).

[56] *Ibid.* art. 9, the so-called 'KYC' or 'know-your-client' requirement.

[57] See discussion on FATF, *supra* n. 44.

[58] Under art. 4, member states may extend the remit of this provision to whichever provisions they see fit.

[59] 2005 Directive, *supra*, art. 3.

[60] *Ibid.* art. 21.

[61] The Criminal Justice Act 1994 (hereinafter 1994 Act) was enacted on 30 June 1994. Most of its provisions were brought into force by ministerial order on 3 November 1994.

The Irish legislation went further than what was required under the first of the European Directives in that it explicitly proscribed money laundering in general, not just that connected with drugs. In contra-distinction to the operation of the 1996 Act, which operates completely independently of criminal proceedings, it is necessary that criminal proceedings are actually in being to avail of the forfeiture provisions in the 1994 Act. Section 3(7) of the 1996 Act now provides that where a confiscation order relates to property frozen under that Act, such injunction shall stand lapsed accordingly. Thus, precedence is given to proceedings under the 1994 Act where possible.

Offences

The offence of money laundering was introduced into Irish law in the 1994 Act. The offence is committed where a person:

(a) conceals or disguises any property which is, or in whole or in part directly or indirectly represents, his proceeds of drug trafficking or other criminal activity, or

(b) converts or transfers that property, or removes it from the state, for the purpose of avoiding prosecution for an offence or the making or enforcement in his case of a confiscation order.[62]

The offence extends to similar action in respect of another person's proceeds of drug trafficking or other criminal activity for the purpose of assisting any person to avoid prosecution for an offence or the making or enforcement of a confiscation order.[63] Equally, it is an offence for any person to handle any property knowing or believing that another has derived it from criminal activity.[64] For the purpose of these offences, 'concealing or disguising property' is given a very broad definition.[65] The same applies to 'converting, transferring or removing'[66] and 'handling' property.[67]

Both the 1994 Act and the 1996 Act allow for seizure of both direct and indirect proceeds of crime. Thus, where assets are transferred to a third party to frustrate the purpose of the legislation, this too may be considered money laundering and form the basis of a confiscation order.

Remedies

Confiscation orders
The 1994 Act introduced a novel procedure whereby the trial court may, on the

---

[62] See the 1994 Act, s. 31(1).
[63] *Ibid.* s. 31(2).
[64] *Ibid.* s. 31(3).
[65] *Ibid.* s. 31(4).
[66] *Ibid.* s. 31(5).
[67] *Ibid.* s. 31(6).

application of the Director of Public Prosecutions (hereinafter DPP),[68] investigate any profit that a person convicted of a drug trafficking offence may have made from such offence. If the conviction is for a drug trafficking offence, this investigation can extend beyond the profits made from the specific offence convicted to profits made from drug trafficking generally. Regarding convictions for any other offence, however, investigation must be limited to any profit made from the specific crime convicted.[69]

In 1999, new legislation was introduced placing a mandatory obligation on the trial court, in every case where a person has been convicted of a drug trafficking offence, to consider whether or not it is appropriate to make a confiscation order, meaning application by the DPP is no longer a pre-requisite.

Where the court issues a judgment as to the value of a profit gleaned from criminal activity under these provisions, it is known as a 'confiscation order'. Such an order has the same effect as a judgment of the High Court for the payment to the state of the sum specified, subject to the proviso that the person concerned can be imprisoned in respect of the confiscation order pursuant to the terms of the 1994 Act.[70] If at any time money falls due to be paid on a confiscation order, the DPP may apply to the High Court to have the defendant imprisoned in default of payment for a period of up to ten years.[71]

---

[68] The Irish Public Prosecutor ('Director of Public Prosecutions' or Stiúrthóra Ionchúiseamh Poiblí), the current incumbent of which is Mr James Hamilton, was established by the Prosecution of Offences Act 1974 to take over much of the work hitherto fore carried out by the Attorney General.

[69] See 1994 Act, s. 9.

[70] *Ibid.* s. 19.

[71] *Ibid.* s. 19(4): see table below as adapted from the sub-section for possible penalties in default of payment: amounts are displayed in the Irish pound or punt, which preceded the euro, and the exchange rate is 1 = IR£ 0.787564.

Table 3.1   Terms of imprisonment for failure to comply with a confiscation order

Amount outstanding under confiscation order	Period of imprisonment
Not exceeding £500	45 days
Exceeding £500 but not exceeding £1000	3 months
Exceeding £1000 but not exceeding £2500	4 months
Exceeding £2500 but not exceeding £5000	6 months
Exceeding £5000 but not exceeding £10 000	9 months
Exceeding £10 000 but not exceeding £20 000	12 months
Exceeding £20 000 but not exceeding £50 000	18 months
Exceeding £50 000 but not exceeding £100 000	2 years
Exceeding £100 000 but not exceeding £250 000	3 years
Exceeding £250 000 but not exceeding £1 million	5 years
Exceeding £1 million	10 years

Any term of imprisonment imposed under these provisions will take place consecutive to the term imposed in relation to the primary offence (if any). However, the imposition of a sentence of imprisonment in default of payment is not automatic or absolute and the court retains discretion in this regard. Moreover, the defendant concerned must be given a reasonable opportunity to make representations to the court on the matter. Nevertheless, in view of the emphatic nature of the legislation, it can be expected that a court would decline to make an order for imprisonment under these provisions only in the most exceptional cases of hardship where the imposition of a further sentence would amount to manifest injustice.

There also exists provision under which the High Court may appoint a receiver over realizable property affected by a confiscation order.[72] Where a receiver is appointed, the court may grant him/her power to take possession and sell any realizable property. The net proceeds of such sale must be applied either in satisfaction or reduction of the amount of the confiscation order. Confiscation orders carry interest at the same rate as that applying to a High Court civil judgment debt.

Restraint orders
Property may be restrained or frozen pending a criminal trial to ensure that it will be available in the event of a confiscation order being made on subsequent conviction.[73] There also exists provision for the appointment of a receiver over the property in appropriate circumstances.[74] The restraint order can be made in anticipation of conviction and/or confiscation on application by the DPP. All realizable property, even property transferred to the person concerned after the making of the order, can be restrained by the court order. Unlike the position with respect to a *Mareva* injunction,[75] there is no statutory pre-requisite of proof that the defendant or another specified person is about to transfer the property, attempt to conceal it somewhere or remove it from the jurisdiction entirely, in a manner which would delay or defeat any subsequent confiscation order.

Where utilized, this legislation has proven quite effective. In one particular case, all the assets of a well-known drug trafficking family were confiscated. This included motor vehicles, cash, real property and funds in various bank accounts, including bank accounts in foreign jurisdictions. The process took

---

[72]   See 1994 Act, s. 20.
[73]   *Ibid.* s. 23.
[74]   *Ibid.* s. 24.
[75]   Ashe and Reid have described the enforcement powers of Criminal Assets Bureau as being like 'a *Mareva* injunction, albeit with added zest': see *Money Laundering, supra* at p. 198, para. 3.

almost seven years, requiring the appointment of a receiver and the effecting of internal confiscation orders abroad by the utilization of international co-operation orders.

However, even before the 1994 Act was fully implemented, it became apparent that its provisions might not suffice to combat the rapidly escalating threat posed by drug trafficking and the related activities of organized gangs, thus paving the way for the 1996 'Summer Crime Package'.[76] This flood of criminal justice legislation discussed above coincided with Ireland's assumption of the presidency of the European Union. Significantly, the Irish Government adopted the war against drug trafficking as one of the key themes of its presidency.

A new forfeiture model
The new measures were intended to provide a remedy for the situation where persons involved in drug trafficking and serious crime were openly enjoying the proceeds of their crimes due to insufficient evidence being available for prosecution.[77] The measures reflected the adoption of a multi-agency approach with the establishment of CAB and, in particular, the more effective enforcement of the taxation and social welfare acts through provision for the exchange of information between the Garda Síochána, the Revenue authorities and the Social Welfare authorities. Together with the 1994 Act the overall effect was to create a statutory mechanism for identifying the proceeds of criminal activity and for denying the benefit of such proceeds to those in possession of them.

The 1994 Act also, *inter alia*, introduced the offences of money laundering and handling the proceeds of crime,[78] imposed duties of identification and record keeping on 'designated bodies' such as banks, insurance companies etc,[79] imposed an obligation on designated bodies to report suspicious transactions to the Gardaí,[80] provided for restraint orders against persons charged,

---

[76]   Comprising the Proceeds of Crime Act 1996 (hereinafter 1996 Act), the Criminal Assets Bureau Act 1996 (hereinafter CAB Act 1996) and the Disclosure of Certain Information for Taxation and Other Purposes Act 1996, as well as consequential amendments to specified Welfare and Social Welfare Acts.

[77]   For a journalistic account of the situation as it prevailed in the summer of 1996, see P. Williams (2006), *The Untouchables: The Dramatic Inside Story of Ireland's Criminal Assets Bureau*, Dublin, Ireland: Merlin Publishing, at Ch. 1, for a vivid description of the frustration of police patrolling supposed slums at being greeted by big houses, expensive cars and wide screen televisions.

[78]   See 1994 Act, s. 31.

[79]   *Ibid.* s. 32.

[80]   *Ibid.* s. 57. Since the Central Bank and Financial Services Authority of Ireland Act 2003, such institutions must also report to the Revenue Commissioners.

or about to be charged, with serious crime,[81] provided for confiscation orders against persons convicted of serious crime[82] and stipulated that the civil standard of proof should apply in relation to issues concerning confiscation.[83] It also provided for the forfeiture of property used in, or intended for use in, the commission of an offence, lawfully seized from a convicted person, which was in his possession or control at the time of being taken into custody or at the time the summons was issued in respect of the offence.[84]

As McCutcheon and Walsh document, the aim of money laundering legislation is to limit the ability to spend illegally acquired funds, which usually take the form of cash, by blocking efforts to enter them into circulation in the legitimate economy, thus removing one of the dominant incentives for crime, while also preserving the integrity of the financial system involved.[85]

THE PROCEEDS OF CRIME ACT 1996

The 1996 Act, arguably the most radical effort to attack the proceeds of crime,[86] has been the subject of a great deal of misconception even among the members of the legal profession. It is this legislation which introduced the process of civil forfeiture in Ireland in 1996, making it no longer necessary to obtain a criminal conviction to proceed with the forfeiture of assets, as had been the case under the 1994 Act. The 1996 Act has shifted the target from profit/benefit to concrete property.

Under the 1996 Act, it is only an injunction which is granted, which must remain in place for seven years prior to the granting of a disposal order, whereas under the 1994 Act a judgment debt is granted in favour of the DPP, which can be executed immediately.

Section 1 of the 1996 Act contains a number of key definitions. It is worth noting at the outset that 'proceeds of crime' is defined as including any property obtained or received at any time, whether before or after the passing of the legislation, and now includes the proceeds of crimes committed outside the jurisdiction.[87] This remedied a lacuna left by the Supreme Court decision in *F. McK. v. A.F.*,[88] which held that the 1996 Act did not apply to property derived

---

81   See 1994 Act, ss. 23 and 24.
82   *Ibid.* Part II.
83   *Ibid.* ss. 4 and 9.
84   *Ibid.* s. 61.
85   See *Confiscation of Criminal Assets*, *supra* at p. 4, para. 3.
86   According to Shane Murphy BL, see *Tracing the Proceeds of Crime*, *supra*.
87   See Proceeds of Crime (Amendment) Act 2005 (hereinafter 2005 Act).
88   *F. McK. v A.F. and Others* [2002] 1 IR 242 (SC).

from crimes committed against the laws of other states. The definitions of 'criminal conduct' and 'property' were accordingly amended in the Proceeds of Crime (Amendment) Act 2005 (hereinafter 2005 Act) to bring the proceeds of extra-territorial criminal activity within the remit of the legislation.

The persons who may make an application under the statute to the High Court include any authorized officer of the Revenue Commissioners and a member of the Garth Síochána not below the rank of Chief Superintendent.[89] Where an application is made as a result of a CAB investigation it will be made in the name of the Chief Bureau Officer of CAB.

Process Leading to Forfeiture of Assets

The interim stage
The first stage is the interim order. As shall be shown below, the interim stage is the most difficult for potential applicants, and once an interim order is secured it is relatively easy to convert it into an interlocutory one. The High Court can make an order prohibiting the respondent, or any specified person having notice of the order, from disposing of or otherwise dealing with specified property or diminishing its value during the period of 21 days from the date of the order.[90] If CAB shows on balance of probabilities that a property is derived from the proceeds of crime, and that that property is worth 13 000 or more, the onus of proof shifts to the respondent property owner to prove otherwise.[91] The order may only be made 'where it is shown to the satisfaction of the Court' that the property concerned constitutes the proceeds of crime. Section 8 of 1996 Act goes on to stipulate, *inter alia*, that an applicant may file an affidavit stating the requisite belief or, if the court so directs, the officer may have to state his or her belief in oral evidence. If the court is satisfied that there are reasonable grounds for that belief, it constitutes evidence of the matters contained within it.

The court may issue such an interim order on an *ex parte* basis,[92] the element of surprise often proving crucial in ensuring the respondent does not make a speedy dispersal of the funds once he or she becomes aware of the investigation. A safeguard is provided, however, in that the court is forbidden

---

[89]   See 1996 Act, s. 1.
[90]   *Ibid.* s. 2(1).
[91]   The test is whether the court is shown, to its satisfaction, that a person is in possession of the property concerned and that such property constitutes, directly or indirectly, the proceeds of crime or was acquired, in whole or in part, with or in connection with property that, directly or indirectly, constitutes the proceeds of crime, where the value of the property is not less than £10 000 (now 13 000): see 1996 Act, s. 8(1).
[92]   See 1996 Act, s. 8(3).

from making any order where there is a 'serious risk of injustice'. Once the High Court is satisfied that this risk has not been established, and that the presumption of illegality mentioned above has not been shifted, it may order the interim freezing of the assets in question.

Even property only partly constituted from the proceeds of crime may be made subject to an interim order.[93] The court may also make such ancillary orders as it considers necessary or expedient in individual cases.[94] Another important safety valve has been provided in that the respondent, or any person claiming ownership of any of the property, can apply to the court to have the order discharged or varied. If it is shown to the satisfaction of the court that the property, or any part of it, is not the proceeds of crime or that the value of the property is less than 13 000, it may discharge or vary the order.[95] It was held in *DPP v. E.H.*, denying an application for living expenses where a large sum of money had been withdrawn shortly before the restraint order was made, that an applicant seeking to have an order varied must go further than simply stating that they need money but must take reasonable steps to show that he or she cannot obtain money elsewhere.[96]

The interim order lapses 21 days from the date of its making unless an application for an interlocutory order in respect of the property in question is brought during that period.[97] A respondent seeking to have the interim order discharged will have to show, also on the civil standard, that the property in question does not represent the proceeds of crime, or that it is not worth 13 000.[98] The High Court can order that compensation be paid where orders lapse or fall to be varied on good cause.

Finally, it was held in *M.F.M. v. M.B. and Others* that the availability of legal aid militates against varying an order for legal expenses under section 6 of the 1996 Act.[99] The very operation of section 6 restricts a defendant's right of access to the court (article 6(3)(c) (right to free legal aid) or article 13 (right

---

93   According to *Money Laundering, supra* at p. 204, para. 3.
94   See 1996 Act, ss 5–7; O'Higgins J in *Murphy* (HC) seems to suggest that this includes appointment of a receiver at the *ex parte* stage of application for an interim order.
95   See 1996 Act, s. 2(3).
96   See *DPP v. H. (E.),* unreported, High Court, 22 April 1997, per Kelly J.
97   See 1996 Act, s. 2(1)(b); see also *ibid.* s. 2(5) (where an application for interlocutory order is brought the interim order lapses upon (a) the determination of the application, (b) the expiration of the ordinary time for bringing an appeal from the determination, or (c) if an appeal is brought, the determination or abandonment of the appeal or any further appeal or the expiration of the ordinary time for bringing any further appeal, whichever is latest).
98   *Ibid.* s. 2(3).
99   See *M.F.M. v. M.B. and Others* [1999] 1 ILRM 540, O'Higgins J. (HC).

to an effective remedy) of the ECHR). The structure of section 6 is no different from any application for legal aid: even under the judgment of Gannon J
in *State (Healy) v. Donoghue* no one is automatically entitled to legal aid, as
applicants have to show both necessity and lack of means.[100]

The interlocutory stage

The pre-conditions which must be met before an interlocutory order will be
granted are similar to those necessary for an interim order. The High Court can
make an interlocutory order where the applicant tenders evidence, admissible
by virtue of section 8 of the 1996 Act, to the effect that a person is in possession or control of property which constitutes the proceeds of crime and such
property has a value of not less than 13 000. Where such evidence is
tendered in support of an application, the court must make the order unless the
respondent introduces evidence to the contrary or the court is satisfied that
there would be a 'serious risk of injustice'.[101]

When an interlocutory order has been issued, it will normally continue in
force until (a) the determination of an application for a disposal order in relation to the property concerned, (b) the expiration of the ordinary time for
bringing an appeal from that determination, (c) if such an appeal is brought, it
or any further appeal is determined or abandoned or the ordinary time for
bringing any further appeal has expired, whichever is the latest, and shall then
lapse.[102] While the interlocutory order is in force, application to have it
discharged may be brought to the High Court by the respondent, or any other
person claiming ownership of any of the property concerned.[103] If it is shown
to the satisfaction of the court that the property, or a specified part of it, is not
the proceeds of crime; or that the order causes some other injustice, the court
may discharge or vary the order as appropriate.[104]

It may happen, of course, that property which forms the subject of an interlocutory order is also the subject of a forfeiture order or a confiscation order
under the 1994 Act, or a forfeiture order under the Misuse of Drugs Act 1977.
In this event, the interlocutory order shall stand varied or discharged as appropriate.[105] The interlocutory order is analogous to that most draconian of equitable remedies: the *Mareva* injunction, and thus applications for such an order
under the 1996 Act must meet similar criteria to that required in *Mareva*

---

[100]   *State (Healy) v. Donoghue*, [1976] IR 325, per Gannon J. (SC).
[101]   See 1996 Act, s. 3(1).
[102]   *Ibid.* s. 3(5).
[103]   *Ibid.* s. 3(3).
[104]   *Ibid.* s. 3(3).
[105]   *Ibid.* s. 3(7).

proceedings. For example, 'substantive relief' must be claimed,[106] substantive relief being a disposal order under section 4 of the 1996 Act. Finally, it was held by the Supreme Court in *McK. v. D.*[107] that the Statute of Limitations 1957 does not apply at any stage of proceedings under the Proceeds of Crime Act 1996. This has since been placed on a statutory footing by virtue of section 10 of the 2005 Act.[108]

Discovery

At any time in the course of an application for an interim or interlocutory order under the 1996 Act, or while any such order is in force, application may be brought for an order compelling the respondent to file an affidavit in the High Court, specifying the property in his or her possession or control or his income or sources of income during such period as the court may specify, not exceeding ten years ending on the date of the application.[109] The Supreme Court has held that an application for an interlocutory order under section 3 of the 1996 Act constitutes a full trial of the issues concerned, which has implications for what will be required in terms of discovery.[110]

This provision formed the subject of detailed legal argument in *M(M). v. D(D).*,[111] the first case in which CAB made an application under the 1996 Act. The respondent in that case challenged the application for discovery under section 9 of the 1996 Act by way of three general headings: (i) that the nature and standard of proof advanced on affidavit against him were unsatisfactory and inadequate to warrant the discovery sought and, in particular, offended against the hearsay rule; (ii) that the relief, if granted, would offend against the respondent's privilege against self-incrimination; and (iii) that the retrospective operation of the order was unconstitutional. Having regard to all the circumstances of the case, Moriarty J granted the order for discovery, subject to the stipulation that the period of disclosure be confined to six years. In deference to the respondent's concerns over self-incrimination, the learned judge also required an undertaking from the DPP not to profit from any disclosure in the proceedings for the purpose of any future criminal prosecution. An appropriate letter to the court was furnished by the DPP. The Supreme Court

---

[106]   See *Caudron v Air Zaire* [1985] IR 716, per Finlay CJ (Henchy and Hederman JJ concurring) (SC).
[107]   *McK. v. D.* [2004] 2 ILRM 419, per Fennelly J (SC).
[108]   See 2005 Act.
[109]   See 1996 Act, s. 9.
[110]   See *The Criminal Assets Bureau v. John Kelly* [2002] 2 ILRM 303, per Murphy J. (SC).
[111]   *M(M). v D(D).*, Moriarty J, Unreported, High Court, 10 December 1996.

agreed with Moriarty J,[112] finding the state's sophisticated version of 'the innocent have nothing to fear' invalid without the assurances outlined above. On the retroactivity point, it was held that the acquisition of assets derived from crime was not an illegal activity before the passing of the 1996 Act and so did not become illegal because of the 1996 Act. Therefore, no law fell to be imposed retroactively.

Receivership

The granting of an interim or interlocutory order can create certain practical problems with respect to the property in question. It may be, for example, that there is a risk that the property will be taken out of the jurisdiction or otherwise dissipated in order to frustrate the confiscation process. Equally, it may happen that the nature of the property is such that it requires active management in order to preserve its value pending the outcome of the confiscation process. The grant of an interim or interlocutory order may result in the abandonment of the property or a failure by the person claiming ownership or possession to preserve its value. Accordingly, the 1996 Act makes provision for the court to appoint a receiver at any time where an interim or an interlocutory order is in force.[113] The receiver may be given such powers as the court thinks appropriate in individual cases, including the power to take possession of the property to which the order relates and, in accordance with the court's directions, to manage, keep possession of, dispose of or otherwise deal with any property in respect of which he or she is appointed.

Living expenses and legal aid

Where an interim or interlocutory order is in force, the court has the power to make orders with respect to the property in like fashion as ancillary orders in proceedings for a *Mareva* injunction.[114] So, for example, if the court considers it essential to do so, it may make orders to enable the respondent to discharge reasonable living or other necessary expenses incurred (or to be incurred) in respect of the respondent or his or her dependants; or orders to enable the respondent or dependants to carry on a business, trade or profession to which any of the property relates. The application of these provisions to the costs of securing legal advice and representation for proceedings under the 1996 Act has given rise to difficulties in a series of cases. This prompted the Department of Justice to implement an *ad hoc* legal aid scheme for the benefit of respondents and defendants in any court proceedings brought by or in the name of CAB including proceedings for a disposal order under the 1996 Act.

---

112   See *M(M). v. D(D)., ibid.*
113   See 1996 Act, s. 7.
114   *Ibid.* s. 6(1).

The disposal stage

The interim and interlocutory orders might be described as essential stages *en route* to a final destination, namely the permanent confiscation of the property in question, which is materialized with a disposal order. When an interlocutory order has been in force in respect of specified property for not less than seven years, an application for a disposal order can be made to the High Court, on due notice to the respondent and other such persons as the court should order.[115] The court must make the order unless it is shown to its satisfaction that the property is not the proceeds of crime. The order will deprive the respondent of his or her rights in the property which automatically transfers to the Minister for Finance or other person to whom the order relates. Where property has vested in the Minister for Finance under these provisions, the Minister can sell or otherwise dispose of it and the proceeds of any such disposition or moneys transferred to him are for the benefit of the Exchequer.[116]

There are certain safeguards built in to the procedure. The court, for example, must give an opportunity to any person claiming ownership of any of the property to be heard and to show cause why a disposal order should not be made.[117] Moreover, a disposal order cannot be made if the court is satisfied that there would be a 'serious risk of injustice'.[118]

Compensation

Section 16 of the 1996 Act contains an important protection for the granting of compensation in certain circumstances. Compensation can be awarded where the aggrieved applicant shows to the satisfaction of the court that he or she is the owner of the property concerned, that one of the specified circumstances exist and that the property does not constitute the direct or indirect proceeds of crime and was not acquired in whole or in part with or in connection with such property. Any sum awarded is payable by the Minister for Finance.

This is a very important provision in that it enables statutory compensation to be paid to any person who has suffered loss as a result of an order having been made in respect of property which emerges not to be the proceeds of crime, thus providing a balance to the provisions in section 8 of the 1996 Act which permits a belief to be admitted in evidence in the interim and interlocutory proceedings.

---

[115]   *Ibid.* s. 4. The application is made by a member of the Garda Síochána not below the rank of Superintendent or an officer of the Revenue Commissioners, authorized in writing by the Revenue Commissioners, to perform the functions conferred upon them by this Act as such officers.

[116]   *Ibid.* s. 4(5).

[117]   *Ibid.* s. 4(6).

[118]   *Ibid.* s. 4(8).

Indeed, in a number of applications the court has regarded section 16 as the equivalent of a suitable undertaking as to damages. In several cases taken by CAB, counsel for the respondent has attempted to extract an undertaking as to damages from the applicant. In all instances it has been refused and the High Court has pointed out that section 16 actually offers greater protection than that which would normally be available through undertakings in comparable *Mareva* proceedings.

THE PROCEEDS OF CRIME (AMENDMENT) ACT 2005[119]

This new legislation was introduced to remedy problems with the 1996 Act, which emerged over the course of nine years of litigation.

First, the 2005 Act cleared up a number of procedural ambiguities which had been left by the 1996 Act. For example, CAB can now take proceedings in its own name, as opposed to the Chief Bureau Officer of CAB being obliged to sue in his own name as had previously been the case. Similarly, the 2005 Act provides that all proceedings can be issued by way of originating notice and new court rules have been approved accordingly. The rebuttable presumptions, discussed in the case law below, were also set out in statutory form in the 2005 Act.

Secondly, it is now possible to make a disposal order under section 4 of the 1996 Act *within* the previous seven-year waiting period, providing it is made on consent. The 2005 Act improved upon the enforcement mechanism available under its 1996 predecessor and, perhaps most importantly, it cleared up any ambiguity as to whether the previous proceeds of crime regime applied overseas. In *F. Mck. v. A.F.*,[120] the Supreme Court held that the 1996 Act did not apply to the proceeds of crimes committed in other jurisdictions. A similar challenge was brought in *Gilligan*.[121] The court in the latter case concluded that while there does exist between sovereign states a recognized 'comity of esteem', requiring one state not to act in a manner clearly to violate the sovereignty of another, this is not a matter of constitutional limitation.[122] It was held by O'Higgins J in *Murphy*[123] that the operation of standard canons of

---

[119] The 2005 Act passed into law and came into effect on 12 February 2005.
[120] See *F. Mck v. A.F.*
[121] See in general *Gilligan*.
[122] English authority lent support for such an approach, for example, a finding that there is no breach of the 'comity of esteem' concept in issuing a world-wide injunction, which operates *in personam: Darby v. Weldon No. 2* [1989] All ER 1002, at p. 1011.
[123] See *Murphy* (HC).

construction determines that the words 'proceeds of crime' include criminal offences committed abroad. However, this contention was overturned in the Supreme Court. The definitions of 'criminal conduct' and 'property' have been amended so that the proceeds of extra-territorial criminality fall within the statute. Provision has also been made to enhance procedures for the exchange of information in the international arena. Furthermore, in terms of enforcement, an enhanced warrant has been introduced by the 2005 Act which includes a tailor made production order designed specifically for CAB.

Finally, the 2005 Act introduced a new remedy called a 'corrupt enrichment order'.[124] This allows the court to direct payment of a specific sum which it holds, on a civil standard, to be the value of a person's enrichment due to corrupt activities. This was primarily designed to address public corruption such as planning irregularities. Corrupt enrichment is defined as deriving 'a pecuniary or other advantage or benefit as a result of or in connection with corrupt conduct wherever the conduct occurred', and 'corrupt conduct' is defined in previous legislation.[125]

PROCEEDS OF CRIME IN THE COURTS

The Irish Constitution and the European Convention on Human Rights

Most of the jurisprudence arising out of innovative counter-organized crime provisions in Ireland revolves around their compatibility with fundamental rights, which are guaranteed by the Irish Constitution[126] and the ECHR.

While the ECHR did not form part of Irish domestic legislation when civil forfeiture was introduced in 1996, most of the protections afforded by the ECHR were already enshrined in the Irish Constitution, some to an arguably higher standard.[127]

In the course of applications made under forfeiture legislation, a number of respondents have challenged its constitutional validity. While the courts have refused to determine any issues on the basis of the ECHR, it should be noted that many points based on the Irish Constitution (Bunreacht na hÉireann) also

---

[124]   Added as s. 16B to 1996 Act: see 2005 Act, s. 12.

[125]   Namely, the Prevention of Corruption Acts 1889 to 2001, the Official Secrets Act 1963 and the Ethics in Public Office Act 1995.

[126]   See Bunreacht na hÉireann, arts 40–44.

[127]   See Donncha O'Connell (2001), 'Ireland', in Robert Blackburn and Jörg Polakiewicz (eds) (2001), *Fundamental Rights in Europe: the European Convention on Human Rights and its Member States (1950–2000)*, Oxford, UK: Oxford University Press, at Ch. 18, pp. 423–74, in association with the Council of Europe.

reflect ECHR arguments. Thus the constitutional objection that an ersatz civil procedure deprives the accused to the right to trial 'in due course of law' under Article 38.1 of the Irish Constitution could equally be based on Article 6 of the ECHR, being the corresponding right to a fair trial. The argument that the requirement to account for one's assets violates the constitutional protection against self-incrimination could similarly be made on Article 6 of the ECHR, for example under the *Saunders v. United Kingdom* principle.[128] The constitutional right of access to the courts mirrors ECHR rights to free legal aid and to an effective remedy.[129] Similarly, the right to hold private property under the Irish Constitution is also protected by Article 1 of Protocol 1 to the ECHR, and retroactive legislation, prohibited by Article 15(5) of the Irish Constitution, is similarly banned by Article 7 of the ECHR.

Murphy is of the opinion that the proceeds of crime legislation can be justified on the same rationale as the old forfeiture powers at common law; the only difference being that the remit of such powers has been extended beyond the person immediately committing such crimes to cover those third parties involved with him or her.[130] He argues that the 1996 Act 'does no more than galvanize previously accepted theories of restraint and forfeiture and direct them in a more streamlined and comprehensive fashion'.[131] However, potential fundamental rights issues have been identified by McCutcheon and Walsh: for example, confiscation without compensation for the property, in the absence of conviction.[132] The right to hold private property without 'unjust attack' is enshrined in Article 40.3.2 of the Irish Constitution. However, it was held by McGuinness J in *Gilligan v. The Criminal Assets Bureau*[133] that while the forfeiture provisions contained in the 1996 Act admittedly affect the property rights of a respondent, the effect involved does not rise to the level of 'unjust attack', which is necessary for the constitutional protection to be triggered, considering that the State must in the first place show that the property at issue constitutes the proceeds of crime. As McGuinness J surmised, 'the right to private ownership cannot hold a place so high in the hierarchy of rights that it protects the position of assets illegal acquired and held'.[134] She also found that the state has a legitimate interest in forfeiture of the proceeds of crime.

---

128   *Saunders v United Kingdom* (43/1994/490/572), 17 December 1996.
129   See arts 6(4) and 13 of the European Convention on Human Rights respectively.
130   See Tracing the Proceeds of Crime, *supra* at p. 163, para. 2.
131   *Ibid.*
132   *Ibid.*
133   See *Gilligan* at p. 237 (HC); aff'd [2001] T.I.T.R. 383 (SC).
134   *Ibid.* para. 136.

Similar forfeiture powers in the 1985 Act were upheld in *Clancy v. Ireland*[135] as reflecting the correct balance between the property rights of individuals and the common good, which was held by McGuinness J in *Gilligan* to include preventing the accumulation and/or use of assets derived from crime.[136]

Objections have been raised to the reverse onus of proof on which forfeiture proceeds and the requirement to produce evidence to rebut a suspicion that property represents the proceeds of crime. It seems there are two pertinent situations where a respondent may seem compelled to talk which should be considered separately for reasons outlined below: first, the situation which arises under section 9 of the 1996 Act; and secondly, that which arises once CAB has satisfied the court that the property at issue represents the proceeds of crime and the respondent must adduce evidence to challenge such proposition.

Under section 9 of the 1996 Act, first, a respondent can be compelled to disclose the extent of his or her assets on pain of contempt proceedings and possible penal sanctions, thus potentially undermining the privilege against self-incrimination. Murphy points out that the section 9 provisions have rarely been invoked by the Irish courts.[137] It was held by the Irish Supreme Court in *Heaney v. Ireland* that the right to silence is not absolute, and that the privilege against self-incrimination is a corollary of the right to freedom of expression, which may be limited in certain circumstances.[138] The court approached the issue as one of balancing the legitimate right of the state to protect itself against the right of the individual not to reveal potentially inculpatory information about himself. Murphy believes the balance struck between the two competing sets of rights in the 1996 Act constitutes a proportionate one.[139] However, it is arguable that to compare the right of the state to protect itself with the right of the public *vis-à-vis* organized crime is not to compare like with like, if only for the fact that the interest of the state at stake in the Offences Against the State legislation is, arguably, a more immediate and more urgent right than that at stake in the fight against organized crime, where perhaps it is a more long-term interest which is engaged. Thus it is submitted that the former interest, that of protecting the state, can be more readily justified.

Furthermore, the Offences against the State Act 1939 was enacted during a state of national emergency, where the very stability of the state was at stake, and so it is to be expected that more stringent measures might be considered

---

135   See *Clancy* (HC).
136   See *Gilligan* at p. 237 (HC).
137   See *Tracing the Proceeds of Crime, supra* at p. 169.
138   See *Heaney v. Ireland,* [1996] 1 IR 580 (SC).
139   See *Tracing the Proceeds of Crime, supra* at p. 168, para. 4.

necessary to counter the threat faced. The Supreme Court held that the right to silence can be curtailed in the public interest, subject to an overriding test of proportionality.[140] The High Court in *Gilligan* concluded that the 1996 Act constitutes a proportionate and legitimate delimitation on constitutional rights in the interests of the common good, considering the extent of the particular malaise it is designed to remedy. The court did, however, express reservations on the operation of section 9 of the 1996 Act, in particular, stating that care must be taken to protect the privilege of a respondent against the revealing of information which could later be used in a criminal prosecution, whether by limiting the purpose for which the information disclosed may be used, or by some other means. McGuinness J also stated that the court should be slow to make an interlocutory order under section 3 of the 1996 Act on the basis of evidence provided under section 8 alone, being without any corroborative evidence.

However, the courts have shown sensitivity to such potential incursion of the fundamental right to silence and the High Court has held that, given the degree of proximity between CAB and the DPP, the former must give an undertaking in any civil forfeiture proceedings that any information adduced therein by means of discovery[141] shall not be used in future criminal proceedings pertaining to the same matter.[142] Secondly, in a situation where a CAB officer has already satisfied the court that the assets at stake are derived from criminal activity, some argue that the privilege against self-incrimination is not, in fact, engaged at all, as the respondent is not *compelled* to adduce evidence on pain of penal proceedings in the same way as in section 9 proceedings. In theory, he or she is free to refrain from defending the source of the property in question and to allow the CAB officer's opinion to stand. It is submitted that such a distinction is one only of form, since in substance the end result may prove just as coercive, if not more: a night in the cells for contempt of court seems imminently more inviting than surrendering the lifeblood of a million euro criminal empire.

Murphy is also of the view that there must be compulsion present, in this case arising from pain of contempt questioning, before the constitutional

---

140   See *In the matter of National Irish Bank Ltd (Under Investigation) and in the matter of the Companies Act 1990* [1999] 3 IR 145 (SC).
141   Under s. 9 of the 1996 Act.
142   See *M. v. D.* (HC), per Moriarty J. He placed heavy reliance on the English precedents in the area including *Re O* [1991] 2 QB 520, and *Istel Ltd v. Tully* [1993] AC 45: see also extract in *Gilligan*, para.119 (HC). *M. v. D.* was followed by McGuinness J in *Gilligan*, who concluded from the evidence in the case before her that the 'degree of nexus' between CAB and the Gardaí was even closer than Moriarty J had imagined, rendering an undertaking along the lines proposed necessary in almost every case where a discovery order was granted.

protection is infringed, as opposed to the approach of the Irish courts in regard to confession evidence, that is to require statements to be given voluntarily and free of compulsion (regardless of the source of such compulsion). The authors agree that the privilege against self-incrimination is not infringed where it falls to a respondent to displace testimony adduced on the criminal source of his or her assets, but for reasons different to those given by Murphy.

In the first place, the legislation does not involve a reverse *burden* of proof, but merely a reduced *standard* of proof. Though the Supreme Court in *Gilligan* found that the onus of proof was in fact reversed, it held that this was justifiable because such reversal only comes into operation after the establishment of certain issues to the court's satisfaction.[143] Furthermore, there is a right to cross-examine. Finally, there is no constitutional infirmity in the procedure whereby the onus is placed on a person seeking property to negate the inference from evidence adduced that a criminal offence has been committed.

If one proceeds on the premise that property forfeiture proceedings are civil in nature, one cannot then seek to apply criminal procedural safeguards, namely, the privilege against self-incrimination, to a civil case. Ashe and Reid urge that orders for discovery should be granted only in the most exceptional of circumstances, since discovery can have a very wide scope and any order granted can have draconian consequences.[144] However, the extent of the search powers available under the regime; the fact that CAB officers remain anonymous and the ability to seize private property, with the right to hold property protected under the Constitution, all support a classification of forfeiture proceedings as criminal. Murphy adduces anecdotal evidence that, in practice, he has never seen an application for restraint or forfeiture based solely on the opinion of one Garda, and that he believes the CAB and the DPP have made a conscious effort to ensure that Garda testimony will not be the sole basis on which forfeiture is based.[145] It has been documented that in light of the paucity of evidence which is usually available regarding the source of property, and in an application for an interim order, the level of proof required in fact amounts to no more than belief.[146]

In *Murphy*[147] it was argued that the admissibility of opinion evidence gives rise to an inequality between the applicant and respondent and that it makes the applicant forming the said opinion a judge in his own case, contrary to the natural justice *nemo iudex* maxim. The High Court rejected this contention,

---

[143] See *Gilligan.*
[144] See *Money Laundering, supra* at p. 207, para. 3.
[145] See Tracing the Proceeds of Crime, *supra.*
[146] See *Money Laundering, supra* at p. 205, para. 2.
[147] See *Murphy* (HC). This point was affirmed by the Supreme Court.

opining that the applicant witness remains just that: a witness. It still falls to the court to decide whether or not to accept his testimony. Ashe and Reid[148] have similarly dismissed the idea that an order can be granted under the legislation based only on the opinion of a Garda, as such opinion will not suffice unless the court is also satisfied there are reasonable grounds for that belief, such reasonable grounds being either set out in the affidavit or manifestly obvious from it. Nonetheless, they stress the importance of the trial court's duty in assigning weight to the evidence, since it is still hearsay.[149] In *Gilligan*, the Supreme Court cautioned that judges should be slow to make an order on the basis of section 8 evidence alone, without any corroborative evidence. The fine toothed combing by Finnegan P in the recent case of *Felix J. McKenna v. MON, BON*,[150] for example, shows the conscientious approach of the judiciary in satisfying themselves that any belief held by a CAB officer is indeed reasonable.

Of course, the burden of proof remains on the applicant. Ashe and Reid also point out that the CAB officer will have the same duty as any applicant in *ex parte* proceedings to be 'full and frank' with the court and to highlight any issues which might be in the respondent's favour. They cite internal guidelines distributed by CAB which encourage this approach, and the practice seems to be to place full information before the court.[151]

The question has been raised as to whether the draconian counter-organized crime legislation is proportionate to the threat faced by the Irish society. Murphy thought so, writing in 1999,[152] as did the Irish Supreme Court in 1998.[153] McGuinness J referred to 'a new type of criminal', organizing rather than committing crimes, with the ability to insulate himself from law enforcement with wealth and a veneer of respectability.[154] Forfeiture under the Offences Against the State Acts, which is subject to less judicial scrutiny than the Proceeds of Crime Act regime, has been upheld.[155] But can it still be justified? McGuinness J in *Gilligan* conceded that the threat posed by this type of offender was smaller than that posed to the State by politically motivated terrorists (presumably referring to the 1985 Act), or at least the latter was perceived by the public as posing a greater threat. It is possible that this point

---

[148]   See *Money Laundering, supra* at p. 205, para. 3.
[149]   *Ibid.*
[150]   Unreported, High Court, 20 November 2006, per Finnegan P.
[151]   See *Money Laundering, supra* at p. 205.
[152]   See *Tracing the Proceeds of Crime, supra* at p.166.
[153]   See *Gilligan* at p. 242 per McGuinness J (HC).
[154]   *Ibid.* at p. 241.
[155]   See *Clancy* (HC).

may be raised in future litigation but Murphy argues that the legislation should withstand constitutional scrutiny.[156]

It has also been argued that the civil forfeiture regime constitutes no more than an effort to punish criminals without establishing guilt, involving ersatz civil proceedings. It was argued that all the trappings of a criminal trial should be present in forfeiture proceedings, including the presumption of innocence, a criminal standard of proof and trial by jury. Murphy dismisses such an analysis, stating that the Irish courts have upheld the civil nature of forfeiture proceedings for years,[157] following the approach of the US Supreme Court to similar American forfeiture provisions.[158] For example, in *Attorney General v. Southern Industrial Trust Ltd and Others*,[159] a procedure whereby a car exported in breach of customs law could be forfeited without any criminal conviction was upheld by the Supreme Court, even though such breach could be based only on the testimony of the Attorney General as to the controlled status of the item in question, such status then being presumed unless otherwise rebutted once such testimony was elucidated. The rationale put forward by the court was that although what was at issue was the establishment of a set of facts underlying a criminal offence, in fact the purpose of proving such facts was not to establish commission of a criminal offence, but to show that the Revenue Commissioners had good title to the car,[160] property law falling, of course, within the realm of civil law.[161] A similar outcome was reached in *O'Keefe v. Ferris*.[162] The Supreme Court upheld the civil nature of the Irish forfeiture provisions in *Gilligan*,[163] in light of, *inter alia*, the fact that there is no provision for the arrest or detention of any person, the admission of persons to bail, the imprisonment for the non-payment of a penalty, the initiation of proceedings by summons or indictment, the recording of a conviction of any form or the entering of a *nolle prosequi*, all elements which would indicate that

---

[156] See *Tracing the Proceeds of Crime, supra* at p. 165.

[157] *Ibid.* at p. 166, para. 1.

[158] See, for example, *United States v. Ursury*, (1996) 518 U.S. 267. See also Chapter 2 of this book.

[159] *Attorney General v. Southern Industrial Trust Ltd and Others* (1960) 94 ILTR 161 (SC).

[160] *Ibid.* This point was made in the High Court by Davitt P at para. 167.

[161] This reasoning was followed in *McLoughlin v. Tuite*, (SC) [1989] IR 82 (hereinafter *McLoughlin*), where it was held that a sanction imposed for failure to make tax returns under the Income Tax Act 1967 should be viewed as a deterrent or incentive, not as a criminal sanction, considering that aside from penalty, none of the other hallmarks of criminal offence mentioned in *Melling v. O'Mathghamhna*, (SC) [1962] IR 1 (hereinafter *Melling*) were present, for example, no particular *mens rea* was required under the provision; *McLoughlin* was followed in *Downes v. DPP* [1987] IR 139.

[162] See *O'Keefe v. Ferris* [1997] 3 IR 463 (SC).

[163] See *Gilligan* (HC) at para. 12.

the 1996 Act created a criminal offence. The court went on to hold that forfeiture is not a punishment *per se* and therefore does not require criminal procedures to be brought about.

The proceeds of crime legislation can be seen as analogous to earlier offences against the state legislation, which allowed for the forfeiture of funds held by illegal organizations, and which forfeiture was upheld.[164] In *Melling v. O'Mathghamhna*,[165] the landmark Irish decision on what makes a trial 'criminal', the Supreme Court elucidated the following as indicia of a criminal trial: detention, search, charge, bail and the imposition of a pecuniary penalty, with liability to imprisonment if the penalty is not paid has all the indicia of a criminal charge. The civil nature of forfeiture proceedings under the 1996 Act were upheld by the Supreme Court in *Gilligan*,[166] having regard to the absence of any charge, remand, bail or any specific penalties.[167] The approach of the court was that the procedure does not exhibit 'all the features of a criminal prosecution',[168] thus proceeding on an assumption that the default model of trial adopted can be presumed to be civil.[169] As Liz Campbell suggests, earlier findings that forfeiture proceedings are civil – which concerned different legislative frameworks to the present one – cannot be applied to the Proceeds of Crime Act 1996 without something of a jump in logic. Furthermore, the conclusion reached by the court involved reliance on the principle that the proceedings at hand bore an *in rem*, rather than an *in personam*, nature, relying on the US authority of *Various Items of Personal Property v. United States*.[170]

---

[164]   See s. 2(1) of the 1985 Act which allowed the Minister for Justice to testify that certain moneys were held by an illegal organization, whereby it fell to any legitimate owner of such monies, if one existed, to apply to the High Court and for an order directing that such monies be paid to him/her: see s. 3(1). Shane Murphy points out that many of the powers contained in this legislation were far more draconian than any contained in current proceeds of crime legislation (see *Tracing the Proceeds of Crime*, *supra* at p. 165). He neglects, however, to take account of the crucial distinction in the powers under which each piece of legislation was promulgated, the Offences Against the State Act having been introduced during a state of national emergency.

[165]   See *Melling* at p. 9 per Lavery J, at p. 23 per Kingsmill Moore J, and at pp. 40–1 per O'Dalaigh J.

[166]   See *Gilligan* (SC).

[167]   *Gilligan* (SC) was heard and decided together with *Murphy v. G.M.* [2001] 4 IR 113 (SC), *supra* n.1.

[168]   See *Gilligan* (HC), p. 217.

[169]   Liz Campbell finds the reasoning adopted by the court 'circular'. She cites, as an example, the fact that the absence of a power to detain under the Proceeds of Crime Act 1996 has been taken to mean that proceedings are civil, when in fact it is probably the legislature's very classification of the regime as 'civil' which meant that powers of detention could not be afforded, see *Theorising Asset Forfeiture*, *supra*.

[170]   *Various Items of Personal Property v. United States* (1931) 282 US 577.

Evidence and Procedure in the Irish Civil Forfeiture Framework

Due to the peculiar nature of organized crime, the legislature were obliged to proceed with great care in formulating the evidential and burden of proof provisions at the heart of the confiscation procedure under the 1996 Act. The difficulty facing those drafting the proceeds of crime legislation in general is that, usually, the funds in question lie in the hands of the principals of criminal gangs. Experience shows that it is very difficult to prosecute such individuals successfully for a variety of reasons, including the way in which they conduct their criminal business and the fear which deters people from giving evidence against them. Furthermore, the methods by which the relevant person acquires, holds and/or attempts to hide the property impugned, are matters which are almost completely within the provenance of that person. Accordingly, admissible evidence pertaining to the property or the methods by which it was obtained has often proven unavailable or difficult to produce. The constitutional right to hold private property places law enforcement under a further obligation to proceed with caution.

On cursory examination, one might be forgiven for thinking that the different phrases used for the granting of an interim order and an interlocutory order were merely the result of drafting license. However, the difference is quite deliberate. The ability of the court granting an interim order based only on affidavit evidence has come to be regarded by some as a statutory intrusion into the common law prohibition against hearsay evidence. However, it is important to bear in mind that the court must decide whether there are reasonable grounds for the belief. The section 8 belief cannot be accepted as evidence of the matters contained within it unless the court is satisfied that there are reasonable grounds for the belief. As such, the court serves more than a mere administrative formality. It has a substantive, justiciable issue to determine. Indeed, the court might require the statement of belief to be given in oral evidence and then proceed to question the grounds underpinning such belief, in order to be satisfied that there are reasonable grounds for that belief.

It is perhaps worth emphasizing that section 2 requires that the court actually satisfy itself that property is the proceeds of crime before an interim order can be granted. It does not, for example, permit an order to be granted merely on the basis of 'evidence ... consisting of or including evidence admissible by virtue of section 8'.[171] Clearly, the legislative intent is to ensure that an interim order can be granted only where there is sufficient objective evidence, on the civil standard of proof, to the effect that the property sought to be restrained is in fact the proceeds of crime. Indeed, it would appear from the judgment of

---

[171]   Proceeds of Crime Act 1996, s. 3(1).

Moriarty J in *M. v. D.*[172] that a section 8 belief by itself might not always prove sufficient. The court may require a certain amount of other objective evidence (in addition to belief) before it is 'satisfied' for the purpose of granting an interim order on an *ex parte* application.

Section 3, governing interlocutory orders, seems to set out a lower threshold than that required for grant of an interim order set out above:

> **3.**—(1) Where, on application to it in that behalf by the applicant, it appears to the Court, on evidence tendered by the applicant, consisting of or including evidence admissible by virtue of section 8—
>> (*a*) that a person is in possession or control of—
>>> (i) specified property and that the property constitutes, directly or indirectly, proceeds of crime, or
>
>   ...
> the Court *shall* make an order ("an interlocutory order") ... [emphasis added]

Before the court can issue an interim order, it must be satisfied with respect to certain matters. Even then, it retains discretion whether or not to issue the order. By contrast, the court *must* issue an interlocutory order once it appears, on the basis of section 8 evidence, that the necessary elements are present. The provision is mandatory and there is no discretion. When considering the differences between the standards contained in the two sections, however, it should be remembered that the respondent at the interlocutory stage will be on notice of the case to be met, having been served with a plenary summons, a notice of motion and supporting affidavits detailing the case.

The standard of proof required to determine any question arising under the statute is the civil standard of 'on the balance of probabilities'.[173] Other provisions exist which might be considered to provide a measure of protection to a respondent, particularly at the interim stage. Proceedings in relation to interim orders, for example, must he heard otherwise than in public.[174] Any other proceedings under the 1996 Act may also be heard otherwise than in public if the respondent or any party to the proceedings apart from the applicant, so requests and the court considers it proper. In practice, most parties do request the court to hold interlocutory and receivership (see below) hearings otherwise than in public, and the courts grant the requests almost as a matter of course. The court may also, if it considers it appropriate to do so, prohibit the publication of information in relation to proceedings under the statute.

CAB, the primary source of most applications under the statute, has a duty to exercise great care so as to ensure that any proceedings taken by it do not

---

[172]   See *M. v. D.* (HC), per Moriarty J.
[173]   See 1996 Act, s. 8(2).
[174]   *Ibid*, s. 8(3).

have the effect of prejudicing any criminal prosecution which may follow. In some cases where the respondent has not appeared, applications have been made by counsel on behalf of the applicant to the court, for orders prohibiting any publication in order to avoid any risk of prejudicing pending or possible criminal prosecutions. Such orders have been regularly granted.

In *McK. v. F.*,[175] Geoghegan J. set out the correct procedure for a trial judge to follow in hearing an application for an order under the statute. First, the section 8 belief should be assessed. If it is decided that there exist reasonable grounds for that belief, then a specific finding should be made that such belief is now evidence of the facts stated therein. Next, the available evidence should be weighed up and a finding made as to whether a *prima facie* case has been made out – if so, the onus of proof will duly shift to the respondent. Following this, the respondent's evidence should be considered in order to decide whether this onus has been discharged. Where the court is satisfied that such burden has been discharged, proceedings should be dismissed. If it has not been so discharged, the court should go on to consider whether a 'serious risk of injustice' exists, and if not, the order should be granted. It was also held in that case that it is necessary for the plaintiff to deliver a statement of claim, where one is required by the defendant.[176]

THE CRIMINAL ASSETS BUREAU

CAB began its mandate on 15 October 1996, and is truly a pivotal creation in the state's attack on the proceeds of crime.[177] The adoption of a novel multi-agency approach, similar to that of the US Drug Enforcement Agency, formed a dominant characteristic of the Government's 1996 response to the upsurge in drug trafficking and organized crime. The Irish model has since been adopted as a template in the UK with the creation of the multi-disciplinary Serious Organized Crime Agency (SOCA).[178]

In contra-distinction to Ireland's National Police Service (An Garda Síochána) (hereinafter Irish Police) and the Revenue Commissioners, CAB is an independent agency, with staff appointed directly by the Minister for Justice and funding provided by the Department of Justice.[179] For the first

---

[175]   See *McK. v. A. F.* (SC), per Geoghegan J. at paras 43–4.
[176]   *Ibid.*; consequently, amendments have been made to ss. 2, 3 and 4 such that interim, interlocutory and disposal orders may be sought by originating motion.
[177]   See *Confiscation of Criminal Assets, supra* at p. 6, para. 2.
[178]   SOCA was created by the Serious Organized Crime and Police Act 2005. It began its mandate on 1 April 2006.
[179]   A point highlighted by Ashe and Reid, *supra*.

time in the history of the state, the resources of the Irish Police, the revenue authorities and the social welfare authorities were combined to produce a more effective weapon to combat organized crime. The vehicle through which these resources would be pooled was a new statutory agency, namely CAB. CAB was established as a body corporate by the Criminal Assets Bureau Act 1996 (hereinafter CAB Act 1996). As an organization it has perpetual succession, an official seal, the power to sue and be sued, and the power to acquire, hold and dispose of land or an interest in land or any other property.[180]

Composition

The distinctive feature of CAB is the fact that it consists of members of the Irish Police, officials from the Revenue Commissioners (both taxes and customs), and employees of the Department of Social, Community and Family Affairs all operating under the guidance of the Chief Bureau Officer of CAB, who is taken from the ranks of senior Garda ('Garda' is a police officer in the Irish Police).[181] Provision is also made for a Bureau Legal Officer[182] and administrative and technical staff.

The Chief Bureau Officer is appointed by the Commissioner of the Irish Police and must be a member of the Irish Police holding the rank of Chief Superintendent.[183] The Bureau Legal Officer is appointed by the Minister for Justice, Equality and Law Reform, with the consent of the Attorney General and the Minister for Finance.[184] Bureau officers, irrespective of which branch of the three services they come from, are appointed by the Minister for Justice, with the consent of the Minister for Finance. However, the appointments are made from police nominated by the Garda Commissioner (equivalent to chief of police in the Irish Police), revenue staff are nominated by the Revenue Commissioners and officers of the Minister for Social, Community and Family Affairs are also nominated by their relevant minister.[185]

The Minister for Justice may only appoint other persons as professional or technical staff once they have consulted the Garda Commissioner and with the consent of the Minister for Finance.[186]

---

[180] See CAB Act 1996, s. 3.
[181] *Ibid.* s. 7(6).
[182] *Ibid.* s. 9(1)(a); the Bureau Legal Officer reports directly to the Chief Bureau Officer.
[183] *Ibid.* s. 7.
[184] *Ibid.* s. 9(1)(b).
[185] *Ibid.* s. 8.
[186] *Ibid.* s. 9.

Anonymity

All reasonable care must be taken to ensure that the identity of any CAB officer, whether from the Revenue Commissioners or the Ministry for Social, Community and Family Affairs, is not revealed.[187] The same applies to any member of the CAB staff. Even where one of the CAB officers is exercising his or her powers or duties in the company of a CAB officer who is a member of the Irish Police, the former shall not be required to identify himself or herself. When exercising any power or duty in writing, he or she does so in the name of CAB.

The anonymity of non-Garda officers (non-police officers) of CAB and CAB staff also extends to court proceedings. Where the officer or staff member is required to give evidence in any such proceedings, the judge or person in charge of the proceedings may, on the application of the Chief Bureau Officer, if satisfied that there are reasonable grounds in the public interest to do so, give such directions for the preservation of the anonymity of the officer or staff member as he or she thinks fit.[188]

CAB Act 1996 makes it a criminal offence to identify non-Garda CAB officers, CAB staff or their families.[189] It is equally an offence to publish their addresses. The legislation also introduces specific prohibitions on assault, obstruction and intimidation of officers, staff and their families.[190]

Powers

Members of the CAB who are taken from the ranks of the Gardaí retain their powers and duties as members of the Irish Police. By the same token, members taken from the revenue officers retain the powers and duties vested in them under the Revenue Acts, while members from the Department of Social, Community and Family Affairs are still governed by the Social Welfare Acts. All such members can exercise their respective powers for the benefit of CAB.[191] Indeed, they do not generally acquire any special powers, or powers over and above those they already enjoy in their respective professional capacities, solely by virtue of joining CAB.

A significant exception, however, exists concerning the power to issue search warrants. Section 14 of CAB Act 1996 confers jurisdiction on District

---

[187]   *Ibid.* s. 10.
[188]   *Ibid.* s. 10(7).
[189]   *Ibid.* s. 11.
[190]   *Ibid.* ss 12, 13 and 15.
[191]   Such powers vested in each individual CAB officer as a member of the Garda Síochána do not extend to the CAB as a corporate entity.

Court judges to issue a warrant for the search of a specified place and any person found at that place.[192] The judge must be satisfied, after hearing evidence on oath from a CAB officer who is a member of the Gardaí, that there are reasonable grounds for suspecting that evidence of, or relating to, assets or proceeds of criminal activities, or pertaining to the identity or whereabouts of such proceeds, is to be found at the place specified. The warrant is valid for seven days. In an emergency situation, a CAB officer, who is a Garda not below the rank of superintendent, may issue a search warrant.[193] This is possible where such member is satisfied that circumstances of urgency give rise to a need for the immediate issue of such warrant and that such circumstances render it impracticable to apply to a judge of the District Court along the usual channel. A warrant issued under this emergency provision is valid for 24 hours only.

Every action of the CAB is subject to the approval of, or appeals to, the Irish courts. It is an offence to obstruct an officer in executing a CAB search warrant.[194] As with the *Anton Pillar* order, which allows search on pain of contempt of court, the penalty must seem relatively light on balance to a would-be obstructer hoarding what could be years of evidence, valuable drug-making materials and large sums of cash.

General Objectives and Functions

As mentioned above, the agency is of a multi-disciplinary character, staffed by personnel from the Irish Police, the Revenue Commissioners and the Department of Social, Community and Family Affairs. This allows it to adopt a three-pronged strategy against organized crime: confiscating the actual proceeds of crime, taxing such proceeds[195] and ceasing/ denying social welfare payments to the owners.

Traditional wisdom held that bringing criminal gains 'within the contemplation'[196] of income tax was wrong in principle as it amounted to the state taking a share in the fruits of criminal activity. As Ashe and Reid point out, however, the new regime grants CAB revenue powers as a 'second-best' option in that where it may not always be possible to freeze/confiscate crimi-

---

[192] See CAB Act 1996, s. 14.
[193] *Ibid.* s. 14(5).
[194] *Ibid.* s. 14(7).
[195] This was first made possible in the Finance Act 1983, which provides for 'gains from illegal sources' (Case IV, Schedule D). This marked a different policy to that adopted by the courts, for example by the Supreme Court decision in *Hayes v. Duggan* [1929] IR 406 (hereinafter *Hayes*).
[196] See *Hayes,* per Kennedy CJ.

nal assets directly, at least the state can settle for taxing them.[197] They identify a potential danger nonetheless in that any strategically minded criminal is unlikely to appeal an initial tax assessment, meaning the state may be tempted to cut its losses and settle for the tax rather than pursuing a more direct attack on illicit profits and potentially losing. They argue it is a near-blending of legitimate work with criminal, tax becoming a regular business expense to the criminal enterprise. Similarly regarding social welfare payments, stopping them may constitute a 'mere rap on the knuckles', but the state can settle for this rather than going for the jugular of the unexplained wealth on which such cessation is based.[198] Nonetheless, such relatively minor penalties cannot be seen as without value as, at the very least, they 'fire a warning shot' to criminals as regards their other assets.

The High Court has held that the statute also applies to proceeds coming from crimes which are committed outside the state[199] because as O'Higgins J reasoned, it would have been very strange if the legislature had intended to make Ireland a safe haven for criminals to enjoy the fruits of exploits which are illegal, if actually committed in the country,[200] especially in light of the legislature's approach in the 1996 Act. CAB's objectives are defined generally as: (i) identification of the assets which derive from crime; (ii) taking appropriate action to deprive those persons the benefit of such assets; and (iii) pursuing any investigation or doing any other preparatory work necessary to the above.[201]

---

197 See Ashe and Reid, *supra* at p. 197, para. 1.
198 *Ibid.* at p. 198, para. 2.
199 See *DPP and Frances Glacken and Felix McKenna v. Ernst Hollmann, Maria Bernadetta Jehle and Uwe Palisch,* unreported, High Court, 29 July 1999, per O'Higgins J.
200 *Ibid* transcript at p. 8.
201 See CAB Act 1996, s. 4. The functions of CAB are defined more specifically at s. 5(1) as the taking of all necessary actions:

(*a*) in accordance with Garda functions, for the purposes of, the confiscation, restraint of use, freezing, preservation or seizure of assets identified as deriving, or suspected to derive, directly or indirectly, from criminal activity,

(*b*) under the Revenue Acts or any provision of any other enactment, whether passed before or after the passing of [CAB Act 1996], which relates to revenue, to ensure that the proceeds of criminal activity or suspected criminal activity are subjected to tax and that the Revenue Acts, where appropriate, are fully applied in relation to such proceeds or activities, as the case may be,

(*c*) under the Social Welfare Acts for the investigation and determination, as appropriate, of any claim for or in respect of benefit (within the meaning of section 204 of the Social Welfare (Consolidation) Act, 1993) by any person engaged in criminal activity, and

Where appropriate, the taking of such actions shall include, subject to any international agreement, co-operation with any police force, tax or social welfare authority of a foreign state. Ashe and Reid stress the growing importance of the CAB's international work, and document the close ties which are maintained between law enforcement officials internationally, both formally and informally.[202]

Revenue Assessment and Collection

Under section 5(1) of the CAB Act 1996, the revenue responsibilities of CAB are to ensure that the proceeds of crime are taxed and that the 'Revenue Acts' are applied appropriately.[203] To this end, its revenue officers are both empowered and obliged to tax profits or gains from an unlawful or unknown source and to deal with the assessment and collection of any tax as defined by the Taxes Consolidation Act 1997.[204]

(d)   at the request of the Minister for Social Welfare, to investigate and determine, as appropriate, any claim for or in respect of a benefit, within the meaning of section 204 of the Social Welfare (Consolidation) Act, 1993, where the Minister for Social Welfare certifies that there are reasonable grounds for believing that, in the case of a particular investigation, officers of the Minister for Social Welfare may be subject to threats or other forms of intimidation...

[202]   See *Money Laundering, supra* at p. 200, para. 3.
[203]   See s 1(1) of CAB Act 1996:

'Revenue Acts' means –
(a)   the Customs Acts,
(b)   the statutes relating to the duties of excise and to the management of those duties,
(c)   the Tax Acts,
(d)   the Capital Gains Tax Acts,
(e)   the Value-Added Tax Act, 1972,
(f)   the Capital Acquisitions Tax Act, 1976,
(g)   the statutes relating to stamp duty and to the management of that duty,
(h)   Part VI of the Finance Act, 1983,
(i)   Chapter IV of Part 11 of the Finance Act 1992,
and any other instruments made thereunder and any instruments made under any other enactment and relating to tax.
"tax" means any tax, duty, levy or charge under the care and management of the Revenue Commissioners.

[204]   See Taxes Consolidation Act 1997, s. 58. The Revenue Commissioners are both empowered and obliged to assess and collect tax on profits or gains from an unlawful or unknown source.

These powers over criminal property were first introduced by the Disclosure of Certain Information for Taxation and other Purposes Act 1996, which made ancillary amendments to facilitate the assessment and collection of taxes by a body such as CAB. One of the most important of these provisions is the amendment to the 1994 Act to permit the exchange of information between the Revenue Commissioners and the Irish Police in appropriate circumstances.[205] Section 12 of that legislation sets out very detailed anonymity provisions in relation to the exercise of relevant powers and functions of authorized officers. Where CAB is concerned, however, more specific provisions are available in the CAB Act 1996.

CAB's application of the Revenue Acts to the proceeds of crime has been extremely effective in depriving persons of the benefit of their suspected crimes. Revenue officers in CAB have benefited from the investigations, enquiries and intelligence gathered by the other two agencies. On the basis of this information they have been able to raise substantial assessments on persons in possession of money or property, who are suspected of having obtained it from drug trafficking or other crime. Where such assessments are challenged, the question of whether or not the impugned profits are the result of crime must, by statute, be disregarded. Unless the person assessed can show that the money or property has been obtained from a lawful source, there is no answer to the tax assessment. The assessment becomes final and conclusive and CAB moves onto the next stage of deciding between the enforcement procedures available to it.

In applying the Revenue Acts generally, the Bureau has collected income tax, capital gains tax, value added tax, money related to the 'Pay-As-You-Earn' (PAYE) payroll deduction system or 'Pay Related Social Insurance' (PRSI) which has been collected and not returned. On the enforcement side, CAB has made use of section 962 of the Taxes Consolidation Act certificates (formerly, the sheriff's certificate under section 485 of Income Tax Act 1967), as well as attachments,[206] the High Court summary judgment procedure and judgment mortgages.

CONCLUSION

Since its formation, CAB has pursued a multi-agency approach in denying persons engaged in criminal activity access to the proceeds of their crimes.

---

[205] See 1994 Act, s. 63A as inserted by Disclosure of Certain Information for Taxation and other Purposes Act 1996, s. 1.
[206] See Taxes Consolidation Act 1997, s. 1002 (formerly Finance Act 1988, s. 73).

The main focus of CAB has been on the proceeds of drug trafficking. Its statutory remit, however, covers all forms of criminal activity. Property targeted includes hard cash but also seemingly legitimate items of real and personal property. Legal obligations of confidentiality, along with the very nature of the work of the Bureau, preclude the furnishing of details of individual cases.

Murphy has praised the introduction of civil forfeiture in Ireland as an innovative move away from traditional crime control strategies of policing and imprisonment, a move which criminologists have advocated for years.[207] CAB brings together the powers and functions of the Irish Police (Garda Síochána), the Revenue Commissioners (both Taxes and Customs) and the Department of Social, Community and Family Affairs in a collective effort to ensure that the full force of the State is brought to bear on persons who engage in drug trafficking and other crime. Property confiscated by CAB using civil remedies has resulted in the Irish Exchequer receiving in excess of 105 million in revenues, with the value of funds still frozen standing in excess of 55 million. It is the civil forfeiture approach which was advocated by the Irish Law Reform Commission in its 1991 Report on Confiscating the Proceeds of Crime.[208]

On the face of it, civil forfeiture seems to have helped enormously in the fight against organized crime in Ireland. In the Dáil (Assembly of Ireland) it has been championed as a real success story, with claims that the work of CAB has resulted in a 'mass exodus of serious criminals' from the jurisdiction;[209] and that it has 'eradicated the top echelon of organized crime' in the country.[210] Ashe and Reid have identified moneys gained through tax evasion as a possible new hunting ground for CAB, since it would fit the 'proceeds of crime' definition. Ultimately, only time will tell how successful this new regime is in actually cutting crime but reactions so far have been very positive.

---

[207]   See *Tracing the Proceeds of Crime, supra* at p. 75, para. 1.

[208]   See Irish Law Reform Commission (1991), http://www.lawreform.ie/publications/data/volume8/lrc_60.pdf (accessed 15 December 2007).

[209]   See Dáil Debates, 8 October 1997, vol. 481, col. 276, per Mr Higgins TD, as quoted in *Theorising Asset Forfeiture, supra.*

[210]   See *Irish Times* (2002), 'Election 2002, The Issues: Crime', http://www.ireland.com/focus/election_2002/issues/crime.htm (accessed 15 December 2007) quoted in Theorising Asset Forfeiture, *supra.*

4. Asset forfeiture in South Africa under the Prevention of Organised Crime Act 121 of 1998

Raylene Keightley*

INTRODUCTION

Civil asset forfeiture has been on the statute books in South Africa for approximately 15 years.[1] A narrow form of civil asset forfeiture was first introduced in 1992. Initially, under the Drugs and Drug Trafficking Act (No. 140 of 1992), a conviction-based scheme of civil forfeiture applied in respect of benefits derived by persons convicted of drug trafficking offences.[2] This regime was

---

*   The views expressed in this chapter are my personal views.
[1]   I use the term 'civil asset forfeiture' in this chapter to refer to asset forfeiture that is implemented by way of a civil legal process which, although it may sometimes operate in parallel with criminal proceedings, has been introduced into the law as an additional law enforcement measure and is not primarily penal in nature. Therefore, I include under consideration the scheme of asset forfeiture which is commonly referred to in South Africa as 'criminal forfeiture', i.e. asset forfeiture which is aimed at stripping convicted persons of the benefit they have derived from their crimes.
[2]   Chapter 5 of the Drugs and Drug Trafficking Act (No. 140 of 1992), which chapter was repealed by s. 37 of the Proceeds of Crime Act (No. 76 of 1996). A conviction-based form of forfeiture is retained in the amended Drugs and Drug Trafficking Act. Section 25 provides that a court convicting an accused person of an offence under the Act shall declare forfeit any scheduled substance, drug or property by means of which the offence was committed or which was used in the commission of the offence. Animals, vehicles, vessels, aircraft, containers or other articles used in the commission of the offence, or used for purposes of the storage, concealment, conveyance or removal of the scheduled substance or drug must also be declared forfeit. This type of forfeiture has a far narrower ambit and is distinct from the civil forfeiture regime established under Prevention of Organised Crime Act (No. 121 of 1998) (hereinafter POCA 1998). For this reason, it is not included for discussion in this chapter. In certain cases it may be possible for the State to elect to proceed under either s. 25 of the Drugs and Drug Trafficking Act or under POCA 1998. For example, in respect of a vehicle conveying drugs or scheduled substances. However, the proceeds of a vehicle forfeited and sold under this Act would not be deposited into the Criminal Assets Recovery Account, which is specifically established under POCA 1998 to receive the proceeds of forfeited assets.

expanded by the Proceeds of Crime Act (No. 76 of 1996), which allowed for
forfeiture in respect of the benefits derived by persons convicted of *any*
offences. However, it was only after 1998, with the enactment of the
Prevention of Organised Crime Act (No. 121 of 1998) (hereinafter POCA
1998), that the implementation of civil asset forfeiture went into full swing.
Effectively, therefore, civil asset forfeiture has been in operation in South
Africa for only a decade.

POCA 1998 is an innovative piece of legislation in that although it retained
the conviction based forfeiture scheme first introduced in the earlier two Acts,[3]
in addition, it established for the first time in South Africa a non-conviction
based forfeiture scheme aimed at the proceeds of unlawful activities and the
instrumentalities of criminal offences.[4]

There had been relatively little practical implementation of the forfeiture
provisions contained in the 1992 and 1996 legislation. In order to ensure that
the innovations introduced by POCA 1998 were implemented, a specialist
implementation agency called the Asset Forfeiture Unit (hereinafter AFU) was
established in 1999. The AFU falls under the National Prosecuting Authority,
a body which was established in terms of the post-1994 democratic constitutional dispensation,[5] and which is headed by the National Director of Public
Prosecutions (hereinafter NDPP).[6] Save for a setback in 1999 regarding the
issue of the retrospective applicability of POCA 1998, which required legislative amendment and caused some delay in rolling out asset forfeiture cases,[7]
the implementation of POCA 1998's asset forfeiture provisions has been

---

   [3]   Under POCA 1998, chapter 5 (hereinafter Chapter 5): see detailed discussion
below.
   [4]   Under POCA 1998, chapter 6 (hereinafter Chapter 6): see detailed discussion
below. By way of an amendment to POCA 1998, introduced in 2004 (Act 33 of 2004),
'property associated with terrorist activities and related activities' is now also covered
under Chapter 6.
   [5]   In terms of the National Prosecuting Authority Act (No. 32 of 1998), read with
s. 179 of the Constitution of the Republic of South Africa (No. 108 of 1996) (hereinafter Constitution).
   [6]   In terms of s. 179(1)(a) of the Constitution, the National Director of Public
Prosecutions (hereinafter NDPP) is the head of the prosecuting authority, and is
appointed by the President of the Republic of South Africa.
   [7]   Three high-profile asset forfeiture cases instituted by the AFU shortly after
POCA 1998 took effect were dismissed by the courts on the basis that neither Chapter
5 nor Chapter 6 had retrospective effect. The NDPP could not, therefore, seek forfeiture in respect of property associated with offences committed prior to POCA 1998
coming into effect: see *NDPP v. Basson* 2002 (1) SA 419 (SCA), *NDPP v. Carolous*
2000 (1) SA 1127 (N) and *NDPP v. Meyer* 1999 (4) All SA 263 (D). The retrospectiv-
ity problem highlighted by these cases was rectified by way of amendment to POCA
1998 in 1999. Section 1(5) of POCA 1998 now expressly provides that:

remarkably speedy. In the period of eight years since POCA 1998 took effect and the AFU was established, a formidable jurisprudence has developed, with decisions on critical issues emanating from the highest courts in the land.

Although the conviction based asset forfeiture scheme had been on the statute books prior to POCA 1998, the lack of widespread implementation of these earlier provisions meant that there was very little pre-POCA 1998 jurisprudence on the many complex issues raised by this scheme of forfeiture.[8] In respect of non-conviction based forfeiture, which was an innovation of POCA 1998, there simply was no pre-POCA 1998 jurisprudence. Consequently, once the asset forfeiture provisions under POCA 1998 were implemented, the courts were faced with the daunting task of interpreting and giving effect to a form of law enforcement that was largely foreign to them. To make matters worse, the asset forfeiture provisions of POCA 1998 are generally accepted as falling somewhat short of being a model of clear legislative drafting.[9] This has increased the scope for uncertainty and has placed a heavy interpretive burden on the courts.

Of further significance in the development of the law has been the role of the Bill of Rights,[10] which was introduced in South Africa in the period shortly preceding the establishment of the National Prosecuting Authority and the adoption of POCA 1998. The Bill of Rights contains far-reaching protections for individual rights, including the protection of property rights,[11] the right to equality,[12] the right to human dignity[13] and the right to freedom and security

---

Nothing in this Act or in any other law, shall be construed so as to exclude the application of any provision of Chapter 5 or 6 on account of the fact that –

    (a) any offence or unlawful activity concerned occurred; or

    (b) any proceeds of unlawful activities were derived, received or retained,

before the commencement of this Act.

[8]   Some judgments by the superior courts were handed down under the Proceeds of Crime Act (No. 76 of 1996). See *Director of Public Prosecutions, Cape of Good Hope v. Bathgate* 2000 (2) SA 535 (C) (hereinafter *Bathgate*); see also *Director of Public Prosecutions v. Aereboe and Others* 2000 1 All SA 105 (N); see also *Bantho and another v. The State*, unreported, Case No. CC138/98 (judgment of the Natal Provincial Division).

[9]   In a recent judgment of the Constitutional Court, *Mohunram & Another v. NDPP and Others,* 2007 (2) SACR 145 (CC) (26 March 2007) (hereinafter *Mohunram*), at para. 25, Van Heerden AJ stated that: 'It is certainly true that POCA, even as amended, is not a model of legislative clarity and coherence.

[10]   The Bill of Rights is contained in Chapter 2 of the Constitution.

[11]   See the Constitution, s. 25.

[12]   *Ibid.* s. 9: the right to equality includes the right to equal protection and benefit of the law.

[13]   *Ibid.* s. 10.

of the person.[14] The Constitution of the Republic of South Africa 1996 (No. 108 of 1996) (hereinafter Constitution) imposes a positive duty on the State to respect, protect, promote and fulfil these rights.[15] This duty clearly includes an obligation on the part of the state to implement appropriate law enforcement measures in the interests of protecting the rights of society at large. In South Africa, which is afflicted by unacceptably high crime rates, this duty is an onerous one.

Where asset forfeiture is implemented as a law enforcement measure, the fulfilment by the state of its public obligation inevitably gives rise to a conflict between its public duty and its duty to respect the individual rights of persons whose property is affected by the asset forfeiture proceedings. Thus, the development of South Africa's asset forfeiture jurisprudence has been shaped by the need to balance the public interest served by asset forfeiture with the private interests directly affected by it.

To date, none of the asset forfeiture provisions in POCA 1998 has been struck down as unconstitutional. Instead, the courts have been guided by constitutional imperatives in determining when asset forfeiture is justifiable. Although the development of the law has occurred on a case-by-case basis, there have been a number of decisions from the highest courts which have had the effect of laying down general principles, and hence introducing a greater measure of certainty, in respect of some key aspects of the law. In other areas, and sometimes notwithstanding pronouncements from the highest courts, uncertainty remains.

In this chapter, the two civil asset forfeiture schemes established under POCA 1998 will be outlined with reference to the relevant case law. In addition, I will attempt to highlight and discuss some of the more important issues that have arisen with regard to the implementation of the asset forfeiture provisions of POCA 1998 and how these issues have been dealt with by the courts.

THE BROAD OBJECTIVES OF ASSET FORFEITURE UNDER POCA 1998: IS THE AMBIT OF ASSET FORFEITURE LIMITED TO ORGANISED CRIME?

The preamble to POCA 1998 (as amended by Prevention of Organised Crime Second Amendment Act (No. 38 of 1999)) outlines in broad terms the underlying objectives of the asset forfeiture provisions of the Act:

---

[14]   *Ibid.* s. 12: this includes the right not to be punished in a cruel, inhuman or degrading way.

[15]   *Ibid.* s. 7(2).

WHEREAS no person *convicted* of an offence should benefit from the fruits of that or any related offence, whether such offence took place before or after the commencement of this Act, legislation is necessary to provide for a *civil remedy* for the restraint and seizure, and confiscation of *property which forms the benefits derived from such offence*;

AND WHEREAS no person should benefit from the fruits of unlawful activities, nor is any person entitled to use property for the commission of an offence, whether such activities or offence took place before or after the commencement of this Act, legislation is necessary to provide for a *civil remedy* for the preservation and seizure, and forfeiture of *property which is derived from unlawful activities* or is *concerned in the commission or suspected commission of an offence* [emphasis added].

The first of the paragraphs cited above relates to the scheme of forfeiture commonly referred to in South Africa as 'criminal forfeiture', and which is catered for specifically in Chapter 5 of POCA 1998 (hereinafter Chapter 5). This description is not technically correct in the sense that the forfeiture procedure under Chapter 5 is expressed to be civil in nature.[16] The common description of this scheme of forfeiture as criminal is because forfeiture under Chapter 5 is dependent ultimately on the conviction of the defendant in the forfeiture proceedings.

The broad objective of Chapter 5 'criminal' forfeiture is to strip the convicted defendant of any benefit (as defined in POCA 1998) that he or she

---

[16]   Chapter 5, s. 13 provides that:

(1)   For the purposes of this Chapter proceedings on application for a confiscation order or a restraint order are civil proceedings, and are not criminal proceedings.
(2)   The rules of evidence applicable in civil proceedings apply to proceedings on application for a confiscation order or a restraint order.
(3)   No rule of evidence applicable only in criminal proceedings shall apply to proceedings on application for a confiscation order or restraint order.
(4)   No rule of construction applicable only in criminal proceedings shall apply to proceedings on application for a confiscation order or restraint order.
(5)   Any question of fact to be decided by a court in any proceedings in respect of an application contemplated in this Chapter shall be decided on a balance of probabilities.

It has been held that a defendant in proceedings under Chapter 5 is not an 'accused person' for purposes of s. 35(3) of the Constitution, which gives every 'accused person' the right to a fair trial. In this respect, therefore, the proceedings are not criminal proceedings, notwithstanding that the proceedings flow from the defendant's criminal conviction and culminates in a judgment against him or her. See *NDPP v. Phillips and Others,* 2002 (4) SA 60 (W) (hereinafter *Phillips*) at para. 40.

derived from the offence in respect of which he or she is convicted, or from related criminal activities. Under this scheme of forfeiture, it is not necessarily the actual proceeds derived from the relevant criminal offences that may be declared to be forfeited. As explained below, forfeiture under Chapter 5 results in a money judgment, in the form of a confiscation order, being granted against a convicted defendant who has benefited from his or her offences. A confiscation order may be satisfied by executing against any property held by such defendant, including property that was legitimately acquired. The underlying premise of Chapter 5 forfeiture is that no person should be entitled to benefit from his or her own wrongdoing.[17] For ease of reference, the present chapter will adopt the label commonly used to refer to the Chapter 5 asset forfeiture scheme, being 'criminal forfeiture'.

The second paragraph from the preamble as cited above relates to the forfeiture scheme established under Chapter 6 of POCA 1998 (hereinafter Chapter 6), which is commonly referred to in South Africa as 'civil forfeiture'. Like forfeiture under Chapter 5, the procedure by which this forfeiture scheme is effected is commonly expressed to be civil in nature.[18] The label of 'civil forfeiture' is derived from the fact that, unlike criminal forfeiture under Chapter 5, a forfeiture order under Chapter 6 is not dependent on the institution or successful conclusion of any criminal prosecution in relation to the offences concerned. In fact, no criminal proceedings at all are necessary for the implementation of forfeiture under Chapter 6. A further distinction between the two forfeiture schemes is that forfeiture under Chapter 6 is focused on tainted property: it can only be granted in respect of the actual proceeds of unlawful activities (or property representing the proceeds) or in respect of property which is an instrumentality (as defined in POCA 1998) of

---

[17]   In *Phillips, ibid.* at para. 43, it was held that:

This is a principle well-known to our common law which has spawned a variety of rules such as those expressed by the maxims *nemo ex suo delicto meliorem suam condictionem facere potest, ex turpi causa non oritur actio, in pari delicto potior est condictio defendentis* and *de bloedige hand neemt geen erf.* Chapter 5 of the POCA extends this principle to the proceeds of crime. The confiscation order merely deprives the criminal of the benefit to which he was not entitled in the first place under general principles of our law. It strips him of the proceeds of his crime and does not punish him for it.

See also *Bathgate,* at para. 87; see also *NDPP v. Mcasa and Another* 2000 (1) SACR 263 (Tk) (hereinafter *Mcasa*).

[18]   See s. 37 under Chapter 6, which is in almost identical wording with s. 13 under Chapter 5.

any of the offences set out in Schedule 1 to POCA 1998 (hereinafter Schedule 1 Offence) or in respect of property associated with terrorist activities.[19] For purposes of this chapter, the forfeiture scheme established under Chapter 6 is referred to as 'Chapter 6 civil forfeiture' or 'forfeiture under Chapter 6'.

The underlying objectives of Chapter 6 civil forfeiture share some similarities with the objectives of criminal forfeiture. Thus, the forfeiture of proceeds of unlawful activities under Chapter 6 also serves the purpose of depriving a wrongdoer of the benefits of wrongful actions. In addition, both forfeiture schemes have a strong deterrent element aimed, not only at the particular wrongdoer involved, but also at society at large.

However, Chapter 6 civil forfeiture has particular features that render it more vulnerable to being held to interfere unjustifiably with individual rights: the absence of the need to prove the commission of an offence beyond reasonable doubt in order to have property declared forfeited; the fact that the forfeiture is concerned with the 'guilt' of the property rather than the wrongdoing of the owner; the availability of only a narrow 'innocent owner' defence being available to property owners affected by forfeiture orders;[20] and the very broad definition of 'instrumentality of an offence', which drastically extends the reach of property that may be vulnerable to forfeiture.[21]

Consequently, to date, it has been with regard to Chapter 6 civil forfeiture, and particularly forfeiture in respect of cases involving 'an instrumentality of an offence', that the courts have been most active in developing a jurisprudence which attempts to bring forfeiture under that Chapter into line with what is held to be constitutionally justifiable.

One illustration of this is the manner in which the courts have dealt with the issue of what the ambit is of the asset forfeiture provisions of POCA 1998.

---

[19]   In the Constitutional Court judgment of *NDPP v. Mohamed No and Others* 2002 (4) SA 843 (CC) (12 June 2002), at para. 17, Ackermann J held that:

Chapter 6 provides for forfeiture in circumstances where it is established, on a balance of probabilities, that property has been used to commit an offence, or constitutes the proceeds of unlawful activities, even where no criminal proceedings in respect of the relevant crimes have been instituted. In this respect, chapter 6 needs to be understood in contradistinction to chapter 5 of the Act. Chapter 6 is therefore focussed, not on wrongdoers, but on property that has been used to commit an offence or which constitutes the proceeds of crime. The guilt or wrongdoing of the owners or possessors of property is, therefore, not primarily relevant to the proceedings.

[20]   See below for further discussion on this feature.
[21]   See below for further discussion on this feature.

This issue is of fundamental significance and involves the question of whether asset forfeiture may be sought only in respect of the 'organised crime' offences established in POCA 1998, or whether asset forfeiture may be sought also in respect of 'ordinary' offences, or cases of individual wrongdoing.

This issue arises due to the fact that POCA 1998 is not solely directed at asset forfeiture. As the name suggests, its broader objective is to combat organised crime. This is clear from a reading of the full preamble of POCA 1998.[22] To this end, the legislation includes chapters that deal with the offences of racketeering,[23] money laundering[24] and criminal gang activities.[25] Money laundering offences were included for the first time in the Proceeds of Crime Act (No. 76 of 1996), but the racketeering and criminal gang related offences were created for the first time in POCA 1998. Notwithstanding the broad objectives set out in the preamble of POCA 1998, the scheme and text of POCA 1998 gives a clear indication that the legislature did not intend to limit the use of the asset forfeiture provisions to the offences specifically established under the legislation.[26]

---

[22] The preamble to POCA 1998 is too long to quote in full. Relevant paragraphs of the preamble dealing expressly with organised crime include the following:

AND WHEREAS there is a rapid growth of organised crime, money laundering and criminal gang activities nationally and internationally and since organised crime has internationally been identified as an international security threat;
AND WHEREAS organised crime, money laundering and criminal gang activities infringe on the rights of the people as enshrined in the Bill of Rights;
AND WHEREAS it is the right of every person to be protected from fear, intimidation and physical harm caused by the criminal activities of violent gangs and individuals;
AND WHEREAS organised crime, money laundering and criminal gang activities, both individually and collectively, present a danger to public order and safety and economic stability, and have the potential to inflict social damage;
AND WHEREAS the South African common law and statutory law fail to deal effectively with organised crime, money laundering and criminal gang activities, and also fail to keep pace with international measures aimed at dealing effectively with organised crime, money laundering and criminal gang activities;
AND BEARING IN MIND that it is usually very difficult to prove the direct involvement of organised crime leaders in particular cases, because they do not perform the actual criminal activities themselves, it is necessary to criminalise the management of, and related conduct in connection with enterprises which are involved in a pattern of racketeering activity; ...

[23] See POCA 1998, chapter 2, ss 2–3.
[24] *Ibid.* chapter 3, ss 4–8.
[25] *Ibid.* chapter 4, ss 9–11.
[26] This is also evident from the preamble itself. In contrast to the repeated refer-

The question of whether the ambit of asset forfeiture under POCA 1998 is limited to the 'organised crime' offences of racketeering, money laundering or criminal gang activities was first raised, and rejected, in the context of Chapter 5.[27] Thereafter, it was rejected in the context of Chapter 6 civil forfeiture in a judgment by the highest court of appeal on non-constitutional matters, the Supreme Court of Appeal (hereinafter SCA). The SCA rejected the finding of the court below that the evasion of personal income tax by a single individual could not be considered 'organised crime' and that the legislation was never intended to be applied in such cases. On the contrary, the court held that POCA 1998 'clearly applies to cases of individual wrongdoing'.[28] This was endorsed expressly by the SCA again in a more recent judgment in which the court

---

ences to organised crime, money laundering and criminal gang activities in other paragraphs of the preamble, those paragraphs citing the need for asset forfeiture make no reference to these specific types of criminal activities and instead adopt broader language, with reference only to 'offences' and 'unlawful activities'.

[27] In one of the early judgments under POCA 1998, *Mcasa* at paras 62 and 64, it was held that:

> An accused who has been convicted of 'an offence' or of 'any other offence' at the same trial and who has derived a benefit from such offences is liable to be subjected to a confiscation order. Equally liable is an accused who has derived a benefit from 'any criminal activity' which the court finds to be sufficiently related to those offences (s 18(1)). Nothing contained in s 18(1) or elsewhere in Chapter 5 suggests that 'an offence', 'any other offence' and 'any criminal activity' are confined to organised crime, money laundering, racketeering and criminal gang activities. Further, not even the general definition (s 1) or the definition section contained in Chapter 5 itself (s 12) defines these terms. They thus must bear their ordinary meaning unless there is a sufficiently clear basis for giving them the special, restrictive meaning ascribed to them by Mr Kemp. Does the preamble lay down such basis? ... It is quite axiomatic that statutory interpretation has to do with deciphering legislative intent. In the instant case we have to determine whether, in the face of the plain language of Chapter 5 (of course, read with the rest of the Act for a full picture and clear perspective), the preamble, in any way, dictates the adoption of the restrictive meaning.

The court held that the preamble did not dictate the adoption of the restrictive meaning and that the kidnapping and extortion charges faced by the defendants fell within the category of offences in respect of which a confiscation order could be granted.

[28] See *NDPP v. (1) R O Cook Properties (Pty) Ltd; (2) 37 Gillespie Street Durban (Pty) Ltd; (3) Seevnarayan* 2004 (2) SACR 208 (SCA) (hereinafter *Cook*) at para. 60. The Supreme Court of Appeal (hereinafter SCA) held that to adopt the restrictive interpretation of the court below would be radically to truncate the scope of POCA 1998. The approach adopted in *Cook* was endorsed subsequently by the SCA in the cases of *Prophet v. NDPP* 2006(1) SA 38 (SCA) at para. 33 and *NDPP v. Van Staden and Others* 2007 (1) SACR 338 (SCA) (hereinafter *Van Staden*), which dealt with the forfeiture of motor vehicles as instrumentalities of drunk driving offences.

considered the use of Chapter 6 civil forfeiture in cases involving motor vehicles as instrumentalities of drunk driving offences.[29] While the court confirmed in this case that the ambit of the asset forfeiture provisions of POCA 1998 extended beyond organised crime, it held that the use of asset forfeiture outside of the ambit of organised crime would not always be appropriate and justified.[30]

In a subsequent decision of the Constitutional Court in *Mohunram v. NDPP*[31] (hereinafter *Mohunram*), however, this issue was reopened and placed sharply under the constitutional spotlight. The case concerned an appeal against a ruling by the SCA granting an order of forfeiture under Chapter 6 in respect of certain business premises that had been used partly to conduct a legitimate business, and partly to conduct an illegal gambling business. The owner of the premises was a juristic person. Mr Mohunran was the sole shareholder in the entity that owned the premises and he was the proprietor of both the legitimate business and the illegal gambling business. The SCA had concluded that the property was an instrumentality of the relevant gambling offences and had ordered its forfeiture.

The issue of the ambit of asset forfeiture under POCA 1998 was raised for the first time in *Mohunram* at the Constitutional Court stage of the proceedings. It was raised by a party that had been allowed to enter the proceedings as *amicus curiae*. The *amicus* argued that on a proper interpretation of the text of POCA 1998, and taking into account the purpose and object of POCA 1998, as set out in the preamble, property could only be declared forfeited as an 'instrumentality of an offence' if it was an instrumentality of one of the organised crime offences established in POCA 1998, being racketeering, money laundering and offences relating to criminal gang activities. Although illegal gambling was listed as one of the Schedule 1 Offences in respect of which the forfeiture of an instrumentality could be granted,[32] the *amicus* argued that

---

29   See *Van Staden, ibid.* at para. 1.
30   *Ibid.* at paras 7 and 8; in para. 7, the court held that:

It must be borne in mind that drunken driving, which does not ordinarily result from organised illicit activity, and presents no special difficulties to detect and prosecute, can attract substantial penalties, and the ordinary criminal law ought to be the first port of call to combat the evil. For the Act exists to supplement criminal remedies in appropriate cases and not merely as a more convenient substitute.

31   2007 (2) SACR 145 (CC) (26 March 2007).
32   The relevant section, being s. 50(1) of POCA 1998, provides that forfeiture may be granted in respect of property which is 'an instrumentality of an *offence referred to in schedule 1*' (emphasis added). Schedule 1 includes a range of common law and statutory offences, such as murder, rape and other sexual offences, assault,

forfeiture would only be competent if, in addition to being a Schedule 1 Offence, the offence was also one of these 'organised crime' offences. For example, in a case where illegal gambling was a predicate offence in respect of money laundering or racketeering.

The decision of the Constitutional Court in *Mohunram* is complex, not least because of the fact that the bench of 11 judges gave three separate judgments, comprising of a minority judgment of five judges (dismissing the appeal and upholding the forfeiture order) and two separate majority judgments, each supported by three judges (both upholding the appeal and dismissing the forfeiture order). Consequently, one of the difficulties with the decision is that there is no clear *ratio* on the fundamental issues considered by the court.

The minority, in a closely reasoned judgment by Van Heerden AJ, were 'unconvinced by the [*amicus'*] contention that Chapter 6 of POCA can reasonably be interpreted so as to apply only to so-called "organised crime offences" '.[33] The first majority judgment by Moseneke DCJ (hereinafter Moseneke DCJ Judgment) found it unnecessary to decide the issue but nevertheless commented that it was 'unable to hold without more that the construction of section 50(1) of POCA advanced by the [*amicus*] is without merit'.[34] The second majority judgment by Sachs J (hereinafter Sachs J Judgment) also did not decide the issue and assumed, without deciding, that 'there was no obligatory jurisdictional requirement that the instrument of an offence be shown to have a connection with organised crime'.[35]

All three judgments recognized that the submissions made by the *amicus* had constitutional implications. As was noted in the Moseneke DCJ Judgment, the contention of the *amicus* was that:

> ... if the meaning given to 'offence' [in the context of 'instrumentality of an offence'] runs wide and well beyond organised crime in a way that includes all the acts of individual wrongdoing listed in Schedule 1, it would be inconsistent, not only with the purpose and text of the statute, but more importantly with the prohibition against unlawful and arbitrary deprivation of property set by section 25(1) of

---

arson, robbery, gambling offences, corruption offences, extortion, child-stealing, kidnapping, breaking and entering, theft, forgery, drug offences, firearms offences and offences relating to dealing in endangered animal species. In addition, it includes a catch-all provision in the schedule including 'any offence the punishment wherefor may be a period of imprisonment exceeding one year without the option of a fine'.

[33] See *Mohunram,* per Van Heerden AJ, with Langa CJ, Madala J, Van der Westhuizen J and Yacoob J concurring, at para. 34; reasons for above are set out at *ibid.* paras 15–33.

[34] *Ibid.* at paras 107–138, per Moseneke DCJ, with Mokgoro J and Nkabinda J concurring.

[35] *Ibid.* at paras 139–155, per Sachs J, with Kondile AJ and O'Regan J concurring.

the Constitution. It would also constitute disproportionate and irrational punishment not permitted by section 12(1)(e) of the Bill of Rights[36] [text in square brackets added; footnotes omitted].

However, by reason of the fact that this constitutional issue had been raised belatedly and only at the Constitutional Court stage of proceedings, the view in all three judgments was that it was not properly before the court and that it would be improper to decide the issue.[37] This leaves the issue unresolved and open for determination in the event of it being raised properly in any subsequent case. Accordingly, it is likely that the Constitutional Court may yet be required to determine the issue of whether, on a proper construction of POCA 1998, the ambit of Chapter 6 civil forfeiture extends to property which is an instrumentality of an 'ordinary' offence rather than one of the 'organised crime' offences described in the Act.

However, assuming for purposes of *Mohunram* that the ambit of POCA 1998 was wide enough to allow for the forfeiture of the instrumentalities of 'ordinary' offences, the court proceeded to consider the question of whether the forfeiture of the premises used by Mr Mohunram for purposes of running his illegal gambling business was constitutionally justifiable. It was in this context that the underlying objective of POCA 1998, as a weapon to combat organised crime, was found by the court to carry significant weight. The court's approach is clearly explained in the following dictum from the minority judgment:[38]

> ... The interpretation of POCA (and more particularly of 'instrumentality of an offence') as reaching beyond the ambit of 'organised crime' and applying to cases of individual wrongdoing could result in situations of clearly disproportionate (and hence constitutionally unacceptable) forfeiture, and courts must always be sensitive to and on their guard against this [footnotes omitted].

The need for a proportionality inquiry to determine the constitutionality of forfeitures in instrumentality cases had already been established in the jurisprudence prior to *Mohunram*.[39] What the Constitutional Court did in *Mohunram* was to recognize that in instrumentality cases the proportionality between means and ends, being between the effect on the individual and the

---

[36]   *Ibid.* at para. 115.
[37]   *Ibid.* at paras. 30–33, per Van Heerden AJ; see also para. 117, per Moseneke J; see also para. 140, per Sachs J.
[38]   *Ibid.* at para. 56, per Van Heerden AJ.
[39]   See SCA in *Cook*; see also the Constitutional Court in *Prophet v. NDPP* 2006 (2) SACR 525 (CC) (29 September 2006) (hereinafter *Prophet*), at para. 58: see detailed discussion below.

public purpose served by the forfeiture, has to be gauged with reference to POCA 1998's underlying objective of combating organised crime. If the forfeiture is not rationally connected to that purpose, it will be disproportionate.

The three judgments in *Mohunram* are in agreement that the objective of combating organised crime is a relevant factor in the proportionality analysis. Where the judgments disagree, is with regard to the weight to be given to POCA 1998's underlying objective in the proportionality analysis, and in the application of the proportionality principle to the facts of the case.

For the minority of the court, '[t]he organised crime element, while significant in assessing whether a forfeiture order should be made in a particular case, is not necessarily decisive'.[40] The majority of the court identified the prevention of organised crime as the 'principle' or 'primary' purpose of POCA 1998, and both majority judgments place primacy on the organised crime element involved in instrumentality forfeitures. The Sachs J judgment held that 'the extent to which the forfeiture manifestly is directed towards preventing organised crime will be highly relevant'.[41] The Moseneke DCJ judgment agreed with the majority in the Sachs J judgment and found that 'the more remote the offence in issue is to the primary purpose of the POCA, the more likely it is that forfeiture of the instrumentality of the crime is disproportionate.'[42] In the case of 'ordinary crime', the Moseneke DCJ judgment held that one of the factors that must be considered is whether the crime has 'some rational link, however tenuous, with racketeering, money laundering and criminal gang activities'.[43]

Although all three judgments recognised the underlying objective of the need to combat organised crime as being a relevant component of the proportionality assessment, both the minority judgment and the Sachs J judgment acknowledged the difficulty in drawing a clear distinction between 'organised crime' and 'ordinary crimes', and noted that 'no bright lines can be drawn' between them.[44]

The minority of the court concluded that while the forfeiture of the property undeniably would have a punitive effect, it was not disproportionate and was justifiable. The majority of the court found that the forfeiture would be disproportionate and that an order of forfeiture could not be justified. In reaching this

---

[40] See *Mohunram*, at para. 74, per Van Heerden AJ: '[t]he criminal activities of an efficient and energetic individual miscreant may well have a more extensive reach and a greater negative social impact'.

[41] *Ibid.* at para. 146, per Sachs J.

[42] *Ibid.* at para. 126, per Moseneke DCJ.

[43] *Ibid.*

[44] *Ibid.* at para. 74 per Van Heerden AJ, and at paras 140 and 146, per Sachs J.

latter conclusion, the majority took into account, *inter alia*, that there was 'no suggestion, still less any proof, that Mr Mohunram ... pursued any wrongdoing connected directly or indirectly to organised crime as envisaged in POCA'.[45] Further, '[t]he offence appears to be relatively far from the heartland of organised crime, while the ordinary criminal penalties seem to have been quite appropriate to deal with it'.[46]

It is not possible within the confines of this chapter to undertake a full analysis of the complex issues that arise for consideration in *Mohunram*. What the case serves to illustrate, is that the Constitutional Court clearly has concerns about the proper use of Chapter 6 civil forfeiture, at least in the context of instrumentality cases. Without resorting to striking down the relevant provisions of POCA 1998, and even without overturning existing authority on the ambit of asset forfeiture under POCA 1998, the Constitutional Court in *Mohunram* demonstrated that it intends to keep a tight rein on the development of the law in this arena.

In assessing the impact that *Mohunram* will have on the future development of this area of the law in South Africa, it is important to highlight at least two matters of relevance. First, much will always depend on the facts of each case as they are presented to the courts. A full reading of the judgments in *Mohunram* indicates that both the majority and minority of the court took into account a range of factors[47] (in addition to the absence of a link with organised crime) in reaching their decisions. The AFU no doubt will be guided by *Mohunram* in the manner in which it presents future cases, and no doubt will select its cases accordingly. The six-five split in the Constitutional Court bench, as well as the fact that there were two different majority judgments, are significant, as this undoubtedly will give rise to debate on the meaning and import of the decision in future cases. It is also significant that the majority in the Sachs J judgment described the case as one that 'may well be a borderline case',[48] and that the Sachs J majority expressly stated that its difference with the minority lay in the application of the proportionality principle, rather than in respect of any question of interpretation of POCA 1998.[49] What is further apparent is that the Constitutional Court is likely to be less rigid in insisting on

---

45   *Ibid.* at para. 129, per Moseneke DCJ. See also a similar comment at *ibid.* para. 150, per Sachs J.
46   *Ibid.* at para. 154, per Sachs J.
47   See in particular *ibid.* at para. 72, per Van Heerden AJ, where the following factors are listed: 'the nature and gravity of the offence, the extent to which ordinary criminal law measures (when properly enforced) are effective in dealing with it, the public impact and potential for widespread social harm and disruption'.
48   *Ibid.* at para. 154, per Sachs J.
49   *Ibid.* at para. 141, per Sachs J.

overt links being drawn with organised crime in certain types of cases, such as those involving drug offences.[50]

Secondly, the arguments by the *amicus* in *Mohunram* focused expressly and specifically on the forfeiture of *instrumentalities* under Chapter 6, rather than on the forfeiture of *proceeds* under Chapter 6, or on criminal forfeiture under Chapter 5. There are significant differences between forfeitures aimed at proceeds of crime and at the benefits derived from criminal activity on the one hand, and forfeitures aimed at instrumentalities on the other. It is far easier to justify the forfeiture of property which a person derived from criminal activity, or to require a convicted defendant to pay to the state an amount equivalent to what he or she benefited from the relevant criminal activity. Of course, Chapter 6 civil forfeitures aimed at proceeds and criminal forfeitures under Chapter 5 must also meet the constitutional imperative of not being arbitrary. However, it is important to bear in mind that the concerns that the Constitutional Court voiced in *Mohunram* about the need for a link between the offence concerned and 'organised crime' are not necessarily applicable, and may be less relevant, in the context of forfeiture in respect of proceeds or of criminal forfeiture.[51]

Unfortunately, however, the doubts raised by some of the judges[52] in the

---

[50]   The Constitutional Court's previous decision in an instrumentality case was *Prophet*, which involved a house in which the owner had set up a small drug laboratory. There was no evidence that he was in any way linked to organised crime, but the court made reference in its decision to the general link between drug offences and organised crime. The Constitutional Court there found that the forfeiture of the house would not be disproportionate and upheld the forfeiture order. In the Sachs J Judgment, the majority sought to distinguish *Mohunram* from *Prophet* on the basis, *inter alia*, that unlike drug manufacturing, the use of gambling machines was not regarded by the law as being inherently harmful; see further *Mohunram*, at paras 147–149, per Sachs J.

[51]   The same issues raised by instrumentality forfeitures, which are dependent on the interpretation given to 'offence' in the definition of 'instrumentality of an offence', do not arise in respect of the forfeiture of proceeds. The definition of proceeds is much wider. It does not refer to 'offences' but instead refers to proceeds of 'unlawful activities', which is defined as meaning 'conduct which constitutes a crime or which contravenes any law'. The wide concept of 'proceeds of unlawful activities' also has application in relation to criminal forfeiture under Chapter 5, albeit for a different purpose. See in this regard, POCA 1998, s. 12(3), which renders the definition of 'proceeds of unlawful activities' applicable for purposes of criminal forfeiture. In addition, it is significant that the same scheme of criminal forfeiture, which currently is contained in POCA 1998, was contained previously in the Proceeds of Crime Act 1996, and that this latter Act was not focused on combating organised crime. Furthermore, as the SCA noted in *Cook,* at para. 66, the risk of unconstitutional application of the provisions of POCA 1998 dealing with the forfeiture of proceeds is smaller than in respect of the provisions dealing with instrumentalities.

[52]   In particular, those who concurred in the judgment of Moseneke DCJ.

Constitutional Court on the ambit of POCA 1998 and on its application outside of organised crime give rise to uncertainty as to how courts in the interim are to deal with these questions. It is not clear what weight the previous SCA judgments, which unequivocally stated that the ambit of POCA 1998 extends beyond organised crime, now carry. Clarity on these issues will be dependent on further litigation, which will have to be taken all the way up to the Constitutional Court.[53]

ASPECTS OF CRIMINAL FORFEITURE UNDER CHAPTER 5

The criminal forfeiture scheme set out in Chapter 5 is modelled closely on that found in the United Kingdom's Criminal Justice Act 1998 and the South

---

[53] Some guidance in this regard appears from a more recent judgment handed down by the SCA. In *NDPP v Vermaak* 2008 (1) SACR 157 (SCA), which also involved a motor vehicle as an instrumentality of drunk driving offences, the SCA interrogated the technical aspects of the rules of precedent applicable in South African law. It held that in view of the fact that the Constitutional Court had left the question of the ambit of POCA 1998 open in *Mohunram*, the SCA was bound to follow its own precedent, as established in *Cook, Prophet* and *Van Staden*, to the effect that POCA 1998 is not confined to organised crime but extends also to individual wrongdoing. Therefore, until this issue is properly revisited by the Constitutional Court, and unless the Constitutional Court decides differently, the courts will follow the precedent set in the SCA and will apply POCA 1998 to 'ordinary' offences. On the question of proportionality, the SCA in *Vermaak* endorsed the view expressed in the two majority *Mohunram* judgments to the effect that the more remote the offence in issue is to the underlying objective of POCA 1998, the more likely it will be that the forfeiture will be disproportionate. See para. 13 of the *Vermaak* judgment. However, the SCA expressly noted that this ought not to be an inflexible approach and that there may be circumstances warranting forfeiture even in cases involving 'ordinary' offences. A final point worth noting about the *Vermaak* judgment is that the SCA's view of what might constitute 'organised' crime appears to be broader than that adopted by the Constitutional Court in *Mohunram*. As discussed earlier, in *Mohunram*, in referring to 'organised crime' offences, the court had in mind the particular offences established under POCA 1998, viz. money laundering, racketeering and criminal gang activities. Although *Vermaak* is a post-*Mohunram* judgment, the SCA elected a different formulation of what is meant by 'oranised crime', viz. 'offences that have organizational features of some kind that distinguish them from individual wrongdoing'. See para. 4 of the *Vermaak* judgment. The SCA made no reference in its formulation of 'organised crime' to the offences established under POCA 1998. It would appear, therefore, that quite apart from the prevailing uncertainty as to whether POCA 1998 should apply beyond the ambit of 'organised' crime, there is yet further uncertainty in the South African jurisprudence as to precisely what this term means.

African courts have found assistance, and have cited with approval, from judgments of the English courts in a number of cases.[54]

The scheme of criminal forfeiture in Chapter 5 encompasses a three-stage
process:

(a) The *restraint* stage, which is directed at preserving assets pending the
    conviction of an accused defendant and the granting of a confiscation
    order.[55]
(b) The *confiscation* stage, which involves an inquiry by the court convicting
    an accused defendant into any benefit that he or she derived from any of
    the offences in respect of which he or she has been convicted or from any
    related criminal activity. If successful, this stage of proceedings culmi-
    nates in a confiscation order, which takes the form of a money judgment
    against the defendant, and in terms of which he or she is required to pay
    a specified sum to the state.[56]
(c) The *realisation* stage, which is initiated in the event of a defendant failing
    to satisfy a confiscation order, and which in essence is a specialised form
    of execution against affected property.[57]

It is impossible in the space available to engage in a detailed discussion of
each of these stages of criminal forfeiture. Therefore, in the discussion that
follows, I will focus only on the more important aspects of the restraint and
confiscation stages of this forfeiture scheme.

The Restraint Stage

The restraint stage of criminal forfeiture proceedings involves the granting of
a 'restraint order', which prohibits any person affected by the order from dealing in any manner with the property to which it applies.[58] The restraint order

---

[54]   See, for example, *Phillips,* at paras 39 and 44, where the court relied on the
decisions in *Her Majesty's Advocate v. McIntosh* [2001] All ER (D) 54 and *Government
of the United States of America v. Montgomery and Another* [2001] 2 WLR 779 in holding that criminal forfeiture was a civil and not a criminal remedy. See also *Shaik and
Others v. The State* 2007 2 All SA 150 (SCA) (hereinafter *Shaik*) at para. 25, where the
court relied on the decision in *R v. Simpson* (1998) 2 CR App R (S) 111 on the issue of
the possibility of multiple restraint orders; and at para. 28, where the court relied on *R
v. Smith* [2002] 1 All ER 367 (HC) in finding that 'benefit' means gross, as opposed to
net benefit.
[55]   See POCA 1998, ss 26–29.
[56]   *Ibid.* ss 18–24.
[57]   *Ibid.* ss 30–36.
[58]   *Ibid.* s. 26.

will be granted over 'realisable property', which includes any property held by the defendant concerned, as well as any property held by any third party who may have received affected gifts[59] from the defendant.[60] It is not necessary for the NDPP to establish a threat of dissipation of property for purposes of obtaining a restraint order.[61]

The purpose of a restraint order is to preserve property on the premise that there is a prospect that the property in question may be realised in satisfaction of a confiscation order.[62] The restrained property effectively is held as security against the confiscation order that is anticipated. For this reason, realisable property is not restricted to property which is tainted by the alleged offence. Even property legitimately acquired by a defendant may be restrained. Similarly, legitimate property held by a third party who received an affected gift from a defendant may also be restrained, as such property is realisable property, and may be subject to realisation in satisfaction of a confiscation order granted against a defendant.[63]

A restraint order may be made over property specified in the restraint order or over all the realisable property of a defendant, whether specified in the restraint order or not. It may also be made over property which will be transferred to the defendant in the future.[64] This means that where such an order is appropriate, the NDPP may seek to restrain all of a defendant's assets, including unknown assets, and may, furthermore, request the court to order the defendant to disclose the whereabouts and other details of any unknown assets.[65]

---

[59]   The definition of 'affected gifts' is contained in POCA 1998, s. 12(1). They include any gifts made by the defendant not more than seven years prior to the institution of the prosecution, and any gift made at any time (including time prior to the seven-year period) if it was a gift of property that was associated with the defendant's alleged offences.

[60]   *Ibid.* s. 14 defines realisable property; under s. 12(2)(a), a person 'holds property' if he or she has any interest in the property. The category of realisable property is widely framed and extends beyond property *owned* by a defendant. It is therefore possible to obtain a restraint order over property which technically may be owned by someone else, provided there is evidence that the defendant has an interest in it. The wide definition of realisable property is necessary in order to deal with criminals who, in an effort to protect their property, place it in the names of family members or other third parties.

[61]   See *Phillips,* at para. 7.

[62]   See *NDPP v. Rautenbach and Others* 2005 (4) SA (603) (SCA) (hereinafter *Rautenbach*), at para. 84, per Navsa JA.

[63]   See POCA 1998, s. 32.

[64]   *Ibid.* s. 26(2).

[65]   *Ibid.* s. 26(7). It has been held that such a disclosure order is 'not to be had simply for the asking', and that the NDPP must make out a case on the facts to satisfy the court that it ought to exercise its discretion in favour of making a disclosure order. See *NDPP v. Rebuzzi* 2002 (2) SA (1) (SCA), at para. 24.

The NDPP may apply for a restraint order even before a criminal prosecution has been instituted. It is a jurisdictional requirement, however, that if the prosecution against the defendant has not yet been instituted, the court must be satisfied that the defendant 'is to be charged with an offence'.[66] A charge sheet is not a prerequisite in this regard nor is it necessary that the prosecution is imminent.[67]

It is a further jurisdictional requirement that it must appear to the court that 'there are reasonable grounds for believing that a confiscation order may be made' against the defendant.[68] The court considering an application for a restraint order is accordingly called upon to assess what might occur in the future,[69] in other words, whether the criminal court may convict the defendant and whether it may find that the defendant benefited from the relevant offences or from related criminal activities.

Early uncertainty regarding what the standard of 'reasonable grounds for believing' entailed was settled by the SCA in two judgments. In *NDPP v. Kyriakou*,[70] the court held that the 'reasonable grounds for believing' standard did not require the NDPP to prove as a fact that a confiscation order will be made, and therefore that there is no room in determining the existence of reasonable grounds for the application of the principles and onus that apply in ordinary motion proceedings.[71] While the *Kyriakou* judgment is useful in determining what the standard of 'reasonable grounds for believing' does *not* mean, it is not particularly helpful in determining what it *does* mean. Further clarity in this regard was provided by the court in *NDPP v. Rautenbach*.[72] In

---

[66]   See POCA 1998, *ibid.* s. 25(1)(b)(i).
[67]   See *Rautenbach,* at paras 20–21, which stated that:

The [NDPP] must set out his case in such a manner that the [defendant] is fairly informed of the case that he or she is called upon to meet (cf *National Director of Public Prosecutions v. RO Cook Properties (Pty) Ltd* et al) but that does not mean that it must be presented in any particular form. What is required is only that the case that is sought to be made out by the [NDPP] is articulated with sufficient clarity to reasonably inform the [defendant] of the case against him or her. [text in brackets as in original text; footnotes omitted]

[68]   See POCA 1998, ss 25(1)(a)(ii) and 25(1)(b)(ii).
[69]   See *Rautenbach,* at para. 25.
[70]   2004 (1) SA 379 (SCA) (hereinafter *Kyriakou*).
[71]   *Ibid.* at para. 9. The SCA also expressly rejected the view of the court *a quo* that the 'discretion to grant a restraint order is to be sparingly exercised and then only in the clearest of cases and where the considerations in favour substantially outweigh the considerations against'.
[72]   2005 (4) SA (603) (SCA).

this judgment,[73] the court held that in determining whether there are reasonable grounds for believing that a confiscation order may be made, a court:

> need ask only whether there is evidence that might reasonably support a conviction and a consequent confiscation order (even if all that evidence has not been placed before it) and whether that evidence might reasonably be believed. Clearly that will not be so where the evidence that is sought to be relied upon is manifestly false or unreliable and to that extent it requires evaluation, but it could not have been intended that a court in such proceedings is required to determine whether the evidence is probably true.

It is apparent from these two judgments that the 'reasonable grounds for believing' standard is relatively light in comparison with the standard that an applicant in ordinary motion court proceedings is required to meet. *Rautenbach* also makes it clear that the NDPP is not required to place all available evidence before the court in support of an application for a restraint order in order to meet the 'reasonable grounds for believing' standard.[74]

Even if the jurisdictional requirements for a restraint order are met, the granting of the order is at the discretion of the court. It has been held that once the requirements are met, a court should not thwart the legislation by purporting to exercise its discretion by refusing to grant the order.[75] There may be circumstances, however, where it would be improper for a court to grant a restraint order even if the jurisdictional requirements are met.[76]

---

[73] *Ibid.* at para. 27.

[74] However, the affidavits filed in support of a restraint application must contain sufficient evidence to allow the court to determine whether there are reasonable grounds for believing that a confiscation order may be made. For an example of a case in which a restraint order was discharged on appeal for failing to set out sufficient evidence in the founding papers to support such a finding, see the SCA case of *Janse van Rensburg v. NDPP*, unreported, Case No. 75/06. The SCA also held in this case that the NDPP was not entitled to place reliance on facts contained in annexures to the founding papers without reference being made to the facts in the founding papers themselves.

[75] See *Rautenbach.*

[76] See *Kyriako*u, at paras 12–13; for example, where the only benefit derived by the defendant is in the form of stolen goods which were subsequently returned to the rightful owners. Although the defendant will have benefited from the offence because he or she received the goods (albeit that they were not retained), in these circumstances it may be that a restraint order ought not, in the proper exercise of the court's discretion, to be granted. It must be noted, however, that this will be entirely dependent on the particular facts in each case. Certainly, it cannot be stated as a general principle that a confiscation order cannot properly be granted in cases where the benefit was lost in this type of situation. It must be borne in mind that at the confiscation stage of the proceedings, the court is required to apply certain evidentiary presumptions relating to the question of benefit. These are discussed in more detail later. In many cases the

A restraint order entails a deprivation of the property rights of persons affected thereby. Not only are they prohibited from dealing in any manner with their property, but the restraint order usually is coupled with an order directing the defendant and other affected persons to surrender their property to a *curator bonis* appointed under section 28 of POCA 1998. Safeguards are provided in Chapter 5 for the protection of a defendant's rights.[77] However, bearing in mind the constitutional protection against the arbitrary deprivation of property rights,[78] courts must be mindful, in exercising their discretion to grant restraint orders, that the rights of affected persons are not unjustifiably infringed thereby.

The protection against the arbitrary deprivation of property requires that there must be a rational relationship between means and ends. In the context of criminal forfeiture, this means that there must be a rational relationship between the purpose served by a restraint order and the effect of the order on the individuals concerned. It has been held that it is not necessary that the amount of the possible confiscation order be ascertained or ascertainable at the restraint stage of proceedings, nor is it required that there must be a correlation between the possible amount of the future confiscation order and the value of the assets under restraint. However, in order to guard against a restraint order amounting to an arbitrary deprivation of property, it has been held that:

---

application of the presumptions may 'save' a restraint order even in circumstances such as that described in the example above, as the possibility always exists that at the confiscation stage of proceedings, the benefit may be found to be greater than the value of the benefit lost. This will be sufficient to justify the granting of a restraint order pending the outcome of the confiscation inquiry. Similarly, the fact that the benefit inquiry extends to an investigation of benefit derived from related criminal activities may also serve to justify the granting of a restraint order in this situation, provided that the NDPP can put up some evidence to indicate that an inquiry into the related criminal activities of the defendant may be appropriate at the subsequent confiscation inquiry.

[77] These include the right to anticipate the return day of the provisional restraint order on 24 hours' notice and to oppose its confirmation (POCA, s. 26(3)(c)); the defendant may request the court to make provision for his or her reasonable legal and living expenses, subject to certain requirements (*ibid.* s. 26(6)); the defendant may apply for an order varying the restraint order if the order will deprive him or her of the means to provide for reasonable living expenses, or will cause undue hardship, and if such hardship outweighs the risk that the property will be lost or destroyed (*ibid.* s. 26(10)); a defendant may apply for the variation or rescission of the order appointing a *curator bonis*, or an order in respect of immovable property, at any time (*ibid.* ss 28(2) and 29(6)). For further discussion of the variation and rescission of restraint orders see *NDPP v. Phillips and Others*, 2005 (5) SA 265 (SCA). A defendant may also appeal against a restraint order: see *Phillips v. NDPP* 2003 (6) SCA 447 (SCA).

[78] See the Constitution, s. 25(1), which provides that 'No one may be deprived of property except in terms of a law of general application, and *no law may permit arbitrary deprivation of property*' (emphasis added).

where there is good reason to believe that the value of the property that is sought to be placed under restraint materially exceeds the amount in which an anticipated confiscation order might be granted then clearly a court properly exercising its discretion will limit the scope of the restraint (if it grants an order at all) for otherwise the apparent absence of an appropriate connection between the interference with property rights and the purpose that is sought to be achieved – the absence of an 'appropriate relationship between means and ends, between the sacrifice the individual is asked to make and the public purpose that [it] is intended to serve' – will render the interference arbitrary and in conflict with the Bill of Rights[79] [footnotes omitted].

Thus while the courts have recognised that it is not always possible to predict what the value of the possible confiscation order might be, sufficient information must be included in the application for a restraint order to satisfy the court that the order that is sought is not materially disproportionate to what may be ordered by the criminal court in the future.

The Confiscation Stage

The confiscation stage of proceedings commences only after a defendant has been convicted. At that stage, the public prosecutor in the criminal case may apply to the criminal court to conduct what is commonly referred to as a confiscation inquiry. The confiscation inquiry is conducted, in the first place, for purposes of determining whether the defendant benefited from any of the offences in respect of which he or she was convicted or from 'any criminal activity which the court finds to be sufficiently related to those offences'.[80] This will be determined according to the civil standard of a balance of probabilities. Section 22(1) of POCA 1998 establishes a *prima facie* evidentiary presumption of benefit in circumstances where the defendant does not have sufficient legitimate sources of income to justify the interests in property that he or she holds. It is open to the defendant to rebut this presumption by placing evidence before the court to justify his or her sources of legitimate income.

---

[79]   See *Rautenbach*, at para. 56; see also ibid. at paras 87–88.
[80]   See POCA 1998, s. 18(1). In *NDPP v. Niemoller*, unreported, Case No. A560/04, 25 November 2004 (judgment of the Witwatersrand Local Division) (hereinafter *Niemoller*), the High Court overturned the decision of a lower court to refuse to conduct a confiscation inquiry. The lower court had justified its refusal on the grounds that the defendant 'had not derived a benefit that would justify an inquiry'. The High Court on appeal held that the very purpose of a confiscation inquiry was to enable the court to determine whether the defendant had derived a benefit or not. The lower court's finding that the defendant had not derived a benefit was the very issue that the inquiry was intended to explore.

If the court conducting the confiscation inquiry finds that the defendant did benefit, then the court may make an order against the defendant for payment to the state of 'any amount that it considers appropriate'.[81] Such an order is commonly referred to as a confiscation order. This instigates the second leg of the confiscation inquiry, aimed at determining whether, and in what amount, a confiscation order ought to be made.

Section 18(2) indicates what the upper limit of a confiscation order may be, being that it may not exceed either the value of the defendant's benefit, or the value of realisable property (being property held by the defendant plus the value of affected gifts given to third parties) if this latter value is less than the value of the benefit. Apart from specifying what the upper limit of a confiscation order may be, however, it lies within the discretion of the court to determine any appropriate amount below the upper limit.

The discretion of the court at a confiscation inquiry accordingly is a wide one,[82] and much clearly will depend on the facts before the court in each case. In exercising its discretion, a court will be mindful of making an order that does not amount to an arbitrary deprivation of property. Thus, as with all other aspects of civil forfeiture under POCA 1998, the confiscation court will have to be satisfied that the order it makes is rationally connected to the purpose sought to be achieved by confiscation orders. In this regard it has been held that the purpose of a confiscation order is to ensure that a defendant disgorges the fruits of his or her criminal conduct, as well as to act as a deterrent. Although the latter purpose may result in punitive consequences for a defendant, this will not of itself render the confiscation order unjustifiable as an arbitrary deprivation of property.[83]

---

[81]   See POCA 1998, *ibid.* s. 18(1).

[82]   See *Shabir Shaik and Others v. The State*, Case No. 248/06 [2006] ZASCA, 6 November 2006, at para. 30.

[83]   For example, in *Shaik*, the defendants argued that a confiscation order in terms of which they were obliged to disgorge both the value of the dividends received from the shares acquired by means of a corrupt scheme, as well as the value of the shares, was disproportionate in that it did not serve the rationale of a confiscation order. The dividends had been used to pay off the purchase price of the shares. The SCA rejected this argument. It held that insofar as there was a punitive element involved in such an order, it was subsidiary to the main objective of the order, which effectively required the defendants to disgorge the gross proceeds of the illicitly acquired shares: *ibid.* para. 30. However, in the same judgment, the court found that to order one of the defendants to pay an amount equivalent to the value of a separate transaction would be solely penal in effect and would serve only to enrich the State. This, notwithstanding that in a mechanistic sense, the value of that transaction could be said to have been proceeds consequent on the unlawful activities. This amount was excluded from the confiscation order: *ibid.* para. 33. An appeal against the SCA's judgment in *Shaik* was rejected by the Constitutional Court in May 2008. The Constitutional Court held that

For purposes of the confiscation inquiry, the court must determine the 'value of a defendant's proceeds of unlawful activities' which is 'the sum of the values of the property, services, advantages, benefits or rewards received, retained or derived by him or her ... in connection with the unlawful activity'.[84] This is not the happiest choice of language for purposes of criminal forfeiture, as it borrows directly from the language of Chapter 6 civil forfeitures. The definition of 'proceeds of unlawful activities' also applies for purposes of both Chapter 6 civil forfeitures and confiscation inquiries.

It has been held that what is required for purposes of a confiscation inquiry is a determination of the value of gross proceeds, rather than net proceeds.[85] It has also been accepted that the fact that a defendant was relieved subsequently of a benefit received has no bearing on the existence of the jurisdictional fact that is necessary for a court to exercise its discretion to make a confiscation order.[86] In this regard it is significant that the phrase 'derived, received or retained' is disjunctive rather than conjunctive. Thus, it has been held that the value of benefits legitimately acquired, but subsequently retained as a result of the defendant's offences can also be included for confiscation purposes.[87] The 'proceeds of unlawful activities' for purposes of a confiscation inquiry have been held to include benefits received both directly and indirectly.[88] Finally, it

---

the general deterrence purposes of POCA 1998 were well served by the confiscation order made by the trial court. The confiscation order was not 'disturbingly inappropriate' and hence was not disproportionate. See the judgment of the Constitutional Court in *Shabir Shaik & Others v. The State* 2008 (5) SA 354 (CC).

[84]   See POCA 1998, s. 19(1).

[85]   See *Shaik*, at para. 28. See also *NDPP v. Johannes du Preez Joubert and Others*, unreported, Case No. 24541/2002 (judgment in the Transvaal Provincial Division) which was cited with approval in *Shaik*.

[86]   See *Kyriakou*, at para. 12. The court noted that the confiscation inquiry involves a determination of benefit derived also from related criminal activities and that the presumptions relating to benefit, set out in s. 22 of the Act, also come into play. In *Niemoller*, at paras 27–28, the court found that a defendant who had received diamonds as part of a police trap, and who was immediately divested of them, had 'received' the benefit of the diamonds for purposes of a confiscation inquiry, even though he was almost immediately divested of the diamonds. Of course, in all of these cases, the court will be entitled to exercise its wide discretion in determining whether the value of the benefit that was received but not retained ought to be included in the amount the defendant is ordered to pay to the State. This will depend very much on the particular facts of the case and on whether such an order will advance the objectives of confiscation.

[87]   See *Shaik*, at para. 27.

[88]   This is made explicit in the definition of 'proceeds of unlawful activities' in s. 1(1) of POCA 1998, although it is not expressly included in s. 19(1). In *Shaik*, the proceeds of the defendants' unlawful activities were held to include benefits derived by a shareholder of a company that was enriched through the shareholder's criminal activities: see *Shaik,* at para. 24.

has been held that a multiplicity of confiscation orders is justified where the benefit has passed through a number of hands, although a court may, in these circumstances, in its discretion decide to 'so phrase its order that the recovery in its total effect will be limited, although made against a number of defendants'.[89]

Section 22(3) of POCA 1998 requires the court to apply certain *prima facie* evidentiary presumptions for purposes of determining the value of the defendant's proceeds. In essence, once it is found that a defendant has benefited, it is presumed that all property held by the defendant at the time of his or her conviction or in the seven years prior to the institution of the prosecution, as well as all expenditure incurred during that period, was derived from, or met out of the proceeds of the defendant's unlawful activities. The effect of these presumptions is to place an evidentiary burden on the defendant to rebut them. If the defendant is unable to do so, then the value of the properties held and expenditure incurred will be included in the value of the proceeds from the defendant's unlawful activities. The presumptions have been held to be 'unobjectionable' by the High Court.[90] However, to date there has been no direct constitutional challenge to the presumptions and no pronouncement thereon by either the Constitutional Court or the SCA.[91]

ASPECTS OF CIVIL FORFEITURE UNDER CHAPTER 6

The inclusion in POCA 1998 of Chapter 6 civil forfeiture was an innovation in terms of law enforcement measures in South Africa. In adopting this scheme of forfeiture, South Africa followed a developing international trend that allows for the forfeiture of property associated with crime without the necessity of a criminal prosecution.

Civil forfeiture under Chapter 6 involves a two stage process:

(a) A *preservation* stage, marked by the granting of a preservation of property order under section 38(1) of POCA 1998 (hereinafter Preservation Order).

(b) A *forfeiture* stage, marked by the granting of a final order in terms of which the property concerned is forfeited to the state.

---

[89] See *Shaik*, at para. 25. This was the effect of the order in the court *a quo* in this case.

[90] See *Phillips*, at para. 51.

[91] See *Kyriakou*, at para. 15, where it was noted that although the defendant had raised a constitutional objection to the presumptions in his affidavit filed at court, the matter was not pursued in argument before the court.

As with criminal forfeiture, the present chapter does not allow for a full and detailed discussion of this forfeiture scheme, and so it will only highlight some of its more significant aspects and in particular those that have been the subject of judicial consideration. As indicated earlier, it is this forfeiture scheme that has been subjected to more searching judicial scrutiny, particularly from the SCA and the Constitutional Court.

Section 38(1) allows the NDPP to apply to a High Court for a Preservation Order, which, like a restraint order, prohibits any person from dealing in any manner with the property concerned. As with criminal forfeiture, provision is made for the appointment of a *curator bonis* to take custody of and to administer the property in appropriate cases.[92]

Section 38(2) provides that the court 'shall' make a Preservation Order if there are 'reasonable grounds to believe' that the property concerned is either an instrumentality of a Schedule 1 Offence, or is the proceeds of unlawful activity.[93] These are the sole jurisdictional requirements for the granting of a Preservation Order and the NDPP is not required to satisfy the court that a forfeiture order will be made subsequently.[94] It has been held, however, that even though the jurisdictional requirements are met, a court is entitled to refuse to grant a Preservation Order where it is apparent to the court on the evidence in the papers before it that it would be unconstitutional for a forfeiture order eventually to be made.[95]

The NDPP is expressly given the power to proceed *ex parte*, or without notice, to any affected person in applying for a Preservation Order. While the NDPP has a similar power under the criminal forfeiture scheme, section 38 of POCA 1998 makes no express provision for the court to grant a provisional Preservation Order. Chapter 5, on the other hand, expressly states that although the NDPP may apply *ex parte* for a restraint order, the court may grant such order in a provisional form, with a return day upon which the confirmation of the order may be opposed.

The provisions of section 38(1) and the distinction between them and the comparable provisions of Chapter 5 gave rise to a constitutional challenge to the section, based on an alleged infringement of the right of access to the courts.[96] The issue was eventually settled after no less than four separate hearings and judgments on the matter, including two in the High Court and two in

---

[92]   See POCA 1998, s. 42.
[93]   *Ibid.* s. 38(2). As noted earlier, since 2004, a Preservation Order (and a Forfeiture Order) may also be made in respect of property associated with terrorist and related activities. This aspect of Chapter 6 has yet to be tested in practice.
[94]   See *Van Staden*, at para. 9.
[95]   *Ibid.*
[96]   See the Constitution, s. 34.

the Constitutional Court.[97] The constitutionality of section 38 ultimately was confirmed by the Constitutional Court.[98]

The purpose of a Preservation Order is to preserve the property that is intended to be made subject to a forfeiture order. A Preservation Order expires within 90 days of the relevant notice of the order being published in the government gazette unless an application for a forfeiture order is pending before the expiry of this period.[99] If an application for a forfeiture order is instituted within this time, the Preservation Order will continue to operate until the forfeiture proceedings are finalised.

Although the Preservation Order may be sought without notice, once a Preservation Order is granted, notice of the order must be given to all persons known to the NDPP to have an interest in the property concerned.[100] The NDPP also is required to give notice of a forfeiture application to all persons who entered an appearance of an intention to oppose after receiving notice of the Preservation Order.[101] Such persons are entitled to appear and oppose the forfeiture application or apply for an order excluding their interest in the property from the operation of the forfeiture order.[102] In practice, opposition to civil forfeiture under Chapter 6 is generally mounted at the forfeiture stage of proceedings. It is possible, however, for a person affected by a Preservation Order to mount a challenge to it either in the form of an

---

[97]   The relevant judgments are: *Mohamed NO and Others v. NDPP and Another* 2002 (4) 366 (W); *NDPP v. Mohamed NO and Others* 2002 (4) SA 843 (CC); *Mohamed NO and Others v. NDPP and Another* 2003 (1) SACR 286 (W); and *NDPP and Another v. Mohamed NO and Others* 2003 (4) SA 1 (CC) (hereinafter *Mohamed*).

[98]   The High Court had found that s. 38 of POCA 1998 was unconstitutional in that it required the NDPP to proceed without notice to interested parties in every case and, further, in that courts could not, under s. 38, grant a provisional preservation of property order with a return day, which would allow interested parties to oppose the preservation of property order (hereinafter Preservation Order). The Constitutional Court interpreted s. 38 as being consistent with the Constitution. It found that although the NDPP was entitled to apply in every case for a Preservation Order without notice, the principle of *audi alteram partem* was not excluded. This means that in considering applications for Preservation Orders, courts can still apply the principles relating to provisional orders and return days: see the 2003 Constitutional Court judgment in *Mohamed, ibid.*, at para. 51. In practice, an assessment is usually made by the AFU in order to determine what form of order will be appropriate, depending on the facts of the case. The options include: proceeding on notice for a final Preservation Order; proceeding without notice for a provisional Preservation Order; or proceeding without notice for a final Preservation Order.

[99]   See POCA 1998, s. 40.
[100]   *Ibid.* s. 39(1).
[101]   *Ibid.* ss 48(2) and 48(3).
[102]   *Ibid.* s. 48(4).

appeal[103] or in the form of an application for a variation or rescission on the grounds set out in Chapter 6.[104]

The jurisdictional requirements for the granting of a forfeiture order are the same those for a Preservation Order, although a different standard is applied. For purposes of a forfeiture order, the court must be satisfied on a *balance of probabilities* that the property concerned is either an instrumentality of a Schedule 1 Offence, or that it is the proceeds of unlawful activities. 'Proceeds of unlawful activities' is defined to mean any property derived, received or retained, whether directly or indirectly, in connection with or as a result of any unlawful activity.[105] The SCA has held that the definition of proceeds, although wide, should, 'subject to necessary attenuation of the linguistic scope of "in connection with", ... be given its full ambit'.[106] The court has also held, however, that the 'connection' referred to in the definition requires some sort of consequential relation between the proceeds and the unlawful activity.[107]

The meaning of 'instrumentality of an offence' has been the subject of more intense consideration by the courts. The definition contained in POCA 1998 is very wide in that an instrumentality of an offence is defined to mean: 'any property which is *concerned in the commission or suspected commission of an offence* at any time before or after the commencement of this Act, whether committed within the Republic or elsewhere'[108] [emphasis added]. This wide definition prompted the SCA in *Cook* to conclude that giving the definition its literal meaning could lead to arbitrary deprivations of property in contravention of the protection afforded under section 25 of the

---

[103]   In *Singh v. NDPP*, unreported, Case No. 268/06, at para. 10, the SCA held that a Preservation Order was appealable.

[104]   POCA 1998, s. 47 sets out the grounds upon which an application for rescission or variation may be granted. They are substantially the same as the grounds set out in respect of criminal forfeiture orders under Chapter 5.

[105]   See *ibid.* s. 1(1) for the full definition, being:

> any property or any service, advantage, benefit or reward which was derived, received or retained, directly or indirectly, in the Republic or elsewhere, at any time before or after the commencement of this Act, in connection with or as a result of any unlawful activity carried on by any person, and includes any property representing property so derived.

[106]   See *Cook*, at para. 67.

[107]   *Ibid.* at para. 72. The court held in this regard that interest earned on funds that were not derived from an illicit source, but which were invested under a fraudulent name in order to avoid income tax, was not consequentially connected to the fraud and therefore was not the proceeds of the fraud. See also *Shaik*, at paras 32–33, in which this approach was endorsed and applied in the context of a confiscation inquiry.

[108]   See POCA 1998, s. 1(1).

Constitution.[109] Forfeitures that do not rationally advance the inter-related purposes of Chapter 6 are unconstitutional.[110] The court found these purposes to include removing incentives for crime, deterring persons from using or allowing their property to be used in crime, eliminating or incapacitating some of the means by which crime may be committed, and advancing the ends of justice by depriving those involved in crime of the property concerned.[111] The court took into account the fact that the second and fourth of these purposes have a penal element, in contrast to the provisions of Chapter 6, which are clearly remedial.[112] The court also took into account the fact that persons with an interest in affected property were only afforded limited protection under the so-called 'innocent owner' provisions of section 52.[113]

For these reasons, the court concluded that a narrow interpretation of the definition of instrumentality was required in order to bring it in line with constitutional requirements. The court held that the property must play a reasonably direct role in the commission of the offence; it should in a substantial sense facilitate the offence.[114] This may be ascertained from the nature of the property or the manner of its utilisation.[115] An incidental relationship between the property and the commission of the offence is not sufficient.[116] An isolated incident involving the property concerned will not be sufficient to establish it as an instrumentality. The more incidents that can be established, the more easily the inference may be drawn that it is an instrumentality.[117]

---

[109] See *Cook*, at para. 15.

[110] *Ibid.* at para. 29.

[111] *Ibid.* at para. 18.

[112] *Ibid.* at para. 17.

[113] *Ibid.* at paras 24 and 25; see further POCA 1998, s. 52 allows a person with an interest in the property to apply to that court to have his or her interest excluded from the operation of the forfeiture order. The applicant must prove that the interest was acquired legally, and that the applicant neither knew nor had reasonable grounds to suspect that the property is the proceeds of unlawful activities or an instrumentality of an offence. As the court noted, s. 52 is more akin to an 'ignorant owner' defence, as once a person becomes aware that the property is proceeds or is an instrumentality, he or she will have no recourse under s. 52 even if they are innocent of the unlawful activities or offences concerned.

[114] See *Cook, ibid.* at para. 32.

[115] *Ibid.* at para. 34. The court noted that reference could be had in this regard to the appointment, arrangement, organization, construction or furnishing of premises to enable or facilitate the commission of a crime.

[116] *Ibid.* at para. 33. Particularly insofar as immovable property as an instrumentality is concerned, the courts have noted that every offence must be committed somewhere. Thus, the more commission of an offence at a particular premises will not make it an instrumentality.

[117] See *NDPP v. Engels* 2005 (3) SA 109 (C), which was cited with approval in *Mohunram*; see *Mohunram*, at para. 51, per Van Heerden AJ.

Having laid down these general principles, the court noted that each case would depend on the facts before it.[118] In *Cook*, the court found that an hotel that had been the site of a variety of criminal offences, including drug offences, over a number of years was not an instrumentality of an offence.[119] However, a residential house in which the owner had established a small drug laboratory was held to be an instrumentality. In *Mohunram*, although the court was divided on the issue of proportionality, there was concurrence in all three judgments that the premises were an instrumentality of the gambling offences. The SCA has also found that vehicles driven by drunk drivers are instrumentalities of the offences associated with drunken driving.[120]

The courts' concern to ensure that the forfeiture of instrumentalities does not have unconstitutional consequences has been developed further. In terms of section 50(1) of POCA 1998, if a court finds on a balance of probabilities that property is an instrumentality of an offence or the proceeds of unlawful activities, it 'shall' grant a forfeiture order. Clearly, were the courts enjoined to grant a forfeiture order in every case where property is shown to be an instrumentality, arbitrary deprivations of property would follow. To avoid section 50(1) having unconstitutional effect, the courts have determined that a proportionality inquiry must be undertaken in each case in which it is found that a property is an instrumentality in order to ensure that there is a rational connection between the forfeiture of the particular instrumentality concerned and the purposes sought to be advanced by such forfeiture. This is now firmly established as part and parcel of the law, and the proportionality principle has been applied in a number of instrumentality cases.[121]

In *Prophet v. NDPP* 2006 (2) SACR 525 (CC) (29 September 2006) (hereinafter *Prophet*), the Constitutional Court identified a number of factors that must be applied in undertaking a proportionality assessment. These include whether the property is integral to the commission of the offence, whether the forfeiture would prevent the further commission of the offence and the social consequences of the offence, whether the innocent owner defence would be available to the owner, the nature and use of the property, and the effect on the respondent of the forfeiture. With regard to this latter factor, of particular

---

[118] See *Cook,* at para. 32.
[119] *Ibid.* at paras 46–50, under the '37 GILLESPIE STREET' section.
[120] See *Van Staden.*
[121] The proportionality analysis was raised in *Cook,* but as the court in that case found that the properties concerned were not instrumentalities of offences, no proportionality analysis was undertaken. Subsequent to *Cook,* the proportionality principle was applied and a proportionality analysis conducted in *NDPP v. Cole and Others* [2004] 3 All SA 765 (W), *Prophet v. NDPP,* 2006 (1) SA 38 (SCA), *Prophet* and *Mohunram.*

significance is whether the property is used as a residence and the effect that forfeiture would have on the residents.[122] However, the fact that the property is used as a residence will not necessarily prevent its forfeiture. This is well illustrated in *Prophet*, where forfeiture was granted notwithstanding that the house in which the drug laboratory was established was used as a residence.

Some of the factors identified by the Constitutional Court in *Prophet*, such as whether the property is integral to the offence and its nature and use, appear to overlap with the factors that must be taken into account in determining whether the property is an instrumentality. This is not helpful to courts attempting to apply what the Constitutional Court has laid down, as it blurs the distinction between the inquiry into instrumentality and the inquiry into proportionality. An additional difficulty for courts is that a variety of other factors were identified and discussed in the three judgments of the Constitutional Court in *Mohunram*. However, in consequence of the decision being split three ways precisely on the issue of the proportionality principle, it will be extremely difficult for courts to know which additional factors identified in *Mohunram* ought to be applied, and what weight they ought to be accorded.

There is one issue in respect of which the Constitutional Court has provided certainty. All three judgments in *Mohunram* were in agreement that the proportionality assessment is a legal one and that the NDPP bears the onus in each case of establishing the proportionality of the forfeiture sought.[123] It is now clear, therefore, that the burden does not rest on the person affected by a forfeiture order to establish that it would be disproportionate, although he or she may be required to adduce evidence to rebut a case made out by the NDPP that the forfeiture is not disproportionate.

Uncertainty still exists, however, with regard to the question of whether a particular 'standard of disproportionality' is required in order to render a forfeiture arbitrary and, if so, what the standard should be. The SCA initially determined (with one judge dissenting) that a standard of 'significant disproportionality' was required.[124] In *NDPP v. Van Staden and others* 2007 (1) SACR 338 (SCA) (hereinafter *Van Staden*), however, the SCA suggested that in the context of non-organised crime offences in respect of which the ordinary criminal law presented a sufficient remedy, such as drunk driving offences, the 'significant disproportionality' standard could not be justified.[125] This

---

[122]   See *Prophet*, at para. 63.

[123]   Concurrence appears from all three judgments in this regard.

[124]   See *Prophet v. NDPP*, at para. 45. Ponnan J dissented, holding that this was 'too strict an evaluative norm' and that it would exacerbate the draconian effect of POCA 1998.

[125]   See *Van Staden*, at para. 8.

suggested that different standards should be applied depending on whether the offence fell within the category of 'organised' crime or 'ordinary' crime.

The question of what standard of disproportionality should be applied was left open by the Constitutional Court when the SCA judgment in *Prophet* went on appeal before it.[126] In *Mohunram*, the minority judgment rejected the approach adopted by the SCA in *Van Staden* to the effect that different evaluative standards should be applied depending on the nature of the offence concerned. The minority in *Mohunram* held that a single evaluative standard ought to be applied, which simply involves the question of whether the property was, in all the circumstances, disproportionate 'in the sense discussed (in the minority judgment)'.[127] The majority judgments did not pronounce on this issue. Consequently, at present, there is no certainty on this issue either in the SCA or in the Constitutional Court.

It is apparent from the discussion on the manner in which the SCA and the Constitutional Courts have approached the proportionality principle that much will depend, in its application, on the facts before the court in each case. Thus, while the general principle regarding the need to apply a proportionality assessment may have been settled, abundant litigation on the issue is to be anticipated. Unfortunately, in view of the lack of consensus in and clear direction from the Constitutional Court, it will be difficult for the courts of first instance, and indeed for the SCA, to pronounce with confidence in matters in which these fundamental issues are raised.

CONCLUSION

Considering the relatively short period during which the civil forfeiture provisions of the POCA 1998 have been applied in South Africa, it is apparent that there has been a significant development of the law in this area. Fundamental issues of constitutionality have been considered and determined by the courts and, with the exception of the uncertainty following in the wake of *Mohunram*, this has given direction to the further implementation of the law. However, POCA 1998 is a complex piece of legislation. There are numerous issues arising out of both criminal forfeiture under Chapter 5 and civil forfeiture under Chapter 6 that have not yet been resolved, and many more that have not yet even been raised. Therefore, the full depths of asset forfeiture law in South Africa have yet to be chartered.

---

[126]   See *Prophet*.
[127]   See *Mohunram*, at para. 74, per Van Heerden AJ.

5. Civil forfeiture – the Australian experience

Sylvia Grono*

INTRODUCTION

Australia is a federation of six states and two territories. The federal government (the Commonwealth) and each state and territory have criminal law powers. The Commonwealth, five of the six states, and both territories have in recent years passed laws providing for the forfeiture of assets and the imposition of pecuniary penalties in relation to criminal conduct which has not been proven to the criminal standard in a criminal court.[1] There is no single Australian model. The Australian Constitution prescribes the powers of the Commonwealth to legislate and also sets out some basic rights. There is no Commonwealth Bill of Rights but the common law has recognized a number of basic rights and Australian Courts will not construe statutory provisions as abrogating important common law rights, privileges and immunities in the absence of clear words or a necessary implication to that effect.[2]

---

* The views expressed herein are the author's personally and do not represent the views of the Australian Government or the Commonwealth Director of Public Prosecutions.

[1] See Proceeds of Crime Act 2002 (Cth) (hereinafter POCA); Criminal Assets Recovery Act 1990 (NSW); Criminal Property Confiscation Act 2000 (WA); Criminal Proceeds Confiscation Act 2002 (Qld); Criminal Property Forfeiture Act 2002 (NT); Confiscation of Criminal Proceeds Act 2003 (ACT); Criminal Assets Confiscation Act 2005 (SA). Tasmania has not passed civil forfeiture legislation; it has legislation providing for forfeiture of the proceeds of crime but it is solely conviction based: Crime (Confiscation of Profits) Act 1993 (Tas).

[2] See *The Daniels Corporation International Pty Ltd v. Australian Competition and Consumer Commission* (2002) 213 CLR 543 at pp. 553 [11], 562–563 [43], 578 [93]–[94], 591–592 [132]; see also *Attorney-General (WA) v. Marquet* (2003) 217 CLR 545 at 598–605; *Coleman v. Power* (2004) 220 CLR 1 [185], [225], [250]–[251].

HISTORY

The Customs Act 1901 (Cth) provides for *in rem* forfeiture of property used in the unlawful importation, exportation or conveyance of prohibited imports.[3] In 1977 these provisions were extended to money or goods in a person's possession as a result of selling or dealing in narcotic goods which were imported unlawfully, or agreeing to import narcotic goods in contravention of the Customs Act. These provisions were administrative. When a vehicle was used in the illegal importation it was forfeited to the Commonwealth. It could then be seized, a notice issued to the owner, and if no claim was made it would be condemned and could be sold by the Commonwealth.

In 1979 provisions were added to the Customs Act which enabled a pecuniary penalty order to be made by a civil court where it could be shown on the balance of probabilities that the defendant had engaged in a prescribed narcotic dealing. Property can be restrained to satisfy the pecuniary penalty.[4]

The *in rem* forfeiture provisions provided no protection to innocent third parties whose property had been used in the importation or conveyance of a prohibited import without their knowledge.[5] Amendments were made in 1995 which enabled an owner to make a claim. If a claim is made the property must be returned unless proceedings are commenced within 120 days in respect of an offence involving the goods. At the completion of the proceedings an order can be made for condemnation of the goods provided the offence is proven and the court is satisfied that in all the circumstances of the case it is appropriate that an order be made for condemnation.[6]

The provisions in the Customs Act are rarely used by the Commonwealth Director of Public Prosecutions (hereinafter CDPP) as lawyers now prefer to rely on the general provisions in the Proceeds of Crime Act 2002 (hereinafter POCA) and, prior to that, the conviction based provisions in the Proceeds of Crime Act 1987.[7] Similar *in rem* forfeiture provisions are contained in the Fisheries Management Act 1991 (Cth)[8] providing for the seizure and forfeiture of foreign fishing vessels. There is no requirement for a conviction.

---

[3]   See Customs Act 1901 (Cth) (hereinafter Customs Act), s. 229.
[4]   See *ibid.* Part XIII, Division 3, ss. 243B and 243E.
[5]   See *Little's Victory Cab Co Pty Ltd v. Carroll*, (1948) VLR 249; see also *Burton v. Honan*, (1952) 86 CLR 169.
[6]   See Customs Act, ss 205D(2), 205D(3)(c).
[7]   See *CDPP Annual Report 2002–2003*, at p. 42 and *CDPP Annual Report 2003–2004*, at p. 46, which show no restraining orders or pecuniary penalty orders were obtained under the Customs Act in those years. There was one condemnation of property valued at $300 000 in 2002–2003 and two of property valued at $17 000 in 2003–2004. A recovery of $4970 has been recorded in the *CDPP Annual Report 2004–2005*.
[8]   See Fisheries Management Act 1991 (Cth), s. 106A.

The New South Wales government introduced civil forfeiture laws in 1990 in relation to drug offences.[9] The Drug Trafficking (Civil Proceedings) Act 1990 (NSW) was extended to cover all 'serious criminal offences'[10] and the legislation was renamed the Criminal Assets Recovery Act 1990 (NSW) (hereinafter CARA) in 1997. It is not necessary for any person to be charged with the serious criminal offence for orders to be obtained under this Act.

Victoria passed legislation which enabled property to be restrained and forfeited where a person was charged with a civil forfeiture offence. Final orders do not depend on a conviction being entered for the offence.[11] Western Australia introduced a civil forfeiture regime in 2000.[12]

The Australian Law Reform Commission (hereinafter ALRC), after reviewing the conviction based Commonwealth confiscation legislation[13] and comparing performance under that legislation with the operation of the CARA in New South Wales, recommended that a non-conviction based regime be introduced by the Commonwealth.[14] The ALRC referred to the 'general underlying principle that persons ought not be permitted to be unjustly enriched at the expense of individuals or society at large by unlawful conduct',[15] and the Commonwealth's response to the ALRC report was the POCA which commenced operation on 1 January 2003.

On 1 January 2003 the Criminal Proceeds Confiscation Act 2002 (Qld) also commenced operation. This Act provided for a civil confiscation scheme and a conviction based scheme. In 2003 and 2004 Victoria also strengthened its confiscation scheme providing for the civil confiscation scheme to apply to a broader range of offences and for tainted property substitution. In 2005 the CARA and the conviction confiscation provisions in the Confiscation of Proceeds of Crime Act 1989 (NSW) were amended following a review of the

---

[9]   See Drug Trafficking (Civil Proceedings) Act 1990.

[10]   See Criminal Assets Recovery Act 1990 (NSW), s. 6(2) (defines serious criminal offences to include a range of drug offences, an offence punishable by imprisonment for five years or more involving theft, fraud, obtaining a financial benefit, money laundering, extortion, violence, bribery, corruption, homicide, tax evasion, illegal gambling, blackmail, perverting the course of justice, forgery and a range of firearm offences).

[11]   See Confiscation Act 1997 (Vic).

[12]   See Criminal Property Confiscation Act 2000 (WA).

[13]   See Proceeds of Crime Act 1987 (Cth).

[14]   See the Australian Law Reform Commission (1999), *Report No. 87, Confiscation That Counts: A Review of the Proceeds of Crime Act, 1987*, Canberra, Sydney, Australia: Australian Government Publishing Services (hereinafter ALRC Report No. 87), at para. 2.74: online version available at http://www.alrc.gov.au/media/1999/mb0616.htm, accessed 20 September 2007.

[15]   *Ibid.* p. 30, para. 2.74.

New South Wales legislation. The Australian Capital Territory and South Australia introduced a civil confiscation scheme in 2003 and 2004 respectively.

RESTRAINT AND CONFISCATION OF PROPERTY UNDER THE PROCEEDS OF CRIME ACT 2002 (CTH)[16]

The principal objects of the legislation are to deprive persons of the proceeds of offences,[17] the instruments[18] of offences and benefits derived from offences, to deprive persons of literary proceeds derived from their notoriety from having committed offences, to punish and deter persons from breaching laws of the Commonwealth, to prevent the reinvestment of proceeds, instruments, benefits and literary proceeds in further criminal activity, and to give effect to Australia's obligations under international treaties relating to money laundering and the confiscation of the proceeds of crime.[19] 'Offence' is an offence against a law of the Commonwealth which can be dealt with on indictment.[20] The legislation will apply to forfeit the proceeds of offences and instruments of offences which are not indictable offences where a Commonwealth offence which is a serious offence has been committed.

There are four distinct procedures that can be followed to confiscate property. They can be referred to for convenience as a conviction based stream, a civil person directed stream, civil asset directed stream and literary proceeds orders. A matter can move between the conviction based stream and the civil stream.

---

[16]   An independent review of the operation of the Act was conducted by Mr Tom Sherman AO. His (2006), *Report on the Independent Review of the Operation of the Proceeds of Crime Act 2002 (Cth)*, Canberra: Commonwealth of Australia (hereinafter the Sherman Report) was tabled in both houses of Parliament on 18 October 2006.

[17]   Proceeds of offences is defined in POCA, s. 329(1) to include property partly derived from the commission of offences and property indirectly derived; *ibid.* s. 330(1) (if property which was proceeds of an offence is sold or disposed of both the original property and anything acquired using proceeds from the disposal are proceeds of the offence); *ibid.* s. 330(4) (if property which is proceeds of an offence is sold to a third party for sufficient consideration it ceases to be proceeds of an offence).

[18]   *Ibid.* s. 329(2) (defines instruments of offences as property 'used in or in connection with the commission of an offence' and property 'intended to be used in or in connection with the commission of an offence'); *ibid.* s. 330(2) (if an instrument is sold then the property which is acquired with the proceeds of sale is an instrument).

[19]   *Ibid.* s. 5.

[20]   See Crimes Act 1914 (Cth), s. 4G (an offence will be an indictable offence if the maximum penalty is more than 12 months' imprisonment unless there is a specific provision in the legislation creating the offence to the contrary).

The legislation also draws a distinction between indictable offences which are not serious offences, serious offences and terrorism offences. An order will only be made to forfeit property which is an instrument of an offence where there has been a conviction for that offence[21] unless the offence is a terrorism offence.[22] Property which is an instrument of an offence which has not been proven to the criminal standard, may still be forfeited if the person is shown to have committed another offence, which is a serious offence, because the person will be unable to satisfy the test to have it excluded from restraint and forfeiture.[23]

Conviction Based Stream

The offence is an indictable offence but not a serious offence[24]
Applications can be made by the CDPP for a pecuniary penalty order[25] or forfeiture order[26] within six months of a person's conviction for an offence. Property which is proceeds of the offence or an instrument of the offence can be forfeited.

Where the offence is an indictable offence but not a serious offence the CDPP can apply for an order forfeiting specified property which is proceeds of the offence or an instrument of the offence.[27] The CDPP is required to give notice of the application to any person who claims an interest in the property and any person whom the CDPP reasonably believes may have an interest in

---

21   See POCA, s. 48(2).
22   *Ibid.* s. 49(1)(c)(iv).
23   See *ibid.* s. 29(2)(a), s. 94(1)(d) (require an applicant for an order excluding property from a restraining order and statutory forfeiture to satisfy the court that the property is not proceeds or an instrument of unlawful activity); see also *ibid.* s. 29(2)(b) (where the offence is not a serious offence the applicant is only required to satisfy the court that the property is not proceeds or an instrument of the offence the person is charged with); see also *infra* n. 81 for discussion of cases relating to serious offences.
24   Serious offence is defined in POCA, s. 338 as an offence punishable by imprisonment for three years or more involving conduct relating to narcotics, money laundering, or where the conduct is intended to cause a benefit for that person or another of at least $10 000 and where the conduct is intended to cause a loss to the Commonwealth or another person of $10 000 or more. Certain offences relating to people smuggling and the harbouring of unlawful immigrants, breaches of the Financial Transactions Reports Act 1988 (Cth) or the Anti-Money Laundering and Counter-Terrorism Financing Act 2006 (Cth) involving at least $50 000 in value, and terrorism offences are also serious offences.
25   See POCA, *ibid.* s. 134.
26   *Ibid.* s. 48.
27   *Ibid.* s. 48.

the property.[28] A person who claims an interest in the property can appear and adduce evidence at the hearing of the forfeiture application. The court has discretion to decide whether an instrument should be forfeited.

Property of the person or under the person's effective control can be restrained before the person is charged with the offence but the restraining order will lapse if the person is not charged with that offence or a related offence within 28 days.[29] The court can refuse to make the restraining order if the court is satisfied that it is not in the public interest to make the order.[30]

The offence is a serious offence

Applications can be made for a forfeiture order or pecuniary penalty order after conviction in the same way that an application is made in respect of a conviction for an indictable offence, which is not a serious offence, but in determining the penalty amount the court assesses the benefit from the offence that the conviction relates to and the benefit from the commission of any other offence that constitutes unlawful activity committed within six years of the application for a pecuniary penalty order or the application for a restraining order whichever is the earlier.[31]

In most cases these proceedings will commence with a restraining order under section 17 over all property of the suspect or specified property of the suspect and property identified as being suspected of being under the suspect's effective control.[32] Property which is restrained six months after the suspect's conviction of an offence, which is a serious offence to which the restraining order relates, is forfeited to the Commonwealth by operation of section 92 of the POCA. To avoid property being forfeited the owner will need to apply to

---

28   *Ibid.* s. 61.

29   *Ibid.* s. 45(2). An application can only be made for a confiscation order in relation to an offence which is not a serious offence after conviction so s. 45(2)(b) has no operation in relation to offences which are not serious offences.

30   See *ibid.* s. 17(4).

31   See *ibid.* s. 121(3) and s. 121(4).

32   Effective control is inclusively defined in the POCA, s. 337. The court can look at the shareholdings, trusts and family, domestic, business and other persons having an interest in the property to determine whether or not property is subject to the effective control of a person. If property was disposed within six years of an application for a restraining order or confiscation order without sufficient consideration it is taken to still be under the effective control of the first person. Rowland J in *Connell v. Lavender* (1991) 7 WAR 9, 22 said effective control contemplates control 'that is practically effective, in the sense that the person has in fact the capacity to control the possession, use or disposition of the property…'. This approach was approved in *DPP v. Toro-Martinez* (1993) 33 NSWLR 82 and applied to the POCA in *Cth DPP v. Hart & Ors (No. 2)* [2005] 2 QdR 246 at 256–258 (hereinafter *Hart*).

have the property excluded from the restraining order[33] or apply to have the property excluded from forfeiture.[34] Once property is restrained the onus of proof shifts to the owner of the property who must satisfy the court that the property is not proceeds of unlawful activity or an instrument of unlawful activity and that a pecuniary penalty order could not be made.

A third party who was not involved in the commission of the offence, may apply to have the property or an interest in the property transferred to them or, if the property is no longer vested in the Commonwealth, an amount paid to them equivalent to the value of their interest in the property. The applicant has to show that the property was not used in connection with any unlawful activity and was not derived from any unlawful activity,[35] or that they were not involved in the commission of the offence, that their interest in the property is not under the suspect's effective control and their interest in the property is not proceeds of the offence or an instrument of the offence.[36]

These provisions are based on the provisions in the Proceeds of Crime Act 1987. The legal onus placed on an applicant for exclusion, the evidential burden and how the onus of proof might be discharged were considered in *DPP v. Brauer*[37] and *Jeffrey v. DPP.*[38]

A conviction can be deemed if the person absconds in connection with the offence.[39]

Civil Person Directed Stream

A person who is referred to in the legislation as a suspect must be suspected to have committed a serious offence within the six years prior to the date of the application for a restraining order. An order is obtained under section 18 over all or specified property of the suspect and specified property suspected of being under the suspect's effective control. An application must be filed for a forfeiture order or pecuniary penalty order within 28 days or the restraining order will lapse. Final orders cannot be made for a period of six months. This gives the suspect, and anyone who may have an interest in the restrained property, an opportunity to apply to exclude the property from the restraining order or to exclude it from forfeiture, by showing that the property was not proceeds of unlawful activity or an instrument of a terrorism offence.

---

[33] See POCA, *ibid.* s. 29.
[34] *Ibid.* s. 94.
[35] *Ibid.* s. 102(3).
[36] *Ibid.* s. 102(2).
[37] [1991] 2 QdR 261 (hereinafter *Brauer*).
[38] (1995) 79 A Crim R 514.
[39] See POCA, ss 331(1)(d), 334.

These provisions are not strictly *in rem* in that to obtain a restraining order the CDPP must satisfy a court that there are reasonable grounds to suspect that the person, who owns the property or is in effective control of the property, committed a serious offence within the preceding six years. To obtain a forfeiture order the CDPP will need to show on the balance of probabilities[40] that the offence has been committed, that the offence was committed within the last six years, unless it is a terrorism offence, that it is a serious offence and that the property has been restrained for six months.[41] The court only needs to consider whether the property has been lawfully acquired if an application is made to exclude it from restraint or forfeiture. The applicant will have the onus of proof on the civil standard.[42] If a pecuniary penalty order can be made against the person who owns the property, or the suspect where the property is under the suspect's effective control, it will not be excluded from restraint.[43] The intention of the legislation is that lawfully acquired property can be restrained and that it should be available to satisfy a pecuniary penalty order if it is owned by the person who will be required to pay the pecuniary penalty or is under that person's effective control.[44]

Civil Asset Directed Stream

Property which is suspected of being the proceeds of an indictable offence, a foreign indictable offence or an indictable offence of Commonwealth concern can be restrained[45] provided that the suspected offence was committed within the preceding six years.[46] It is not necessary to identify the owner of the prop-

---

40 *Ibid.* s. 317.
41 *Ibid.* s. 47.
42 See *Hart.*
43 See POCA, s. 29(4).
44 *Ibid.* Part 2-4, Division 4.
45 See POCA, s. 19. 'Indictable offence of Commonwealth concern' is an offence against a law of a State or Territory: (a) that may be dealt with on indictment (even if it may also be dealt with as a summary offence); and (b) the proceeds of which were (or were attempted to have been) dealt with in contravention of a law of the Commonwealth on:
    I.   importation of goods into, or exportation of goods from, Australia; or
    II.   a communication using a postal or telegraphic or telephonic service within the meaning of paragraph 51(xx) of the Constitution; or
    III. a transaction in the course of banking (other than State banking that does not extend beyond the limits of the State concerned).
46 The six-year time limit does not apply to terrorism offences. Property suspected of being an instrument of a terrorism offence can also be restrained. The Sherman Report, *supra*, recommends that the six-year time limit be extended to 12 years: see the Sherman Report, *ibid.*, Recommendation D1 p. 72.

erty nor is it necessary for the order to be based on a finding as to the commission of a particular indictable offence.[47] The CDPP must give notice of the restraining order to anyone who is suspected of having an interest in the property.

If the restraining order has been in force for six months, and the court is satisfied that the CDPP has taken reasonable steps to identify and notify persons with an interest in the property, and no application has been made for the property to be excluded from the restraining order, or any application to exclude property has been withdrawn, the CDPP will be able to obtain a forfeiture order without having to show that the property is proceeds of an indictable offence, foreign indictable offence or indictable offence of Commonwealth concern. If an application is made for the property to be excluded the court will need to be satisfied that the property is proceeds of one or more indictable offences, foreign indictable offences or indictable offence of Commonwealth concern but the court will not need to make a finding that a particular person committed any offence or as to the commission of a particular offence. A finding that some offence or other of the kind specified in the legislation was committed is sufficient.[48]

Literary Proceeds Orders

A restraining order can be obtained over a suspect's property or property under a suspect's effective control where the court is satisfied that there are reasonable grounds to suspect that the suspect has committed an indictable offence or a foreign indictable offence and that the person has derived literary proceeds.[49] In this way property can be secured to enable a literary proceeds order to be recovered.

Literary proceeds is defined as a benefit the person derives from the commercial exploitation of their notoriety from the commission of the offence or the notoriety of another person involved in the commission of the same offence.[50] The court can make an order that a person pay to the Commonwealth an amount, if the court is satisfied on the balance of probabilities that a person committed an indictable offence, or a foreign indictable offence, and that the

---

[47]   See POCA, s. 19(4): refers only to indictable offence even though property which is the proceeds of a foreign indictable offence or an indictable offence of Commonwealth concern can be restrained; see also *DPP v. Garcia and Others* [2004] QDC 523 [94], where it was submitted that the DPP was required to identify the particular foreign indictable offence and that the Court was required to make a finding as to the commission of the particular offence where a foreign offence was being relied on.
[48]   See POCA, *ibid.* s. 49.
[49]   *Ibid.* s. 20; see *DPP (Cth) v. Corby* [2007] 2 QdR 319.
[50]   See POCA, *ibid.* s. 153.

person derived literary proceeds in relation to the offence.[51] The benefit must have been derived after 1 January 2003. The court has discretion in deciding whether to make a literary proceeds order.

Moving Between Streams

Matters may commence with a civil person directed restraining order under section 18 but if the person is convicted of a serious offence to which the restraining order relates, the restrained property will be forfeited six months after the conviction by operation of section 92 of POCA even though there may be a pending civil based forfeiture application or pecuniary penalty application.

If a conviction based forfeiture order is made or property is statutorily forfeited under section 92 and the conviction is later quashed on appeal, an application can be made to confirm the order and the court may confirm the forfeiture if the court is satisfied that a civil based forfeiture order could be made.[52]

Procedure for Obtaining Restraining Orders and Confiscation Orders

The state courts that have jurisdiction to deal with criminal matters on indictment have jurisdiction to make orders under POCA. In most states this is the District or County Court. The Supreme Courts in each state will also have jurisdiction.

Applications are made by the CDPP. An application for a restraining order must be supported by an affidavit of an authorised officer[53] stating that the officer suspects that the offence has been committed and if the property is not owned by the suspect that the property is under the suspect's effective control. The CDPP can be required to give an undertaking as to damages on behalf of the Commonwealth[54] and the practice is to offer this undertaking.[55] If the restraining order is under section 18 the officer will also have to state that he

---

51   *Ibid.* s. 152.

52   *Ibid.* s. 110.

53   Members of the Australian Federal Police, Australian Crime Commission, Australian Securities and Investment Commission, officers of Customs or a member or officer of an agency specified in the regulations are authorised officers. Officers of the Australian Taxation Office were specified in regulation 3A as authorised officers on 4 October 2006.

54   See POCA, s. 21.

55   Not all state legislation has a similar provision to POCA, s. 21; see *Mansfield v. Director of Public Prosecutions for Western Australia* (2006) 228 ALR 214 (hereinafter *Mansfield*). Recently the High Court held that where there was no express provi-

or she suspects that the offence is a serious offence and that the offence was committed within the preceding six years. If the restraining order is under section 19 the officer will have to state that he or she suspects that the property is proceeds of an indictable offence, foreign indictable offence or indictable offence of Commonwealth concern.

The affidavit needs to set out the grounds for the officer's suspicion in sufficient detail and appropriately sourced so that a judge can determine whether the officer has reasonable grounds for his or her suspicion.

Hearsay is admissible on the application for a restraining order but will not be admissible on an application for forfeiture order or pecuniary penalty order unless it comes within one of the exemptions in the Evidence Act which applies to civil proceedings in the jurisdiction in which the application is brought.[56]

If the offence is a serious offence the court must make the restraining order if the relevant grounds are made out. There is no discretion and the court cannot refuse to make the order on the grounds that it is not in the public interest to make the order. If the offence is an indictable offence that is not a serious offence, the court may refuse to make the order if the court is satisfied that it is not in the public interest to make the order.[57] The offence does not need to have been committed after the commencement of the POCA.[58]

The application for a restraining order may be made *ex parte*.[59] The nature of these types of orders means that the applications are normally made *ex parte* unless the property has already been seized by police or restrained under another provision. Notice of the order and a copy of the affidavit relied on are then given to the owner of the property. Notice of the order is given to anyone

---

sion relating to undertakings in the Criminal Property Confiscation Act 2000 (WA) and where the legislative provisions for making a freezing order were permissive not mandatory, the court could require an undertaking as a condition of making the order.

[56] See *Chief Executive Officer of Customs v. Labrador Liquor Wholesale Pty Ltd and Others* (2003) 216 CLR 161 (the High Court held that s. 92 of the Evidence Act 1977 (Qld) which only applied to civil cases applied to 'Customs prosecutions' and 'Excise prosecutions' under the Customs Act 1901 (Cth) and Excise Act 1901 (Cth) where there was a provision that these prosecutions 'may be commenced prosecuted and proceeded with in accordance with any rules of practice (if any) established by the Court for Crown suits in revenue matters or in accordance with the usual practice and procedure of the Court in civil cases or in accordance with the directions of the Court or a Judge'. The High Court also held that the criminal standard of proof applied as the legislation had not clearly and unequivocally removed or deprived the defendant of the normal protection of requiring the Crown to prove an offence beyond reasonable doubt).

[57] See POCA, ss. 17(1), 17(4), 17(5), 18(1), 18(5), 19(1), 19(5).

[58] *Ibid.* s. 14 (provides that the POCA is intended to have retrospective effect).

[59] *Ibid.* s. 26(4).

who the CDPP believes may have an interest in the property. If the order was made *ex parte* a person may apply within 28 days of receiving notice of the application to have the order revoked.[60] Although the court must consider the application for a restraining order without notice being given, the court may before finally determining the application direct the CDPP to give notice.[61] A provision in the Criminal Proceeds Confiscation Act (Qld) 2002 which required the court to hear an application for a restraining order without the owner of the property being present or having notice of the application was held to be constitutionally invalid as 'it was such an interference with the exercise of the judicial process as to be repugnant to or incompatible with the exercise of the judicial power of the Commonwealth'.[62]

The proceedings on an application for a restraining order, forfeiture order, pecuniary penalty order and literary proceeds order are not criminal proceedings. This is the position whether the orders are conviction based and made at the time of sentence or civil based. The POCA specifies that the rules of evidence applicable in civil proceedings apply, and those applicable only in criminal proceedings do not apply to proceedings under the POCA.[63] The legislation also specifies that any question of fact to be decided by a court on an application under the Act is to be decided on the balance of probabilities.[64] The standard of proof in proceedings for a pecuniary penalty or forfeiture order will be the balance of probabilities as explained by the High Court in *Briginshaw v. Briginshaw*[65] and *Rejfek v. McElroy.*[66]

In assessing benefits obtained from offences courts have accepted that it is

---

[60]   *Ibid.* s. 42.

[61]   *Ibid.* s. 26(5).

[62]   In *Re Criminal Proceeds Confiscation Act 2002 (Qld)* [2004] 1 Qd R 40 at para. 58. At the time of the application the Criminal Proceeds Confiscation Act (Qld) 2002 did not have provisions which allowed the court to direct the applicant to give notice or to enable a person to apply to revoke the order. The legislation has now been amended.

[63]   See POCA, s. 315.

[64]   *Ibid.* s. 317(2).

[65]   (1938) 60 CLR 336 at pp. 361–362 per Dixon J: 'The seriousness of an allegation made, the inherent unlikelihood of an occurrence of a given description, or the gravity of the consequences flowing from a particular finding are considerations which must affect the answer to the question whether the issue has been proved to the reasonable satisfaction of the tribunal.'

[66]   (1964–65) 112 CLR 517 at p. 521 per Barwick CJ, Kitto, Taylor, Menzies & Windeyer JJ:

But the standard of proof to be applied in a case and the relationship between the degree of persuasion of the mind according to the balance of probabilities and the gravity or otherwise of the facts of whose existence the mind is to be persuaded are

not in the nature of criminals to keep records or be completely truthful and that the courts' assessment of benefit derived must necessarily be based on a 'rough and ready' approach.[67]

Applications for restraining orders, revocation orders and exclusion from restraint are interlocutory proceedings.[68]

The CDPP has been ordered to make discovery of documents in the course of proceedings for confiscation orders but the court has also recognized that the CDPP should not be required to make discovery prior to examinations.[69] The defendant in proceedings to recover a penalty is not required to provide discovery or answer interrogatories.[70] The defendant can, however, be compelled to produce documents and answer questions at an examination.[71]

Magistrates have jurisdiction to make restraining orders and forfeiture orders where the orders relate to an offence that the person has been convicted of before a magistrate.[72]

Protection of Legitimate Interests in Property

Revocation

An owner of property or person claiming an interest in property can appear on an application for a restraining order over the property and oppose the order. If a person was not notified of the application for a restraining order they may apply to the court to revoke the order. The application must be made within 28 days of the person being notified of the order. This period can be extended by a court order for up to three months. The order continues in force until it is

---

not to be confused. The difference between the criminal standard of proof and the civil standard of proof is no mere matter of words: it is a matter of critical substance. No matter how grave the fact which is to be found in a civil case, the mind has only to be reasonably satisfied and has not with respect to any matter in issue in such a proceeding to attain that degree of certainty which is indispensable to the support of a conviction upon a criminal charge...

[67]   See *R v. Fagher* (1989) 16 NSWLR 67; see also *State of Queensland v. Hirst* [2003] QSC 266; see also *NSWCC v. Kelly & Ors (No. 2)* [2003] NSWSC 154.

[68]   See *DPP (Cth) v. Hart* [2004] 2 QdR 1.

[69]   See *DPP (WA) v. Centurion Trust Co Ltd* [2004] WASC 74; see also *"B" and Others v. State of Western Australia and Another* [2002] WASC 298.

[70]   See *R v. Associated Northern Collieries* (1910) 111 CLR 738; this privilege will not apply to corporations: see *TPC v. CC(NSW) Pty Ltd (No. 4)*, (1995) 131 ALR 581 and *TPC v. Abbco Ice Works Pty Ltd* (1994) 1223 ALR 503 at pp. 534, 549–550.

[71]   See discussion below on 'Examinations' under the heading 'Information gathering'.

[72]   See POCA, s. 335(6); indictable offence is defined to include an offence that may be dealt with on indictment even if there has been an election to have it dealt with summarily.

revoked, and it cannot be revoked unless the court is satisfied that there are no grounds on which to make the order at the time of considering the application to revoke the order.[73] The CDPP and the applicant can adduce additional material to the court.[74]

Excluding property from restraint

If a person was given notice of the application for a restraining order they can apply within 14 days of being given notice of the application to have property excluded from the restraining order.[75] If the person was not given notice of the application they can apply at any time to exclude property from the restraining order.[76] The test that is to be satisfied by an applicant to exclude property from restraint has already been referred to above.[77] The court must not hear an application to exclude property from restraint until the CDPP has been given a reasonable opportunity to conduct an examination of the applicant.[78]

Recovery from forfeiture

The provisions that apply to a person who is applying to exclude property from forfeiture vary depending on the provision under which the property is to be forfeited or has been forfeited. There is no prohibition on a person who has been unsuccessful in an application to exclude property from restraint applying to exclude the same property from forfeiture.

1. Conviction based forfeiture (offence is not a serious offence) A person who has notice of the forfeiture application can appear on the hearing of the application and oppose forfeiture or apply to exclude the property prior to forfeiture. If the person was not given notice of the application for a forfeiture order they can apply within six months of the forfeiture order being made. The applicant will have to satisfy the court that: (a) he or she was not involved, in any way, in the commission of the offence that the forfeiture relates to; and (b) the property is not proceeds or an instrument of the offence.[79]

2. Conviction based forfeiture (serious offence) Property is forfeited to the

---

73   *Ibid.* s. 42.
74   See *DPP (Cth) v. Tan* [2004] NSWSC 856.
75   See POCA, s. 30.
76   *Ibid.* s. 31.
77   See discussions above under 'Conviction based stream' where offence is a serious offence, 'Civil person directed stream' and 'Civil asset directed stream'.
78   See POCA, s. 32; see also discussion below on 'Examinations' under the heading 'Information gathering'.
79   See POCA, s. 73(1)(e).

Commonwealth six months after a person's conviction of a serious offence[80] if at that time the property is covered by a restraining order that relates to the offence and the property has not been excluded from forfeiture under section 94.

The person who is convicted of the offence can apply for exclusion from forfeiture under section 94. The convicted person must satisfy the court that the property: (a) is not proceeds of unlawful activity; (b) is not an instrument of unlawful activity; and (c) the property was lawfully acquired. 'Proceeds of unlawful activity' is defined to include property partly acquired with the proceeds of unlawful activity.[81]

Third parties can apply under section 104 for an order under section 102 for recovery of property from forfeiture or the payment of an amount equal to the value of their interest in the property. Under section 102(2) and (3), the third party must satisfy the court that: (a) they were not involved, in any way, in the commission of the offence; (b) their interest in the property is not subject to the effective control of the person who was convicted of the offence; and (c) their interest in the property is not proceeds of the offence or an instrument of the offence. Alternatively, relief is available if the court is satisfied that: (a) the property was not used in or in connection with any unlawful activity and was not derived from any unlawful activity; (b) they acquired the property lawfully; and (c) they are not those convicted of the offence to which the forfeiture relates.

---

[80]   *Ibid.* s. 92.

[81]   See *DPP (Cth) v. Studman* (2005) 155 ACrimR 515 (an application to exclude property from restraint and forfeiture was dismissed where it was conceded that the property was not proceeds of the offence which the conviction related to but was otherwise proceeds of unlawful activity being an offence under the Financial Transactions (Reports) Act 1989 and used in connection with offences under that Act but not the offence the conviction related to. 'Unlawful activity' is defined in s. 338 as 'an act or omission that constitutes: (a) an offence against a law of the Commonwealth; or (b) an offence against a law of a State or Territory that may be dealt with on indictment (even it may also be dealt with as a summary offence in some circumstances); or (c) an offence against a law of a foreign country.' An appeal from this decision was dismissed by the New South Wales Court of Appeal *DPP (Cth) v Studman* [2007] NSWCA 285; see also *DPP (Cth) v. Wei-Liang Tu* [2005] NSWSC 772 (varying and inconsistent accounts about the source of funds were not sufficient to satisfy the court on the balance of probabilities that the funds were lawfully derived); see also *Brauer* (an owner of a yacht, who was unable to explain the use of a yacht during a period when it was left in the hands of someone who was involved in illegal drug activity, was unable to satisfy the court that the yacht had not been used in connection with any unlawful activity for the purpose of having it excluded from forfeiture under a similar provision in the Proceeds of Crime Act 1987 (Cth)); see also *DPP (Vic) v. Le* [2007]

3.   Civil person directed[82] or asset directed forfeiture[83]   A person can apply
for an exclusion order if a forfeiture order that could specify the person's property has been applied for but not yet made. If they were not given notice of the
application for a forfeiture order they can apply for an exclusion order within
six months of the making of the order.[84]

If the applicant is the person on whose commission of an offence the order
would be based the court must be satisfied that the property: (a) is not proceeds
of unlawful activity; or (b) if the offence is a terrorism offence, that the property is not an instrument of any terrorism offence.

If the applicant is a third party the court must be satisfied that: (a) the applicant was not involved in the commission of any offences that the forfeiture
relates to; (b) the property is not proceeds of unlawful activity; and (c) if the
offence is a terrorism offence that the property is not an instrument of any
terrorism offence.

Compensation

A court can make a compensation order where: (a) a court made a forfeiture
order;[85] and (b) the order specifies the applicant's property as proceeds of an
offence to which the forfeiture order relates; and (c) the court is satisfied that
when the property became proceeds of the offence, part of the property was
not acquired using proceeds of any offence.

A compensation order specifies the proportion of the property that was
lawfully acquired and directs the Commonwealth to pay to the applicant that
proportion of the proceeds from the sale of the property after deducting the
Official Trustee's costs in connection with the sale and the restraining order.[86]

HCA 52 (a wife applied to exclude property from forfeiture on the basis that she had
an interest as a joint tenant with her husband in the property). Her husband was
convicted of drug trafficking, the jointly owned property had been used in the commission of the offences without the knowledge of the applicant wife. The court declared
that the wife had an interest as tenant in common in the property as to a one-half share
and excluded the wife's interest in the property from automatic forfeiture.

[82]   See POCA, s. 47.
[83]   *Ibid.* s. 49.
[84]   *Ibid.* s. 74.
[85]   Forfeiture order is defined as an order under ss. 47, 48 and 49. Statutory
forfeiture under s. 92 is not a forfeiture order so a compensation order under s. 77
cannot be made if the property has been forfeited six months after conviction for a serious offence; see *NSWCC v. Kelly and Others (No. 2)* [2003] NSWSC 154 for the
approach taken to quantifying and making a hardship order to protect infants under the
Criminal Assets Recovery Act 1990 (NSW) (hereinafter CARA); an appeal was
dismissed: *NSWCC v. Kelly and Others (No. 2)*, (2003) 58 NSWLR 71.
[86]   See POCA, s. 77.

Hardship

Where a civil based forfeiture order has been made a court must make an order directing the Commonwealth to pay a specified amount to a dependant of the person whose property was forfeited if the court is satisfied that: (a) the forfeiture order would cause hardship to the dependant; (b) the specified amount would relieve that hardship; and (c) if the dependant is at least 18 years old, the dependant had no knowledge of the person's conduct that is the subject of the forfeiture order.[87]

Access to restrained property[88]

 A court may allow reasonable living expenses of the person whose property was restrained and their dependants' reasonable living expenses to be paid out of restrained property. Reasonable business expenses and specified debts incurred in good faith can also be paid out of restrained property.

Before a court can make provision for payment of any expenses out of restrained property, the person whose property is restrained will need to apply and satisfy the court that: (a) he or she disclosed all interests in property and liabilities; (b) the debt does not or will not relate to legal costs in connection with the proceedings under the POCA or proceedings for an offence; and (c) he or she cannot meet the expense or debt out of property that is not covered by a restraining order.

INFORMATION GATHERING

Examinations[89]

If a restraining order is in force the court may make an order for the examination of any person about the affairs[90] (including the nature and location of any

---

87   *Ibid.* s. 72, for the reason outlined in *supra* n. 85 this section will not apply to statutory forfeiture under s. 92. The section specifies that it does not apply to conviction based forfeiture orders under s. 48.

88   *Ibid.* s. 24; see *Mansfield* (when considering the Criminal Property Confiscation Act 2000 (WA) where there was no provision for payment of legal expenses the court could exempt property from a freezing order on condition that it be spent for legal expenses). Under the Commonwealth scheme people whose property has been restrained can apply for legal aid and the legal aid commission can be reimbursed out of restrained assets: see POCA, Part 4-2. In the Proceeds of Crime Act 1987 (Cth) payments could be made out of restrained property for reasonable legal expenses. This caused difficulties for both the court and the DPP: see ALRC Report No. 87, *supra.*

89   See POCA, *ibid.* Part 3-1.

90   See *NSWCC v. Murchie* (2000) 49 NSWLR 465 and *Meredith v. State of*

property) of the person whose property is restrained or a person who claims an interest in that property, a person whom the restraining order states to be a suspect, or the spouse of a person whose property is restrained or the suspect.

The examinee cannot refuse to answer questions on the grounds of self-incrimination or claim legal professional privilege. The answers and documents produced at the examination are not admissible in evidence against the examinee in civil or criminal proceedings other than criminal proceedings for giving false or misleading information, proceedings on an application under the POCA, or proceedings ancillary to such an application or enforcement of a confiscation order. Although there is no derivative use immunity stated in the Act the common law implies an obligation to only use the information for the purposes of the POCA.[91]

Examinations are conducted in private before an approved examiner.[92] The publication of the transcript of the examination and the discussion of the examination by the examinee and the examinee's legal representative can be restricted.[93]

Search Warrants

A magistrate may issue a search warrant[94] to an authorized officer for the search of premises if he or she is satisfied that there are reasonable grounds for suspecting that there is at the premises or will be within the next 72 hours evidential material[95] or tainted property.[96]

Queensland [2006] 1 QdR 334 for a discussion of the meaning of 'affairs' in similar legislation.

[91] See *DPP (Cth) v. Hatfield* [2006] NSWSC 195.

[92] Retired Judges and members of the Administrative Appeals Tribunal can be appointed as approved examiners. The DPP appears and usually asks the questions with the approved examiner asking additional questions and ruling on any objections. Questions of law arising in the examination can be referred to the court that made the examination order.

[93] Examiners routinely make directions restricting the discussion of the examination by the examinee with other potential examinees.

[94] See POCA, s. 225.

[95] *Ibid.* s. 338 (evidential material is defined as evidence relating to property in respect of which action has been taken or can be taken under the Act, evidence relating to benefits derived from the commission of an indictable offence or literary proceeds).

[96] *Ibid.* s.338 (tainted property is defined as proceeds of an indictable offence or an instrument of an indictable offence); see also *ibid.* (indictable offence is defined as an offence against a law of the Commonwealth); see also *ibid.* (the extended definition of proceeds of an indictable offence in ss 329 and 330 means that property which is partly derived from the commission of an indictable offence and property acquired with the proceeds from the sale of property acquired or partly derived from proceeds of an indictable offence will be tainted property).

The warrant must state the nature of the property in respect of which action can be taken or has been taken, the nature of the action and the kinds of tainted property or evidential material that is to be searched for as well as a number of other matters set out in section 227.[97] Warrants can be obtained by telephone in urgent cases[98] and searches can be conducted without a warrant in emergency situations but the circumstances must be serious and urgent.[99]

If tainted property is seized under a search warrant the property must be returned if an application is not made for a restraining order or forfeiture order within 14 days.[100] Evidential material must also be returned if proceedings in respect of which it might afford evidence are not commenced within 60 days.[101] This period can be extended by a magistrate. Things seized under a search warrant can be made available to officers of other enforcement agencies if it is necessary for investigating or prosecuting an offence or recovering the proceeds or an instrument of an offence.[102]

Production Orders

A magistrate may make an order requiring a person to produce one or more property-tracking documents to an authorized officer or to make the same available to an authorized officer for inspection.[103] Under section 202(5), property-tracking documents can be, for example, documents relevant to identifying, locating or quantifying property of a person who is charged or

---

[97]   The requirement to state the nature of the property in respect of which action can be taken and the nature of the action in circumstances where investigators were searching for property and evidence of effective control of property was considered in *Unlimited Business Consultants (Qld) Pty Ltd ACN098523 490 v. Commissioner, Australian Federal Police* [2003] FCA 706 (17 June 2003).

[98]   See POCA, s. 229.

[99]   *Ibid.* s. 251.

[100]   *Ibid.* s. 260.

[101]   *Ibid.* s. 256.

[102]   *Ibid.* s. 228(2); enforcement agency is defined as the Australian Federal Police, Australian Crime Commission, Australian Securities and Investment Commission, Australian Customs Service or an agency specified in the regulations to be a law enforcement, revenue or regulatory agency for the purposes of the Act. The Australian Taxation Office was specified in reg. 4A of the Proceeds of Crime Amendment Regulations (2006) (no. 4) as a revenue agency on 4 October 2006. As a consequence the provision of documents to state police or foreign law enforcement agencies would not be authorised by s. 228(2). The Sherman Report, *supra* Recommendation No. 1 pp. 29, 69 recommends that POCA be amended to contain a clear mandate that information acquired under the legislation relating to any serious offence can be passed to any agency having a lawful function to investigate that offence.

[103]   See POCA, *ibid.* s. 202.

intended to be charged with an indictable person, or a person who is suspected on reasonable grounds of engaging in a terrorism offence or conduct constituting a serious offence in the preceding six years. They may also be documents relevant to identifying, locating or quantifying proceeds of an indictable offence or an instrument of an indictable offence of which a person has been charged or is proposed to be charged, or proceeds of a serious offence or instrument of a serious offence the person is reasonably suspected of committing within the last six years, and proceeds or instruments of terrorism offences.

At least 14 days is allowed for the production of such documents. A person is not excused from producing a document under a production order on the grounds that it would tend to incriminate the person or expose them to a penalty, that it would breach an obligation not to disclose the existence or contents of the document or that it would disclose information that is the subject of legal professional privilege. The document is not admissible in evidence in criminal proceedings against the person producing it.[104]

The order can specify that a person is not to disclose the existence of the production order. A breach of the order is an offence punishable by up to two years' imprisonment.

Monitoring Orders

A judge may make an order requiring a financial institution to provide information about transactions conducted during a particular period, not exceeding three months, through a specified account. It is an offence to disclose the existence of the order. A monitoring order enables the investigating agency to find out about transactions as they occur or soon afterwards.

Notices to Financial Institutions

A small number of senior police officers and officers in the Australian Crime Commission can issue a written notice to a financial institution requiring the institution to provide to an authorized officer any information or documents relevant to determining whether an account is held by an identified person, whether the person is a signatory to an account, the current balance of an account, details of transactions on an account over a period of up to six months, details of related accounts and transactions conducted on behalf of a specified person. The notice can only be issued to determine whether to take action under the Act or in rela-

---

[104]   *Ibid.* s. 206(1); legal professional privilege could be claimed if a search warrant under s. 225 was used to seize the document instead of a production order.

tion to proceedings under the Act. This is one of the most commonly used information-gathering tools by the Australian Federal Police as it enables information to be obtained quickly to determine whether a person who is being investigated has money in any bank accounts.[105]

Access to Tax Information

The Commissioner of Taxation may disclose information acquired under the provisions of a taxation law to an authorized officer of a law enforcement agency if he is satisfied that the information is relevant to the making, or proposed or possible making of a proceeds of crime order.[106]

Access to Financial Transaction Reports

Law enforcement agencies are able to access the database maintained by the Australian Transaction Reports and Analysis Centre (AUSTRAC). This database contains information extracted from reports of significant cash transactions by cash dealers in Australia, reports by travellers where $10 000 or more is carried in or out of Australia and reports of international funds transfer instructions.[107]

PRESERVATION OF RESTRAINED PROPERTY

Under the POCA the court can order[108] that the Official Trustee be given custody and control of restrained property. Dealings with property can be restrained and the order registered by way of caveat or other notice on a public register where that is available. The Official Trustee is able to recover his costs of managing the property after forfeiture. Orders can be varied and commonly are varied to enable property to be sold or leased with the proceeds of sale being restrained or rent being applied to make mortgage repayments.[109] Wasting property can be sold.[110]

---

[105] *Ibid.* s. 213; information-gathering powers are also contained in the Australian Crime Commission Act 2002 (Cth): see Australian Crime Commission Act 2002, s. 12(1A) (information obtained in the course of investigation by the Australian Crime Commission may be disseminated for the purpose of confiscation proceedings).
[106] See Taxation Administration Act 1953 (Cth), s. 3E.
[107] See Financial Transaction Reports Act 1988 (Cth) and Anti-Money Laundering and Counter-Terrorism Financing Act 2006 (Cth).
[108] See POCA, s. 38.
[109] *Ibid.* s. 39.
[110] *Ibid.* s. 278 (authorizes the sale of restrained property where the cost of

Although there are provisions protecting the Official Trustee from any claims for damages in relation to the management of restrained property the Commonwealth may be liable to pay compensation pursuant to the undertaking[111] given by the CDPP when the restraining order was obtained if the loss was suffered whilst the property was restrained.

In one case a restraining order was varied to give the Official Trustee custody and control of a pharmacy in circumstances where it became apparent that the approval for the premises to be used as a pharmacy would have been revoked if the defendant pharmacist continued to operate the pharmacy pending forfeiture or a pecuniary penalty order being made. This would have caused a substantial depreciation in the value of the business. A variation to the restraining order enabled the Official Trustee to take custody and control of the pharmacy, and employ a registered pharmacist until the pharmacy was sold as a going concern.

WHERE DOES FORFEITED PROPERTY GO?

The net proceeds from the sale of forfeited property and money paid in satisfaction of pecuniary penalty orders are paid into the Confiscated Assets Account. Money can be paid out of this account to foreign governments and states in recognition of the contribution they made to a recovery in a particular case pursuant to the equitable sharing program or to satisfy the Commonwealth's obligations in respect of a registered foreign forfeiture order or pecuniary penalty order or an order registered under section 45 of the International War Criminal Tribunals Act 1995 (Cth). Payments are also made to legal aid commissions.[112] The Minister may approve funding out of the account for programs for crime prevention measures, law enforcement measures, measures relating to treatment for drug addiction and diversionary measures relating to illegal use of drugs.

There is no provision in the POCA for forfeited property or money paid by way of pecuniary penalty order to be returned to the victim. In Commonwealth matters the victim is often another Commonwealth agency but in cases involving breaches of the Corporations Act by directors and financial advisers where there are identifiable victims the recovery provisions in the Corporations Act

---

controlling the property is likely to exceed its value and where the property is likely to lose value); a notice is issued to the owner and any person who has an interest in the property. An objection can be lodged and the court can then order the sale or destruction of the property.

[111] See *Re Cannon*, [1999] 1 QdR 247; see also *McCleary v. DPP(Cth)* (1998) 157 ALR 301.

[112] See *supra* n. 88.

will normally be used rather than the provisions in the POCA so that any money recovered can be returned to the company or investors. In some cases the POCA is used where either there are no identifiable victims or for other reasons that make the POCA provisions more appropriate. There is provision in the Crimes Act 1914 (Cth) for a compensation order to be made at the time of sentence in favour of a person who has suffered a loss as a result of the offence but there is no mechanism for restraining property prior to the making of the compensation order nor are there any provisions to facilitate the recovery of these orders which are enforced as a civil judgment.

RECOVERY OF PECUNIARY PENALTY ORDERS

Property of a suspect and property under a suspect's effective control can be restrained so that it will be available to satisfy a pecuniary penalty order. When a pecuniary penalty order is made against a person and property belonging to that person is restrained, a charge is created over the property at the time the pecuniary penalty order is made to secure the payment of the pecuniary penalty to the Commonwealth.[113] If property is under the person's effective control the CDPP can obtain a declaration that all or part of the property is available to satisfy the pecuniary penalty order and the order can be enforced against the property as if it was the person's own property. If the property was restrained a charge would then be created over the property. Where property has been restrained declarations can be obtained at the time the pecuniary penalty order is made for the Official Trustee to sell the property and apply the proceeds to payment of the pecuniary penalty and directions can be made for the Official Trustee to sign documents to give effect to the direction.

Pecuniary penalty orders can be enforced as a civil debt but are not provable in bankruptcy proceedings. Bankruptcy will not discharge a liability to pay a pecuniary penalty order and property that has vested in a trustee in bankruptcy can be restrained and applied to satisfy a pecuniary penalty order. There are no provisions in the POCA for imprisonment for failing to pay a pecuniary penalty order.

EFFECT ON SENTENCE

The court is not to have regard to any order forfeiting the proceeds of the offence or to a pecuniary penalty order that relates to the offence when passing sentence

---

[113]　See POCA, s.142.

on a person in respect of the offence. A court is to have regard to a forfeiture order to the extent that it forfeits property which is not proceeds of the offence. The court may have regard to any cooperation by the person in resolving action under the POCA.[114]

STAY OF PROCEEDINGS

As provided in the legislation, the mere fact that criminal proceedings have been commenced is not a ground on which a court may stay proceedings under the POCA. This and similar provisions in the Queensland and Western Australian legislation, however, have been interpreted as not removing the court's inherent power to stay proceedings in the interests of justice and stays have been granted where some specific prejudice justifying the stay has been demonstrated.[115]

CONSTITUTIONAL CHALLENGES

Challenges to the forfeiture provisions in the Customs Act and Fisheries Management Act on the basis that they constituted an acquisition of property other than on just terms were unsuccessful.[116] The High Court upheld forfeiture laws in customs and fisheries legislation as penalties or sanctions with respect to a head of power other than section 51(xxxi) of the Australian Constitution.[117]

Challenges to the statutory forfeiture provisions in the Proceeds of Crime Act 1987 which provided for the statutory forfeiture of all restrained property six months after conviction of a serious offence were also unsuccessful.[118] Arguments that these provisions went beyond what was incidental to a primary

---

[114]   *Ibid.* s. 320.
[115]   In *State of Queensland v. Henderson* unreported QSC S1246 of 2003 16 May 2003, *State of Queensland v. Bush* (2003) QSC 375, and *Queensland v. Cannon* (2003) QSC 459 stays were refused as no specific prejudice justifying the stay in the circumstances of the cases had been demonstrated; in *Queensland v. Shaw* (2003) QSC 436, *State of Queensland v. O'Brien and Falzon* unreported QSC S3879 of 2004, 22 June 2006, *DPP (Cth) v. Queensland Jewellery and Gift Company Pty Ltd and Others* [2006] QDC 373 and *DPP (Cth) v. Jo and Others* [2007] QCA 251 stays were granted.
[116]   The Constitution authorises the acquisition of property by the Commonwealth on just terms.
[117]   See *Re DPP ex parte Lawler and Anor* (1994) 179 CLR 270; see also *Burton v. Honan* [1952] 86 CLR 169.
[118]   See *Della Patrona v. DPP(Cth) [No. 2]* (1993) 38 NSWLR 257.

head of power, in this case the trade and commerce power in section 51(i) of the Australian Constitution 1900 (Cth), were rejected by the Court of Appeal.[119] The argument that it imposed a sanction which was a cruel and unusual punishment was also rejected.[120] McPherson JA when considering the conviction based provisions in the POCA referred to the lengthy history of legislative forfeiture provisions.[121]

---

[119]   *Ibid.* at pp. 268–269, paras 48–49:

48.   The complaint that the forfeiture provision could operate harshly in a particular case is one to be addressed to Parliament, not to a court judging the constitutionality of the provision. Parliament has in any case provided for a facility of exemption of what might be called 'untainted' property, provided such facility is exercised before six months after conviction. In the present case, the appellant had ample opportunity before and after her conviction, to seek such exemption. She failed to do so within time. The facility provided robs the appellant of the argument that the sanction imposed by the Act (as part of the chosen means of enforcing the will of Parliament as to prohibited imports) is unconnected with the power, or disproportional to its proper exercise.
49.   Because I am of the opinion that the challenged terms of s30 of the Act are properly described as incidental to the exercise by Federal Parliament of its powers. under s51(i) of the Constitution, no question of requiring the support of s51(xxxix) arises. ...

[120]   *Ibid.* pp. 269–270.
[121]   See *Hart,* at para. 16:

There is a lengthy history of the use of legislative provisions like these as adjuncts to enforcing customs and excise duties, trade and navigation laws, anti-slave trading measures, and other activities prohibited by Parliament. Courts of admiralty and exchequer developed special procedures *in rem* against forfeited goods to give effect to such legislation, which in modern times have been held to be still available to common law courts in the United States: see discussion in *C J Hendry Co v. Moore* (1943) 318 US 133 and cf *Willey v. Synan* (1935) 54 CLR 175, 185–186. In *Burton v. Honan* (1952) 86 CLR 169, 180–181, the High Court held that legislation providing for such statutory forfeitures of the property of other, even apparently innocent, persons was within the competence of the Commonwealth Parliament and fell outside the ambit of s. 51(xxxi) of the Constitution requiring acquisition of property to be on just terms. 'It has', their Honours said there, 'no more to do with the acquisition of property for a purpose in respect of which the Parliament has power to make laws within s. 51(xxxi) than has the imposition of taxation itself, or the forfeiture of goods in the hands of the actual offender'. See also *DPP v. Toro-Martinez* (1993) 33 NSWLR 82, 101–103. The judicial tendency to adopt narrow interpretations of legislation that radically restricts property rights, although not without weight as a consideration, cannot control the unambiguous meaning and effect of the provisions of s. 29(4) and s. 317(1).

In *Silbert (as Executor of the estate of Stephen Retteghy dec'd) v. Director of Public Prosecutions (WA)*[122] the High Court considered the constitutional validity of provisions, which deemed a person who died after being charged but before conviction, to have absconded and to be convicted for the purposes of the Crimes (Confiscation of Profits) Act 1988 (WA).[123] It was argued that the deeming of a conviction was invalid because it precluded the court from making sufficient inquiry into whether the deceased had committed the offence. This argument was rejected because the court was required to be satisfied that the offence had been committed before making a forfeiture order. The court had a discretion to exercise in making a pecuniary penalty order and the reference to a conviction merely described the circumstances in which the operative provisions in the legislation were enlivened: 'There is no legislative determination of guilt of an offence; there is no legislative conviction of a person accused of crime.'[124]

HAS CIVIL FORFEITURE MADE A DIFFERENCE?

Experience has shown that the introduction of the civil forfeiture provisions on 1 January 2003 has made a difference in that:

(a)   restraining orders can be obtained at an earlier stage in the investigation and in some cases restraining orders can be served at the same time as the operation becomes overt with the execution of search warrants at the suspect's premises;[125]

(b)   property suspected of being proceeds of foreign offences can be restrained quickly;[126] and

(c)   action can be taken where the property is located in Australia but the person suspected of committing the offence may not have been identified or is outside of Australia but is unlikely to be extradited to Australia for trial.

---

[122]   (2004) 205 ALR 43 (hereinafter *Silbert*).

[123]   Similar provisions are contained in the Criminal Property Confiscation Act 2000 (WA), Confiscation Act 1997(Vic), Criminal Assets Confiscation Act 1996 (SA), and Criminal Proceeds Confiscation Act 2002 (Qld).

[124]   See *Silbert*, para.13.

[125]   Delay between the date when search warrants are executed, a prosecution brief completed and charges are laid can be significant in complex fraud investigations.

[126]   See cases of *Gaborit*, *Lambert* and *Rahardja* at pp. 90, 91 and 94 of the *CDPP Annual Report 2003–2004*.

It is too early to know what the impact of civil forfeiture will be on the value of property confiscated as it is not unusual for there to be a delay of two or three years between the date when property is restrained and the date when the property is sold after forfeiture or a pecuniary penalty is made.[127] An analysis of the numbers of restraining orders obtained and the value of restrained property indicates a significant increase in orders and the value of restrained property after 1 January 2003 when the civil forfeiture provisions were introduced.

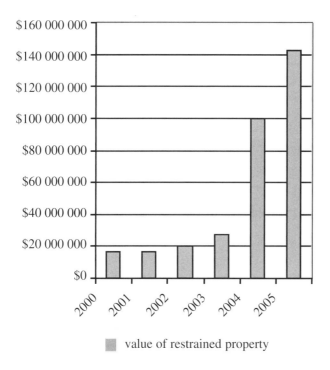

value of restrained property

Figure 5.1   Value of property restrained by the DPP as at 30 June 2000 through to 30 June 2005[128]

---

[127]   The Sherman Report, *supra* has noted that recoveries are running at 45 per cent higher than under the conviction-based regime.
[128]   Figures are taken from the *CDPP Annual Report 1999–2000, 2001–2002, 2003–2004* and *2004–2005*.

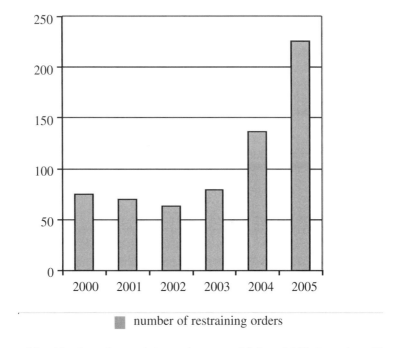

Figure 5.2   Number of restraining orders as at 30 June 2000 through to 30 June 2005[129]

COMPARISON WITH STATE LEGISLATION[130]

Australian Capital Territory

The Australian Capital Territory's Confiscation of Criminal Assets Act 2003 provides for conviction based orders and a civil forfeiture regime which is very similar to the POCA. Applications for restraining orders, forfeiture orders and pecuniary penalty orders are made by the Director of Public Prosecutions (ACT).

---

[129]   Figures are taken from the *CDPP Annual Report 1999–2000, 2001–2002, 2003–2004* and *2004–2005*.
[130]   At the time of writing Tasmania had not introduced civil confiscation legislation.

New South Wales

New South Wales has conviction based legislation.[131] Applications under this legislation are made by the New South Wales office of the Director of Public Prosecutions. The civil based CARA is administered by the New South Wales Crime Commission not the DPP (NSW). The POCA is similar to the CARA and was substantially modeled on the New South Wales civil scheme but incorporates some of the features of the Proceeds of Crime Act 1987. CARA has been amended to incorporate forfeiture of assets held under a fraudulently acquired identity[132] and to provide for a confiscation order to be made against a third party to recover proceeds of crime that have been used to pay for legitimate activities or services on behalf of the third party where that person knew or ought reasonably to have known that the money was proceeds of illegal activity.[133] The Public Trustee is responsible for the administration and sale of restrained and forfeited property. Money recovered under the CARA can be applied to the Victims Compensation Fund, applied in aid of law enforcement, used for victims support programs, crime prevention projects and for drug rehabilitation.

Victoria

The Confiscation Act 1997 (Vic) provides for civil forfeiture and conviction based forfeiture. Applications are made by the Victorian Director of Public Prosecutions although in some instances applications can be made by a police officer to a magistrate. There is provision for a police officer to obtain a freezing order over money in a bank account pending an application by the DPP for a restraining order.

The Victorian legislation provides for tainted property substitution. Where property used in the commission of a crime is not available for forfeiture the court may order that property of the same nature or description in which the offender has an interest to be substituted. Property can be restrained to enable a compensation order to be paid. If property is forfeited and a compensation order is made a victim can recover compensation from the proceeds of the forfeited property.

A restraining order can only be obtained if a person is charged or to be charged within 48 hours, or the property is suspected of being tainted property of an offence which is a civil forfeiture offence. Civil forfeiture orders and civil pecuniary penalty orders can be made based on a finding of guilt to the

---

131   See Confiscation of Proceeds of Crime Act 1989 (NSW).
132   See CARA, s. 9A.
133   *Ibid.* s. 27(2)A.

civil standard where the offence is an offence under Schedule 2 to the legislation. Evidence in support of an exclusion application is not admissible in criminal proceedings[134] and the civil proceedings can be stayed until completion of the criminal proceedings.[135]

South Australia

The Criminal Assets Confiscation Act 2005 (SA) is similar to the POCA. Applications are made by the Director of Public Prosecutions (SA) although police officers can obtain a freezing order over bank accounts from a magistrate for up to 72 hours.[136] Conviction based instrument substitution declarations can be made if the court is satisfied that the convicted person had an interest in the property when the offence was committed, the property is of the same nature as property that was an instrument of the offence and that property is not available for forfeiture.[137] Money which is recovered is available for the costs of administering the Act and for the Victims of Crime Fund.

Queensland

The Criminal Proceeds Confiscation Act 2002 (Qld) is similar to the POCA and CARA. A scheme for confiscation without conviction is set out in chapter 2 of the legislation and a separate scheme for confiscation after conviction is set out in chapter 3. Applications for orders under chapter 2 are made by the Office of the Director of Public Prosecutions on behalf of the state and supported by affidavit from a police officer or officer from the Crime and Misconduct Commission. Property is forfeited to the state and the proceeds are paid into consolidated revenue.

Western Australia

The Criminal Property Confiscation Act 2000 (WA) provides for the confiscation of: unexplained wealth;[138] criminal benefits;[139] crime-used property;[140]

---

[134]   See Confiscation Act 1997 (Vic), s. 20(5).
[135]   *Ibid.* s. 20(7).
[136]   See Criminal Assets Confiscation Act 2005 (SA), Part 2.
[137]   *Ibid.* s. 48.
[138]   See Criminal Property Confiscation Act 2000 (WA) s. 144.
[139]   *Ibid.* s. 145.
[140]   *Ibid.* s. 146.

crime-derived property;[141] and property owned, effectively controlled or given away by a person declared to be a drug trafficker.[142]

Drug trafficking declarations can be made when a person is convicted of a confiscation offence committed after the commencement of the Criminal Property Confiscation Act 2000 (WA). All property owned or controlled by a person at the time the declaration is made and all property the person gave away before the declaration was made is 'drug trafficker's property'.[143] A freezing notice can be obtained from a justice of the peace[144] by the Director of Public Prosecutions or a police officer if a person is charged or is likely to be charged within 21 days and the person could be declared to be a drug trafficker, or there are reasonable grounds for suspecting that the property is crime-used or crime-derived. Objections can be made to the freezing notice by people who have an interest in the property and for release of confiscated property.

An unexplained wealth declaration can be obtained if a court is satisfied that it is more likely than not that the total value of the person's wealth is greater than the value of the person's lawfully acquired wealth.[145]

Money which is recovered is applied to the administration of the Act, law enforcement purposes, programs for the prevention of drug-related criminal activity and abuse of drugs, support services for the victims of crime and to carry out operations for identifying and locating property which can be confiscated.

Northern Territory

The Criminal Property Forfeiture Act 2002 (NT) states in section 10(2) and (3) that property of a person involved in criminal activities or taken to be involved in criminal activities is forfeited to the territory to the extent provided for in the Act to compensate the community for the costs of deterring, detecting and dealing with the criminal activities and that crime-used or crime-derived property is forfeited to deter criminal activity and prevent the unjust enrichment of persons involved in criminal activity.

---

[141]   *Ibid.* s. 148.
[142]   *Ibid.* s. 159.
[143]   *Ibid.* s. 8.
[144]   *Ibid.* s. 34.
[145]   The Sherman Report, *supra* p. 37 rejected the submission that similar provisions be included in POCA commenting that 'to introduce these provisions would represent a significant step beyond the national and international consensus in this area'. It also noted that the use of the provisions had been relatively low.

Police can seize property if it is suspected that it is an instrument, or proceeds of crime, or owned or effectively controlled by a person charged with an offence who could be declared a drug trafficker.[146] A restraining order would then need to be obtained.

This legislation is similar to the Western Australian legislation and includes provisions for the Director of Public Prosecutions (NT) to apply to the Supreme Court for an unexplained wealth declaration[147] and for crime-used property substitution declarations.[148] Hearsay is admissible on applications for final orders.[149]

CONCLUSION

My impression that the POCA has been more effective and successful than the conviction based Proceeds of Crime Act 1987 which preceded it has been confirmed by the independent review of the operation of the POCA[150] which noted that recoveries were 45 per cent higher under the POCA than its predecessor with $22 million received in actual recoveries from proceeds and instruments of crime and 416 restraining orders issued over property of the value of $184 million since 1 January 2003.

A number of recommendations were made by Mr Sherman for changes to the POCA, mostly of a technical nature. The most significant recommendations were that the POCA should contain a clear mandate for agencies to pass on information acquired under the POCA to other agencies, the Australian Taxation Office be given the same access and coercive powers under the POCA as other agencies, the Confiscated Assets Account be made a normal income and expenditure account with greater flexibility for payments and greater accountability to Parliament, the processing of legal aid claims be made more flexible and efficient, and the limitation period be extended from six to 12 years for civil based action.

As part of the review of the operation of POCA comments were invited on the operation of POCA from a range of agencies and organizations. No submission furnished to the review suggested that POCA should be fundamentally reassessed.[151]

---

[146] See Criminal Property Forfeiture Act 2002 (NT), s. 39.
[147] *Ibid.* s. 71.
[148] *Ibid.* s. 81.
[149] *Ibid.* s. 143.
[150] See in general the Sherman Report, *supra.*
[151] *Ibid.* p. 12, para. 2.41.

6. Civil asset forfeiture in Canada

James McKeachie and Jeffrey Simser*

A substantial proportion of criminal activity makes money, consumes money or both.[1]

INTRODUCTION TO CIVIL ASSET FORFEITURE[2]

Over the past 20 years, there has been considerable attention paid to the relationship between money and unlawful activity, both domestically and internationally.[3] Civil asset forfeiture or non-conviction based forfeiture is an important element of this discussion. This chapter canvasses civil asset forfeiture in Canada. The authors of this chapter have been at the forefront of Canadian developments in policy, law and litigation since 2000. The chapter covers the theoretical underpinnings, legislative techniques and practical implications of non-conviction based forfeiture. As Canada develops, one looks to burgeoning jurisprudence in other countries. Wherever possible, relevant cases from the United States (US), Australia, Ireland, South Africa and the United Kingdom (UK) have been included in the footnotes.

---

*   The views expressed herein are those of the authors personally and do not represent the views of the government of Ontario or its Ministry of the Attorney General.

[1]   See Mariano-Florentino Cueller (2003), 'The Tenuous Relationship Between the Fight Against Money Laundering and the Disruption of Criminal Finance', *J Crim L & Criminology*, **93**, 311, at p. 323. This 154-page article provides a very interesting critique of the current investigative, prosecutorial and regulatory system designed to interdict international criminal finance.

[2]   Many people refer to civil forfeiture and civil asset forfeiture interchangeably, we prefer to use the phrase 'civil asset forfeiture' because it more accurately describes the forfeiture scheme, namely the *in rem* nature of the civil proceeding that is non-conviction based, as opposed to an *in personam* proceedings.

[3]   See H. Morais (2005), 'Fighting International Crime and Its Financing: The Importance of Following a Coherent Global Strategy Based on the Rule of Law', *Vill L Rev*, **50**, 583.

The US, which has had civil asset forfeiture since 1789, began to actively apply existing civil asset forfeiture laws from the mid-1980s following Congressional reforms in 1984 as part of the 'war on drugs'.[4] New South Wales was the first commonwealth jurisdiction to apply civil asset forfeiture, particularly from 1990 onwards. Ireland reacted to two very public and contro- versial murders (of police officer Gerry McCabe and journalist Veronica Guerin) with a civil asset forfeiture law in 1996.[5] Post-apartheid South Africa brought forward legislation in 1998 as a result of finding that the earlier apartheid government had not provided the country with adequate means to fight organized crime.[6] Ontario was the first Canadian jurisdiction to enter the fray with the Remedies for Organized Crime and Other Unlawful Activities Act 2001 (amended in 2007 and renamed the Civil Remedies Act 2001 (here- inafter Civil Remedies Act)). As discussed in this chapter other Canadian provinces have or are following Ontario. Finally, there have been significant developments in the UK,[7] Australia[8] and New Zealand.[9]

Generally, civil asset forfeiture is a legal technique whereby the courts are invited to address property derived from or instrumental in unlawful activity. Civil asset forfeiture proceedings are brought to civil court by civil lawyers (not the police or criminal prosecutors)[10] who invite the court to examine the origin and use of specific property. If the court finds that property constitutes proceeds or an instrument, it can be forfeited to the state. The proceeding is brought *in rem,* literally against the thing, in contrast to an *in personam*

---

4   See Chapter 2 of this book on the law and practice in the US.
5   See Chapter 3 of this book on the law and practice in Ireland.
6   See Chapter 4 of this book on the law and practice in South Africa.
7   See Chapters 7 and 8 of this book on the law and practice in the UK.
8   See Chapter 5 of this book on the law and practice in Australia.
9   Some portions of this chapter as well as a comparative analysis of the origins and operation of civil asset forfeiture laws can be found in: J. Simser (2006), *Anti- Money Laundering Techniques: Civil Asset Forfeiture,* Money Laundering Symposium, Osgoode Hall Law School, 11 February 2006; see also J. Simser (2005), *Civil Asset Forfeiture in Common Law Jurisdictions,* Money Laundering Symposium, Osgoode Hall Law School, 29 January 2005.
10   This is not true of all jurisdictions. Currently, Manitoba designates a police chief to bring a proceeding under the Criminal Property Forfeiture Act 2003. In some jurisdictions, like the US Federal System, the distinction between the prosecutor and the civil asset forfeiture attorney appears to have less significance. In Ireland, a police- led agency, established by the Criminal Assets Bureau Act 1996 operates the civil asset recovery system. In Australia, one tends to see specialized civil agencies. In the UK, it appears to be moving away from a specialized civil agency. In Ontario and British Columbia, specialized civil lawyers in the Ministry of the Attorney General bring cases.

proceeding, which is brought against the person.[11] In an *in rem* proceeding, the property itself is the defendant or respondent. The person who held title or possession is a necessary party. The court is asked to take jurisdiction over the property to preserve it for litigation and ultimately to rule on its title. There are no criminal penalties, fines or imprisonment imposed in the proceeding. Finally, legislatures like Ontario declare their legislative intent in classifying the regime as civil and remedial.[12]

Civil asset forfeiture is a legislated response to the societal problem that a large portion of unlawful activity is carried out for purely economic gain. Civil asset forfeiture is a property-based approach to a societal problem; there is no punishment or stigmatization of people, only the removal of property. The form of that response and its rationale varies from jurisdiction to jurisdiction. In the Republic of Ireland, courts are invited to make inquiries respecting title to property: can a person claim title to property with an illicit provenance? The courts have answered 'no'. Where there is an ascertained victim, the money is returned to them. Where the specific victim cannot be ascertained, the void in title is filled by forfeiture to the state.[13] In either case, the primary goal is to return to the *status quo ante*, at least as far as property is concerned.[14] In the UK, the courts have upheld the state's interest in removing illicit assets from circulation.[15] South African courts have held that civil asset forfeiture is a valid and legitimate technique to address money laundering and organized crime.[16] In some jurisdictions, like Western Australia, the state may seek the

---

[11]   See D. Smith (2006), *Prosecution and Defence of Forfeiture Cases*, Newark, New Jersey, US: Matthew Bender (hereinafter *Prosecution and Defence of Forfeiture Cases*), ch. 16, which discusses the consolidated *in personam* New York statute found at Art. 13A of the New York Civil Practice Law and Rules as well as various *in rem* statutes and forfeiture provisions under state law and under para. 14-140 of the Administrative Code of the City of New York.

[12]   See Civil Remedies Act, s. 1. See also *Clingham v. Royal Borough of Kensington and Chelsea* [2002] UKHL 39 (House of Lords) considered the issue of clarification in reviewing 'anti-social behaviour orders'. The court found that the relevant standard of proof was in fact 'civil'.

[13]   See for example: *Gilligan v. Criminal Assets Bureau* [1998] 3 IR 185 (HC) and discussion in Chapter 3 of this book.

[14]   See A. Kennedy (2004), 'Justifying the Civil Recovery of Criminal Proceeds', *J Financial Crimes*, **12**, 8 (hereinafter Justifying Civil Recovery of Criminal Proceeds); see also M. Gallant (2005), *Money Laundering and the Proceeds of Crime: Economic Crime and Civil Remedies*, Cheltenham, UK and Northampton, MA, US: Edward Elgar.

[15]   See *Re Assets Recovery Agency and Walsh* [2004] NIQB 21, aff'd [2005] NICA 6 (Court of Appeal) (hereinafter *Walsh*): see references to the Court of Appeal case in Chapter 7 of this book. Leave to appeal denied, House of Lords, 7 July 2005. A challenge in Strasbourg was also unsuccessful, see *Walsh v. UK* [2006] ECHR 1154.

[16]   See *National Director of Public Prosecutions v. Mohamed NO and Others*

forfeiture of untainted property to ensure that the benefits of unlawful activity are stripped from the defendants.[17]

The cornerstone of the criminal law, *mens rea*, is not part of civil asset forfeiture law. Criminal law is, by design, punitive. Civil asset forfeiture law is not. Non-conviction based forfeiture does embrace a number of traditional civil law concepts: preventative, remedial and reparative justice. Concepts drawn from the law of property (valid title to property), tort (compensation to victims) and equity (unjust enrichment) are combined into a judicially controlled process.

HOW DOES CIVIL ASSET FORFEITURE WORK?

Civil asset forfeiture proceedings are brought *in rem* by the appropriate government authority.[18] The proceedings are judicially controlled,[19] generally under the auspices of the jurisdiction's rules of civil procedure. Notice is given to parties with a known interest to the property: titleholders, mortgagors and so on. The state bears the burden, as plaintiff or applicant, of establishing its

---

[2003] 1 SACR 561 (Constitutional Court). See also *National Director of Public Prosecutions v. Mohunram and Others* [2007] ZACC 4 (Constit Court); affirming *Mohunram and Another v. National Director of Public Prosecutions & Another* CCT 19/06, 26 March 2007 (South African Constitutional Court) [2006] 1 SACR 554 (S.C.A.); see references to this series of cases in Chapter 4 of this book.

[17]   See *DPP (WA) v. Bridge and Others* [2006] WASC 36 (Bridge had stolen $100 000, which was squandered on a trip and on shares in a diamond venture that failed. The court allowed the state to enforce a 'criminal benefits declaration' against other assets).

[18]   In Australia, for example, there are federal and state civil asset forfeiture laws. The federal proceedings are launched by the Director of Public Prosecutions. In New South Wales, an agency, the New South Wales Crime Commission, brings the proceeding; see Chapter 5 of this volume in general for the practice in Australia.

[19]   In the US there are federal 'administrative' forfeiture proceedings: 38 per cent of cases are uncontested, leading to forfeitures of $456 million. 29 per cent of forfeitures are civil and contested ($348 million) and the remaining 33 per cent ($400 million) are conviction-based: see S. Cassella (2007), 'The Case for Civil Forfeiture: why *In Rem* Proceedings are an Essential Tool for Recovering the Proceeds of Crime', 25th Cambridge International Symposium on Economic Crime, 27 September 2007, at p. 5: see for further reference Chapter 2 of this book. Property can be seized under a judicially authorized warrant. Notice is given to owners. If they choose not to contest, the property can be forfeited without a court order (there are some limitations to this: realty cannot be forfeited in this manner). See for example, *Prosecution and Defence of Forfeiture Cases*, *supra* para. 2.05, which attempts to explain the process of a typical civil asset forfeiture case, although it does not reflect the amendments under the Civil Asset Forfeiture Reform Act 2000.

case on a balance of probabilities.[20] The theory used in the court varies from jurisdiction to jurisdiction and case to case. Cases regarding proceeds of unlawful activity may involve tracing of funds from unlawful activity into an asset. The simplest case may involve the cash proceeds of drug deals, where they are found on a courier who is transporting the money from one place to another. The money is unexplained wealth in the hands of the courier. If that courier is able to place, layer and integrate their illicit profits into the financial system, the case becomes more complex.[21]

If the state satisfies the court that the property ought to be subject to forfeiture, the parties claiming an interest then have an opportunity to show the court that their interests in the property ought to be protected. This can occur in any number of ways. The wife of an alleged insider trader convinced the court that her personal jewellery ought to be exempted from the proceeding.[22] As each jurisdiction has evolved, specialized rules have been developed for each situation.[23] Each type of unlawful activity lends itself to particular types of interests. For example, in Canada marijuana hydroponic indoor growing operations are conducted in houses, which are often financed with a bank mortgage. The courts will protect that interest where there is no evidence of knowledge of what use the property would be put.[24]

---

[20] See *State of Queensland v. Brooks* [2005] QSC 390 is an interesting factual example; the state met the burden on some assets and failed on others. *State of Queensland v. Brooks* [2005] QSC 204 is a related case.

[21] Cases are factually interesting as money laundering can take an endless variety of forms, some of which are not intended. In *US v. Betancourt* (2005) 422 F. 3d 240 (5th Cir), the proceeds of drug money were traced into the purchase of a lottery ticket in Houston. Betancourt had bought the ticket with a neighbor, and they agreed to split the winnings. Betancourt's 50 per cent share of the $5 million winning ticket was forfeited.

[22] See *Teresita Tan v. DPP* [2004] NSWSC 952 (SC); there are numerous related cases including *CDPP v. In the Matter of Specified Property of Universal Lionshare and Another* [2005] NSWSC 91 and *DPP v. Tan* [2003] NSWSC 717 and [2004] NSWSC 856.

[23] Some of the provisions of the Civil Asset Forfeiture Reform Act 2000 passed by the US Congress can be traced to cases like *US v. 92 Buena Vista Avenue* (1993), 507 US 111: see references to this case in Chapter 2 of this book.

[24] In *AG (Ont.) v. Marihuana Growing Equipment et al.* [2005] OJ 6008 (Ont. S.C.J.) (hereinafter *Marihuana Growing Equipment*), Ingram J ruled that 'as there was no suggestion that the bank was aware of or party to the unlawful activities carried out on the property, the Crown shall take the property subject to the interests of the Toronto Dominion Bank'.

RECENT DEVELOPMENTS IN CANADA

Constitutional Background

Canada is a federation of ten provinces and three territories with both provincial and federal levels of legislative authority, which colours the landscape of forfeiture in Canada. Canada's Constitution Act 1867 gives the Canadian Parliament the power to legislate criminal law and criminal procedure, except for the constitution of the criminal courts, under section 91(27), while each provincial legislature has exclusive power to legislate 'property and civil rights' under section 92(13). In Canada, offences under the Criminal Code of Canada (hereinafter Criminal Code) are prosecuted by lawyers acting on behalf of the provincial Attorneys General; whereas offences under the Controlled Drugs and Substances Act (hereinafter CDSA) are prosecuted by lawyers acting on behalf of the federal Attorney General. In some cases, with charges from both the CDSA and the Criminal Code that would be prosecuted by different levels of government, either the federal or provincial prosecution services delegate authority to the other to prosecute the whole of the case.

In a number of countries that have civil asset forfeiture legislation the fundamental argument against civil asset forfeiture is that the state is trying to carry out a criminal law purpose in a civil law forum; the criminal law having greater protection for individuals than are available in civil law. In Canada, this is seen not only as a fundamental issue between civil and criminal law but also as a constitutional issue as between the legislative authority of the federal parliament and the provincial legislatures.[25]

Criminal Law Background

This chapter is not meant to be a complete review of Canadian criminal asset forfeiture law and therefore should not be taken as being comprehensive. For a complete review there are excellent texts available.[26] This review will deal primarily with the Criminal Code.

Canada has two primary statutes that govern the punishment of criminal offences, the Criminal Code and the CDSA. Under these statutes, there is a

---

[25]   This issue went to the highest court in Canada, the Supreme Court of Canada, with a hearing held on 12 November 2008 in *Attorney General of Ontario v. $29,020 in Canadian Currency et al.*

[26]   See R. Hubbard, T. Murphy, F. O'Donnell and P. DeFreitas (eds) (2004), *Money Laundering and Proceeds of Crime*, Toronto, Canada: Irwin Law (hereinafter *Money Laundering and Proceeds of Crime*); see also P. German (1998), *Proceeds of Crime*, Toronto, Canada: Thomson Carswell, a looseleaf publication.

scheme for criminal asset forfeiture. There are essentially four methods for exercising criminal asset forfeiture.

First, under section 462.37 of the Criminal Code a person who has been convicted of a 'designated offence'[27] or is found guilty but receives an absolute or conditional discharge is subject to criminal asset forfeiture as part of their sentence. Criminal asset forfeiture is not available for offences that are strict summary offences or that are hybrid offences prosecuted summarily.

Criminal asset forfeiture is made only upon application by the prosecutor, where the court is satisfied upon a balance of probabilities that the property is the 'proceeds of crime'[28] and that the offence was committed in relation to the property. Where the prosecutor does not satisfy the court that the property was in relation to the proven offence, then where the prosecutor proves beyond a reasonable doubt that the property is proceeds of crime then the court may forfeit the property. The offence for which forfeiture may be ordered can be one committed in Canada or outside of Canada, if the act or omission if it had occurred in Canada would have been an offence. The property can be located either inside or outside of Canada. Where a court cannot make an order of forfeiture of the property because of some defect with respect to the property a 'fine in lieu of forfeiture' may be ordered.[29] If the fine is not paid then a consecutive jail term, determined by statute, shall be ordered.

Secondly, under section 462.38 of the Criminal Code there is a stand-alone application for forfeiture of property for the situation where a proceeding for a designated offence has been commenced but that the accused person has either absconded from the jurisdiction or died. The court must be satisfied beyond reasonable doubt, *inter alia*, that the property is proceeds of crime.

Thirdly, under section 490.1 of the Criminal Code forfeiture of property may also be made upon application after conviction of a person for an

---

[27]   See Criminal Code, s. 462.3: a 'designated offence' to be '(*a*) any offence that may be prosecuted by indictment under this [Criminal Code] or any other Act of Parliament, other than an indictable offence prescribed by regulation, or (*b*) a conspiracy or an attempt to commit, being an accessory after the fact in relation to, or any counselling in relation to, an offence referred to in paragraph (*a*)'.

[28]   See Criminal Code, s. 462.3: 'proceeds of crime' means 'any property, benefit or advantage, within or outside Canada, obtained or derived directly or indirectly as a result of (*a*) the commission in Canada of a designated offence, or (*b*) an act or omission anywhere that, if it had occurred in Canada, would have constituted a designated offence'.

[29]   See Criminal Code, s. 462.37 (3): the defects are that the property '(*a*) cannot, on the exercise of due diligence, be located; (*b*) has been transferred to a third party; (*c*) is located outside Canada; (*d*) has been substantially diminished in value or rendered worthless; or (*e*) has been commingled with other property that cannot be divided without difficulty'.

indictable offence where the court is satisfied that the property is 'offence-related property'. 'Offence-related property' is any property, within or outside Canada, by means or in respect of which an indictable offence under the Criminal Code is committed, that is used in any manner in connection with the commission of an indictable offence under the Criminal Code, or that is intended for use for the purpose of committing an indictable offence. Similar 'offence-related property' provisions exist in the CDSA. The wording of the section seemed to allow that if a person was convicted of one offence then 'offence related property' from any number of occurrences were open to forfeiture. 'Offence-related property' has been limited to the property that is specific to the offence proven.[30]

Fourthly, under section 490(9) of the Criminal Code, where property has been seized by the police and is not required for proceedings the court is required to either return the property to the person from whom it was taken, if they had the property lawfully, or forfeit it where the person did not have it lawfully. This is in essence a section that is meant to deal with property that has been seized but that has not been dealt with in a proceeding or there has been no proceeding brought. Courts have held that section 490(9) is an independent basis for forfeiture.[31]

The burden of proof is on the prosecutor to establish that the property is unlawfully in the possession of the party from whom it was seized on a beyond a reasonable doubt standard.[32] Originally, this section dealt merely with the disposition of property that was not dealt with during criminal proceedings or for which criminal proceedings had not been commenced. It was seen as a shorter route to forfeiture, however courts have decided that the proceedings are to be conducted as if they were a criminal trial.[33] Anecdotally, this has significantly reduced the use of section 490(9) as a means of criminal asset forfeiture. While this procedure does not put a person at risk of a criminal conviction, the Federal Prosecution Service (now the Public Prosecution Service of Canada) has conceded that the Canadian Charter of Rights and Freedoms (hereinafter Charter of Rights) applies.[34]

---

[30]   A narrow approach has been adopted by the courts to mean property related to the specific offence under the CDSA not any offence-related property. See *R. v. Hape* 2005 CanLII 26591 (ON C.A.) at paras 31–42. All CanLII cases are available online at www.canlii.org.

[31]   See *Money Laundering and Proceeds of Crime, supra* at pp. 159–178.

[32]   See *R. v. West* 2005 CanLII 30052 (ON C.A.) (hereinafter *West*), at paras 22 and 23.

[33]   See *West*, at para. 27.

[34]   See *R. v. Raponi* 2004 SCC 50 at para. 50, on the basis of *R. v. Daley* 2001 ABCA 155.

Although the Charter of Rights is to be applied, the force upon which it is to be applied is blunted.[35]

International Assistance for Criminal Asset Forfeiture

When asked to assist other countries using criminal asset forfeiture there are two avenues for Canada to provide assistance: bringing a criminal proceeding in Canada or seeking enforcement of foreign forfeiture orders through the Mutual Legal Assistance in Criminal Matters Act 1985, a federal statute. First, under the Criminal Code 'proceeds of crime' can be property either inside or outside of Canada that is derived from a designated criminal offence committed within Canada or outside of Canada, if the same occurrence having occurred in Canada would be a designated criminal offence. The most difficult way for Canada to assist other countries to recover proceeds of crime is to prosecute a criminal offence committed elsewhere in the world and then seek forfeiture of the assets located in Canada.[36]

The second way for Canada to lend assistance in criminal matters is through the application of the Mutual Legal Assistance in Criminal Matters Act 1985 sections 9.3 (seizure orders) and 9.4 (forfeiture orders). The other jurisdiction in these cases must have seizure and forfeiture orders already granted in their own jurisdiction in order to proceed under either of the two sections.

International Assistance in Civil Asset Forfeiture

Currently, there is no civil asset forfeiture equivalent to the Mutual Legal Assistance in Criminal Matters Act 1985. The provincial jurisdictions in Canada that have civil asset forfeiture all contemplate that property in their jurisdiction is subject to forfeiture even if unlawful activity occurred outside of their jurisdiction that would have been an offence if it had occurred in Canada or in the province. Ontario has the advantage of being able to proceed either by application or action. An application under Ontario law is a proceeding, which is based on affidavit evidence. Civil forfeiture statutes, including Ontario's, have provisions allowing inter-jurisdictional agreements, which allow for the sharing of information and assets. This approach was pioneered by officials with the Asset Recovery Agency in Belfast working with the Criminal Assets Bureau in Dublin.

---

[35] See *West*, at para. 46.
[36] See *supra* n. 29.

Civil Asset Forfeiture

There are seven provinces in Canada that have passed a form of civil asset forfeiture. The seminal statute, Ontario's Civil Remedies Act,[37] permits the Attorney General to bring four types of civil proceedings: civil asset forfeiture for proceeds of unlawful activity, a similar process for instruments of unlawful activity, instruments of unlawful activity related to road safety[38] and *in personam* conspiracy proceeding. The statute was recently amended by Bill 128 and then Bill 203, which received Royal Assent on 15 December 2005 and 4 June 2007 respectively. Alberta's Victims Restitution and Compensation Payment Act 2002 has unproclaimed provisions to strengthen the ability of the Crown to enforce Criminal Code restitution orders. Manitoba has taken a unique approach, a police-led forfeiture regime, under the Criminal Property Forfeiture Act 2004. Saskatchewan's Seizure of Criminal Property Act 2004, which is similar to Manitoba's law, came into force on 3 November 2005. British Columbia's Civil Forfeiture Act 2005 was given Royal Assent in late 2005.[39] In 2007, Québec passed an Act Respecting the Forfeiture, Administration and Appropriation of Proceeds and Instruments of Unlawful Activities and Nova Scotia passed their Civil Forfeiture Act 2007.

Ontario

The Civil Remedies Act has a statement of legislative intent in Part I of the statute. The purpose of the law is to provide civil remedies that will assist in four ways: first, compensating persons who suffer pecuniary and non-pecuniary losses as a result of unlawful activities; secondly, to prevent persons who engage in unlawful activities and others from keeping property that was acquired as a result of unlawful activity; thirdly, to prevent property from being used to engage in unlawful activity; and fourthly, to prevent injury to the public that may result from conspiracies to engage in unlawful activities.

Under Part II of Civil Remedies Act, the Superior Court of Justice, in a proceeding commenced by the Attorney General of Ontario, is authorized to make an order forfeiting property to the Crown in right of Ontario if the court finds that the property is the proceeds of unlawful activity, except where to do

---

[37]   Formerly, the Remedies for Organized Crime and Other Unlawful Activities Act, 2001.

[38]   Part III.1 of the Civil Remedies Act, adds a separate type of instrument. It relates specifically to 'vehicles' used in 'vehicular unlawful activity'. This specifically deals with vehicles that are used or intended to be used by people with two or more suspensions related to drinking and driving offences. Part III.1 was proclaimed on 20 February 20 2008.

[39]   Royal assent was received on 24 November 2005.

'would clearly not be in the interest of justice'. Under section 2 of Civil Remedies Act, 'unlawful activity' is defined as any breach of the laws of Canada, Ontario, other provinces and other countries if the activity had occurred in Ontario. Provision is made to protect the interests of 'legitimate owners', whose definition includes someone who acquired the property before the unlawful activity occurred for fair market value.

Part II also creates statutory interlocutory orders for the preservation of property that is the subject of a proceeding. The courts in Ontario have accepted the common law *Mareva* injunction;[40] however, the legislature decided that the Attorney General should have access to a statutory injunction to preserve property. Unlike the common law *Mareva* injunction, where the standard is a strong case, the statutory standard is a reasonably held belief in the nexus between unlawful activity and the proceeds that is being sought to be preserved.[41]

Where property is subject to an interlocutory order there is a mechanism to permit the property to be used to cover reasonable legal expenses to defend title to the said property. Reasonable legal expenses are regulated at the legal aid rate for civil lawyers in the province. Legal expenses are also limited to a portion (on a sliding scale) of the preserved asset, which is always under 25 per cent of the liquidated value of any preserved assets. In the Criminal Code there is provision to use the preserved property for not only legal expenses to defend the person against the criminal charge(s) but also living expenses. Legal expenses under the Criminal Code scheme pay faint attention to the legal aid rate[42] and appear to only be limited by the absolute amount of the property that was preserved.

Property forfeited to the Crown under Part II of Civil Remedies Act is converted to money and paid into a special purpose account.[43] Payments may be made out of a statutorily created special purpose account to compensate

---

[40] See *Mareva Campania Nariera SA of Panama v. International Bulk Carriers SA* [1980] 1 All ER 213, [1975] 2 Lloyd's Rep 509 (hereinafter *Mareva*), which was accepted in Ontario and Canada in *Liberty National Bank & Trust Co. v. Atkin* (1981), 31 O.R. (2d) 715, 121 D.L.R. (3d) 160 (OHC) and *Aetna Financial Services v. Feigelman* [1985] 1 S.C.R. 2 (SCC).

[41] Civil Remedies Act, s. 4(2) states: 'Except where it would clearly not be in the interest of justice, the court shall make an order... if the court is satisfied that there are reasonable grounds to believe that the property is proceeds of unlawful activity.'

[42] See the Criminal Code, s. 462.34(5) requires the court to 'take into account the legal aid tariff of the province'. Expenses are rarely, if ever, limited to that tariff rate by the courts. See *R. v. Marsh* 2003 CanLII 1009 (ON S.C.) where approximately six times the legal aid rate was paid to one of three counsel, the other two receiving approximately four times and twice the rate and an articling student was paid nearly double the rate for students.

[43] See Civil Remedies Act, s. 6.

persons who suffered pecuniary or non-pecuniary losses as a result of the unlawful activity and for other specified purposes. Claims for compensation are adjudicated administratively by independent adjudicators.

Under Part III of Civil Remedies Act, the Superior Court of Justice, in a proceeding commenced by the Attorney General of Ontario, is authorized to make an order forfeiting property to the Crown if the court finds that the property is an instrument of unlawful activity. An 'instrument' is property that is likely to be used to engage in unlawful activity, which in turn is intended to result in the acquisition of other property or in serious bodily harm to someone.[44] Provision is made to protect the interests of 'responsible owners'. 'Responsible owner' is a defined term meaning a person who either had no knowledge of the use the property was being put or if having knowledge then did everything reasonable to stop the activity or inform the proper authorities about the activity.[45] Part III also contains provisions that are similar to the provisions in Part II that deal with interlocutory orders, the payment of reasonable legal expenses, the payment of money from forfeited property into a special purpose account and the payment of compensation and other purposes from the special purpose account.

Part III.1 of Civil Remedies Act was enacted as a result of Bill 203; vehicles may be forfeited where it is shown that the vehicle was or is likely to be used to engage in vehicular unlawful activity. The vehicle must be shown to be owned or in the care or control of a person who has two prior suspensions in the past ten years for vehicular unlawful activity. These amendments are aimed at removing motor vehicles from the roadways of Ontario that are used by people who habitually drink and drive. There are also sections that deal with the protection of responsible vehicle owners. While awaiting adjudication of the government's claim against the vehicle, the public can be made safe in a number of ways including impounding of the vehicle or the requirement that an ignition interlock device be installed before being returned.

Finally under Part IV of Civil Remedies Act, in a proceeding commenced by the Attorney General of Ontario, the Superior Court of Justice is authorized to make any order that the court considers just if it finds that two or more persons conspired to engage in unlawful activity, one or more of the parties to the conspiracy knew or ought to have known that the unlawful activity would be likely to result in injury to the public, and injury to the public has resulted from or would be likely to result from the unlawful activity.[46] For example, an

---

44   *Ibid.* s. 7(1).
45   *Ibid.*
46   *Ibid.* s. 13(1).

order could require a party to the conspiracy to pay damages to the Crown in right of Ontario for any injury to the public resulting from the unlawful activity and, for the purpose of preventing or reducing the risk of injury to the public, an order could require any person to do or refrain from doing anything specified in the order.[47] Part IV also authorizes interlocutory orders for the purpose of preventing or reducing the risk of injury to the public. If the Crown receives money pursuant to an order for the payment of damages, the money must be paid into a special purpose account and payments may be made out of the account for specified purposes.

For clarity sake, the Civil Remedies Act states that the standard to be applied in making decisions generally under the statute is the civil standard (a balance of probabilities). The Supreme Court of Canada recently decided in *F.H. v. McDougall* that there will only be one standard of proof required in civil proceedings whether or not the allegations are of a criminal nature.[48] This would suggest that there is a stigma attached to a civil *in personam* proceeding accusing a person of a criminal act(s). Under the Civil Remedies Act, it is not the person who holds title that is being tried or is being penalized for some wrongdoing, if that were to be the case then it would be an *in personam* proceeding. The Civil Remedies Act is an *in rem* proceeding, against the property; it merely examines the origins or uses of property. Property is not stigmatized in any legally recognized way that requires protection. If the provenance of the property is found to be of unlawful origin then the title is void and the property is forfeited to the state. As of the writing of this chapter, no conspiracy proceeding has been commenced under the Civil Remedies Act; it is, however, arguable that the evidence would have to be clear and convincing to establish the Attorney General's case in a conspiracy proceeding on a balance of probabilities.

---

47   *Ibid.* s. 13(4).
48   See *F.H. v. McDougall*, 2008 SCC 53:

[40] Like the House of Lords, I think it is time to say, once and for all in Canada, that there is only one civil standard of proof at common law and that is proof on a balance of probabilities. Of course, context is all important and a judge should not be unmindful, where appropriate, of inherent probabilities or improbabilities or the seriousness of the allegations or consequences. However these considerations do not change the standard of proof. I am of the respectful opinion that the alternatives I have listed above should be rejected for the reasons that follow.

[49] In the result, I would reaffirm that in civil cases there is only one standard of proof and that is proof on a balance of probabilities. In all civil cases, the trial judge must scrutinize the relevant evidence with care to determine whether it is more likely than not that an alleged event occurred

The Civil Remedies Act extensively uses Ontario's Rules of Civil Procedure (hereinafter Rules) for procedural issues and does not seek to create a new legal framework for civil asset forfeiture in Ontario. For example, the Rules set out what notice provisions are to be used to let a necessary party know that there is a proceeding before the courts. Where notice cannot be served personally, the Rules set out what steps are to be taken for substitutional service or to deem service to have been made.[49]

Bill 128 The Law Enforcement and Forfeited Property Management Statute Law Amendment Act 2004 amends a number of statutes including the Civil Remedies Act. Generally speaking, the amendments relate to the handling, management and disposition of property preserved or forfeited under the Civil Remedies Act. The court's power to manage and in some cases dispose of property during the interlocutory stages of a proceeding is clarified. The statute also creates a mechanism to sell or dispose of property, which formerly had been addressed under the Escheats Act. There are provisions to clarify the Attorney General's ability to collect information, particularly in aid of victim compensation. There are also technical personal information sections to conform to the Personal Health Information Protection Act 2004.

Bill 203 The Safer Roads for a Safer Ontario Act 2007 amended the Highway Traffic Act 1990 and Civil Remedies Act. Besides adding Part III.1 to the Civil Remedies Act, it also made a number of technical changes including formalizing the fact that proceedings under section 15.6 of Civil Remedies Act are *in rem* rather than *in personam* proceedings. This is simply a codification of law as affirmed in the *Attorney General of Ontario v. $29,020 in Canadian Currency et al.* (hereinafter *Chatterjee*) decisions.[50] Persons who have an interest in property are required to be notified of a proceeding, but unless they file a notice of appearance they do not become parties under section 15.5. The name of the Remedies for Organized Crime and Other Unlawful Activities Act 2001 was formally changed to the Civil Remedies Act 2001.

---

[49]   Other jurisdictions make mixed or even minimal use of the Rules. Manitoba's Criminal Property Forfeiture Act 2004, s. 8 stipulates that the rules of discovery do not apply. The unproclaimed civil forfeiture provision at Alberta's Victim Restitution and Compensation Payment Act 2001, s. 4 stipulates the form of proof for an *ex parte* order in a fashion similar to Ireland's Proceeds of Crime Act 1996. See further discussions under sub-heading 'Alberta' below in this chapter.

[50]   [2005] CanLII 24251 (Ont. S.C.J.) (hereinafter *Chatterjee*); affirmed [2007] OJ No. 2102; 2007 ONCA 406 (CanLII).

Alberta

Alberta's Victims Restitution and Compensation Act 2001 gives the Minister of Justice and Attorney General for Alberta (hereinafter Minister) the power to restrain and dispose of property in the civil courts. Part of the statute permits the Minister to launch an action[51] to obtain restitution or compensation for victims. A peace officer must investigate the underlying matter, have reasonable grounds to believe that an illegal act[52] has been committed and reasonably believe property has been acquired as a result of that illegal act. Property must be restrained *ex parte*[53] based on an affidavit of the investigating officer. If the court finds that there are reasonable grounds to believe that the property has been acquired by illegal means,[54] the property can be restrained through a variety of means.[55] Powers are given to the police to detain property for up to 72 hours without judicial authorization;[56] an arrest power is also granted in the statute to backstop the property detention. The court is given a broad range of powers to review the restraint.[57] Failure to comply results, as well, in forfeiture.[58]

Following the restraint, a disposal hearing is held by the courts to determine whether the property was acquired by illegal means, what interests the parties may have and what entitlements the victims may have. The statute creates some procedural rules (substitutional service), but other rules presumably rely on the standard rules of civil procedure. A respondent forfeits his or her interest if he or she fails to comply with procedural steps,

---

[51]   Compare this with the option of either an application or action in Ontario: generally applications are conducted through affidavit evidence and take less time to move through the courts.

[52]   See Victims Restitution and Compensation Act 2001, s. 3(2) (hereinafter VRCA 2001); *ibid.* s. 1(2) includes contraventions and offences under the Criminal Code, the CDSA or other statute (Federal or Alberta) as specified in regulation. To date there has not been such a designation.

[53]   This was an issue in *Re The Criminal Proceeds Confiscation Act 2002 (Qld)* [2003] QCA 249.

[54]   'Illegal act' and the preconditions for a proceeding are both defined, but not 'illegal means'.

[55]   The court is given broad jurisdiction to make orders that normally would be in the purview of the Rules of Civil Procedure, including directions on parties, service, method of service and so on.

[56]   See VRCA 2001, s. 6(6): failure to comply with the officer can result in six months' imprisonment or a $10 000 fine or both.

[57]   Although the court is not given the grounds to deal with property interests (e.g. of legitimate owners).

[58]   See for example, VRCA 2001, s. 12(e): forfeiture ordered where the failure to comply with directions of a peace officer was without reasonable excuse and subject to a court order otherwise.

such as answering questions on examination. In a disposal hearing, the Minister must establish that the property has been acquired by illegal means. Then a respondent bears the onus to show his or her interest, that he or she has not been involved in an illegal act in respect of the restraint[59] and if purchased after the property was acquired by illegal means, he or she must have done so without knowledge of its[60] provenance. Where the Minister fails to meet the onus, the court is to revoke the restraint and may provide compensation for loss suffered as a result of the restraint of the property.[61] If the Crown meets its test the property can be disposed of in a variety of ways.[62] The standard of proof is the balance of probabilities. Part 2 of the statute also provides for restitution assistance post conviction. These provisions apply a variety of civil remedies to ensure that victims can be compensated and failure to comply can lead to fines and imprisonment. Finally, there are confiscation proceedings whereby the court can order the value of the property, earned by illegal acts, paid over the state for use in the grants program. This type of order would be made where there are no identifiable victims.

Manitoba

Manitoba's Criminal Property Forfeiture Act 2004 permits a police chief[63] to seek a forfeiture order for proceeds and instruments in Manitoba. A motion to preserve property can be made and within 10 days, notice must be given to the owner, the person in possession of the property, persons with registered interests as well as persons known to have an interest. Subject to legitimate property interests,[64] the court under section 14(1) is to forfeit

---

[59]   The use of 'illegal means' is intentionally not employed here, and there may be some question as to the statutory definition of 'illegal act'.

[60]   See VRCA 2001, s. 13(1)(b): it is for the respondent to show he/she did not know and would not reasonably be expected to know that the property had been acquired by illegal means.

[61]   *Ibid.* s. 14(a); this conflicts with *ibid.* s. 48 to some extent, which states that 'no costs and no payment of expenses may be awarded against the Minister...'; note also *ibid.* s. 47 does not permit an action against the Crown unless provided for in the statute.

[62]   The property can be returned, can be sold with a portion of a sale returned, or sold with proceeds (or a part thereof) to victims. This must be done in the proceeding. Any remaining money goes to the Crown for use in its grant process.

[63]   See Manitoba's Criminal Property Forfeiture Act 2004, s. 1: defined as a municipal chief or a Royal Canadian Mounted Police commanding officer or a special constable in charge of police services for a First Nation Community. The latter provision, given the federal jurisdiction over the property and civil rights of First Nation aboriginals, could have interesting operational implications.

[64]   *Ibid.* ss. 15–17: generally institutions or rights holders prescribed by regulation, such as banks, credit unions, trusts, insurance companies or government.

property it finds to be proceeds or an instrument of unlawful activity (unless to do so would clearly not be in the interest of justice).

There are some unique and interesting wrinkles in the Manitoba law. The rules of civil procedure apply except for the pre-trial discoveries and examinations.[65] The impact of this provision is not yet known. There are also presumptions, which apply to property belonging to members of criminal organizations as defined by the Criminal Code, or belonging to a corporation with such a person or such a person having significant interest, or transferred to another for consideration significantly less than fair market value by either of the above. If the above was found to be so, in the absence of evidence to the contrary, their property is deemed to be proceeds of unlawful activity.[66] Finally, all net funds from a forfeiture proceeding are directed to the Victim's Assistance Fund. In 2007, a number of significant amendments were introduced by Bill 14, the Criminal Property Forfeiture Amendment Act, which if passed will bring Manitoba's forfeiture law in line with the British Columbia and Ontario models.

Saskatchewan

Saskatchewan's Seizure of Criminal Property Act 2005 enables a police chief to apply to the court for a forfeiture order for proceeds and instruments. A motion to preserve property may be brought without notice for a period not exceeding 10 days.[67] Application for forfeiture must name the following as respondents and notice be given to the owner of the property: any person in possession of the property; any persons with prior registered interests; and any other person known to have an interest in the property.[68] A forfeiture order shall be made (unless it clearly would not be in the interests of justice) if the court finds the property to be proceeds or an instrument of unlawful activity.[69] Protection from forfeiture is provided to legitimate owners.[70] The issues respecting the disposition of forfeited property and the post-forfeiture distribution of money are dealt with by regulation.[71]

British Columbia

The Civil Forfeiture Act 2005 came into force on 19 April 2006. It received

---

[65] *Ibid.* s. 8.
[66] *Ibid.* s. 11.
[67] See Seizure of Criminal Property Act 2005, s. 6.
[68] *Ibid.* s. 3.
[69] *Ibid.* s. 7.
[70] *Ibid.* ss. 8–10.
[71] See Seizure of Criminal Property Regulations, R.R.S. c. S-46.001.

Royal Assent on 24 November 2005. British Columbia's Civil Forfeiture Act 2005 is very similar to Ontario's Civil Remedies Act. The statute creates a 'Director' reporting to the Solicitor General who is responsible for gathering information, bringing proceedings and managing the distribution of property forfeited under the statute.[72] Where the director is satisfied that property is proceeds or an instrument of unlawful activity, they may apply to court for forfeiture.[73] The director can apply for interim preservation orders freezing property, which the court shall grant (unless to do so would not be in the interests of justice) if it is satisfied there are reasonable grounds to believe the property is proceeds or an instrument.[74] The court may make protection orders to address property interests in instruments held by an 'uninvolved property holder' in instruments cases.[75] One difference between British Columbia's and Ontario's laws is that instruments in British Columbia are defined as property that has been used or that is likely to be used. Following forfeiture, the director may apply to the court seeking orders directing the disposition of property.[76] Forfeited funds are deposited in a specially created civil asset forfeiture account.[77] Payments out of the account may be made to administer the statute (which includes victim compensation), prevent unlawful activities, remediate the effect of unlawful activities and for other prescribed purposes.[78]

One particularly intriguing aspect of the British Columbia legislation can be found in its definition of 'proceeds'. Generally, civil asset forfeiture of proceeds occurs when the state shows that all or part of the property's provenance relates to unlawful activity. In addition, some jurisdictions like the UK have an entirely separate process to address the value created by crime.[79] For example, a court may make a finding that a drug dealer has earned a set amount of money from his or her crime. That amount, once determined, becomes a debt due to the state. Untainted assets can then be attached in order to discharge the debt. In British Columbia, these two systems (traceable property and value-based orders) appear to be combined into an *in rem*

---

[72] See Civil Forfeiture Act 2005, ss 21–22.
[73] *Ibid.* s. 3.
[74] *Ibid.* s. 8.
[75] *Ibid.* ss 12–13.
[76] *Ibid.* s. 14.
[77] *Ibid.* ss 25 and 26.
[78] *Ibid.* s. 27.
[79] See Proceeds of Crime Act 2002, s.76(7), which states if a person benefits from criminal conduct his benefit is the value of the property obtained. In Australia, these are far reaching: see for example *State of Queensland v. Brooks*, [2005] QSC 390 and a companion case [2005] QSC 204.

forfeiture process. Tainted assets can be forfeited. Untainted assets can be forfeited, where the interest in property is 'the equivalent in value to the amount of the increase in value, of the whole or the portion of the interest in property if the increase in value results directly or indirectly from unlawful activity'. Parsing this section is difficult. Could the 'Director' in British Columbia seek to attack untainted equivalent assets? This is an intriguing possibility. One challenge, though, in aggressively using this provision lies in section 6 of the Civil Forfeiture Act 2005, which vests a broad residual discretion to refuse to make an order where it 'is not in the interest of justice'. This threshold is lower for the court than in Ontario.

Nova Scotia
Nova Scotia passed two companion statutes in 2007 respecting civil forfeiture and property management. The Civil Forfeiture Act, 2007 is patterned largely on the Ontario and British Columbia model. Courts are empowered to freeze and forfeit proceeds and instruments in a civil proceeding. The definition of instruments is similar to British Columbia's in that property, which has been used or is likely to be used, can be adjudged an instrument by the court. There is a statutory protection for 'uninvolved interest holders' based on an 'interests of justice' test. The proceeds architecture contemplates protecting interests through partial orders of forfeiture; the court can make such attributions as it sees fit as between interests. The Assets Management and Disposition Act, 2007 empowers a statutorily created 'manager of assets' who can bring civil forfeiture proceedings and who can manage property that is the subject of a civil or in some cases criminal proceeding.[80]

Québec
Québec's Act Respecting the Forfeiture, Administration and Appropriation of Proceeds and Instruments of Unlawful Activity 2007 (hereinafter Forfeiture Act), creates a civil asset forfeiture scheme.[81] Québec's civil law tradition differs from the other jurisdictions discussed in this chapter.[82] The

---

[80]   In this respect, Nova Scotia has followed Québec's approach discussed below. Property management powers are given in respect of conviction-based proceedings brought under Criminal Code sections: 83.13, 462.331 or 490.81 (management orders); 462.33 or 490.8 (restraints); or 83.14, 199, 462.37, 462.38, 462.43, 490, 490.01, 490.02 or 490.1 (forfeitures).

[81]   The Forfeiture Act was granted Royal assent on 11 December 2007 and came into force on 1 September 2008.

[82]   Compare the discussion of the civil law tradition of Macau, see Chapter 11 of this book.

laws of property and obligations in Québec are informed by Roman law and would be far more recognizable to a continental lawyer than a barrister in London.[83] The civil asset forfeiture scheme, however, appears to have been derived from common law models; while very unique, the law appears to have been informed by other jurisdictions like Ontario. The Forfeiture Act attempts to wed common law ideas somewhat anchored in admiralty concepts to a different civil system. The Act had two stated purposes: to introduce civil asset forfeiture to Québec and to manage all forfeited property (both conviction and non-conviction based).

The Attorney General may bring proceedings for forfeiture of property that 'is in whole or in part directly or indirectly derived from or used to engage in unlawful activities'.[84] The court grants forfeiture where it is 'convinced' by the Attorney General. For instruments, the Attorney General must show that the owner, holder or possessor 'participated in the unlawful activities or was aware that the property was used to engage in such activities or could reasonably have been unaware that the property was so used'.[85] Unlawful activities include offences under the Criminal Code and the CDSA as well as 'penal offences' under Acts determined by the government. Presumably, the latter will be done by regulation.[86] One wrinkle has been added here: under section 7 of the Forfeiture Act, if the property derives from such a designated offence (as opposed to a Criminal Code offence), the court must be satisfied that the commission of such an offence resulted in substantial economic gain. This appears to be a safeguard: designated offences will generally not have the same gravity as offences under the Criminal Code; requiring the proof of substantial economic gain will temper the use of these provisions.[87] There is a dual criminality provision[88] and the Forfeiture Act applies to property in Québec. In Québec, possessors, holders and owners of property have certain assumed rights. The Forfeiture Act permits a court in an incidental application to declare those assumed rights unenforceable.

There are notice provisions prescribed in the Forfeiture Act. The owner, holder and possessor as well as anyone with rights in the property are to be

---

83   See H. Kelada (2006), *Civil Code du Québec, Texte Annote,* Toronto, Canada: Thomson Carswell, a looseleaf publication; see also J.G. Castel (1962), *The Civil Law System of the Province of Québec,* Toronto, Canada: Butterworths.

84   Forfeiture Act, s. 4.

85   *Ibid.* s. 7.

86   A similar approach was taken in the Prohibiting Profiting from the Recounting of Crimes Act 2002 (Ontario): see Ontario Regulation 235/03 in particular.

87   The types of provisions that may be designated could include consumer fraud offences, environmental offences or other similar offences.

88   Forfeiture Act, s. 3.

served. This type of provision is fairly typical in a civil asset forfeiture statute[89] although it seems somewhat incongruous beside provisions incorporating the rules of civil procedure (as Québec's law does). The rules of civil procedure typically have extensive rules and procedures on parties, notice, service and other procedural matters.

There are three kinds of property interests addressed by the statute. A forfeiture hearing plus an incidental hearing is required for those with presumptive property rights (possessors, holders and the owner). Third party rights held in good faith, including those with a secured creditor interest, are to be protected by the court; the Attorney General can ask the court to specify the amount of any secured debt. Finally, if proceeds have made their way to a third party, the property retains its nature as proceeds unless the owner can show that she was not 'or' could not reasonably have been aware of its unlawful nature at the time the rights were acquired. This disjunctive test could mean that nominee arrangements could flourish to evade the application of the statute. There is no limitation on how the property was acquired. So the heirs of a deceased outlaw motorcycle gang member could inherit his illicit wealth.[90] The court can, however, rule that a right is fictitious and deny a third party claim on that basis.

The Forfeiture Act contains some interesting presumptions. For a person claiming a presumptive right of good faith in property, the Attorney General must hold an incidental hearing to have that right declared unenforceable. The court will be asked to declare the property interest 'fictitious, simulated or unlawful' and hence unenforceable. The court may 'presume' unenforceability where the holder is related[91] through family or in the case of corporation control. For proceeds, property is presumed to derive from unlawful activity 'where the value of the defendant's patrimony is significantly disproportionate to the defendant's lawful income'. The Attorney General, in order to avail themselves of this presumption, must also show that the defendant either:

---

[89]   See for example Civil Forfeiture Act 2005 (British Columbia), s. 4.

[90]   Contrast this with Australian provisions, where death is a trigger that leads to forfeiture. The constitutionality was tested and the provisions upheld in *DPP (WA)* v. *The Public Trustee on Behalf of the Estate of the Late Stephen Retteghy* [1998] WASC 347 (SCWA); see also *Silbert* v. *DPP* [2004] HCA 9 (High Court, Australia).

[91]   See s. 10: being related to the owner as 'the owner's spouse, a blood relative of the owner up to the second degree, a person connected to the owner by marriage or a civil union up to the second degree, a person living under the same roof as the owner, a partner of the owner or a legal person of which the owner is a director or that the owner controls'.

1. frequently participates in unlawful activities likely to result in personal economic gain;
2. participates in the unlawful activities of a criminal organization within the meaning of the Criminal Code or acts in association with such an organization; or
3. is a legal person one of whose directors or officers participates in the unlawful activity of a criminal organization within the meaning of the Criminal Code or a legal person in which a person who participates in such activity holds a substantial interest.[92]

Proving the criminal organization aspects to get to this presumption will pose an interesting challenge. A conviction in a separate criminal proceeding gives rise to a presumption. This presumption has an interesting wrinkle: section 12 of the Forfeiture Act allows the court to presume a person convicted of a criminal offence to have participated in that unlawful activity except if they are discharged. The discharge exception, however, does not appear to apply to the criminal organization provisions under section 11. Under the Criminal Code:

> a criminal organization means a group, however organized, that
> *a.*   is composed of three or more persons in or outside Canada; and
> *b.*   has as one of its main purposes or main activities the facilitation or commission of one or more serious offences that, if committed, would likely result in the direct or indirect receipt of a material benefit, including a financial benefit, by the group or by any of the persons who constitute the group.[93]

A group that forms randomly for the immediate commission of a single offence is not a criminal organization. Proving a criminal organization offence, at least from a prosecutor's perspective, has proven difficult and led to mixed results.[94] That said, the Manitoba statute provides for a similar presumption.[95]

Typically, a civil asset forfeiture statute provides a court with the power to preserve property so that the *status quo* is maintained, against possible dissipation, while property title is litigated. In some instances the state avails itself of the existing legal standard; the UK applies the *Mareva* injunction

---

[92]   *Ibid.* ss 11(1)–11(3).
[93]   See the *Criminal Code*, s. 467.1(1).
[94]   See for example *R. v. Lindsay* (2004) 182 CCC (3d) 301 (SCJ) which dealt with a challenge to the provision based on *Canadian Charter of Rights and Freedoms* (hereinafter Charter of Rights), as well as *R. v. Accused No. 1* [2005] BCJ No. 2701 (BCSC) and *R. v. Smith* [2006] S.J. No.184 (Sask QB).
[95]   See Criminal Property Forfeiture Act 2004, s. 11.

standard to preservation orders.[96] Other jurisdictions apply a statutorily created standard.[97] The Québec Forfeiture Act is unique in this respect. Section 14 of the Forfeiture Act allows the Attorney General to seek a seizure in accordance with the existing civil rules; this is essentially the British model. However, as a precondition the Attorney General must show to the court that 'there is a reason to fear that the forfeiture of the property would otherwise be jeopardized or that the property would otherwise be destroyed, severely damaged or squandered'. In this regard, the reasoning of the South African courts in a series of challenges to their *ex parte* preservation powers might be useful to authorities. The court was faced with a challenge to the preservation powers under the civil asset forfeiture scheme in South Africa; the court held that an *ex parte* preservation power was essential to the overall scheme and was constitutionally justified.[98]

The Forfeiture Act also grants to the Attorney General legal authority to administer and deal with property that is either forfeited civilly or seized and restrained under a federal statute. This is a technical area that bears paying attention to. Ontario and the federal government have found it necessary to pass statutes in this regard.[99] There are also provisions addressing forfeited money and its relationship to the consolidated revenue fund. Again these provisions are critical to the successful operation of a civil asset forfeiture scheme.

CIVIL ASSET FORFEITURE LITIGATION IN CANADA

In *Attorney General of Ontario v. $78,000 (in rem)*, Mr Justice Crane analyzed Ontario's Civil Remedies Act and ordered the forfeiture of $78 000.[100] The respondent was a passenger in a motor vehicle[101] stopped

---

[96]   See *ARA v. Szepietowski* [2007] EWCA 766.

[97]   See for example Division 3, Part 4 of the Criminal Property Confiscation Act 2000 (Western Australia), s. 43(1)(b): for example, the DPP may apply for a freezing order on an *ex parte* basis if they can show that court that they are likely to seek an examination order within 21 days. Examination orders are compelled interrogatories ordered by the court under Part 5 of the statute.

[98]   There are a series of decisions but the relevant analysis can be found at para. 52 of *NDPP v. Mohamed NO and Others* [2003] 1 SACR 561 (Constitutional Court).

[99]   See the Seized Property Management Act 1993 (federal) and the Law Enforcement and Forfeited Property Management Statute Law Amendment Act 2005 (Ontario).

[100]   See *Ontario (Attorney General) v. $78,000 et al*, 2003 CanLII 16958 (ON S.C.) (hereinafter *$78,000*).

[101]   The driver chose not to participate in the proceedings.

in northwestern Ontario *en route* to Manitoba. The respondent conceded that the stop was lawful, but that the subsequent search (which led to finding $78 000 in the trunk) was not. The respondent sought to exclude the evidence produced by the search under section 24(2) of the Charter of Rights. The court refused to exclude the evidence, given the 'borderline breach' of the respondent's rights and his reduced expectation of privacy. As part of the factual substratum, the court noted that the story of the passenger was not credible: he claimed to be attending a Winnipeg wedding, but the car rental agreement would require him to drive back to Toronto in the 'order of 24 hours of continuous, non-stop driving'.[102] The distance from Toronto to Winnipeg through Thunder Bay by car is 2263 kilometres each way.

In the forfeiture application brought by the Crown, the court found that a *prima facie* case for forfeiture had been established. The respondent then challenged the proceeding on the grounds that the $78 000 was legitimate business money. He claimed that he had borrowed the money and was taking it to Winnipeg to buy items from a bankrupt company. The court, weighing all of the evidence and noting that the respondent did not adduce affidavits from the mystery lenders, rejected the respondent's assertion as 'totally incredible'. Forfeiture was ordered.

Another Ontario case is *Attorney General of Ontario v. Marihuana Growing Equipment et al.*[103] The forfeiture application was brought against real property used in an outdoor marijuana growing operation, on the primary basis that the real property was an instrument of unlawful activity.[104] The court held that the Attorney General had met the two part test for instruments in s. 7(1) of the Civil Remedies Act. Since one of the owners of the property admitted during cross-examination on her affidavit that she had been running a marijuana growing operation on the property, the first element required to find that the property was an instrument of unlawful activity was established: 'as it was not only intended to be used for unlawful activity, it was used for unlawful activity'.[105] The second part of the test, that the unlawful activity was intended or would likely result in the acquisition of other property was easily met, because the marijuana growing operation produced marijuana, which the owners sold to acquire more property, being money. The court issued a forfeiture order, subject to the interest of a third party lien holder (a bank) who claimed the right as a 'responsible

---

[102]   See *$78,000*, para. 13.
[103]   See *Marihuana Growing Equipment*.
[104]   Ontario had unsuccessfully argued that the real property was traceable as proceeds of earlier marijuana operations.
[105]   See *Marihuana Growing Equipment*, para. 18.

owner' (as per sections 7(1) and 8(3) of Civil Remedies Act) to protection from forfeiture.

The Supreme Court of Canada in *Martineau v. Minister of National Revenue* (hereinafter *Martineau*) addressed the validity of a customs forfeiture statute.[106] A customs officer alleged that Martineau made false statements and owed \$315 458 for the deemed value of goods. This process is known as an ascertained forfeiture. Martineau challenged the decision and the customs sought a civil discovery of Martineau. He objected, saying that the discovery would violate his right against self-incrimination under the Charter of Rights.[107] In an interlocutory motion, the court ruled that as the customs proceeding was civil not penal, Martineau could not avail himself of the right against self-incrimination (which applies only to criminal proceedings).[108]

In a unanimous decision by Fish J, the court upheld the findings of the lower courts that forfeiture under the Customs Act 1985 was achieved through civil, as opposed to criminal, proceedings. The court analyzed the issue in the light of three criteria: the objectives of the statute, the purpose of the sanction and the process leading to the imposition of the sanction.

In reviewing the legislative scheme, Fish J focused not on the nature of the act but the nature of the proceedings themselves. Martineau had argued that the customs officer imputed that he had made false statements, which in turn gave rise to criminal and civil consequences. Martineau argued that the choice of proceeding (civil asset forfeiture or prosecution) ought not to govern. If the consequences can be penal, then the constitutional analysis must invoke the right against self-incrimination. The court disagreed, finding that the analysis must focus not on the act but rather on the proceeding itself. A single act can give rise to more than one consequence; some consequences may be penal, others civil.

The appellant argued that the purpose of the custom's sanction was 'to *punish* the offender in order to produce a *deterrent effect* and *redress a wrong done to society*'[109] [emphasis added by the court]. The court rejected this argument for three reasons: first, the forfeiture mechanism is designed

---

[106] *Martineau v. Minister of National Revenue* [2004] SCC 81 (hereinafter *Martineau*). Indeed, the Court of Appeal applied this case in *Chatterjee*. Conviction-based forfeiture decisions like *R. v. Raponi* [2004] SCC 50 have not tended to shed much light on the issue of civil asset forfeiture.

[107] See Charter of Rights, s. 11(c): 'any person charged with an offence has the right ... not to be compelled to be a witness in proceedings against that person in respect of the offence'.

[108] The Supreme Court and the Court of Appeal upheld the decision: (2002), 216 FTR 218 (2003), 310 NR 235 (Fed CA).

[109] See *Martineau*, at para. 34.

to ensure compliance with the Customs Act, not to punish; secondly, while ascertained forfeiture has a deterrent effect, that in and of itself does not make the proceeding criminal; thirdly, the forfeiture provisions are not meant to redress a wrong done to society and do not factor in the principles of criminal liability or sentencing.[110] The court noted the following in the civil asset forfeiture proceeding: no one is charged, no information is laid, no one is summoned to a court of criminal jurisdiction, no criminal record results. At worst, a defendant risks a financial consequence from a civil action.[111]

In reviewing jurisprudence, the court noted with approval that the US Supreme Court had recognized the validity of civil asset forfeiture statutes since 1789.[112] Modern jurisprudence in the US on civil asset forfeiture developed out of 19th century cases on customs (the main source of public revenue prior to the advent of income tax in the 20th century) and piracy.[113] Martineau argued that the magnitude of the ascertained forfeiture ($315 458) was six times larger than a fine for false reporting, and therefore constituted a true penal consequence. The court held that a fine is a consequence distinct from civil asset forfeiture. Arguably one of the most relevant passages, from a civil asset forfeiture perspective, was given at paragraph 63 of the judgment: '[I]n addition, forfeiture is an *in rem* proceeding in which the subject is the thing itself. In such a proceeding, the guilt or innocence of the owner of the forfeited property is irrelevant.' In *Martineau*, the Supreme Court of Canada has signalled that civil asset forfeiture mechanisms are alive and well in Canada.

The constitutional validity of Ontario's Civil Remedies Act was reviewed at the trial level by Loukidelis J of the Superior Court of Justice in *Chatterjee*.[114] In this case, police stopped a vehicle for a routine traffic offence, and arrested the driver when it was discovered that he was in violation of the conditions of his release on bail in a pending criminal case. A search of the vehicle incident to the arrest turned up $29 020 in cash that 'smelled of marihuana'. Also in the car was equipment associated with the indoor growing of marihuana, which the respondent said he found and kept

---

[110]   *Ibid.* paras 35–39.
[111]   *Ibid.* para. 45.
[112]   Citing *Helvering v. Mitchell* (1938), 303 US 391.
[113]   See for example, *The Palmyra* (1827), 25 US 1 and *Cliquot's Champagne* (1865), 70 US 114. In the 20th Century, jurisprudence has dealt with prohibition (*Van Oster v. Kansas* (1926) 272 US 465), drugs (*Calero-Toledo v. Pearson Yacht Leasing* (1974) 416 US 663), and prostitution (*Bennis v. Michigan* (1996), 516 US 442): see Chapter 2 of this book generally for references to these cases.
[114]   See *Chatterjee*.

while cleaning out the apartment he had shared with his best friend. The forfeiture application commenced by the Attorney General alleged the currency was proceeds and/or instruments of unlawful activity. The driver of the vehicle then brought a motion challenging the constitutionality of Civil Remedies Act. He argued the statute was: (1) an invalid attempt by the province to legislate in relation to the criminal law;[115] and (2) violated the Charter of Rights. Both grounds were rejected by the court.

First, the court accepted the Crown's argument that the Civil Remedies Act fell within the province's power to legislate in relation to property and civil rights, the administration of justice, and over matters of a local nature in the province:

> the real purpose of the *Civil Remedies Act* is to disgorge unlawful financial gains to compensate victims and to suppress the conditions that lead to unlawful activities by removing incentives. The case law is clear that provincial governments possess the legislative authority to pursue both of these goals.[116]

The court expressly relied on *Martineau* in holding (at paragraph 52 of the decision) that civil asset forfeiture proceedings create a valid, *in rem* civil mechanism, which is entirely different from a criminal proceeding. The court suggested that a stand-alone civil asset forfeiture statute would be *ultra vires* the federal government. Conviction based forfeiture and forfeiture to support clear federal areas, like customs, would be valid; a general civil asset forfeiture provision like Ontario's statute could not be passed by the federal government.[117] The court's ruling is consistent with civil asset forfeiture jurisprudence, which rejects defence assertions that the law is 'criminal' not really 'civil' in its operation.

Mr Chatterjee, the driver of the vehicle, argued that the operation of the statute violated his constitutional rights under the Charter of Rights. Those rights include section 7 (life, liberty and security of person), section 8 (search and seizure), section 9 (arbitrary detention) and section 11(d) (presumption of innocence). The Charter of Rights arguments were rejected for various reasons, the main grounds being: it is people, not property that are protected by the Charter of Rights. The court noted that no penalty

---

[115] In Canada, property and civil rights are matters for the province (Constitution Act 1867, s. 92(13)); criminal law is a matter for the federal government (*ibid.* s. 91(27)).

[116] See *Chatterjee*, para. 47; see in general Constitution Act 1867, *ibid.* s. 91(27) and s. 92(13).

[117] The court cited *R. v. Zelensky* [1978] 2 SCR 90 and P. Hogg (1997), *Constitutional Law of Canada*, Scarborough, Ontario, Canada: Thomson Canada, a looseleaf publication, at pp. 18–25.

attaches to a person and therefore little or no stigma can be experienced by an individual, and because civil asset forfeiture does not create a criminal offence, the civil standard of proof suffices.

The Court of Appeal for Ontario on 30 May 2007 released its judgment in *Chatterjee*. The constitutional judgment of Loukidelis J was affirmed by a unanimous panel and the forfeiture of the property in question was upheld. The Court found that the Civil Remedies Act was not an infringement on the criminal law jurisdiction of the federal government and solely dealt with the civil consequences of unlawful activity. It noted that the Northern Ireland Court of Appeal in *Walsh v. Director of the Assets Recovery Agency* came to the same decision dealing with a civil asset forfeiture law as the Supreme Court of Canada did in *Martineau* when dealing with the Customs Act.[118] It also noted that if the Civil Remedies Act intruded at all into the federal jurisdiction in criminal law, it was only incidentally as is likely to happen in any federal state. As the Supreme Court of Canada did in *Martineau*, the Ontario Court of Appeal found that there was no breach of section 11 of the Charter of Rights, as no person was charged with an offence.

Canada's highest court, the Supreme Court of Canada, granted leave to appeal the Ontario Court of Appeal's decision in *Chatterjee*, and the appeal was heard on 12 November 2008. The issue is whether Part II, the proceeds sections of the Civil Remedies Act, are *ultra vires* the province's legislature.

The Supreme Court of British Columbia in *British Columbia (Civil Forfeiture Act, Director) v. Tse et al.* on a hearing for interim preservation dealt with the issue of a building being a proceed of the illegal activity.[119] In that case, the judge accepted that it was a reasonable inference that, where a property has a mortgage and illegal activity was being carried out in the building, some of the money earned from the illegal activity was used to pay down the debt of the building. So the building was not only an instrument that facilitated the illegal activity within but was also proceeds of the illegal activity.

ACADEMIC COMMENTARY

There has been little by way of academic commentary on civil asset forfeiture in Canada.[120] A 2003 article examined the effect of forfeiture on third

---

[118]   See *Walsh*.

[119]   *British Columbia (Civil Forfeiture Act, Director) v. Tse et al.* [2007] BSC 995 (CanLII).

[120]   Professor Beare shared her concerns about Ontario's legislation at the Standing Committee of the Legislative Assembly on Justice and Social Policy Issues

parties. The analysis in the article is, in part, out of date; civil asset forfeiture laws in Ontario and Alberta are pejoratively referred to as 'so-called
forfeiture' laws.[121] An otherwise authoritative text on proceeds and money
laundering considers provincial civil asset forfeiture laws 'potentially
invalid'.[122] Their analysis was offered to the court in at least one challenge;
the court came to a different view.[123]

Arguably, the most thoughtful analysis to emerge comes from Professor
Gallant in Manitoba. In a comprehensive book, she has examined civil asset
forfeiture in the larger context of economic crime, largely from the UK
perspective.[124] A 2004 article focuses on the Alberta and Ontario legislation.
Professor Gallant considers the 'crime control' models, which apply civil
asset forfeiture and takes particular note of Ontario's and Alberta's emphasis on restitution to victims. Jurisdictions like UK and Ireland, in her view
unconstrained by the Canadian division of powers issue, freely ascribe to
civil asset forfeiture as part of crime control. Even though other jurisdictions
lack a Canadian division of powers, they must still satisfy the courts that
non-conviction forfeiture regimes are properly within the civil law.

She later developed this argument into a position on the *Chatterjee* case
discussed above; the Court of Appeal completely disagreed with her position.[125] The argument, in each instance, is identical to the argument considered in the Canadian courts on division of powers.[126] If non-conviction
based forfeiture is ersatz civil law, it would fail as completely in the UK or
Ireland as it would in the face of a division of powers argument in Canada.

---

on 20 February 2001; the Ontario *Hansard* is available at www.ontla.on.ca. See T.
Gabor (2003), *Assessing the Effectiveness of Organized Crime Control Strategies: A
Review of the Literature,* Ottawa, Ontario, Canada: Department of Justice, at pp.
27–31, which notes civil asset forfeiture in the US but does not note the Canadian
versions: available online at http://www.justice.gc.ca/en/ps/rs/rep/2005/rr05-5/rr05-
5.pdf, accessed 28 December 2007.

[121]   See K. Davis (2003), 'The Effect of Forfeiture on Third Parties', *McGill LJ*,
48, 183, at p. 183. The author counselled the use of the Escheats Act and the Fines and
Forfeitures Act to challenge forfeitures under the Remedies for Organized Crime and
Other Unlawful Activities Act 2001; in an amendment subsequent to the article by way
of the Civil Remedies Act, s. 15.4 explicitly states that those two above statutes do not
apply. There is some doubt as to whether the provisions would have applied in any
event.

[122]   See *Money Laundering and Proceeds of Crime, supra* at p. 651.

[123]   See *Chatterjee.*

[124]   Note particularly, M. Gallant, *supra* n. 14, ch. 3.

[125]   See M. Gallant (2006), '*Ontario (Attorney General) v. $29,020 in Canadian
Currency*: A Comment on Proceeds of Crime and Provincial Civil Forfeiture Laws',
Crim LQ, **52**, 64.

[126]   See *Chatterjee.* See also M. Gallant (2005), 'Civil Law May Be the Best Way
to Deal With Money Laundering', 25:23 *Lawyer's Weekly* **13**, 21 October 2005.

In Ireland, the UK and South Africa, the question has been carefully considered by courts at the trial and appellant level.[127] Those jurists as well as commentators[128] have not focused on criminology concepts of crime control, but rather on legal concepts.

The central question is when is it appropriate for government to apply the remedial concepts underlying civil law as opposed to the penal concepts underlying criminal law? Unlawful activity with a profit motivation is a highly complex problem that refuses to stand still.[129] A fairly robust legislative architecture is required to address the issue, irrespective of its theoretical moorings.

---

[127]   In Ireland, see *Gilligan v. Criminal Assets Bureau* [1998], 3 IR 185; in the UK, see *Walsh v. Assets Recovery Agency* [2005] NICA 6 Affirming [2004] NIQB 21; in South Africa, see *NDPP v. Mohamed No and Others* [2003] 1 SACR 561. See Chapters 3 and 4 of this book for the position in Ireland and South Africa respectively.

[128]   See Justifying Civil Recovery of Criminal Proceeds, *supra*.

[129]   For an excellent look at one aspect of economic crime, see Moises Naim (2005), *Illicit*, Toronto, Canada: Doubleday.

7. Assets recovery under the Proceeds of Crime Act 2002: the UK experience

Angela V.M. Leong*

INTRODUCTION

The United Kingdom (UK) government recognised that the profits from serious organised crime were so great that the deterrent effect of even a lengthy imprisonment was insignificant, as the convicted criminals knew that the illicit gains would be available to them on their release. Various confiscation and money laundering provisions were established under the Drug Trafficking Offences Act 1986, the Criminal Justice Act 1988 and the Drug Trafficking Act 1994. However, these early confiscation regimes had not made a significant impact on criminal assets and there were only few prosecutions and convictions for money laundering offences. As a result, the whole assets recovery system was reviewed in 2000 and policy implications were generated for the Proceeds of Crime Act 2002 (hereinafter POCA 2002), which created the Assets Recovery Agency (hereinafter ARA) and consolidated the criminal law with regard to money laundering and confiscation. More importantly, POCA 2002 has established the new civil recovery and taxation regimes under which property obtained through unlawful conduct can be recovered without the need for a criminal conviction. This chapter examines the development of confiscation legislation, and discusses their limitations. It also focuses on assessing the laws, policies and operational experiences of the civil recovery and taxation regimes under POCA 2002.

CONFISCATION LEGISLATION PRIOR TO POCA 2002

The UK Home Office observed, 'organised criminal activity is a particular

---

* The views expressed herein are the author's personally and do not represent the views of the ARA. Some of the analysis in this article has been drawn from Angela V. M. Leong (2007), *The Disruption of International Organised Crime: An Analysis of Legal and Non-Legal Strategies*, UK: Ashgate Publishing.

kind of serious criminal activity which in Great Britain is primarily focused on drug trafficking and money laundering'.[1] Thus, the UK legislation focuses on confiscation and money laundering provisions in order to target the proceeds of criminal activity. The confiscation regime and the law described in this section are obsolescent. Confiscation for offences committed on or after 24 March 2003 has to be made under POCA 2002,[2] while confiscation for offences committed before 24 March 2003 will still be made under the previous legislation until the old law works out of the system completely.

The Confiscation Regime

Confiscation and forfeiture measures were designed to deprive the wrongdoers the fruits of their wrongs. There were three different types of asset recovery available under the traditional criminal legislation in the UK, namely (i) forfeiture of property, (ii) forfeiture of cash at borders under the Drug Trafficking Act 1994[3] (hereinafter DTA 1994), and (iii) confiscation following criminal conviction. Forfeiture was an ancient legal concept. Until the late nineteenth century, all of a convicted felon's property was automatically forfeited to the Crown. However, this concept was abolished by the Forfeiture Act 1870. The power to forfeit property was introduced again in the 1950s for dealing with illicit articles, such as pornography. Powers of forfeiture were still found in the Misuse of Drugs Act 1971, the Powers of Criminal Courts Act 1973, the Customs and Excise Management Act 1979 and the Immigration and Asylum Act 1999. In addition, forfeiture powers were also available on application of a customs officer under section 42 of DTA 1994 to recover cash at borders that represented the proceeds of drugs trafficking, or was intended for use in drugs trafficking, without the need for criminal conviction.

In *R v. Cuthbertson*[4] (also known as the 'Operation Julie' case; hereinafter *Cuthbertson*), the defendants were convicted of offences of conspiring to produce and supply the drug 'LSD' (Lysergic Acid Diethylamide, also known as 'acid'). The House of Lords held that forfeiture powers under section 27 of the Misuse of Drugs Act 1971 were restricted to the physical items used to commit the offence. Besides, the defendants had not been convicted of 'an offence under the Act' but of statutory conspiracies contrary to the Criminal Law Act 1977. As per Lord Diplock, '... section 27 can never have been

---

[1]   See Home Office, *Home Affairs Committee Third Report on Organised Crime: Minutes of Evidence and Memoranda* (HC Paper (1994–95) 18–II) (hereinafter Third Report), at p. 80, para. 22.

[2]   Proceeds of Crime Act 2002 (hereinafter POCA 2002).

[3]   Hereinafter DTA 1994.

[4]   [1980] 2 All ER 401 (HL) (hereinafter *Cuthbertson*).

intended by Parliament to serve as a means of stripping the drug traffickers of the total profits of their unlawful enterprises.'[5] As a result of this ruling, the drug trafficking proceeds of over £750 000 were released even though these funds were traced into the hands of the offenders, and then restrained. *Cuthbertson* was a turning point for the modern law of confiscation. Following this case, the Hodgson Committee was formed to review the limited forfeiture powers in recovering the proceeds of crime. The UK Government recognised that the profits from drug trafficking were so great that the deterrent effect of even a lengthy imprisonment was insignificant. Based on the Hodgson Report, the confiscation regime was enacted in the UK in 1986.[6]

Confiscation Proceedings

The first confiscation legislation was introduced under the Drug Trafficking Offences Act 1986[7] (hereinafter DTOA 1986), which was amended and consolidated by DTA 1994. It imposed a mandatory obligation on the court to confiscate the proceeds of drug trafficking offences.[8] It was a conviction-based system

---

    [5]   *Ibid.* at p. 406.
    [6]   See Derek Hodgson (1984), *Profits of Crime and their Recovery,* London, UK: Heinemann.
    [7]   Hereinafter DTOA 1986.
    [8]   A drug trafficking offence is defined in DTA 1994, s. 1(3) as:

(a)   an offence under section 4(2) or (3) or 5(3) of the Misuse [1971 c. 38.] of Drugs Act 1971 (production, supply and possession for supply of controlled drugs);
(b)   an offence under section 20 of that Act (assisting in or inducing commission outside United Kingdom of offence punishable under a corresponding law);
(c)   an offence under–
    (i)   section 50(2) or (3) of the Customs [1979 c. 2.] and Excise Management Act 1979 (improper importation),
    (ii) section 68(2) of that Act (exportation), or
    (iii) section 170 of that Act (fraudulent evasion), in connection with a prohibition or restriction on importation or exportation having effect by virtue of section 3 of the Misuse of Drugs Act 1971;
(d)   an offence under section 12 of the Criminal [1990 c. 5.] Justice (International Co-operation) Act 1990 (manufacture or supply of substance specified in Schedule 2 to that Act);
(e)   an offence under section 19 of that Act (using ship for illicit traffic in controlled drugs);
(f)   an offence under section 49, 50 or 51 of this Act or section 14 of the Criminal Justice (International Co-operation) Act 1990 (which makes, in relation to Scotland and Northern Ireland, provision corresponding to section 49 of this Act);
(g)   an offence under section 1 of the Criminal [1977 c. 45.] Law Act 1977 of conspiracy to commit any of the offences in paragraphs (a) to (f) above;

of confiscation with discretionary statutory assumptions, which allowed the Crown Court to make certain assumptions after a person had been convicted of a drug trafficking offence. The Crown Court was allowed to assume that all assets acquired and all transfers and expenditure made in the six years prior to the institution of proceedings, and all property currently held by the defendant were proceeds of drug trafficking. The onus was on the defendant to prove to the civil standard that his wealth had been legitimately acquired in the relevant period, if it was to be excluded from the assessment.[9] The court had the discretion not to apply these statutory assumptions if they would lead to a serious risk of injustice. In addition, the prosecution had the power to require the defendant to submit information as to the source of his assets. If the court was satisfied that the source of the assets was not drug trafficking, the statutory assumptions cannot be relied on.[10]

Once the court decided that the defendant had benefited from drug trafficking, it then calculated the value of benefits (the amount to be recovered)[11] and the amount available to satisfy the confiscation order (the amount to be realised).[12] If the defendant established to the civil standard that the amount to be realised was less than the total amount of his benefit, then the court was obliged to make a confiscation order of the amount to be realised, or a nominal amount if the amount that might be realised is nil.[13] Any realisable property[14] in the possession of the defendant, regardless of whether it had been

---

(h)   an offence under section 1 of the Criminal [1981 c. 47.] Attempts Act 1981 of attempting to commit any of those offences; and

(i)   an offence of inciting another person to commit any of those offences, whether under section 19 of the Misuse of Drugs Act 1971 or at common law;

and includes aiding, abetting, counselling or procuring the commission of any of the offences in paragraphs (a) to (f) above.

Note that simple possession of drugs is not a drug trafficking offence.

[9]   See the following: *R v. Comiskey* [1991] Crim LR 484; *R v. Redbourne* (1993) 96 Cr App R 201; *R v. Barwick* [2001] Crim LR 52; *R v. Barnham* [2005] EWCA Crim 1049; *R v. Ripley* [2005] EWCA Crim 1453.

[10]   See *R v. Johnson* (1990) 91 Cr App R 332.

[11]   The amount to be recovered is the amount the court assesses to be the proceeds of drug trafficking.

[12]   The amount to be realised is the total value of all the realisable property held by the defendant at the time the confiscation order is made, together with the value of gifts caught by section 8(1) of DTA 1994.

[13]   See the following: *R v. Comiskey* [1991] Crim LR 484; *R v. Barwick* [2001] Crim LR 52; *R v. Smith* [2001] UKHL 68; *R v. Versluis* [2004] EWCA Crim 3168; *R v. McKinnon* [2004] Crim LR 485; *R v. Atobrah* [2005] EWCA Crim 3321; *R v. Barnham* [2005] EWCA Crim 1049; *R v. Ripley* [2005] EWCA Crim 1453.

[14]   Realisable property means free property which the defendant holds or has given to another person. Property is free unless it is the subject of a forfeiture or depri-

legally or illegally obtained, could be used to satisfy the order. A confiscation order was an *in personam* order,[15] thus the government did not have the right of possession of the defendant's property in cases of non-payment, unless the property was being handed over pursuant to a receivership order, or the defendant had expressly consented to the property being forwarded to the court.

Where the court considered that it required further information before determining whether the defendant had benefited from drug trafficking, or the amount to be recovered, it could postpone the confiscation proceeding for a period not exceeding six months from the date of conviction.[16] The application for postponement of the confiscation determination must be made before the defendant was sentenced. A defect in the procedure for obtaining a postponement could result in a confiscation order being quashed, if it was unfair to the defendant. In *R v. Williamson*[17] confiscation orders were quashed by the Court of Appeal where the judge had failed to postpone the confiscation hearing prior to sentencing.

The Criminal Justice Act 1988[18] (hereinafter CJA 1988) extended the confiscation legislation to include all non-drug indictable offences, and specified summary offences from which peculiarly high profits could be gained. However, there were no mandatory statutory assumptions in such cases to catch the proceeds of the whole course of criminal activity other than those acquired in the course of the offence for which the defendant was convicted. Under CJA 1988, it was the duty of the Crown Court to consider confiscation when a defendant was convicted in any proceedings before the Crown Court or magistrates' court of a 'relevant offence'.[19]

---

vation order under other legislation. Realisable property also includes any business operated by the defendant as a sole proprietor or his share in a partnership or limited company.

[15] A confiscation order in UK, contrary to that in US, is an *in personam* order against the defendant himself rather than an *in rem* order against the defendant's realisable property. See also Chapter 2 of this book.

[16] See the following: *R v. Kelly* [2000] Crim LR 392; *R v. Miranda* [2000] Crim LR 393; *R v. Lingham* [2000] Crim LR 696; *R v. Gadsby* [2001] EWCA Crim 1824; *R v. Jagdev* [2002] EWCA Crim 1326; *R v. Pisciotto* [2002] EWCA Crim 1592; *R v. Knights and Maguire* [2003] EWCA Crim 2222.

[17] [2003] EWCA Crim 644; see also the following: *R v. Steele and Shevki* [2001] 2 Crim App R (S) 40; *R v. Ross* [2001] 2 Crim App R (S) 484; *Sekhon and Others v. R* [2002] EWCA Crim 2954; *R v. Haisman, Lant and Miller* [2003] EWCA Crim 2246.

[18] Hereinafter CJA 1988.

[19] A 'relevant offence' is defined as an offence listed in Sch. 4 to the CJA 1988, if convicted before a magistrates' court; or an indictable offence, other than a drug trafficking offence, if convicted before a Crown Court (including offences taken into consideration).

There were two types of confiscation, namely (i) conviction determination, and (ii) course of criminal conduct determination. A conviction determination enabled the court to confiscate benefit arising only from the offences the defendant was convicted of, along with any offences taken into consideration. Such proceedings could be triggered by the prosecutor or the court. A course of criminal conduct determination could only be triggered by the prosecutor with written notice containing a declaration that the case was one where it was considered appropriate for the assumptions to be made. This determination not only allowed the court to confiscate benefit arising from offences the defendant was convicted of and any offences taken into consideration (that is, the conviction determination), but also offences with which the defendant had not been charged or convicted. A defendant was considered to have followed a course of criminal conduct if he was convicted in the current proceedings of at least two 'qualifying offences';[20] or was convicted of one qualifying offence, and had been convicted of at least one other qualifying offence during the previous six years. If the court decided to make a confiscation order under CJA 1988, it had to decide how much money was available to satisfy the order. The amount the defendant was required to pay under the confiscation order must not exceed the value of the benefit, or the amount that might be realised, whichever was less at the time the order was made. Any realisable property[21] in the possession of the defendant, regardless of whether it had been legally or illegally obtained, could be used to satisfy the order. The procedure for obtaining a postponement of the confiscation determination was the same as that under DTA 1994.

The Criminal Justice (International Co-operation) Act 1990 enabled mutual legal assistance in confiscation, furthered drug money laundering offences, and contained provisions for drug cash seizure on import or export. The Criminal Justice Act 1993[22] (hereinafter CJA 1993) put in place criminal provisions dealing with money laundering in compliance with article 3 of the United Nations Convention Against Illicit Traffic in Narcotic Drugs and Psychotropic Substances[23] (hereinafter Vienna Convention), and enhancement to all crime confiscation provisions. Parliament, under CJA 1993, expressly made the civil standard of proof that the proceeds were of criminal provenance

---

[20]   A 'qualifying offence' refers to a relevant offence committed after 1 November 1995, and from which the court is satisfied that the defendant has benefited.
[21]   Realisable property is the total value of all the realisable property held by the defendant at the time the confiscation order is made, together with the value of gifts caught by CJA 1988, s. 74(10).
[22]   Hereinafter CJA 1993.
[23]   Available online at http://www.cicad.oas.org/Lavado_Activos/eng/Conventions/convention_1988_en.pdf, accessed 24 December 2007.

sufficient for a confiscation order to be made.[24] DTA 1994 consolidated the provisions of DTOA 1986 and the Criminal Justice (International Co-operation) Act 1990, as well as strengthened the confiscation legislation by replacing discretionary assumptions in drug-trafficking cases with mandatory assumptions, as recommended by the First Report of the Home Office Working Group on Confiscation in 1991.[25] In other words, the court was allowed to assess and confiscate not only the proceeds of the particular drug-related offence for which a person had been convicted, but also all the income arising from drug trafficking for a period of six years before the offence.

It was contended in *Welch v. UK*[26] that the confiscation provisions had raised a strong indication of a regime of punishment, and thus the statutory assumptions were inconsistent with the presumption of innocence. It was held that since a confiscation hearing was not a trial of the defendant for a criminal offence, the presumption of innocence should not apply. The Judicial Committee of the Privy Council in *McIntosh v. Lord Advocate*[27] took the view that since confiscation proceedings followed a conviction, article 6 of the European Convention on Human Rights[28] (hereinafter ECHR) did not apply, thus no derogation from the presumption of innocence was involved. This ruling was followed by the European Court of Human Rights[29] and the House of Lords.[30] The Second Report of the Home Office Working Group on Confiscation in 1992 recommended that discretionary assumptions for non-drug trafficking cases be introduced in the Proceeds of Crime Act 1995. The Proceeds of Crime Act 1995 provided greater powers of investigation, as inserted in CJA 1988, and further alignment of all crime provisions with DTA 1994.

---

[24]   See *R v. Dickens* [1990] 2 QB 102.

[25]   The Home Office Working Group on Confiscation was established following the Home Affairs Committee's Seventh Report on *Drug Trafficking and Related Serious Crime* (HC Paper 370 (1988–89)).

[26]   [1995] 20 EHRR 247; see also *R v. Ko Chi Yuen* [1994] HKLY 198.

[27]   [2001] 3 WLR 107.

[28]   Hereinafter ECHR.

[29]   See *Phillips v. United Kingdom* [2001] Crim LR 817; see also discussion of this case in Chapter 11 of this book.

[30]   See *R v. Benjafield* [2002] 2 WLR 325; see also *R v. Rezvi* [2002] 1 All ER 801. In addition, the state must remain within reasonable time limits, see *Attorney General's Reference (No. 2 of 2001)* [2003] UKHL 68; see also the following: *R (Lloyd) v. Bow Street Magistrates' Court,* [2004] 1 Cr App R 11; *Crowther v. United Kingdom* (Application No. 53741/00) (*The Times*, 11 February 2005); *Re Saggar* [2005] EWCA Civ 174. See also Chapter 11 of this book.

Restraint Orders

The purpose of a restraint order was to freeze a defendant's assets so that they might be used to satisfy a confiscation order. Restraint orders under DTA 1994 and CJA 1988 were obtained in the High Court, and the proceedings were subject to the Civil Procedure Rules. Section 26(1) of DTA 1994 and section 77(1) of CJA 1988 provided that a restraint order might prohibit any specified person or persons from dealing with any realisable property held by him, subject to such conditions and exceptions as may be specified in the order. But the ownership of the restrained assets belonged to the specified person. Section 26(2) of DTA 1994 and section 77(3) of CJA 1988 stated that a restraint order might apply to all realisable property (whether the property was specified in the order or not) held by or being transferred to the specified person after the making of the order. In other words, the court had the power to restrain any other person or body holding assets in which the defendant had an interest, including limited companies.[31] Besides, the assets could be anywhere in the world. The court also had the power to make an order requiring the defendant to repatriate all assets held abroad within the jurisdiction,[32] or alternatively, the defendant was required to co-operate with the management receiver appointed by the court under section 26(7) of DTA 1994 and section 77(8) of CJA 1988 in repatriating the assets. Receivers appointed by the court were independent officers of the court, and had wide ranging powers including (i) taking possession of property, (ii) preserving, managing or dealing with property, (iii) starting, carrying on or defending legal proceedings in respect of property, (iv) realising part of the property as necessary to meet their remuneration and expenses, and (v) requiring the defendant and any person holding realisable property to take all reasonable and necessary steps to enable the receivership to be conducted properly.

Under section 25(1) of DTA 1994, the High Court might grant restraint and charging orders when the following conditions were satisfied:

(a)   proceedings had been instituted in England and Wales against the defendant for a drug trafficking offence, or an application had been made by

---

[31]   Although a limited company is a legal entity on its own, and its assets will not normally constitute 'realisable property' of the defendant within the meaning of DTA 1994 and CJA 1988, it was held in *Re H and others* [1996] 2 All ER 391 that when the limited company has been used to facilitate or conceal the criminal activity, the court could lift the corporate veil and treat the assets of the company as realisable property of the defendant. Also see the following: *Salomon v. Salomon* [1987] AC 22; *Adams v. Cape Industries plc.* [1991] 1 All ER 929; *R v. Omar* [2004] EWCA Crim 2320; *R v. Stannard* [2005] EWCA Crim 2717; *R v. K* [2005] EWCA Crim 619.

[32]   See *DPP v. Scarlett* [2001] 1 WLR 515.

the prosecutor in respect of the defendant under sections 13, 14, 15, 16 or 19 of DTA 1994;

(b) the proceedings had not, or the application had not, been concluded; and

(c) the court was satisfied that there was reasonable cause to believe[33] that

    (i) in the case of an application under section 15 or 16 of DTA 1994, that the court would be satisfied as mentioned in section 15(4) or, as the case may be, 16(2) of DTA 1994; or

    (ii) in any other case, that the defendant had benefited from drug trafficking.

Similar provisions were found in section 76(1) in Part VI of CJA 1988 (as amended by the Proceeds of Crime Act 1995), which gave the High Court the power to grant restraint orders in relation to defendants against whom criminal proceedings had been or were to be instituted for criminal offences other than drug trafficking offences.

A restraint order would not be required in all cases. Decisions regarding whether or not to apply for an order, and the timing of an application were of strategic importance to a case. A restraint order might be made prior to the confiscation order, or made for the first time after a confiscation order had been granted but prior to it being satisfied. There was no minimum monetary value for restraint. An application for restraint orders was part of the statute, and there was no express provision in DTA 1994 or CJA 1988 requiring the prosecutor to establish a risk of dissipation of assets as a condition to obtaining an order. However, in *Re AJ & DJ*, the Court of Appeal held that it was necessary for the prosecutor to establish a risk of dissipation.[34] In fact, the longer the prosecutor delayed in making his application for a restraint order, the more difficult it would be to establish the fact that there was a risk of assets being dissipated. The defendant or any third parties who held or had an interest in the realisable property, or held property which was a gift caught by the legislation might apply for the variation or discharge of the restraint order.

Charging Orders

Unlike the restraint orders, charging orders did not prevent the property in question being sold. A charging order only gave the prosecuting authority an

---

[33] In proving the requirement for reasonable cause to believe, the prosecutor has a lesser burden than having to establish the defendant has a case to answer. It will suffice to show reasonable grounds for believing that the defendant has committed a drug trafficking offence, as an inference can be drawn in relation to his benefit from drug trafficking. See *Lister v. Perryman* (1870) LR 4 HL 521; *Johnson v. Whitehouse* (1984) RTR 38.

[34] See *Re AJ & DJ* (unreported) 9 December 1992, Court of Appeal.

interest in the property to which it related, and any purchaser would take the property subject to the Crown's interest. Section 27(5) of DTA 1994 and section 78(5) of CJA 1988 specified the types of property that could be the subject of charging orders, including (a) land in England and Wales; or (b) securities of any of the following kinds: (i) government stock, (ii) stock of any body (other than a building society) incorporated within England and Wales, (iii) stock of any body incorporated outside England and Wales or of any country or territory outside the UK, being stock registered in a register kept at any place within England and Wales, and (iv) units of any unit trust in respect of which a register of the unit holders was kept at any place within England and Wales. If a confiscation order had been made, the charge must not exceed the amount of the order, whereas if no confiscation order had been made, the charge could extend to the full value of the property in question. Thus, the extent of the charge depended largely on the stage of the proceedings.

Like the restraint orders, charging orders under DTA 1994 and CJA 1988 were obtained in the High Court, and the proceedings were subject to the Civil Procedure Rules. Section 25(1) of DTA 1994 and section 76 of CJA 1988 provided that charging orders might be made in precisely the same circumstances as restraint orders. Nevertheless, both orders could not be granted in respect of the same property,[35] as stated in section 26(3) of DTA 1994 and section 77(4) of CJA 1998. Section 27(8) of DTA 1994 and section 78(8) of CJA 1988 provided for an application for the variation or discharge of a charging order made by the defendant or any party affected by it.

LIMITATIONS OF THE EARLY CONFISCATION REGIME

A range of statutory provisions has been in place in UK since 1986 to deal with money laundering, and to allow confiscation of the proceeds of criminal activity, as discussed above. However, these early regimes had not made any significant impact on criminal assets and there were only few prosecutions and convictions for money laundering offences. The UK Cabinet Office observed that 'these powers have developed in a piecemeal fashion, are not well understood, and are spread across a range of statutes with differences in the treatment of the proceeds of drugs and non-drugs crime'.[36] There were significant deficiencies in their application.

---

35   See *Re a Defendant, The Times*, 7 April 1987.
36   See Cabinet Office (June 2000), *Recovering the Proceeds of Crime*, London, UK: Cabinet Office (Performance and Innovation Unit) (hereinafter PIU Report), at para. 1.15. The full report is available at http://www.cabinetoffice.gov.uk/strategy/downloads/su/criminal/crime.pdf, accessed 20 September 2007; see also Chapter 8 of this book.

Limitations of the Confiscation Regime

DTA 1994 imposed a mandatory obligation on the court to confiscate the proceeds of drug trafficking offences. It was a conviction-based system of confiscation with discretionary statutory assumptions, which allowed the Crown Court to make certain assumptions after a person had been convicted of a drug trafficking offence. The major weakness of this early legislation was that only the proceeds of drug trafficking could be confiscated, and it failed to attack the proceeds of non-drug trafficking crime. Furthermore confiscation was only possible after conviction.

CJA 1988 then extended the confiscation legislation to include all non-drug indictable offences and specified summary offences from which peculiarly high profits could be gained. Though confiscation may be in respect of both drug trafficking and non-drug trafficking crime, it was still only possible after an offence had been proved to a criminal standard, being beyond reasonable doubt. Thus, the assets of the masterminds of the organised crime groups could not be confiscated because they would often distant themselves from the crimes; as a result, there would not be enough evidence to convict them. In fact, few people had the expertise in the process of deciding on benefit and realisable assets, and many found it confusing and unattractive.[37] In the *Home Affairs Committee Third Report on Organised Crime* (hereinafter Third Report), the Regional Crime Squads[38] suggested that the government should consider similar legislation like the Racketeer Influenced and Corrupt Organisations Act 1970[39] (hereinafter RICO) in the US. RICO combines both civil and criminal law together into removing the proceeds of crime, and does not rely on the individual being convicted, but allows civil forfeiture on the balance of probabilities without a prior criminal conviction.

Another weakness identified by the Third Report was that the rate of recovery of sums ordered to be confiscated was much lower than the sums ordered. 'For orders made under the Drug Trafficking Offences Act 1986 between April 1987 and March 1993, the figures were £43.4 million ordered and £14 million recovered. For orders under the Criminal Justice Act 1988 (ie for other serious crime), accurate statistics were not available for the first two years of operation, but for subsequent years (April 1991 to March 1993) the figures were

---

[37]   See Michael Levi and Lisa Osofsky (eds) (1995), *Crime Detection and Prevention Series: Paper 61: Investigating, Seizing and Confiscating the Proceeds of Crime*, London, UK: Home Office Police Research Group, at p. (vii).

[38]   See Regional Crime Squads, *Home Affairs Committee Third Report on Organised Crime: Minutes of Evidence and Memoranda* (HC Paper (1994–95) 18-II) (hereinafter *Home Affairs Committee Third Report*), at p. 135.

[39]   Hereinafter RICO.

£1.7 million and £0.5 million respectively'.[40] The Home Office explained that appeals, complications in property sales, receivers' costs and overvaluation of property assets had contributed to the low figures in sums recovered. The Third Report recommended that a full study on the rate of recovery of confiscated funds was necessary to evaluate the effectiveness of the confiscation regime. In fact, the confiscation regime has been kept under regular review by the Home Office Working Group on Confiscation.

Similar results in the report titled *Recovering the Proceeds of Crime* by the Performance and Innovative Unit of the UK Cabinet Office published in 2000 (hereinafter PIU Report) also showed that the confiscation regime was not making a significant impact on criminal assets. Between 1994 and 1998, confiscation orders were made in only 20 per cent of drugs cases and only 0.3 per cent of other serious crime cases. The collection rate was also significantly lower than the amounts ordered to be confiscated, on average only 40 per cent of the amounts ordered by the courts to be seized were collected in drugs cases, and the average collection rate for other serious crime was only 30 per cent.[41] According to the Asset Recovery Strategy Committee, unenforced confiscation orders amounted to over £130 million in 2001. Such poor performance was due to a lack of available resources and skills, poor procedures and limited inter-agency co-operation. There were also inappropriate restrictions on the ability of courts to restrain defendants from disposing of their assets.

Another issue raised in the Third Report was the use of confiscated funds. It was criticised that confiscated funds placed in the Treasury's Consolidated Fund were not made available specifically for the fight against organised crime, and that only international drug-related confiscated funds placed in the Seized Assets Fund were directly devoted to the fight against drug trafficking. It was proposed that confiscation funds be made available to agencies fighting serious crime. However, the Crown Prosecution Service indicated that there might be the danger of distorted police priorities in focusing on cases where money was likely to be recovered.[42]

Investigation, Prosecution and Trial Process

Financial investigation, in addition to traditional investigation techniques, is an important tool for asset identification and recovery. Financial investigators

---

[40]   See Home Affairs Committee, *Home Affairs Committee Third Report on Organised Crime* (HC Paper (1994–95) 18-I), at p. xlix, para. 137.

[41]   See PIU Report, *supra* at pp. 29–31.

[42]   See Crown Prosecution Service, *Home Affairs Committee Third Report on Organised Crime: Minutes of Evidence and Memoranda* (HC Paper (1994–95) 18-II), at p. 252.

need to be involved at an early stage to identify and freeze assets for confiscation. However, under the traditional law enforcement structure, financial investigation was not seen as central in the whole investigation process, and the career path for financial investigators had been quite uncertain. Financial investigators from Her Majesty's Customs and Excise[43] and Serious Fraud Office were sometimes involved at an early stage, while police service financial investigators did not come into the picture until a relatively late stage, sometimes even after the charge. There were also differences in the allocation of budget for financial investigation among different agencies. Some law enforcement agencies might not have the necessary resources to conduct financial investigations. Her Majesty's Customs and Excise spent about 2.3 per cent of the total National Investigation Service budget on financial investigation (which was about 0.3 per cent of its overall budget for Customs and Excise), while only between 0.05 per cent and 0.3 per cent of the total budget was allocated specifically for financial investigations within the police forces.[44] Furthermore, given the complexity and the sophistication of the cases, financial investigation required specialist skills. However, there was no universally recognised qualification, and the standard of training in financial investigation varied greatly among agencies. As a result, 'financial investigation is underused, undervalued and underresourced in the UK. There is also a shortage of people with the right skills, and little cross-agency co-operation or sharing of best practice.'[45] It was recommended that greater emphasis should be put on financial investigation to make it central to UK law enforcement investigations, a national training programme on financial investigation should be established, and wider investigative powers (such as compulsory disclosure orders and general bank circulars) should be made available to law enforcement agencies as well as civilian financial investigators.

The question of disclosure of information, and the intimidation of witnesses might prevent the prosecution of members of organised criminal groups.[46] Most successful prevention and prosecution of organised criminal activity depended on intelligence gathered from informants and through surveillance. However, the requirement to disclose such information to the courts would have serious implications on the effectiveness of investigation, and possible revelation of capabilities of police methods might prevent prosecutions from

---

43   Her Majesty's Customs and Excise (hereinafter HMCE) were merged with the Inland Revenue to form Her Majesty's Revenue and Customs (hereinafter HMRC) on 18 April 2005.

44   See PIU Report, *supra* at p. 53, para. 7.8.

45   *Ibid.* at p. 51, para. 7.2.

46   See Royal Commission on Criminal Justice (1993), *Report of the Royal Commission on Criminal Justice* Cm 2263, London, UK: HM Stationery Office.

going ahead. In addition, under the current evidential rules in the Regulation of Investigatory Powers Act 2000, the content of telephone taps or other intrusive devices, which is often essential to prove a connection between the defendant and the set of people performing the predicate acts, is not admissible in court as evidence.[47] This has led to the question of whether the recognition of the concept of 'criminal organisations' or 'racketeering' is necessary in the UK criminal law.

Law enforcement agencies sometimes find it difficult to get witnesses to co-operate in organised crime trials, because organised criminals are ready to use threat or violence to intimidate the witnesses or jurors so as to prevent prosecutions.[48] Witness and jury protection schemes have been set up since the Diplock type trials in Northern Ireland to ensure that the best evidence is given in court, thus increasing the number of successful prosecutions.[49] Though various witness protection schemes exist in different law enforcement agencies, their arrangements and standards are different.[50] A more effective national witness protection programme with common standards and national guidelines is necessary for improving the support and protection to witnesses.[51]

---

[47]   See A. Tomkins (1994), 'Intercepted Evidence: Now You Hear Me, Now You Don't', *Modern Law Review*, **57**, 941.

[48]   An offence of witness intimidation has been introduced under s. 51 of the Criminal Justice and Public Order Act 1994. Under ss. 39 to 41 of the Criminal Justice and Police Act 2001, it is a criminal offence if a person knowingly performs an act intended to intimidate another person who is or may be a witness in civil or criminal proceedings and the penalty is up to five years' imprisonment.

[49]   See Steven Greer (1994), *Supergrasses: A Study of Anti-Terrorist Law Enforcement in Northern Ireland*, Oxford, UK: Oxford University Press; see also Steven Greer (2001), 'Where the Grass is Greener? Supergrasses in Comparative Perspective' in Roger Billingsley, Teresa Nemit and Philip Bean (eds) (2001), *Informers, Policing, Policy and Practice*, Devon, UK: Willan Publishing.

[50]   See Home Office (1998), *Speaking Up for Justice: Report of the Interdepartmental Working Group on the Treatment of Vulnerable and Intimidated Witnesses in the Criminal Justice System*, London, UK: Home Office.

[51]   See Home Office (2004), *One Step Ahead: A 21st Century Strategy to Defeat Organised Crime* Cm 6167, London, UK: HM Stationery Office, at para. 6.4; see also Nicholas Fyfe and James Sheptycki (eds) (2005), *Facilitating Witness Co-operation in Organised Crime Cases: An International Review* (Home Office Online Report 27/05), available at http://www.homeoffice.gov.uk/rds/pdfs05/rdsolr2705.pdf, accessed 20 September 2007.

CURRENT ASSETS RECOVERY AND DISRUPTION STRATEGIES

Proceeds of Crime Act 2002

In 2000, the Performance and Innovative Unit of the UK Cabinet Office published the PIU Report, which reviewed the anti-money laundering and confiscation regimes.[52] It identified the weaknesses in the whole assets recovery system and generated policy implications for POCA 2002. The new era focuses on depriving the organised criminals of their illicit gains, and disrupting funding for future activities, thus showing crime will not pay.

> Most crime is committed for profit – about 70 per cent of recorded crime is acquisitive. Asset deprivation attacks criminality through this profit motive. In the same way that starving a thriving small business of capital hampers its growth, removing assets from criminal enterprises can also disrupt their activities. Removing unlawful assets also:
> * underpins confidence in a fair and effective criminal justice system and shows that nobody is above the law;
> * removes the influence of negative role models from communities;
> * deters people from crime by reducing the anticipated returns;
> * improves crime detection rates generally; and
> * assists in the fight against money laundering.[53]

Some of the main proposals suggested by the PIU Report and later implemented in POCA 2002 are summarised as follows: (i) the creation of a new agency with lead responsibility for asset recovery and containing a 'Centre of Excellence' for financial investigation training; (ii) the consolidation of existing laws on confiscation and money laundering into a single piece of legislation; (iii) the introduction of new civil recovery proceedings without the need for a criminal conviction; (iv) the use of Inland Revenue[54] functions by the new agency in relation to criminal gains; (v) the development of gateways for the exchange of information between the new agency and the other authorities; and (vi) the assurance of sufficient trained staff in all the agencies involved in asset recovery so that the system can function efficiently.

The POCA 2002 received Royal Assent on 24 July 2002, and it contains 12

---

[52] See PIU Report, *supra*.
[53] *Ibid.* at p. 6, para. 1.10; see also Guy Stessens (2000), *Money Laundering – A New International Law Enforcement Model,* Cambridge, UK: Cambridge University Press.
[54] As from 18 April 2005, the Inland Revenue merged with HMCE to form HMRC.

parts. Part I creates the ARA.[55] Part II makes provisions for confiscation in England and Wales. Parts III and IV make similar provisions for Scotland and Northern Ireland respectively. Part V sets out new provisions for the civil recovery proceedings in the UK, and provisions for the search, seizure and forfeiture of cash. Part VI empowers the Director of ARA to exercise functions of the Inland Revenue. Part VII consolidates, updates and reforms the criminal law in the UK with regard to money laundering. Part VIII sets out wider powers for use in criminal confiscation, civil recovery and money laundering investigations.[56] Part IX deals with the relationship between confiscation and insolvency proceedings. Part X provides for the disclosure of information to and by the Director of ARA and the Scottish Ministers. Part XI provides for co-operation in investigation and enforcement between the jurisdictions of the UK and overseas authorities. Part XII deals with miscellaneous and general matters.[57]

When considering POCA 2002, the Home Office took into account human rights safeguards, consonant with the standards in the ECHR and the Human Rights Act 1998[58] (hereinafter HRA 1998), that are necessary to reach an appropriate balance between the right of the individual to legal enjoyment of property and the right of society to reclaim illegally derived assets. Such safeguards include 'a £10,000 *de minimis* threshold; the burden of proof remaining with the State; the provision of civil legal aid; compensation provisions; and organisational management arrangements to ensure that the civil forfeiture route is not adopted as a "soft option" in place of criminal proceedings'.[59] The hierarchical structure in the legislature intended that confiscation should be the primary means of depriving criminals of the proceeds of their activities with civil recovery as the initial alternative and taxation being utilised as a 'last resort'. The Revised Guidance by the Secretary of State to the Director of ARA in February 2005, however, indicated that criminal investigations and civil recovery and/or taxation investigations and proceedings can be instituted at the same time into unrelated criminality.[60]

---

[55]   The Assets Recovery Agency.

[56]   See Angela V. M. Leong (2006), 'Financial Investigation: A Key Element in the Fight against Organised Crime', *Company Lawyer*, **27** (7), 219.

[57]   *Explanatory Notes to the Proceeds of Crime Act 2002*, London, UK: The Stationery Office Ltd, available at http://www.opsi.gov.uk/ACTS/en2002/2002en29.htm, accessed 20 September 2007.

[58]   Hereinafter HRA 1998.

[59]   See PIU Report, *supra* at p. 40, para. 5.24.

[60]   See Home Office (2007), *Proceeds of Crime Act 2002 Section 2 (Director's Functions: General) Revised Guidance by the Secretary of State to the Director of ARA*, London, UK: Home Office, 7 February 2005: online version available at http://www.assetsrecovery.gov.uk/NR/rdonlyres/A5FC7AD6-2E59-41F2-B3E2-44795202E04E/0/SOSrevisedguidanceFeb2005.pdf, accessed 27 December 2007.

The Assets Recovery Agency

The ARA, established on 13 January 2003, is a non-ministerial department headed by a new office holder, 'the Director' (hereinafter Director), who is appointed by the Secretary of State. The Director reports to the Home Secretary, in consultation with the Secretary of State for Northern Ireland and the Scottish Ministers as necessary. The office of the Director is a corporation sole, which has legal personality and can hold property, bring legal proceedings and employ staff.[61] The Director may employ staff to assist him/her in carrying out his/her functions, and enter into contractual arrangements. The Director may delegate the exercise of his/her functions to his/her staff and to others working on a contractual basis.[62] ARA has three strategic aims[63] which are consistent with the Government's Asset Recovery Strategy[64] published in November 2001:

1. to disrupt organised criminal enterprises through the recovery of criminal assets, thereby alleviating the effects of crime on communities;
2. to promote the use of financial investigation as an integral part of criminal investigation, within and outside the Agency, domestically and internationally, through training and continuing professional development; and
3. to operate the Agency in accordance with its vision and values.

ARA is a non-prosecuting authority which carries out three distinct operational functions, namely: criminal confiscation, civil recovery and taxation. The civil recovery and taxation powers are unique to ARA as designated under POCA 2002. Cases are referred to ARA by law enforcement agencies for assessment before adoption for civil recovery or taxation investigations. ARA was intended to become a centre of expertise capable of handling high value and complex confiscation cases on referral from law enforcement and prosecution agencies. ARA also took the lead in developing the Joint Asset

---

[61] See POCA 2002, s. 1(3).

[62] *Ibid.* s. 1(4).

[63] See ARA (2004), *Annual Report 2003/04 and Business Plan 2004/05*, London, UK: ARA (hereinafter *ARA Report 03/04*), at p. 5.

[64] The aims of the Government's Asset Recovery Strategy are: (i) to make greater use of the investigation of criminal assets in the fight against crime; (ii) to recover money that has been made from crime or which is intended for use in crime; (iii) to prevent criminals and their associates from laundering the proceeds of criminal conduct, and detect and penalise such laundering where it occurs; and (iv) to use the proceeds recovered for the benefit of the community. Details of the Asset Recovery Strategy and Committee can be found at http://www.homeoffice.gov.uk, accessed 30 April 2006.

Recovery Database (JARD)[65] funded by the Recovered Assets Incentives Fund. The Financial Investigation Centre of Excellence is an integral part of ARA, which discharges the Director's statutory obligations in providing training and accreditation to financial investigators, and promotes the use of financial investigation as part of criminal investigation. ARA recognises the importance of working in partnership, and has developed and maintained a series of memoranda of understanding with key stakeholders. The number of staff has increased from 131 in March 2004 to 162 in March 2005, 201 in March 2006 and 219 in March 2007.[66]

Confiscation Regime Under POCA 2002

Confiscation proceedings

Part II of POCA 2002 makes a consolidated and updated set of provisions for confiscation in England and Wales. It introduces the concept of 'criminal lifestyle',[67] and will eventually replace the separate drug trafficking and criminal justice legislation. As a result of HRA 1998 and decisions in the European Court, confiscation for offences committed before 24 March 2003 has to be made under previous DTA 1994 and CJA 1988, and ARA can only assist in these cases. For offences committed on or after 24 March 2003, ARA has the power to undertake and adopt a confiscation investigation with support from the referring law enforcement agency. In addition, wider investigative powers

---

[65] JARD provides a central information management system for monitoring performance in asset recovery, and a comprehensive record of all the assets under restraint nationally.

[66] See the following: *ARA Report 03/04*; ARA (2005), *Annual Report 2004/05 and Business Plan 2005/06,* London, UK: ARA (hereinafter *ARA Report 04/05*); ARA (2006), *Annual Report 2005/06 and Business Plan 2006/07,* London, UK: ARA (hereinafter *ARA Report 05/06*); ARA (2007), *Annual Report 2006/07 and Business Plan 2007–08,* London, UK: ARA (hereinafter *ARA Report 06/07*).

[67] See POCA 2002, s. 75 states that a person has a criminal lifestyle if the offence (or any of the offences) concerned is: (i) an offence specified in Sch. 2 to the legislation which include a drug trafficking offence, or a money laundering offence under ss. 327 or 328, or an offence specified by the Secretary of State relating to people trafficking, arms trafficking, counterfeiting, intellectual property, pimps and brothels, blackmail, or an attempt, conspiracy, incitement or aiding, abetting, counseling or securing one of the above; or (ii) an offence committed over a period of at least six months and the offender's total benefit is not less than £5000; or (iii) the conduct forming part of a course of criminal activity. Conduct forms part of a course of criminal activity if the defendant has been convicted of three or more other offences on the same occasion and from which he has benefited, or the defendant has at least two previous convictions on separate occasions within six years of the most recent proceedings, and the total benefit is not less than £5000.

under Part VIII of POCA 2002 will be available to all confiscation investigations, no matter which legislation the confiscation procedure is under. Therefore, confiscation proceedings are now an integral part of all acquisitive crime proceedings with the objective that the criminal justice process will not be regarded as concluded until confiscation proceedings have been considered.

The purpose of confiscation proceedings is to recover the financial benefit that an offender has obtained from his criminal conduct. A confiscation order is made by the Crown Court and requires the defendant (who has been convicted following a criminal trial) to pay a particular sum that the court calculates to be the amount recoverable. Thus, although a confiscation order is an *in personam* order, it does not apply to particular items of property, and the defendant can satisfy the confiscation order with both legitimate and illicit income. The court must proceed to make a confiscation order if (i) the defendant is convicted of an offence or offences in proceedings before the Crown Court, or he is committed to the Crown Court for sentencing or with a view to a confiscation order being considered, and (ii) if the prosecutor, the Director or the court believes it is appropriate to do so.[68] The court then decides whether the defendant has a criminal lifestyle. If the defendant has a criminal lifestyle and has benefited from his general criminal conduct,[69] then the four statutory assumptions[70] are applied in determining the defendant's benefit from crime, unless the court decides that applying the assumptions would give rise to a serious risk of injustice, or the defendant can prove these assumptions are incorrect. If the court decides that the defendant does not have a criminal lifestyle, then his benefit is the amount which he has obtained from the particular criminal conduct[71] including the value of the property and any pecuniary advantage.[72]

---

[68]   *Ibid.* s. 6(1) to (3).

[69]   General criminal conduct is defined in POCA 2002, s. 76(2) as all the defendant's criminal conduct and it is immaterial whether conduct occurred or whether property constituting a benefit from conduct was obtained before or after the passing of the legislation.

[70]   The four assumptions contained in POCA 2002, s. 10 are (i) any property transferred to the defendant after the relevant day was obtained as a result of his general criminal conduct, (ii) any property held by the defendant at the time after his conviction was obtained as a result of his general criminal conduct, (iii) any expenditure incurred by the defendant after the relevant day was met by property obtained as a result of his general criminal conduct, and (iv) any property obtained by the defendant was free of any other interests in it. The relevant day is defined in s. 10(8) as the first day of the period of six years before the proceedings against the defendant were started.

[71]   Particular criminal conduct is defined in POCA 2002, s. 76(3) as conduct that constitutes offences of which the defendant was convicted and offences taken into consideration when deciding the defendant's sentence.

[72]   *Ibid.* s. 76(4) to (7).

Once the court has determined the amount of the defendant's benefit, the court must decide the recoverable amount (which is an amount equal to the defendant's benefit from the conduct concerned),[73] and then make a confiscation order requiring him to pay that amount. If the defendant shows that the available amount[74] is less than that benefit, the recoverable amount is the available amount or a nominal amount if the available amount is nil.[75] The standard of proof in relation to criminal lifestyle, benefit from general criminal conduct and recoverable amount is on a balance of probabilities. A court may proceed with confiscation proceedings in the absence of a defendant who has been convicted,[76] or who has neither been convicted nor acquitted provided that two years have elapsed from the time of absconding.[77] The court may postpone the confiscation proceedings on one or more occasions for up to a total of two years from the date of conviction.[78] The application for the postponement of the confiscation determination must be made before the defendant is sentenced. In enforcing the confiscation order, the court may appoint an enforcement receiver, whose primary purpose is to realise assets in satisfaction of a confiscation order, but they will inevitably have to manage assets pending realisation. The enforcement receiver is a court appointed officer with wide powers[79] and independent of the prosecutor and the defendant. He has the right to have his fees paid from the proceeds of realisation of the defendant's assets.

Restraint orders

A restraint order[80] can be obtained to freeze a defendant's assets, and prohibit the defendant from dealing with any realisable property[81] held by him, so that assets will be available to satisfy any confiscation order that might be made against him by the Crown Court upon his being convicted of a criminal offence. The general rule is that if a restraint order is made before a bankruptcy order, then the restraint order will have priority over any assets subject to both orders. Where the court has made a restraint order, it may at any time appoint

---

73 *Ibid.* s. 7(1).
74 The available amount is the value of all the defendant's free property, minus certain prior obligations of the defendant's such as earlier fines, plus the value of all tainted gifts made by the defendant as described in section 77.
75 See POCA 2002, s. 7(2).
76 *Ibid.* s. 27.
77 *Ibid.* s. 28.
78 *Ibid.* s. 14.
79 *Ibid.* s. 51.
80 *Ibid.* s. 41.
81 *Ibid.* s. 83.

a receiver[82] to take possession of any realisable property, and to manage or otherwise deal with any property in respect of which he is appointed. The receiver has wide powers and is independent of the prosecutor and the defendant.[83] The receiver's costs will be paid from assets under his control, and if they are insufficient, it will rely on an indemnity from the prosecutor. For offences that occurred before 24 March 2003 (whether or not joined with other offences that occurred after this date), restraint powers under the previous DTA 1994 and CJA 1988 are used. The restraint powers under POCA 2002 are only available for those offences committed on or after 24 March 2003.

There are three main differences between the restraint regime under POCA 2002 and those of the old legislation. The first difference is the venue of the application: applications for restraint orders under POCA 2002 are made to the Crown Court, whereas such applications were made to the High Court under previous legislation. The second difference is the timing of the application: applications under POCA 2002 can be made at an earlier stage as the power to make a restraint order is triggered by the start of a criminal investigation and, therefore, there are reasonable grounds to believe that the alleged offender has benefited from his criminal conduct. Under the old procedure, applications are made when a defendant has been, or is about to be, charged. The third difference is the legal costs: funds restrained under the new regime cannot be released to the defendant to pay for legal expenses incurred in relation to the offences in respect of which the restraint order is made,[84] while such restraint did not exist under the old regime.

Civil Recovery and Forfeiture Proceedings Under POCA 2002

The concept of civil recovery is similar to the civil forfeiture power under RICO, which does not rely on the individual being convicted, but instead allows civil forfeiture on irrefutable presumptions without a prior criminal conviction. The idea of having a civil forfeiture power in the UK was suggested by the Regional Crime Squads in 1995,[85] and it was again recommended by the PIU Report in 2000. Following the PIU Report, the Home Office proposed that:

> with appropriate safeguards, more extensive civil forfeiture powers should be introduced to England and Wales. The Home Office proposals envisage the powers being

---

[82]   *Ibid.* s. 48.

[83]   *Ibid.* s. 49. For an insider's perspective of the work of receivers under POCA 2002, see Chapter 8 of this book.

[84]   *Ibid.* s. 41(4).

[85]   See *Home Affairs Committee Third Report*, at p. 135.

used where there is strong evidence that the property has criminal origins, but insufficient evidence for the criminal conviction of the owner.[86]

During the establishment of the civil recovery regime in the UK, experience was drawn from RICO in the US, the Criminal Assets Recovery Act 1990 in New South Wales,[87] the Proceeds of Crime Act 1996 and Criminal Assets Bureau Act 1996 in the Republic of Ireland.[88]

Part V of POCA 2002 contains two separate non-conviction based civil systems for removing the proceeds of crime. The first system deals with the civil recovery proceedings of property which has been obtained through unlawful conduct. This procedure can only be initiated by ARA through High Court proceedings. The second system is a cash forfeiture system for amounts of cash discovered by police or customs officers during searches. Part V expands the provisions for the search and seizure of cash, which is reasonably suspected of having been obtained through unlawful conduct or of being intended for use in such conduct. The forfeiture of such cash involves magistrates' court proceedings.

Civil recovery proceedings

The civil recovery procedure under Part V of POCA 2002 enables ARA to recover in civil proceedings before the High Court property which is, or represents, property obtained through unlawful conduct in England, Wales and Northern Ireland.[89] ARA receives cases referred by the law enforcement agencies where (i) criminal investigation has been carried out but insufficient evidence has been uncovered to pursue criminal charges, or (ii) a decision not to institute criminal proceedings is made due to public interest criteria, or (iii) confiscation proceedings have failed due to procedural faults, or (iv) where the defendant is beyond the reach of criminal proceedings because that person is

---

[86]   See PIU Report, *supra* at p. 35, para. 5.1.

[87]   See the Australian Law Reform Commission (1999), *Report No. 87, Confiscation That Counts: A Review of the Proceeds of Crime Act, 1987*, Canberra, Sydney, Australia: Australian Government Publishing Services, online version available at http://www.alrc.gov.au/media/1999/mb0616.htm, accessed 20 September 2007; see further references to this report in Chapter 1 of this book. The New South Wales scheme imposes a reverse onus on defendants to prove the lawful provenance of their restrained assets. Also see David Lusty (2002), 'Civil Forfeiture of Proceeds of Crime in Australia', *Journal of Money Laundering Control*, **5** (4), 345. For further more on Australia, see Chapter 5 of this book.

[88]   The Criminal Assets Bureau also exercises the Irish Revenue legislation to proceeds of criminal activity. See further Chapter 3 of this book.

[89]   See POCA 2002, s. 240(1). However, POCA 2002, s. 282(2) prohibits civil recovery proceedings being taken in respect of cash only, where the appropriate mechanism should be cash forfeiture.

dead or abroad and there is no reasonable prospect of securing his extradition, or that the person has been convicted of an offence abroad but has recoverable property in the UK. A respondent who absconds would not usually result in any delay in the civil recovery proceedings as long as he was served with the relevant pleadings, and judgment can be entered against the respondent in his absence.

Certain criteria must be met before cases can be adopted by ARA for civil recovery investigations including (i) the case must normally be referred by a law enforcement agency or prosecution authority, (ii) recoverable property must have been identified and have an estimated value of at least £10 000, (iii) recoverable property must be acquired within 12 years, (iv) there must be significant local impact in the communities, and (v) there must be evidence of criminal conduct that is supported on the balance of probabilities.[90] It was held in *ARA v. Green*[91] that:

1. In civil proceedings for recovery under Part 5 of the Act the Director need not allege the commission of any specific criminal offence but must set out the matters that are alleged to constitute the particular kind or kinds of unlawful conduct by or in return for which the property was obtained.
2. A claim for civil recovery cannot be sustained solely upon the basis that a respondent has no identifiable lawful income to warrant his lifestyle.

ARA has the burden to prove on a balance of probabilities that any matters alleged to constitute unlawful conduct[92] have occurred, and that the property sought to be recovered is property, or represents property, that has been obtained through that unlawful conduct. The respondent has a reverse onus to prove the lawful provenance of his assets, and has to produce evidence that either refutes any allegation of unlawful conduct or an allegation that property is recoverable. Property is obtained through unlawful conduct if a person obtains it by or in return for the conduct.[93] In deciding whether any property has been obtained through unlawful conduct, it is immaterial whether or not any money, goods or services were provided in order to put the person in question in a position to carry out the conduct, and it is not necessary to show that

---

[90]   See *ARA Report 04/05, supra* at p. 10.
[91]   [2005] EWHC 3168 (Admin), at para. 47.
[92]   POCA 2002, s. 241(1) states that conduct occurring in any part of the UK is unlawful conduct if it is unlawful under the criminal law of that part. Unlawful conduct, as stated in s. 241(2), also includes conduct which occurs in a country outside the UK and is unlawful under the criminal law of that country, and if it occurred in a part of the UK, would be unlawful under the criminal law of that part.
[93]   *Ibid.* s. 242(1).

the conduct was of a particular kind if it is shown that the property was obtained through conduct of one of a number of kinds, each of which would have been unlawful conduct.[94] Thus, the property is still recoverable even if it is not possible to prove that particular property was derived from a particular type of crime.

Recoverable property is property[95] obtained through unlawful conduct.[96] Recoverable property may be followed into the hands of a person obtaining it on a disposal.[97] In addition, where the 'original property' obtained through unlawful conduct is or has been recoverable, any property which represents this 'original property' is also recoverable property.[98] In other words, if the person tries to conceal the proceeds by mixing them with legitimate funds, the portion of the mixed property which is attributable to the recoverable property represents the property obtained through unlawful conduct and remains recoverable.[99] The other portion of the mixed property which is not recoverable is described as 'associated property'.[100] Besides, where a person who has recoverable property obtains further property consisting of profits accruing in respect of the recoverable property, the further property is recoverable.[101] However, property is not recoverable if the property was acquired 12 years ago from the date on which the Director's cause of action accrued,[102] or if the victims of theft obtain a declaration that they own the property.[103] Other exemptions are found under section 282 of POCA 2002.

ARA may apply for freezing injunctions under Part 25.1(1)(f) of the Civil Procedure Rules to preserve assets for the purpose of meeting a recovery order, if there is a real risk of imminent dissipation of such assets. Alternatively, ARA may apply for a property freezing order whereby investigation can continue after such order is granted.[104]

If the case involves ongoing businesses or a substantial amount of overseas property, ARA may apply for an interim receiving order (hereinafter IRO) (whether before or after commencing civil recovery proceedings) for the

---

94   *Ibid.* s. 242(2).
95   *Ibid.* ss. 316(4)–(7): property includes all types of property whether in the UK or abroad.
96   *Ibid.* s. 304(1).
97   *Ibid.* s. 304(3).
98   *Ibid.* s. 305.
99   *Ibid.* s. 306.
100   *Ibid.* s. 245(1).
101   *Ibid.* s. 307.
102   *Ibid.* s. 288(1).
103   *Ibid.* s. 281.
104   See Serious Organised Crime and Police Act 2005, s. 98 inserts the provision for property freezing order into POCA 2002, s. 245A; see also Chapter 8 of this book.

detention, custody or preservation of property, and the appointment of the interim receiver.[105] The High Court may grant an IRO if the court is satisfied that there is a good arguable case that the property to which the application relates is or includes recoverable property and associated property whereby the identity of the person who holds the associated property cannot be established.[106] An application for an IRO may be made without notice to the person whose property it is going to affect, if the circumstances are such that notice would prejudice any right of the enforcement authority to obtain a recovery order.[107] An IRO is a type of worldwide freezing injunction prohibiting the person to whose property the order applies from dealing with the property, and also requiring him to repatriate property or documents abroad to the UK. The interim receiver is responsible for establishing the owner of the property, the whereabouts of the property and the extent of the property.[108] The interim receiver is a court appointed officer with wide powers, and independent of ARA and the respondent. However, ARA is responsible for the costs of the interim receivers.

Recovery orders are orders against specified property, and require that the property subject to the order is sold and the proceeds realised.[109] If the court is satisfied that any property is recoverable, then the court must make a recovery order which vests the property in the trustee for civil recovery.[110] The functions of the trustee are: (i) to secure the detention, custody or preservation of any property vested in him, (ii) to realise the value of the property to the benefit of ARA, and (iii) to perform any other functions conferred on him by Part V POCA 2002.[111] It is the duty of ARA to nominate a suitably qualified person for the appointment[112] and the trustee, in performing his functions, acts on behalf of ARA, and must comply with the directions given by ARA.[113]

Cash forfeiture proceedings

POCA 2002 replaces and extends the powers under DTA 1994 for the search, seizure and forfeiture of cash.[114] It not only extends this power to include cash

---

[105]   See POCA 2002, s. 246(1) and (2), and Chapter 8 of this book.

[106]   *Ibid.* s. 246(5) and (6); also see *R (Director of the ARA) v. Keenan,* (2005) NIQB Ref No. COGC5362.

[107]   See POCA 2002, s. 246(3).

[108]   *Ibid.* s. 247 and Sch. 6.

[109]   *Ibid.* s. 266.

[110]   *Ibid.* s. 266(1) and (2).

[111]   *Ibid.* s. 267(3).

[112]   *Ibid.* s. 267(2).

[113]   *Ibid.* s. 267(4).

[114]   Part III of the Criminal Justice (International Co-operation) Act 1990 introduced the power for the police and customs officers to seize cash discovered on import

related to all unlawful conduct, but allows the forfeiture of cash which has an entirely legitimate origin as long as the court is satisfied that the cash is intended for use in unlawful conduct.[115] Cash forfeiture proceedings are civil proceedings and the civil standard of proof (balance of probabilities) applies, and no conviction is required for the forfeiture of the cash to be ordered. Unlike the previous legislation, POCA 2002 provides for seizure of cash inland anywhere in UK rather than only at the borders. In other words, cash held in any safety deposit box may be seized if there are reasonable grounds for suspicion. POCA 2002 also establishes a new power to search any person or any article in his possession[116] if a customs officer or the police have reasonable grounds for suspecting that the person is carrying cash,[117] which is recoverable property or is intended for use in unlawful conduct, and the amount of which is not less than the minimum amount.[118] The officers may detain the person for as long as necessary for the search,[119] but the power does not include an intimate search or strip search.[120] The officers may also search premises for cash if they are lawfully on the premises,[121] but the legislation has not provided a new power of entry. The officers may seize any cash if they have reasonable grounds for suspecting that it is recoverable property or intended for use in unlawful conduct, and the amount of which is not less than the minimum amount.[122] The powers of search and seizure will normally require the approval of a justice of the peace (in England, Wales and Northern

---

or export which was reasonably suspected of being derived from or intended for use in drug trafficking. An application for the forfeiture of the case might subsequently be made in a magistrates' court. These provisions had been consolidated into Part II of DTA 1994.

[115]   In *Commissioners of Customs and Excise v. Duffy* [2002] EWHC 425, it was held that the court was entitled to aggregate to cover 'smurfing', a technique used in order to avoid the creation of any records or detection, whereby large amount of cash transactions is broken into smaller ones, so that each transaction is below the threshold-reporting requirements.

[116]   See POCA 2002, s. 289(2).

[117]   Cash is defined in POCA 2002, s. 289(6) as '(a) notes and coins in any currency, (b) postal orders, (c) cheques of any kind, including travellers' cheques, (d) bankers' drafts, (e) bearer bonds and bearer shares, found at any place in the United Kingdom'; see also s. 289(7): 'Cash also includes any kind of monetary instrument which is found at any place in the United Kingdom, if the instrument is specified by the Secretary of State by an order made after consultation with the Scottish Ministers.'

[118]   The minimum amount was originally £10 000 as specified in POCA 2002 (Recovery of Cash in Summary Proceedings: Minimum Amount) Order 2002, but the threshold is reduced to £5000 in 2004. The limit was further reduced to £1000 with effect from 31 July 2006.

[119]   See POCA 2002, s. 289(4).

[120]   *Ibid.* s. 289(8).

[121]   *Ibid.* s. 289(1).

[122]   *Ibid.* s. 294.

Ireland) or a sheriff (in Scotland), or if that is not practicable, the approval of a senior officer (police inspector or equivalent).[123] The exercise of such powers is governed by the Code of Practice issued by the Secretary of State.[124] Where a search takes place without prior approval, and either no cash is seized, or cash is seized but not detained for more than 48 hours, a written report justifying such search must be submitted by the officer who exercised the power to a person appointed by the Secretary of State.[125]

Cash, which has been seized, may be detained for an initial period of 48 hours.[126] This period can be extended with an order made by a magistrates' court or a justice of the peace, on application by the officers, for a period of no longer than three months in the case of the initial order. Further orders may be granted for up to a maximum of two years. In addition, cash detained for more than 48 hours should be paid into an interest bearing account,[127] unless the cash is required as evidence of an offence or as evidence in the forfeiture proceedings.[128] While cash is detained, an application for the forfeiture of the whole or any part of it may be made to a magistrates' court by the Commissioners of Customs and Excise or a constable.[129] Any person who claims ownership of the detained cash may apply for it to be released before a forfeiture order is made.[130] An appeal against the forfeiture order can also be made to the Crown Court within the period of 30 days of the order by way of a rehearing.[131]

Taxation Powers Under POCA 2002

As the Al Capone case illustrated, tax offences can be key in dealing with organised crime. For years, Al Capone evaded prosecution for his racketeering and other criminal activities, but was found guilty in 1931 of tax evasion and sentenced to 11 years' imprisonment, US$80 000 in fines and court costs. Many criminal organisations generate substantial revenues, especially through drug trafficking, and most illicit proceeds have gone untaxed, which greatly destabilise the financial systems in the UK. A number of jurisdictions have tried to 'fiscalise resources from participants in drug markets, and integrate

---

[123]   *Ibid.* s. 290.
[124]   *Ibid.* s. 292, and POCA 2002 (Cash Searches: Code of Practice) Order 2002, Statutory Instrument No. 3115 of 2002.
[125]   See POCA 2002, ss. 290(6)–(8).
[126]   *Ibid.* s. 295(1).
[127]   *Ibid.* s. 296(1).
[128]   *Ibid.* s. 296(3).
[129]   *Ibid.* s. 298(1).
[130]   *Ibid.* s. 301(1).
[131]   *Ibid.* s. 299.

this drug revenue into their system of rule'.[132] In view of the potential of using tax enforcement laws as a means of deterring and punishing criminals, the Proceeds of Crime Act 1996 and the Criminal Assets Bureau Act 1996 have established the framework for the exchange of information between the revenue authorities and the department of social welfare in the Republic of Ireland. Under section 5 of the Criminal Assets Bureau Act 1996, the Criminal Assets Bureau has the functions under the Revenue Acts to ensure that the proceeds of criminal activity or suspected criminal activity are subject to tax. Indeed, taxation powers have been a major source of recovered funds from suspected criminals in both Ireland and Australia.[133]

In the UK, criminal organisations were estimated to have generated between £6.5 billion and £11.1 billion in 1996, and some of these revenues were untaxed.[134] Although the Inland Revenue has the power to raise assessments and enforce removal of assets against those shown to have undeclared income and wealth, these powers are generally of little use against individuals suspected of benefiting from crime. Tax cannot be collected where a source of the income (including criminal activity) cannot be identified. The PIU Report suggested that there should be:

- increased proactive investigation and removal of criminal assets by the Inland Revenue and tax inspectors located in the new [National Confiscation Agency];[135]
- the facilitation of greater exchanges of information on criminality between Inland Revenue and law enforcement, including new statutory gateways; and
- the correction of tax law anomalies to enable the Inland Revenue to tax income, even where a source (such as crime) cannot be identified.[136]

Part VI of POCA 2002 empowers the Director to exercise functions of the Inland Revenue in relation to income, gains and profits arising or accruing as a result of criminal conduct[137] without a conviction. Before the Director can

---

[132]   See Hans Van Der Veen (2003), 'Taxing the Drug Trade: Coercive Exploitation and the Financing of Rule', *Crime, Law & Social Change*, **40**, 349, at p. 349.

[133]   See further Chapters 3 and 5 of this book.

[134]   See PIU Report, *supra* at p. 90, para. 10.1.

[135]   The proposed new agency responsible for achieving criminal confiscation and civil forfeiture results under POCA 2002 is the ARA.

[136]   See PIU Report, *supra* at p. 10, para. 1.40.

[137]   Criminal conduct is defined in POCA 2002, s. 326 as conduct which constitutes an offence in any part of the UK, or would constitute an offence in any part of the UK if it occurred there, but does not include conduct constituting an offence relating to a matter under the care and management of the Board of Inland Revenue.

take over general 'Revenue' functions[138] and carry out taxation investigations, certain qualifying conditions must be satisfied. The Director must have reasonable grounds to suspect that income, gains or profits accruing to a person or a company in respect of a chargeable period are chargeable[139] to the relevant tax, and arise or accrue as a result of the person's or another's criminal conduct.[140] The relevant taxes include, but are not limited to, income tax, capital gains tax, corporation tax and inheritance tax. Once the qualifying condition is met, the Director is then required to serve a notice on the Board of Inland Revenue, which enables the Director to carry out the normal taxation functions of the Inland Revenue for the specified period.[141] Section 318 of POCA 2002 gives more details in relation to the Revenue functions regarding employment.

A major difference between the assessments raised by the Inland Revenue and those initiated by the Director is that the former is required to specify the source of income in question, while the Director can raise income tax assessments under section 29 of the Taxes Management Act 1970, where the Director discovers a loss of tax even though the source of income in question cannot be identified. This provides for a new 'no-source' assessing power.[142] However, if the case is transferred back to the Inland Revenue from the Director, any 'no-source' assessment is invalid.[143] All appeals against the actions arising from the exercise by the Director of its Revenue functions will be addressed to the Special Commissioners, excluding access to the General Commissioners.[144] There are similar provisions and conditions in relation to inheritance tax functions.[145] In exercising the 'Revenue' functions, the Director must apply all interpretations of the law and concessions published by the Board of Inland Revenue.[146] The authority of the Director is not just limited to the proceeds of unlawful conduct, but applies to the whole of the respondent's property. ARA's settlement policy also applies to taxation cases.

---

138   General 'Revenue' functions under POCA 2002, s. 323(1) include '(a) income tax; (b) capital gains tax; (c) corporation tax; (d) national insurance contributions; (e) statutory sick pay; (f) statutory maternity pay; (g) statutory paternity pay; (h) statutory adoption pay; (i) student loans.'
139   Income must be chargeable to tax under one or other of the legal headings or 'schedules' of tax. See Income and Corporation Taxes Act 1988 in general for schedules of taxes; see further, *ibid.* s. 18(1) 'Schedule D' provides for a charge to tax in respect of income from trade, profession and vocation.
140   See POCA 2002, s. 317(1).
141   *Ibid.* s. 317(2).
142   *Ibid.* s. 319.
143   *Ibid.* s. 319(3).
144   *Ibid.* s. 320.
145   *Ibid. ss.* 321 and 322.
146   *Ibid.* s. 324.

In general, taxation cases are expected to take 12 to 18 months to reach conclusion particularly where the subject chooses to exercise their rights of appeal.[147] In addition, tax inspectors from the Special Compliance Office of the Inland Revenue are seconded to ARA to enhance sharing of information and experience.

HOW EFFECTIVE ARE THE CIVIL RECOVERY AND TAXATION POWERS?

Evaluation of the Civil Recovery Regime

Between 2003 and 2004, ARA's targets included the disruption[148] of 35 criminal enterprises at all levels of criminality, obtaining orders and issuing tax assessments to the value of at least £10 million and realisation of confiscation receipts to the value of at least £5 million. During this period, ARA managed to disrupt 24 criminal enterprises, freeze £14.1 million worth of property by the High Court and restrain £4.4 million. The reason for the shortfall was mainly the result of the length of time taken to progress civil recovery cases through the courts which was longer than initially expected.[149]

Between 2004 and 2005, ARA's targets included the disruption of 35 criminal enterprises at all levels of criminality, adoption of a further 35 cases, early restraint of assets to the value of £15 million, obtaining recovery orders and issuing tax assessments to the value of at least £15 million and realisation of receipts in civil recovery and taxes cases to the value of £10 million. ARA achieved three out of the five main targets, including the disruption of 36 criminal enterprises, adoption of 51 cases and early restraint of £17 million of assets. However, the impact of legal challenges[150] delayed the progress of the civil recovery cases in the High Court resulting in only £5.6 million in civil recovery orders and tax assessments granted and £4.7 million in receipts collected.[151] Other reasons for the lengthy litigation process included the issue

---

[147]   Further guidance in respect of ARA's policy on the application of Part VI powers and the conduct of taxation cases is available at http://www.assetsrecovery.gov.uk/WhatWeDo/Tax, accessed 20 September 2007.

[148]   According to ARA, disruption is: (a) the freezing of assets through a restraint or freezing order, Mareva injunction or IRO; or (b) where freezing has not taken place either (i) making a confiscation or recovery order; or (ii) obtaining voluntary settlement/payment, where no order has been made; or (iii) undertakings given not to deal with assets; or (c) the issue of a tax assessment.

[149]   See *ARA Report 03/04*, at Annex A.

[150]   See *ARA Report 04/05,* at pp. 15–17.

[151]   *Ibid.* Annex A.

of legal aid and the fact that section 252(4) of POCA 2002 expressly prevented the use of frozen property for paying legal expenses. Courts were reluctant to hear the case unless the respondent had legal representation, thus a new provision to modify its effect was introduced in SOCPA 2005.[152]

Between 2005 and 2006, ARA's targets became more challenging including the disruption of 70 criminal enterprises at all levels of criminality, adoption of a further 100 cases, early restraint of assets to the value of £25 million, obtaining recovery orders and issuing tax assessments to the value of at least £16 million and realisation of receipts in civil recovery and taxes cases to the value between £6 to £12 million. Once again, ARA achieved, indeed over performed, in three of the five main targets, including the disruption of 100 criminal enterprises, adoption of 108 cases and early restraint of £85.7 million of assets. However, only £4.6 million in civil recovery orders and tax assessments were granted and only £4.1 million in receipts were collected.[153]

In 2006, ARA was heavily criticised for not meeting its targets and failing to raise enough money to cover its budget.[154] A common criticism was that in the first three years of its existence ARA cost over £60 million but only managed to retrieve some £8 million.[155] In February 2007, the National Audit Office published a damning report which found that no feasibility study was carried out before ARA's creation to assess its likely performance or appropriate targets. There were still four police forces which had not yet referred a single case to ARA. Case management information was considered poor. There was no central database of cases, and staff referred to different systems which held contradictory and incomplete information.[156] As a result, ARA went through major reforms and reorganisation in order to increase its performance. ARA

---

[152]   The Proceeds of Crime Act 2002 (Legal Expenses in Civil Recovery Proceedings) Regulations 2005 (Statutory Instrument No. 3382 of 2005).

[153]   See *ARA Report 05/06*, at Annex A, p. 59

[154]   See "Assets Recovery Agency 'failing'", *British Broadcasting Corporation News* (hereinafter *BBC News*), 14 June 2006, available at http://news.bbc.co.uk/1/hi/uk_politics/5077846.stm, accessed 20 September 2007; see also 'Agency aims to take crime gains', *BBC News*, 14 June 2006, available at http://news.bbc.co.uk/1/hi/uk_politics/5078624.stm, accessed 20 September 2007 (both articles collectively hereinafter BBC Reports).

[155]   See Angela V. M. Leong (2006), 'Civil Recovery and Taxation Regime: Are These New Powers under the Proceeds of Crime Act 2002 Working?', *Company Lawyer*, **27** (12), 362 (hereinafter *Civil Recovery and Taxation Regime*); see also Anthony Kennedy (2006), 'Civil Recovery Proceedings under the Proceeds of Crime Act 2002: The Experience So Far', *Journal of Money Laundering Control*, **9** (3), 245.

[156]   See David Hencke (2007), 'Assets Recovery Agency in a mess, says watchdog', *The Guardian Newspaper*, 21 February 2007, online version available at http://www.guardian.co.uk/uk_news/story/0,,2017972,00.html, accessed 27 December 2007 (hereinafter ARA News Article).

also took a more active role in communicating and educating law enforcement agencies and other stakeholders on the application of civil recovery and taxation proceedings so as to increase the quality of the referrals.

Between 2006 and 2007, ARA met its targets for the first time. During this period, the key performance indicators included the disruption of 90 to 125 criminal enterprises at all levels of criminality, adoption of a further 110 to 160 civil recovery and taxation cases, adoption of 15 POCA 2002 criminal confiscation cases, early restraint of assets to the value of £49 to £65 million, obtaining recovery orders and issuing tax assessments to the value of between £12.5 to £23.5 million, and realisation of receipts in civil recovery and taxes cases to the value between £9.5 to £16 million. ARA exceeded almost every baseline target including the disruption of 114 criminal enterprises, adoption of 45 POCA 2002 criminal confiscation cases, early restraint of £73.6 million of assets, £16.6 million in civil recovery orders and tax assessments and collection of £15.9 million in receipts. The only target that was narrowly missed was the adoption of a further 109 civil recovery and taxation cases.[157]

Reasons for Variances

There are several factors which explain the shortfall of the civil recovery regime. Since civil forfeiture is a significant extension of the government's powers to deal with the proceeds of crime without a conviction to the criminal standard, there have been several legal challenges. Some fundamental concerns in relation to the civil recovery proceedings include the lack of proportionality,[158] the breaching of the presumption of innocence and the double jeopardy rule.[159] The impact of such legal challenges has delayed the

---

[157] See *ARA Report 06-07*, at p. 9.

[158] See *McIntosh v. Lord Advocate* [2001] 2 All ER 638; *R (The Director of the ARA) v. He & Cheng* [2004] EWHC 3021 (Admin) (hereinafter *He & Cheng*). The issue of proportionality has to be considered on an individual case basis. However, both the High Court and the Court of Appeal in England and Wales, and Northern Ireland ruled that civil recovery proceedings is generally regarded as a proportional response, and breaches to arts 1 and 8 of Protocol 1 of ECHR were justified and proportionate to the harmful activities against which the proceedings were aimed, and in the public interest.

[159] The double jeopardy rule states that a person should not be prosecuted twice for the same offence, and that conviction shall be a bar to all further criminal proceedings. However, if that can be circumvented, there is no independent rule in English Law against double punishment. In fact, UK has not signed or ratified the double jeopardy protocol to ECHR. See *Connelly v. Director of Public Prosecutions* [1964] AC 1254; see also *Wymyss v. Hopkins* (1875) LR 10 QB 378; see also *R v. W* [1998] STC 550 (CA (Crim Div)); see also *R v. Smith* [2001] UKHL 68; see also Peter Alldridge (2002), 'Smuggling, Confiscation and Forfeiture', *Modern Law Review*, **65**, 781.

progress of civil recovery cases. In *Walsh v. The Director of the Assets Recovery Agency*[160] and *R (The Director of the Assets Recovery Agency) v. He & Cheng*,[161] the respondents argued that civil recovery proceedings should be categorised as criminal rather than civil, and should attract all the safeguards guaranteed by article 6 of ECHR. It was held that civil recovery procedure is to recover property obtained through unlawful conduct, but not to penalise or punish any person who is proved to have engaged in such conduct. Therefore, civil recovery proceedings under Part V of POCA 2002 should be classified as civil rather than criminal,[162] and does not contravene articles 6 and 7 of ECHR. Similar rulings were held in *R (Director of the Assets Recovery Agency) v. Belton*[163] by the High Court in Northern Ireland. Furthermore, the government argued that the civil recovery proceedings are classified as civil in nature, and it may be brought against any person (whether or not he is the person who committed the unlawful conduct) who holds or controls the recoverable property. Thus, the civil recovery proceedings do not contravene the spirit of the presumption of innocence, nor the double jeopardy rule.[164]

The lack of understanding and experience of civil recovery proceedings among law enforcement agencies and interim receivers also hindered the progress of the civil recovery cases. The law enforcement agencies are confused with the criteria for civil recovery and confiscation proceedings which often result in overlap of resources. Until 31 May 2006, ARA had received in total 397 referrals from different law enforcement agencies and authorities. Only about 50 per cent of all referrals were adopted by ARA which reflects the low quality of the referrals received by ARA.[165] Furthermore, the interim receivers have not yet fully utilised their new powers under POCA 2002.

Civil recovery investigations have also been obstructed by the lack of international powers. Part XI of POCA 2002, which empowers ARA to seek and

---

[160]   [2005] NICA 6 (hereinafter *Walsh*); see also *R (The Director of the ARA) v. Charrington* [2005] EWCA Civ 334 (hereinafter *Charrington*).

[161]   See *He & Cheng*.

[162]   The European Court of Human Rights ruled in a number of cases that civil forfeiture is classified as civil proceedings, see *Agosi v. UK* (1987) 9 EHRR; see also *Air Canada v. UK* (1995) 20 EHRR 150; see also *Butler v. UK* (2002) Application No. 41661/98; see also *Webb v. UK* (2004) Application No. 56054/00. Other Italian cases include *M v. Italy* 70 DR 59 (1991); *Raimondo v. Italy* (1994) 18 EHRR 237; *Arcuri v. Italy* (2001) Application No. 54024/99.

[163]   (2005) NIQB Ref No. COGF5334.

[164]   See Anthony Kennedy (2004), 'Justifying the Civil Recovery of Criminal Proceeds', *Journal of Financial Crime*, **12** (1), 8 (hereinafter Justifying Civil Recovery), at p. 18.

[165]   See *Civil Recovery and Taxation Regime, supra* at p. 366.

provide overseas co-operation in asset freezing and recovery, only came into effect in January 2006. However, even after the enactment of Part XI, the mutual recognition of asset freezing and confiscation orders among overseas authorities involves a lengthy process, and the standard of proof required might be higher than the balance of probabilities since civil recovery proceedings do not exist in every jurisdiction.

Evaluation of the Taxation Regime

ARA adopted seven cases for taxation between 2003 and 2004, and estimated assessments were issued between 2004 and 2005 in six cases with a total amount in excess of £1 million. The tax, National Insurance contributions, and penalties totalled over £500 000.[166] ARA has successfully obtained taxation production orders under section 23 of the Taxes Management Act 1970, and has developed a good working relationship with the Special Commissioners. As at 31 March 2006, the ARA tax team were working on 24 cases, in which seven freezing orders were granted in five cases, and estimated assessments were issued in 12 cases with a total of £3.2 million.[167] Between 2006 and 2007, seven cases have been completed with receipts of £0.5 million.[168] However, compared to the Irish system, the taxation powers under POCA 2002 have not been fully utilised.[169]

Taxation proceedings have certain advantages over civil recovery and confiscation proceedings, which include: (i) taxation deals with 'income' rather than 'property', which means that assets acquired prior to or after the period of criminality can be seized in settlement of the debt; (ii) tax assessment is not constrained by the prerequisites for civil recovery proceedings, which requires the proceeds be tangible, accessible, linked to criminality and acquired within the last 12 years; (iii) criminal proceeds do not have to be specifically identified or quantified; (iv) assessments can cover up to 20 years instead of 12 years in civil recovery proceedings; (v) future earnings can be used to settle the debt; (vi) the costs of tax cases will generally be lower as there are no searches and no receivers involved during the investigation; and (vii) it can be easier to deal with smokescreens, such as 'front' companies, in certain instances.[170]

However, there are certain shortcomings in initiating the taxation proceedings. The investigation, assessment, determination and enforcement of a tax

---

166   See *ARA Report 04/05*, at p. 20.
167   See *ARA Report 05/06*, at p. 29.
168   See *ARA Report 06/07*, at p. 13.
169   On the Irish experience, see Chapter 3 of this book.
170   See *Civil Recovery and Taxation Regime, supra* at p. 367.

debt involve a cumbersome and lengthy process, which is expected to take at least 12 to 18 months to reach a conclusion. Assets cannot be frozen or restrained for repaying tax debts, and no Part VIII investigation powers under POCA 2002 are available for taxation investigations. The complexity of tax cases also makes forecasting the outcome of the cases almost impossible; in fact, the taxation process is less certain compared with the procedures for confiscation and civil recovery proceedings. In addition, the potential yield from confiscation and civil recovery proceedings will almost invariably be higher than that from taxation. The highest yield from taxation, including penalty and interest, would be at a maximum of only 80 per cent of the criminal proceeds, due to the fact that criminals are entitled to the same personal allowances and consideration has to be given to the expenses or costs under tax assessments. Therefore, criminals are, in effect, allowed to benefit from a percentage of their proceeds. Furthermore, revenue confidentiality rules limit the amount of publicity on taxation cases, thus reducing the deterrent value.[171]

Taxation powers under Part VI of POCA 2002 have raised a number of legal issues in taxing the proceeds of crime, which is commonly seen as being untaxable. First of all, the qualifying condition requires the Director to have reasonable grounds to suspect that there has been income which arises to a person and from criminal conduct, and that income is chargeable to income tax or is a chargeable gain. In other words, the income derived from the criminal conduct must somehow fit into one of the schedules of income taxes under the Income and Corporation Taxes Act 1988 (hereinafter ICTA 1988). The most relevant in this case would be a charge of tax in respect of income from trade, profession and vocation under Schedule D, being section 18(1) of the ICTA 1988. This means that those activities, which are capable of being a trade but merely tainted with illegal activities, would satisfy this qualifying condition.[172] However, the real problem lies with those activities which can never be done legally and are not capable of being a trade, as there is no supply of goods and services. Crimes, such as burglary, theft, robbery, excise duty evasion and advance fee fraud fall into this category. Nevertheless the situation could be reconciled by defining burglary, theft and robbery as a vocation, and income from excise duty evasion is chargeable to tax as it could be accompanied with the buying and selling of smuggled goods, which underlay the evasion. Whether such tax cases would be successful depends on how far ARA pushes the boundaries of the case law.

---

[171] *Ibid.*

[172] See *Minister v. Smith* [1927] AC 193; see also *PC and Lindsay Woodward and Hiscox v. Commissioners of Inland Revenue* 16 TC 43; see also *Mann v. Nash* 16 TC 523; see also *Southern v. AB* 18 TC 59.

Secondly, the 'no-source' provision under section 319 of POCA 2002 contradicts the qualifying condition that the Director must have reasonable grounds to suspect that there has been income which is chargeable to income tax or is a chargeable gain, and this income has a causative link to criminality, when the Director does not even know the source of the income.[173] Thirdly, similar concerns as to whether articles 6 and 7 of ECHR apply to the taxation jurisdiction will depend on whether the raising of an assessment to income tax constitutes a 'criminal charge'.[174] In fact, there are many more issues under Part VI of POCA 2002 that need to be clarified, and perhaps more political and public support is required to move this new taxation regime forward.

On 30 June 2006, Her Majesty's Revenue and Customs[175] (hereinafter HMRC) announced the creation of a new Criminal Taxes Unit that will use taxation 'as a way of disrupting crime'. Sir David Varney, Chairman of HMRC, said: 'it will use every method of taxing and penalising suspected criminals, taking away their profits made from crime. The new Criminal Taxes Unit will aim to ensure that suspected criminals who have gained from their criminal activity are made to pay their fair share of tax.'[176]

REVIEW OF ASSETS RECOVERY SINCE POCA 2002

POCA 2002 represents a powerful opportunity to disrupt and deter serious organised crime to a substantial extent provided that it is used as a routine investigative process against a wide range of criminality. According to the Joint Review published by Her Majesty's Inspector of Constabulary (HMIC),[177] there has been some positive feedback regarding the new assets recovery regime.

---

[173]   See Tamara Solecki (2003), 'Taxing the Untaxable?', *Taxation* (27 November 2003) 216; see also Patrick Hunt (2001), *Criminal Assets Bureau and Taxation Matters*, Taxation Conference of the Bar Council of Ireland, 21 July 2001.

[174]   See the following: *Georgiou v. UK* [2001] STC 80; *Customs and Excise Commissioners v. Han and another and other appeals* [2001] STC 1188; *King v. Walden* [2001] STC 822; *Ferrazzini v. Italy* [2001] STC 1314; *King v. UK (No.2)* [2004] STC 911; P. Baker (2000), 'Taxation and the ECHR', (2000) *British Tax Review* 211; Peter Alldridge (2003), *Money Laundering Law: Forfeiture, Confiscation, Civil Recovery, Criminal Laundering and Taxation of the Proceeds of Crime,* Oxford, UK: Hart Publishing, at pp. 250–253.

[175]   Formerly the Inland Revenue and HMCE.

[176]   See Phillip Inman (2006), 'Criminal taxes hit squad aims to give fraudsters the Al Capone treatment', *The Guardian*, 30 June 2006, available online at http://business.guardian.co.uk/story/0,,1809376,00.html, accessed 20 September 2007.

[177]   See Her Majesty's Chief Inspector of Constabulary (2004), *Payback Time –*

There is a universal acceptance of POCA 2002 which has worked its way up for managerial and political attention. There is also a growing body of expertise in financial investigation and asset recovery which led to the success of several significant cases. However, since POCA 2002 is a fairly new piece of legislation, there are some areas of deficiencies which need to be changed and improved. In general, asset recovery, confiscation and money laundering are still widely regarded as highly complex and specialised activities divorced from the mainstream business. Full integration into force-level priorities and objectives is the exception rather than the rule. In fact, implementation and adoption of the new powers has been patchy and inconsistent across the criminal justice system, thus improvements in the strategic framework of objectives and targets, awareness levels, partnership approaches, the use of intelligence and enforcement are required to move the whole asset recovery strategy forward.

The uncertainty about the way POCA 2002 could be used reflects some incoherence in the national framework for setting objectives and targets and monitoring performance on asset recovery. It was suggested in the Joint Review that one body, perhaps the National Criminal Justice Board or Concerted Inter-agency Criminal Finances Action Group (CICFA),[178] should take the responsibility in securing clarity, consistency and coherence in the strategic framework of targets and objectives. Asset recovery should feature mainstream objectives rather than only marginally in the overall performance framework for criminal justice. In order to boost the capacity and incentive to assets recovery, the Recovered Assets Incentive Fund (RAIF) was set up by the Home Office between 2003 and 2004 to resource crime reduction and asset recovery activity. In February 2004, a new incentive scheme was finally set up to give the police a direct financial incentive to recover assets. 'They will receive a third of all assets above £40 million recovered next year, increasing to 50 per cent in 2005–06. The maximum benefit available to the police will be £43 million in 2004–05, rising to £65 million in 2005–06.'[179] In February

---

Joint Review of asset recovery since the Proceeds of Crime Act 2002, UK: Her Majesty's Inspector of Constabulary (hereinafter Joint Review): available online at http://inspectorates.homeoffice.gov.uk/hmic/inspections/thematic/pt1/?version=1, accessed 27 December 2007.

[178] CICFA is a non-statutory multi-agency group set up in 2002 to co-ordinate, monitor, manage and drive achievement of asset recovery targets. It is chaired by HMCE with members from ARA, HMCE, Association of Chief Police Officers of England, Wales and Northern Ireland, Crown Prosecution Service, Inland Revenue, National Crime Squad, National Criminal Intelligence Service, Financial Services Authority, Home Office, Department of Constitutional Affairs, Northern Ireland Office and Department of Public Prosecutions (Northern Ireland).

[179] See House of Commons Hansard, Written Ministerial Statements for 'Money Laundering Report System', session 2003–2004, vol. 419, 25 March 2004, column 65

2005, the Home Office announced that the incentive scheme would be extended to asset recovery agencies including HMRC, ARA, Serious Organised Crime Agency[180] (hereinafter SOCA) and Department of Constitutional Affairs (DCA) from 2006. On one hand, it is important to clarify and communicate proactively how the incentive scheme works; on the other hand, it is necessary to emphasise that asset recovery must be regarded as a crime fighting tactic rather than an income generating tool.

Due to the disparate nature of data collection and the confusion that arises from the mixed use of pre-POCA legislation and POCA provisions, it is difficult to assemble meaningful and validated statistics for analysing the current level of POCA successes and monitoring the performance of the overall asset recovery strategy. The lack of an effective measuring mechanism has also been criticised by the National Audit Office.[181] Indeed, it is naïve to evaluate the efficacy of POCA 2002 and anti-money laundering strategies simply by adding up the amounts of money that have in fact been successfully seized and recovered or the number of prosecutions and convictions of money laundering offences. It is not just how much it removes that matters but from whom it is removed. Successful disruption of criminal role models will have a deterrent effect and send the message to the local communities that 'crime does not pay', hopefully, this will eventually deter criminal intent and improve public confidence in the criminal justice system. However, 'disruption' should not be confused with the meaning of 'intervention' which is a means to an end. Nor should 'disruption' be confused with the effect of 'displacement' which only relocates criminal activities to areas or jurisdictions with weaker law enforcement rather than reducing further criminal activities. 'Money laundering is intrinsically global. If one country or jurisdiction tightens its regulation on money laundering and the financing of terrorism, these activities will quickly shift to a less regulated environment.'[182]

WS; details can be found at http://www.parliament.the-stationery-office.co.uk/pa/cm200304/cmhansrd/vo040325/wmstext/40325m03.htm, accessed on 20 September 2007.

[180]   The Serious Organised Crime Agency was established on 1 April 2006 under SOCPA 2005 with the remit to lead the fight against organised crime and to reduce the harm to UK caused by serious organised crime at all levels. It is a non-departmental public body reporting to the Home Office and incorporates National Crime Squad, National Criminal Intelligence Service, the investigative and intelligence work of HMRC on serious drug trafficking, and the Immigration Service's responsibilities for organised immigration crime.

[181]   See ARA News Article, *supra*.

[182]   See Eduardo Aninat, Daniel Hardy and R. Barry Johnston (eds) (2002), 'Combating Money Laundering and the Financing of Terrorism', *Finance and Development*, **39**, 3, at p. 44.

Most countries in Europe and the US have comprehensive anti-money laundering laws, but places like China, Southeast Asia, and Africa continue to provide wide opportunities for money laundering and terrorist financing.[183] Therefore, it is important to establish meaningful and representative indicators for measuring the effect of disruption, and consistency in data collection is required to monitor the performance of POCA 2002 so that the necessary resources can be deployed accordingly.

The Joint Review also identified a common problem of low levels of awareness of asset recovery issues among operational officers and that the mystique around financial investigation still remains. It is only recently that law enforcement agencies have been able and willing to commit the necessary resources to asset recovery. The courts and prosecutors have yet to become entirely comfortable with this body of law. There are also problems in case management and communications between the Crown Prosecution Service lawyers and police financial investigators. Courts are ill-equipped to enforce confiscation orders against hidden assets, especially those hidden abroad. Thus the Crown Prosecution Service and the courts need to be geared up to manage the greater volume of such cases as well as improving their enforcement activity. The awareness level also needs to be raised so that police officers feel confident to use the new powers under POCA 2002.

Improvement is also required in the partnership approach, which is both a strength and a weakness. When different law enforcement agencies work together effectively, the results can be spectacular. However, it also means that officers are operating on a crowded playing field with lots of potential for disjointed effort. Indeed, continuous effort is required to make criminal asset recovery an inclusive and seamless process. In addition to sharing intelligence, it needs to be effectively managed, co-ordinated and disseminated. There is also 'the need for asset recovery and financial investigation to be embedded within the National Intelligence Model, and possibly made the subject of a Code of Practice within the scope of the Police Reform Act'.[184]

THE WAY FORWARD[185]

Whether success or failure, it no longer matters as the ARA has been merged

---

[183] See J. M. Winer, T. J. Roule (eds) (2002), 'Fighting Terrorist Finance', *Survival*, **44** (3), 87, at pp. 98–99. On the confiscation laws in China and Taiwan, see generally Chapters 9 to 12 of this book.

[184] See Joint Review, *supra* at p. 11, para. 19.

[185] See in general, Angela V. M. Leong (2007), 'The Assets Recovery Agency: Future or No Future?', *Company Lawyer*, **28** (12), at p. 379.

with the SOCA in April 2008 after only five years in existence. On 11 January 2007, the government announced that the ARA would be abolished and the SOCA would take over the assets recovery function and there may be additional powers for prosecutors to seize money.[186] The Financial Investigation Centre of Excellence has now been moved to the new National Policing Improvement Agency. This new approach against organised crime adopted by SOCA will have an impact on the overall asset recovery regime. The rationale behind the merger, according to the government, is to streamline the work done by law and order agencies so as to achieve better economies of scale. However, whether the under-performance of ARA is a contributing factor to its disappearance is debatable.

Although ARA initially stays as a discrete entity within SOCA similar to the Child Exploitation and Online Protection Centre (CEOP) and all staff have the opportunity to transfer to SOCA, there are some concerns at both the organisational and operational levels. The establishment of SOCA through the integration of the National Crime Squad, the National Criminal Intelligence Service, the investigative and intelligence work of HMRC on serious drug trafficking and the Immigration Service's responsibilities for organised immigration crime in 2006 has posed major challenges to the different structural organisations and system procedures within the existing agencies. Indeed, the different components of SOCA are still adjusting through the difficult process of integrating various practices and cultures. The incorporation of ARA, yet another different set of procedures, practices and culture, has created further tensions at SOCA. In addition, staff morale is always an issue which needs to be addressed carefully in any merger.

Since SOCA concentrates on 'Level 3' criminality, being organised crime operating nationally and across borders, there is the worry that the merger could mean a narrowing of the focus. Nevertheless some argue that the intelligence-led UK wide SOCA could be a perfect outfit for asset recovery. The merger will require new legislation, which also gives the civil powers currently held solely by ARA to other criminal prosecutors in the Crown Prosecution Service, HMRC and the Serious Fraud Office. As a result, there might be potential legal challenges since civil recovery proceedings currently classified as civil in nature[187] is no longer initiated by a non-prosecuting

---

[186]   See Lords' Hansard text for 11 January 2007 (pt 1) 'Crime: Assets Recovery Agency', available at http://www.publications.parliament.uk/pa/ld200607/ldhansrd/text/70111-wms0001.htm, accessed 20 September 2007; see also 'Assets Recovery Agency Abolished' *BBC News* (11 January 2007), available at http://news.bbc.co.uk/1/hi/northern_ireland/6249769.stm, accessed 20 September 2007.

[187]   Civil recovery proceedings under Part V of the Proceeds of Crime Act 2002 point towards a civil classification because: (i) no police investigative powers are avail-

authority. There is no doubt that expectations are high but whether the merger between ARA and SOCA is going to work, only time will tell.

To conclude, criminal law is only one weapon against organised crime, and that much can be achieved under the civil law and taxation law provided that they are properly implemented and enforced. Though some jurisdictions have more advanced confiscation, money laundering and civil forfeiture regimes than others, many lessons are still to be learnt and many issues remain to be addressed and resolved. Ideally, a global civil forfeiture structure would be necessary for improving mutual legal assistance between different jurisdictions in the civil recovery arena.

able to the Director of ARA; (ii) civil procedural rules are applied and proceedings are initiated in the format of a claim form in the High Court; (iii) liability for an individual is limited to the recoverable property based on the balance of probabilities; (iv) the ARA does not have prosecuting authority and civil recovery proceedings are not brought by the Crown Prosecution Service; and (v) the Parliament's intention is to adopt the civil model of forfeiture to tackle the proceeds of crime. See Justifying Civil Recovery, *supra* and the following cases: *Walsh*; *Charrington, Director of the ARA v. Singh* [2005] EWCA Civ 580; *He & Cheng*; *R (Director of the ARA) v. Belton* (2005) NIQB Ref No. COGF5334.

8. Is the patient expected to live? UK civil forfeiture in operation

Sara Dayman*

INTRODUCTION

The commencement in 2003 of the Proceeds of Crime Act 2002 (hereinafter POCA 2002) introduced to the United Kingdom (UK) the concept of civil recovery proceedings against assets derived from the profits of crime. Home Office estimates, based on data supplied by law enforcement bodies, suggested in 1999–2000, that there were 'some £440 million of criminal assets that could be targeted by civil forfeiture across 400 individual cases'.[1]

In order to target the aforesaid £440 million of criminal assets a budget of some £15 million was granted in March 2003 to the newly formed Assets Recovery Agency (hereinafter ARA), the government department established to carry out such civil recovery proceedings. By September 2004 the ARA Resource Accounts 2003–04[2] made it clear that the cost and impact of pioneering the new legislation had been underestimated. The ARA's opening operational and financial plans had been based on the operational experience of HM Customs and Excise (now HM Revenue and Customs) in criminal asset forfeiture work. Those assumptions failed to reflect the mix, complexity (both in terms of case weight and the level of legal challenge) or length of civil recovery cases being handled by the ARA. Nor did they reflect the costs actually

---

*   The views expressed herein are the author's personally and do not represent the views of BDO Stoy Hayward LLP.

[1]   See Cabinet Office (June 2000), *Recovering the Proceeds of Crime*, London, UK: Cabinet Office (Performance and Innovation Unit) (hereinafter PIU Report), at para. 3.5; the full report is online at http://www.cabinetoffice.gov.uk/upload/assets/www.cabinetoffice.gov.uk/strategy/crime.pdf, accessed 20 December 2007. See generally Chapter 7 of this book.

[2]   See Assets Recovery Agency ('hereinafter ARA') (15 October 2004), ARA Resource Accounts 2003–04 (for the year ended 31 March 2004), London, UK: The Stationery Office; available online at http://www.assetsrecovery.gov.uk/NR/rdonlyres/C45C6396-879B-46B4-841F-16308B410629/0/ResourceAccounts0304.pdf, accessed 19 December 2007.

being incurred, notably in terms of external legal costs which are dependent on those other factors.

In particular, the receivers' costs provided for in the original plan reflected the experience of HM Customs and Excise in respect of management receivers in confiscation cases. It took no account of the significantly more extensive powers exercised by an interim receiver under POCA 2002, in carrying out their investigative and management functions. Indeed the interim receiver's investigative functions go beyond any power vested in or duly placed upon receivers in any other field. They amount to a duty to investigate the circumstances of the case on behalf of the court, independent of the parties and are more akin to the function of a reporting judge in civil law jurisdictions.[3]

In June 2006, some three years after the inception of the ARA, its 2005/2006 report indicated that it recovered only £4.3 million in 2005/2006, whilst its running costs were £18 million. However, the report also confirmed that £85.7 million of assets had been frozen since its inception although the ARA was 'still striving to turn these early intervention results into final recovery orders'.[4] Blame was attributed to human rights issues.[5] Interestingly, this view was countered by the Head of JUSTICE, a leading UK legal and human rights organisation who stated that the ARA should be given more time to achieve its objectives and not be expected to take 'short cuts' in due process.[6]

In late 2006 the National Audit Office selected the ARA as a subject for one of their Value for Money studies, which examine and report on the economy, efficiency and effectiveness of government departments and other public bodies. The National Audit Office published a report of its findings on 21 February 2007.[7] The report heavily criticised the failure of the ARA to meet its targets and to become self-financing by 2005–06.

---

[3]   See Ian Smith, Tim Owen and Andrew Bodnar (2007), *Smith, Owen & Bodnar on Asset Recovery, Criminal Confiscation and Civil Recovery*, 2nd edn, Oxford, UK: Oxford University Press, at para. III.1.109.

[4]   See ARA (June 2006), ARA Annual Report 2005/06, London, UK: The Stationery Office (hereinafter ARA Annual Report); available online at http://www.assetsrecovery.gov.uk/NR/rdonlyres/8D8413B8-B0FE-4A9F-AA02-2E2A9771A809/0/ARAAnnualReport06_new.pdf, accessed 19 December 2007.

[5]   See ARA (June 2006), ARA Annual Report 2005/06, London, UK: The Stationery Office (hereinafter ARA Annual Report); available online at http://www.assetsrecovery.gov.uk/NR/rdonlyres/8D8413B8-B0FE-4A9F-AA02-2E2A9771A809/0/ARAAnnualReport06_new.pdf, accessed 19 December 2007.

[6]   Available on www.politics.co.uk accessed 14 June 2006.

[7]   See National Audit Office (21 February 2007), 'The ARA: Report by the Comptroller and Auditor General, HC253, Session 2006–07', London, UK: The Stationery Office; available online at http://www.nao.org.uk/publications/nao_reports/06-07/0607253.pdf, accessed 19 December 2007.

On 11 January 2007, the Home Office laid a written ministerial statement before Parliament setting out Government proposals to merge the ARA with the Serious Organised Crime Agency (hereinafter SOCA), and to extend to prosecutors the power to launch civil recovery action under the POCA 2002. On 30 October 2007 the Serious Crime Act 2007 received Royal Assent. It is anticipated that it will be enacted in April 2008.

Under the provisions of the Serious Crime Act 2007 the ARA will be disbanded and its civil recovery powers will be transferred in England and Wales to SOCA, the Director of Public Prosecutions (hereinafter DPP), the Serious Fraud Office (hereinafter SFO) and the Revenue and Customs Prosecutions Office (RCPO). In Northern Ireland, civil recovery powers will be transferred to SOCA, SFO and DPP for Northern Ireland. The Civil Recovery Unit in Scotland is not affected by this and remains intact with no further extension of its powers to any other body.

The political view of the demise of the ARA is reflected thus: 'What we have is an Assets Recovery Agency announced with a fanfare of publicity by the Prime Minister, yet the reality is that it's costing us nearly £20m to run, whilst it's only recovering little over £4m each year'.[8] A more objective view might be that the UK system typifies the present global approach to civil forfeiture by its reliance on a public sector agency which was under funded, set unrealistic targets and given insufficient time to meet its stated objectives.

However, it is not the purpose of this chapter to carry out a post mortem of the demise of a civil forfeiture agency in the UK; those findings are contained within the report of the Committee of Public Accounts.[9] For the reality is that teething troubles aside, the case law that has evolved thus far sets the bench-mark for a positive and innovative civil forfeiture regime.

WHY DID THE UK ADOPT CIVIL FORFEITURE?

Where We Started From

In common with many jurisdictions, the concept of forfeiture is age old, and provided the basis for the UK criminal confiscation regime which commenced

---

[8]   See comments by Grant Schapps MP in, Grant Schapps MP (12 June 2006), 'Report into the Underperformance of the Assets Recovery Agency', London, UK: House of Commons, at p. 10, para. 3; available online at http://www.shapps.com/reports/AssetsRecoveryAgency-underperformance.pdf, accessed 19 December 2007.

[9]   See House of Commons Committee of Public Accounts (12 October 2007), 'Assets Recovery Agency: Fiftieth Report of Session 2006–07, HC 391', London, UK: The Stationery Office; online version at http://www.publications.parliament.uk/pa/cm200607/cmselect/cmpubacc/391/391.pdf, accessed 19 December 2007.

with the enactment of the Drug Trafficking Offences Act 1986 (enacted early 1987). Whilst forfeiture powers had been used for some time by the law enforcement agencies for the purpose of removing items for which it was an offence to possess and which had been instrumental in the carrying out of the crime, for example drug-making equipment, the failure of an attempt to utilise that legislation in order to recover the proceeds of drug trafficking highlighted the lack of confiscation legislation available in 1981. A table of the ensuing criminal confiscation legislation is summarised here.

Limited civil forfeiture powers were also introduced by section 42 of the Drug Trafficking Act 1994, which enabled customs officers to seize cash at borders that represented the proceeds of drugs trafficking or was intended for use in such drug trafficking.

However, by 1999 it became apparent that, despite the UK's extensive powers to confiscate the proceeds of crime, its 'confiscation track record was poor. Very little was being ordered to be confiscated and even less collected.'[10] Accordingly, the Government commissioned a review of the regime under a nine-month study by the Cabinet Office's Performance and Innovation Unit (hereinafter PIU Report), which reported in June 2000.

In summary, the PIU Report stated its concluding strategy as follows:

- ensure the conclusions in this report are implemented;
- raise the priority given to asset confiscation;
- set demanding targets;
- align incentives and promote co-operation between law enforcement bodies;
- devise and oversee a programme of financial investigation training;
- maximise effective use of resources outside the public sector;
- define the indicators that need to be tracked to measure progress; and
- change the culture in the criminal justice system so that it is understood that the law has not been satisfied until criminals have been deprived of their unlawful gains.[11]

As a result of the PIU Report, the existing criminal confiscation legislation was consolidated and civil recovery legislation was introduced by the enactment of POCA 2002 in 2003. Civil forfeiture had arrived in the UK.

---

10   See PIU Report, *supra* at para. 4.18. See also Chapter 7 of this book.
11   *Ibid.* at para. 1.22.

Table 8.1   Confiscation legislation leading to civil forfeiture under POCA 2002

Year	Legislation	Purpose of legislation
1986	Drug Trafficking Offences Act	*Confiscation provisions for drug trafficking offences and first drug money laundering offence*
1987	Criminal Justice (Scotland) Act	
1988	Criminal Justice Act 1988	*Confiscation provisions for all non-drug indictable offences and specified summary*
1990	Criminal Justice (International Co-operation) Act	*Mutual legal assistance, further drug money laundering offences and drug cash seizure on import or export*
1993	Criminal Justice Act	*(Other forms of) money laundering offences and enhancements to all crime confiscation provisions*
1994	Drug Trafficking Act	*Consolidating the drug provisions and removing mandatory confiscation*
1994	Criminal Justice and Public Order Act	*Bringing forward the date from which Criminal Justice Act 1993 confiscation provisions apply*
1995	Proceeds of Crime Act	*Further alignment of all crime confiscation provisions with Drug*
1995	Proceeds of Crime (Scotland) Act	*Trafficking Act 1994: notably use of assumptions in crime lifestyle cases*
1996	Proceeds of Crime (NI) Order	
1998	Crime and Disorder Act	*Amendment to Criminal Justice Act 1988 for confiscation orders on committal for sentence*

Creation of a New Government Agency

POCA 2002 established a new government agency, the ARA, whose core role was to deal with the reduction of crime through civil recovery proceedings. It was headed by a new office holder, the Director (hereinafter Director), as appointed by the Home Secretary. The ARA was a small, non-ministerial department which commenced operations in February 2004. It was based in London, with a further office in Belfast, Northern Ireland. A separate office in Edinburgh, Scotland operates as the Civil Recovery Unit. In written evidence submitted in July 2006 to the Northern Ireland Affairs Committee the ARA reported that it employed 200 people in respect of both the London and Belfast offices with a budget of £15.5 million.

The ARA set out in its Annual Report 2005/06 its three strategic aims:[12]

1. To disrupt organised crime enterprises through the recovery of criminal assets, thereby alleviating the effects of crime on communities.
2. To promote the use of financial investigation as an integral part of criminal investigation within and outside the Agency, domestically and internationally, through training and continuing professional development.
3. To operate the Agency in accordance with its vision and values.

CIVIL RECOVERY – THE PRACTICAL PROCESS

The POCA 2002 allowed the Director to initiate proceedings in one of two ways: to serve a 'claim form' under section 243(2) or to apply to the court for an 'interim receiving order' (hereinafter IRO) under section 246. If the Director chooses to proceed by way of a claim form then the assets the subject of that claim were at risk, and the ARA had to ensure that their case was ready to proceed. However, if the Director applied to the court for an IRO (possibly and preferably without notice), then the assets would be frozen.

It quickly became apparent that the prime legislative tool available to the ARA was the IRO. Thus, as the key instigator of the civil recovery process, any assessment of the UK processes relies on an understanding of the IRO, and the role of the interim receiver appointed thereunder.

---

[12]   See ARA Annual Report, *supra* at p. 7.

Interim Receiving Order – How the Process Works

Operational overview of civil recovery process 2003–2006

The ARA was dependent upon case referrals submitted by law enforcement; it could not initiate its own cases. Once it adopted a case for civil recovery, it would commence a *covert* investigation utilising the powers available to its staff under Part 8 of POCA 2002: production orders,[13] search and seizure warrants,[14] disclosure orders,[15] customer information orders[16] and account monitoring orders.[17]

For the duration of the ARA investigation the assets were at risk of dissipation as the legislation only provided until January 2006[18] for the assets to be frozen by means of an IRO. At this point the ARA investigative powers cease and the duty of taking whatever further steps needed to establish the facts about the property was placed on the interim receiver acting under the court's direction. Prior to this amendment, the ARA had been successful in persuading the courts to grant freezing orders. However, the ARA could not apply for investigative orders under POCA 2002 while property was subject to a freezing order. In practice, the ARA therefore could only use such freezing orders on the basis that they promptly issued a claim form in respect of its civil recovery proceedings. The principal regime therefore utilised for the three-year period prior to this amendment was that provided by POCA 2002 – the IRO.[19]

When the ARA believed it had, by its own investigations, established a good arguable case, it would make application to the High Court for an IRO. The IRO is an order which provides for the detention, custody or preservation of property *and* for the mandatory appointment of an interim receiver. Given the covert nature of the investigation and the consequent risk of dissipation, such application is almost invariably made without notice to the respondents holding the alleged recoverable property.

---

[13]   See Proceeds of Crime Act 2002 (hereinafter POCA 2002), s. 345.
[14]   *Ibid.* s. 352.
[15]   *Ibid.* s. 357.
[16]   *Ibid.* s. 363.
[17]   *Ibid.* s. 370.
[18]   See s. 98(1) of Serious Organised Crime and Police Act 2005 (hereinafter SOCPA) which added new ss. 245A to 245D to POCA 2002 creating property freezing orders for England, Wales and Northern Ireland; see also s. 98(2) of SOCPA introduced ss. 225A–225F to POCA 2002 creating prohibitory property orders for Scotland. These have now been implemented by secondary legislation, POCA 2002 (Legal Expenses in Civil Recovery Proceedings) Regulations 2005, Statutory Instrument No. 3382 of 2005 (hereinafter POCA 2005 Regulations), which came into force on 1 January 2006.
[19]   See POCA 2002, s. 246.

In its application the ARA must nominate one of a limited panel of private sector specialists, usually insolvency practitioners or forensic accountants, to act. The panel was established under a government procurement exercise and its encumbents act on discounted rates, akin to those established by the legal aid scheme. The costs of the interim receiver are met by the ARA, although the interim receiver is required initially to meet the costs of the third party agents that he or she may instruct, for example valuation agents, solicitors or personal protection officers, and then seek reimbursement from the ARA.

The UK civil recovery legislation is unique in its establishment of a dual role for its court appointed interim receiver. Whilst the interim receiver performs an essential management function in respect of the property over which he or she is appointed, the interim receiver is also responsible for the continuance of the investigation. Once the interim receiver is in office, the investigative powers of the ARA cease and the interim receiver's role is as a court appointed expert, independent of the ARA and of the respondents in carrying out an *overt* investigation to establish not only whether the property referred to in the order is indeed recoverable property, but also whether or not any other property is recoverable. In order to carry out his or her role, the interim receiver not only has extensive *specific* powers provided by Schedule 6 to the POCA 2002 but may also 'take any other steps the court thinks appropriate'.[20] Each of the powers specified in Schedule 6 are set out below followed with commentary where appropriate.

Seizure[21]
The power to seize property is essential to allow the interim receiver to take control of the alleged recoverable property specified in the order, *or* in respect of which he or she may form a reasonable belief that it may be additional recoverable property. It is incumbent on the interim receiver to take a practical view when dealing with property under this provision; it may be sufficient to leave items with the respondent providing that the interim receiver is satisfied as to the adequacy of insurance and storage provided.

Information[22]
Schedule 6 provides the following regime in respect of information gathering:

(1) Power to obtain information or to require a person to answer any question.

---

[20] *Ibid.* s. 247(1)(b).
[21] *Ibid.* Sch. 6, para. 1.
[22] *Ibid.* Sch. 6, para. 2.

(2) A requirement imposed in the exercise of the power has effect in spite of any restriction on the disclosure of information (however imposed).

(3) An answer given by a person in pursuance of such a requirement may not be used in evidence against him in criminal proceedings.

(4) Sub-paragraph (3) does not apply —

    (a) on a prosecution for an offence under section 5 of the Perjury Act 1911, section 44(2) of the Criminal Law (Consolidation) (Scotland) Act 1995 or Article 10 of the Perjury (Northern Ireland) Order 1979 (false statements), or

    (b) on a prosecution for some other offence where, in giving evidence, he makes a statement inconsistent with it.

(5) But an answer may not be used by virtue of sub-paragraph (4)(b) against a person unless –

    (a) evidence relating to it is adduced, or

    (b) a question relating to it is asked,

by him or on his behalf in the proceedings arising out of the prosecution.

In practice, this power is widely exercised by the interim receiver in terms both of obtaining oral and written evidence in consideration of the ARA's case. In relevant circumstances, interviews may be tape-recorded in order that the court may be provided with a transcript of the proceedings.

The interim receiver's overt investigation will require substantiation of the ARA case whether by interview of the author of the application for an IRO or by full delivery up of all documentation relied upon therein. Similarly, the respondents to the case must submit for interview and be required to arrange for documentation to be given up to the interim receiver. It is not only the parties to the action who are obliged to comply with this direction, but it extends to any government department, corporate entity, individual or professional adviser to comply.

Entry, search, etc[23]

Schedule 6 provides the interim receiver with the following powers to enter and search premises:

(1) Power to –

    (a) enter any premises in the United Kingdom to which the interim order applies, and

    (b) take any of the following steps.

---

[23] *Ibid.* Sch. 6, para. 3.

(2) Those steps are –
    (a) to carry out a search for or inspection of anything described in the order,
    (b) to make or obtain a copy, photograph or other record of anything so described,
    (c) to remove anything which he is required to take possession of in pursuance of the order or which may be required as evidence in the proceedings under Chapter 2 of Part 5.
(3) The order may describe anything generally, whether by reference to a class or otherwise.

Bearing in mind the covert nature of the ARA investigation and the subsequent appointment of the interim receiver on a without notice application, the first indication that the respondent(s) will have of the matter is the attendance at his or her property, be it residential or commercial, by the interim receiver and his or her staff to secure the papers and carry out, where appropriate, a search and seizure operation. As these are civil proceedings, the police may not attend with a receiver on the property unless there is an imminent or actual breach of the peace. It is often the case that risk assessments made in respect of the holder of the property, its locality or associates would necessitate personal security guards for the protection of the receiver and staff on the premises. Whilst this may be a costly process, this is often a far more effective approach, as the presence of local police who may be well known to the holder of the property, can prove inflammatory. It should also be noted that the right of entry rests with the interim receiver, *not* with the police.

Whilst POCA 2002 provides only for the premises of identified alleged recoverable property to be searched, the court may allow the inclusion of other premises that are not recoverable but which hold essential evidence to be searched, for example those of solicitors or accountants.

Supplementary[24]
Ancillary and other orders may be made subject always to protection for legal professional privilege:

(1) An order making any provision under paragraph 2 or 3 must make provision in respect of legal professional privilege (in Scotland, legal privilege within the meaning of Chapter 3 of Part 8).
(2) An order making any provision under paragraph 3 may require any person –

---

24 *Ibid.* Sch. 6, para. 4.

(a) to give the interim receiver or administrator access to any premises which he may enter in pursuance of paragraph 3,

(b) to give the interim receiver or administrator any assistance he may require for taking the steps mentioned in that paragraph.

Management[25]

Schedule 6 provides for specific powers to manage seized and frozen property:

(1) Power to manage any property to which the order applies.

(2) Managing property includes –

    (a) selling or otherwise disposing of assets comprised in the property which are perishable or which ought to be disposed of before their value diminishes,

    (b) where the property comprises assets of a trade or business, carrying on, or arranging for another to carry on, the trade or business,

    (c) incurring capital expenditure in respect of the property.

Part of the interim receiver's function is to secure the detention, custody or preservation of the property to which the IRO applies (section 247(1) of POCA 2002). Schedule 6 to POCA 2002 (paragraph 5), together with the IRO itself, provides the interim receiver with powers to manage the respondents' assets including power to continue the trade of a business and a power of sale regarding assets that are perishable or diminishing in value. The period between the appointment of the interim receiver and the making of a civil recovery order can be two years or more and therefore this management function should be considered as a long-term commitment. In practice the initial phase of the appointment will consist of securing the assets subject to the IRO to prevent dissipation and thereafter establishing control and monitoring systems to ensure that they are being preserved.

The types of management issues faced are wide ranging and could consist of:

(a) management of properties: rental collections, negotiation of rental increases, establishment of tenancy agreements, dealing with tenants, property maintenance, compliance with legislation regarding landlord and tenant and health and safety;

(b) management of businesses: formal business reviews to establish solvency of business, production of management accounts, control of expenditure to verifiable trading creditors, establishment of trading

---

[25] *Ibid.* Sch. 6, para. 5.

controls to monitor trading during the appointment, winding up of insolvent entities;

(c) general issues: payment of mortgages/finance agreements to preserve equity, provision of living expenses to respondents, insuring assets, dealing with respondents on a daily basis, preparation for litigation.

The interim receivers currently utilised within the UK are mainly accountants experienced in the above situations, having developed the required skills from dealing with insolvency and business restructuring matters. At the moment, the ARA does not have the appropriate skills to deal with these issues and for it to do so would result in tying up financial investigators in dealing with issues they are not competent to deal with, outsourcing work on a piecemeal basis or recruiting a staff base with the appropriate skills and experience.

Additionally, in cases where the court decides that property dealt with during the course of proceedings is not recoverable or associated property, the owner of that property may apply for compensation.[26] Should the court be satisfied that the applicant has suffered loss as a result of the IRO it may require the ARA to pay compensation.[27] The use of external interim receivers with their specialist skills mitigates the possibility of such a claim arising, however, should this happen then the ARA has the ability to look to those receivers to recover any compensation by negligence claims. This would not be possible if the matter was dealt with internally by the ARA by way of property freezing orders.

The Interim Receiver's Report

The interim receiver is required to report his or her findings to the court and to serve copies also on the ARA and any person who holds the recoverable property and is affected by the report, being especially the financial institutions which have interests in the property.[28] The report so issued must be decisive and conclusive in its findings, given that it provides an assessment of the evidence provided by the ARA and the respondents and will adduce new evidence brought as a result of the interim receiver's own investigations. On the basis of that report the ARA will decide whether or not to issue a claim for civil recovery. The interim receiver remains in office with retained powers of management and investigation until the process is complete.

---

[26] *Ibid.* s. 283(1).
[27] *Ibid.* s. 283(5).
[28] *Ibid.* s. 255.

Civil Recovery Progress

Although the ARA built up a substantial pipeline of cases, their ability to bring these to fruition either by means of settlement or trial was stalled by various major issues which are summarised under the following headings:

(a) lack of provision for defendants' legal expenses;
(b) delays in provision of or non availability of information;
(c) international provisions; and
(d) challenges to the new legislation.

Lack of provision for defendants' legal expenses

Prior to the POCA 2002, criminal confiscation legislation allowed for the payment of defendants' legal fees from restrained funds. The PIU Report had identified a concern in the dissipation of restrained assets to pay their legal fees in defending the criminal case, sometimes at very high rates. This is illustrated at Table 8.2 on page 70 of the PIU Report as reproduced herein below.

As a result, POCA 2002 contained (until legislative amendment in January 2006)[29] a provision which prohibited respondents in civil recovery proceedings from using assets restrained under an IRO for payment of their legal fees.

Table 8.2   Analysis of receivership costs and defence costs

Case	Assets (£000s)	Receiver's Costs (including legal) (£000s)	Receiver's Costs (including legal) (%)	Defence Costs (£000s)	Defence Costs (%)
1	1 680	46	3	826	49
2	1 690	104	6	340	20
3	4 440	573	8	811	18
4	2 700	96	4	175	6
5	3 900	166	4	174	4
Total	**14 410**	**985**	**7**	**2 326**	**16**

---

[29] Schedule 6 to SOCPA provided powers for secondary legislation to allow for legal funding expenses to be excluded from the scope of property freezing orders and interim receiving orders (IRO): see POCA 2005 Regulations for detailed rules for its application.

It was envisaged that this provision would force respondents to use legal aid from the Legal Services Commission (hereinafter LSC). However, as the LSC did not have specific funding to meet this obligation, respondents had to make application to the LSC under a means test. Not only were such applications slow, but many were ultimately rejected due to the level of living expenses, however moderate, that they received under the terms of the IRO, in order that mortgages might be met to preserve the assets.

The lack of legal fees and hence representation for respondents proved significant. In many instances respondents were therefore unable to obtain legal advice to clarify the order and its effects. Of more concern was the inability of the interim receiver to complete investigations satisfactorily as respondents would often understandably refuse interview without legal representation. In an attempt to prevent substantive delay in submission of reports, interim receivers were forced at times to submit reports, albeit with the consent of all parties, without the benefit of interview with the respondent.

In order to address the issue the legislative amendment to POCA 2002 was made in January 2006. The amendment allowed for public funding to be made available where appropriate, but if not, the respondent could make application to the court to utilise frozen assets to meet legal costs, in accordance with the regulations introduced by the amendment. In practical terms, unless there are cash funds available within the receivership the process remains slow and cumbersome whilst assets are sold and proceeds made available to meet legal expenses, unless those acting on behalf of the respondent will defer settlement of their fees until sale.

Delays in provision of or non availability of information
The interim receiver is required to examine financial transactions and records over a period of up to 12 years.[30] The recoverability and accessibility of these records are the 'lifeblood' of any financial investigation, not only in respect of identifying property obtained by unlawful conduct, but also property acquired legitimately. Financial records are required from a large number of sources, ranging from banks and building societies to information held by government departments.

Often current financial records are readily accessible and easily accessed via electronic data, at other times records may have been microfiched or sent to off-site storage. Major problems are encountered by the interim receiver in obtaining these historic financial records as there is no priority given by the holders of the records to deliver them up within as short a time frame as possible.

---

[30]   See POCA 2002, s. 288.

Additionally, other issues can emerge from the outset, with third parties questioning the necessity to provide information under the terms of the order, to failing to understand how crucial the provision of information is to the process. Often commercial organisations do not provide sufficient resources to deliver up information, as this is clearly a non-profit making side to their operations and therefore investment of resources is of a low priority. Typically then, delays are encountered in obtaining responses which in some cases can be up to 12 months from the original request despite constant reminders and threats of litigation. This has the knock on effect in delaying the submission of final reports.

There is much work still to be done to engage institutions into understanding that the provision of information on a timely basis are the actions of a good 'corporate citizen', instead of not providing sufficient resources to address what will become increasingly more demanding requests for information and documents. The issue has been addressed largely by increased familiarity with the legislation by recipients and by use of already existing relationships with financial institutions which provide reassurance in light of new and largely untested legislation.

International provisions

Part 11 of POCA 2002 enables international co-operation to take place. This was only enacted in January 2006.[31] In practical terms it is meaningless. At present there are two recognised systems of international co-operation, neither of which is available to the ARA as a governmental body: in *criminal investigations* the regime of letters of request is recognised in many jurisdictions and is widely used for assistance in criminal investigations; in *civil proceedings* there is similarly a wide-reaching regime regularly in use by individuals or corporate entities engaged in civil litigation.

In practice it is the interim receiver who to date has had the only success in seizing property from foreign jurisdictions, for example Ireland and Spain, by use of powers of attorney, a practical utilisation of the asset forfeiture legislation introduced from like experience by management receivers in criminal confiscation. Thus, there is arguably a regime in place which enables the interim receiver to progress investigations on an international level, but not the ARA.[32]

---

[31]   The remaining provisions of Part 11 of POCA 2002 which required implementation came into force on 1 January 2006 by Order in Council, SI 2005/3181. This Order makes detailed arrangements for the Director to be able to provide assistance to other jurisdictions for the purpose of civil recovery as well as criminal confiscation.

[32]   See House of Commons Select Committee on Northern Ireland Affairs (1 March 2006), 'Northern Ireland Affairs – Minutes of Evidence', London, UK: Northern

In summary, there are at present no international treaties or conventions in place that enable assistance to civil investigations into the proceeds of criminal activity. The only exception is the amendment passed in Ireland at the request of the Criminal Assets Bureau allowing them to assist any assets recovery internationally.[33]

Challenges to the new legislation

The legislation has inspired challenges and was doing so well before it was enacted. The lack of provision for legal expenses for defendants (see above) has, however, inevitably hampered the development of any such challenges. To date the challenges which have arisen include the following:

(a) whether civil recovery constitutes a criminal penalty and thereby attracts associated safeguards;
(b) definition of the 'proceeds of unlawful conduct';
(c) jurisdiction;
(d) provision of legal expenses;
(e) disclosure;
(f) delay.

Not criminal

In the Northern Ireland High Court case of *In the Matter of the Director of the Assets Recovery Agency and Cecil Stephen Walsh* argument was made that proceedings were criminal and should therefore attract the associated safeguards.[34] Coghlin J found that the process was a civil one and stated that:

> The purpose of the legislation is essentially preventative in that it seeks to reduce crime by removing from circulation property which can be shown to have been obtained by unlawful conduct thereby diminishing the productive efficiency of such conduct and rendering less attractive the 'untouchable' image of those who have resorted to it for the purpose of accumulating wealth and status.[35]

Jurisdiction

The POCA 2002 operates in England, Wales, Northern Ireland and Scotland. IROs granted in each of these jurisdictions confine the operation of the order to the jurisdiction of the court which granted it. This apparent limitation of

---

Ireland Affairs Committee Publications, questions 201–205; online version available at http://www.parliament.the-stationery-office.co.uk/pa/cm200506/cmselect/cmniaf/886/6030104.htm, accessed 19 December 2007.

[33] For more on Ireland, see Chapter 2 of this book.
[34] [2004] NIQB 21 (1 April 2004). See also Chapter 3 of this book.
[35] *Ibid.* para. 19.

jurisditional power has been challenged, and in some instances exploited by institutions or professionals requested to render assistance to the interim receiver.

Where it can be shown that the subject of the request is out of the jurisdiction but is for example also, by virtue of their professional practice, subject to the jurisdiction of the court which granted the order then such person is liable to proceedings for contempt. In this respect, professionals operating across two or more jurisdictions may open themselves to contempt proceedings which would otherwise have had no teeth.

Disclosure

The interim receiver is, invariably, granted a power to obtain information or to require a person to answer any question. This power is essential in the interim receiver's ability to perform his or her investigative duties. Legal professional privilege is the only defence to non-compliance. The power is therefore a far reaching one and has been challenged by defendants, private individuals, professional advisors and even government agencies. These challenges are met with the same robust warning of contempt proceedings to follow in the event of further non-compliance. By pursuing all persons irrespective of their identity with equal vigour, the interim receiver enhances his or her credibility with the court as its truly independent officer. Such an approach must therefore increase the weight of the interim receiver's findings.

Contested Trials and Issues: Legislation That Sets the Benchmarks

With legal representation in place, many cases have moved to a contested trial. In all of these reported cases, whether in England, Scotland or Northern Ireland, it is the report of the interim receiver and the interim receiver's oral evidence and cross-examination on which the ARA relies in support of their claim.[36] The court has provided invaluable guidance in terms of both the evaluation of the interim receiver's methodology and status which may be summarised in the following extracts.

Objectivity of Interim Administrator

> The approach of the interim administrator to quantification adopted a version of the familiar methodology of analysing verified sources of income year by year, setting against the annual receipts known and established applications of cash, and deriv-

---

[36] See *The Scottish Ministers against Marie Buchanan and Others* [2006] CSOH 121.

ing a deficiency of explained revenue required to fund the respondents' expenditure. … Since any cash expenditure that was not funded by a bank withdrawal would necessarily increase the deficiency, the position might be thought to be as favourable to the respondents as it could be.[37]

Interim receiver's report fundamental to claim

The report of … the interim receiver … sets out most of the material on which the director now relies in support of her claim.… Generally she has unearthed extensive and plausible evidence.…[38]

Did the court have power to order an exclusion from the IRO to meet the costs of a forensic accountant?

I entirely accept that the statutory objective in section 252(6) must bear heavily on the issue of whether it is appropriate in any particular case to provide such an exclusion taking into account the role of the interim receiver. But there may be cases where the fair trial rights of the defendant under common law or the Convention require that an exclusion should be made in respect of such costs and the Court must be free to do so.[39]

Role of the interim receiver and import of evidence?

The role of the interim receiver is that of a court appointed expert to investigate the origin and owner of assets and to report to the court on those assets. In the absence of evidence to the contrary such a report will be compelling evidence in any application based upon it. Its detailed contents relating to accounting matters are accepted as fact unless shown otherwise.[40]

Status of the interim receiver

In my judgment [the interim receiver] is akin to an officer of the court and is reporting and giving evidence to the court in that capacity independent of the parties. Further, in principle I am prepared to accept that the Receiver's findings as to recoverable property should be given considerable persuasive weight by the court and to that extent [the interim receiver's] report enjoys special status.[41]

---

[37]   *Ibid.* at para. 29.

[38]   See *John Szepietowski v. The Director of ARA* [2006] EWHC 3228 (Admin), at para. 4.

[39]   See *Director of The Asset Recovery Agency Re Fleming and Others* [2006] NIQB 70 (11 October 2006), at para. 8; contrast POCA, s. 252(6) ('The power to make exclusions must be exercised with a view to ensuring, so far as practicable, that the satisfaction of any right of the enforcement authority to recover the property obtained through unlawful conduct is not unduly prejudiced.')

[40]   See *The Director of ARA v. William Wilson and Christine Wilson* [2007] NIQB 49, at para. 10.

[41]   See *The Director of ARA v. Fabian Jackson* [2007] EWHC 2553 QB.

Extension of 12-year limitation period

> 83. Does section 32(1)(b) [of Limitation Act 1980] apply here? In my judgment, it does. In my judgment, if facts relevant to the ARA's right of action in relation to both 6 Holland Road and Ashford House have been deliberately concealed from the ARA by JS, section 32(1)(b) establishes that the limitation period does not begin to run against the ARA until it has discovered the concealment or could with reasonable diligence have discovered it.
>
> 84. In my judgment, this construction of the section 32(1)(b) makes sense. Were it otherwise, the defendant to an action brought by the ARA under Part 5 of POCA could conceal facts relevant to the ARA's right of action for an indefinite period and then, when the facts were timeously discovered by the ARA, rely on section 27A to assert that it was too late for the ARA to do anything about it. Such a result, in my judgment, is not consistent with the intention of Parliament when enacting Part 5 of POCA.[42]

Settlement

To date, few claims have come to fruition although the ARA is now actively pursuing settlement under a new policy introduced in late 2004. Whilst provision for settlement is to be encouraged in appropriate cases, this must be balanced against a perception that too heavy a reliance on such a system deals inadequately with the issue of civil forfeiture by avoiding litigation of the salient issues.

A further dilemma is in allowing terms of settlement which would allow significant assets to not only be legitimised or even retained, for example by allowing real property believed to have been purchased by the proceeds of crime to be refinanced to meet the terms of such settlement. In addition, there is the ensuing public perception that the negative role model is not removed from the local community, nor his profits of crime recovered. This is contrary to the expectations of the Government in establishing civil forfeiture.[43]

LEGISLATIVE CHANGES TO THE CIVIL RECOVERY REGIME

Property Freezing Order

Although POCA 2002 did not specifically provide for freezing orders, the ARA were successful in persuading the courts that, in certain simple cases, an

---

[42]   See *The Director of ARA v. Szepietowski and Others* [2007] EWCA CIV 766 (CA), at paras 83–84, per Wall LJ; see further paras 119–120, per Moore-Bick LJ.

[43]   See PIU Report, *supra* at p. 16, para. 3.2.

IRO and interim receiver was not necessary and that a freezing order should be granted instead. Quite apart from the additional burden of management of assets which was then placed on the ARA, it was also encumbent on them to quickly issue a claim form for civil recovery which had the effect of cessation of the ARA's investigative powers. In Scotland, the courts would not allow a freezing order regime.

In order to extend and sanction the freezing order regime the ARA obtained a new concept, being the property freezing order (hereinafter PFO), using the vehicle of the Serious Organised Crime and Police Act 2005. The introduction of PFOs in January 2006 reduced the ARA's reliance on interim receivers, and the PFO allows the ARA to retain its investigative powers whilst the assets are frozen.

As the first such orders have only recently been obtained, there have not yet been many documented challenges. As with the prior freezing order applications, it is to be expected that the ARA will be required to submit claim forms in a timely fashion. Without the impartial report of the interim receiver it is inevitable that both claimant and respondent will require the assistance of a single joint expert at additional cost to the ARA. Property management will also require further resources to be made available to the ARA as at present no such expertise exists. Compensation is available to respondents under section 283 of POCA 2002 in the event that the ARA's application for civil recovery is unsuccessful. In the event of such application the Agency would have to demonstrate that decisions taken in respect of management of assets be they property portfolios or trading entities have been made on an informed and objective basis.

Incentivisation Scheme

In 2003/04 the Home Office established a Recovered Assets Incentivisation Fund, whereby funds were committed to it for projects dealing with asset recovery matters. In early 2005 the incentivisation scheme was extended to include the ARA, with effect from 2006/07. As a result the ARA will recover 50 per cent of the assets that they recover (net of receivers' fees). Of the 50 per cent recovered, the ARA have decided to share this fund in equal shares with the referring law enforcement agency, thus decreasing the monies available to build the ARA, but ensuring that the goodwill of the referrers is retained.

The Northern Ireland Experience

The impact and success of any civil forfeiture regime has much to do with the attitude and response of the general public. In order to maximise the potential of such a regime, it is critical that people within the community are prepared to engage in the process and to support the structures put in place to implement it. Nowhere has this been more evident than in Northern Ireland.

The introduction of the ARA in Northern Ireland followed the conclusion of over three decades of political and civil unrest in the province. The nature of the political and social issues surrounding this unrest has already been extensively reported upon in the media and it is not necessary to comment further on the underlying issues. However, for the purposes of this chapter it is important to note that the numerous paramilitary groups that were active during the period were also involved in a wide range of criminal activities not directly related to terrorism. These include armed robberies, smuggling, drug trafficking, extortion and money laundering.

With the successful implementation of the Peace Process, it was intended that the various paramilitary organisations would cease their activities and disband. Although the majority of these organisations are no longer active, the criminal activities perpetrated by their former members have continued. In a survey undertaken by the Statistics and Research Branch of the Northern Ireland Office in January 2007,[44] it was reported that 71 per cent of those surveyed thought that paramilitary organisations were mainly responsible for committing offences related to organised crime. Due to the sophistication and complexity of the structures within these paramilitary organisations, criminal convictions have often been difficult to secure against their members. This has led to a general perception that the individuals involved are beyond the law.

However, under the civil forfeiture regime, ARA has been able to progress referrals made by the various law enforcement agencies in the region. By taking action against well-known paramilitaries ARA has shown that there are sanctions against those who may have thought themselves to be untouchable. ARA's actions in Northern Ireland have resulted in a much higher level of awareness within the general public: 80 per cent in Northern Ireland in comparison with only 46 per cent in Great Britain.[45] Furthermore, 82 per cent

---

[44] See Northern Ireland Office Statistics and Research Branch (2007), 'Views on Organised Crime: Findings from the January 2007 Northern Ireland Omnibus Survey', *Research and Statistical Bulletin 7/2007*, Belfast, Northern Ireland: Northern Ireland Office; online version available at http://www.nio.gov.uk/views_on_organised_crime__findings_from_the_january_2007_northern_ireland_omnibus_survey-2.pdf, accessed 19 December 2007.

[45] See Northern Ireland Office Statistics and Research Branch (February 2007), 'Public attitudes towards crime and recovery of assets by the ARA in Northern Ireland: Findings from the January 2006 Northern Ireland Omnibus Survey', *Research and Statistical Bulletin 6/2006*, Belfast, Northern Ireland: Northern Ireland Office, at p. 5, Findings 15; online version available at http://www.nio.gov.uk/public_attitudes_towards_crime_and_recovery_of_assets_by_the_assets_recovery_agency__findings_from_the_january_2007_northern_ireland_omnibus_survey.pdf.pdf, accessed 19 December 2007.

of those surveyed said that wealth confiscation was as important as a prison sentence when dealing with criminals and 89 per cent also supported ARA having the powers to pursue this wealth.

It is clear from the public response and the media coverage of its actions,[46] that ARA has had a significant positive impact in Northern Ireland. In the future, the merger of ARA with the SOCA should ensure that its positive contribution will continue. Despite the unique challenges that exist in Northern Ireland, ARA has successfully shown that crime does not pay.

CONCLUSION

> The research showed that prison is regarded only as an 'occupation hazard or an unlikely risk' [but] asset recovery action, under which the State seizes the proceeds of the trade, appeared to cause much more worry for the drug trade.[47]

This describes some of the findings in a report commissioned by the Home Office published in November 2007. Such research continually underlines the need and worth of asset forfeiture. The research underlined the fact that criminals 'run the illegal drug trade in Britain increasingly as if it were a legitimate business, employing salaried staff to increase efficiency'.[48]

In order for civil forfeiture to survive in the UK it will need similar levels of funding and resourcing as those employed by the organised crime business. The PIU report recognised that the public sector needed to maximise effective use of the private sector for provision of the enhanced skill sets necessary to deal with these complex and in-depth investigations.

As discussed, the courts have also recognised the importance of the objective role of the interim receiver in the process. Civil forfeiture will survive in the UK, but only if appropriate transfusions of funding and resourcing are made available to the agencies tasked with taking it forward.

.

---

[46]   'ARA is an asset worth keeping' editorial comment, *Belfast Telegraph*, Monday 25 February 2008.

[47]   See Richard Ford (2007), 'How drug gangs are taking a leaf out of legitimate business manual', *The Times*, 21 November 2007: online version at http://www.timesonline.co.uk/tol/news/uk/crime/article2910484.ece, accessed 19 December 2007.

[48]   *Ibid.* at para. 1.

PART III

Forfeiture of criminal property in Chinese societies: prospects for modern forfeiture laws

9. The confiscation system in mainland China

Xing Fei and Kung Shun Fong

INTRODUCTION

This chapter seeks to give a brief introduction to the confiscation system in Mainland China within the context of the current legal system. The term 'confiscation' appears in many legal documents in China with different natures and purposes but it is most relevant in two main areas: criminal law and administrative law. In analysing these confiscation powers, this chapter is divided into the following parts. The first part introduces and analyses confiscation in Chinese criminal law, where confiscation of property as a penalty co-exists with confiscation of illegal assets as a disciplinary measure. The second part discusses confiscation of illegal gains as a punishment in Chinese administrative law. It will examine the legal status of this punishment and its application in authorized and delegated legislation. Finally, the third part analyses problems of the current system and the prospect for improvement. The inconsistencies and proliferation of confiscation and the lack of co-ordination among different branches of law are possible obstacles for future international co-operation in combating corruption, being an important concern of society, and for China as it strives to meet international standards.

CONFISCATION IN CRIMINAL LAW

The criminal law in Mainland China derives from three major sources: the penal code and its amendments, specific penal acts and legally binding interpretations of the penal code and acts.[1] The bulk of Chinese criminal law is

---

[1]   By the narrowest meaning, sources of law are rules binding on the court in its adjudication. According to some scholars, sources of Chinese criminal law are the criminal code, specific criminal act and supplementary criminal provisions in other laws: see Zhang Mingkai (hereinafter Zhang) (2003), *Criminal Law*, 2nd edn, Beijing, China: Law Press. Zhang thinks supplementary criminal provisions in other laws are of

mainly contained in the penal code promulgated in the 1997 Criminal Law of the People's Republic of China (hereinafter 1997 Criminal Law). From 1997 to 2006 the Standing Committee of the National People's Congress (hereinafter NPCSC) passed six amendments to the 1997 Criminal Law and three specific criminal statutes on illegal trading of foreign currency, illegal religious groups and internet safety respectively. The specific criminal statutes are named as 'decisions' by the NPCSC.[2] Legally binding interpretations include both legislative interpretations by the NPCSC and judicial interpretations by the Supreme People's Court (hereinafter Supreme Court) or the Supreme People's Procuratorate or jointly by these two judicial organs.[3] These judicial interpretations may have different titles, such as interpretation, circular, reply and so on, and may be binding generally on all cases in respect of the same criminal law problem or on a specific case, depending on the concrete circumstances of the document, such as the nature of the question, whom the addressee is, and whether it is a set of compiled rules of judicial interpretation. In short, the laws on confiscation of property not only appear in primary legislation, but can also be found in most types of other legal sources.[4]

Confiscation of Property as a Penalty – The Law

The 1997 Criminal Law has two parts and 452 articles. There are five chapters in part one entitled 'General Provisions' and 11 chapters in part two entitled

---

little significance since the codification of the 1997 Criminal Law (hereinafter 1997 Criminal Law). The present authors agree with Zhang as in the broader sense legislative and judicial interpretations of the code and acts could be regarded as part of these statutes. When talking about confiscation of property, legislative and judicial interpretations are quite important and illuminating as a legal source and thus they will be raised separately in this chapter.

   [2] See Huang Taiyun (2006), *Reading and Understanding the Legislation: Amendments and Legislative Interpretations of the Criminal Law*, Beijing, China: People's Court Press; see also Huang Taiyun (2007), *Criminal Judicial Interpretation*, Beijing, China: Law Press (hereinafter *Criminal Judicial Interpretation*).

   [3] See *Criminal Judicial Interpretation, ibid.*

   [4] In addition to provisions of the criminal code and judicial interpretations invoked in this chapter, confiscation of property appears in Amendments III, IV, V, and VI to the 1997 Criminal Law and one specific criminal statute – the 1998 Decision on Illegal Trading of Foreign Currencies. Legislative interpretations by the Standing Committee of the National People's Congress (hereinafter NPCSC) do not address the penalty directly but make interpretations on certain articles of the criminal code involving this penalty, such as in its legislative interpretation in 2004, where the NPCSC clarified the definition of credit card and Article 196 of the 1997 Criminal Law and its Amendment V regulated crimes on credit card fraud with confiscation of property as a penalty.

'Specific Provisions'. Chapter III of Part One is entitled 'Punishments', in which Article 32 (also the first article of this chapter) sets out that 'punishments are divided into principal punishments and supplementary punishments'. Articles 33 and 34 stipulate respectively that there are five principal punishments (public surveillance, criminal detention, fixed-term imprisonment, life imprisonment and the death penalty), three supplementary punishments (fine, deprivation of political rights and confiscation of property) and that 'supplementary punishments may be imposed independently'.[5] These three articles are the background and starting point for understanding confiscation of property within the framework of criminal penalties.

The article that provides a definition for the penalty confiscation of property is Article 59, which also imposes conditions on confiscation if and when such penalty is to be ordered. Article 59 provides as follows:

> Article 59: Confiscation of property refers to the confiscation of part or all of the property personally owned by a criminal. Where confiscation of all the property of a criminal is imposed, the amount necessary for the daily expenses of the criminal himself and the family members supported by him shall be taken out.
>
> When a sentence of confiscation of property is imposed, property that the criminal family members own or should own shall not be subject to confiscation.[6]

Articles 36 and 60 also provide that confiscation of property shall be executed after the criminal has paid compensation to the victim and his legitimate debts. Article 212 provides that for offences from Articles 201 to 205, the criminal's evaded or defrauded tax shall be recovered before confiscation of property.

Among other similar provisions, below are three examples of articles in the 1997 Criminal Law on specific crimes with express stipulation of confiscation of property as a penalty:

> Article 239(1): Whoever kidnaps another person for the purpose of extorting money or property or kidnaps another person as a hostage shall be sentenced to fixed-term imprisonment of not less than 10 years or life imprisonment and also to a fine or confiscation of property; if he causes death to the kidnapped person or kills the kidnapped person, he shall be sentenced to death and also to confiscation of property.[7]

---

5 See 1997 Criminal Law: hard copy version available as *Criminal Law of the People's Republic of China* 1998 (hereinafter *Criminal Law of PRC*), Beijing, China: China Procuratorial Press, at p. 20.

6 *Criminal Law of PRC, ibid.* at pp. 30–31.

7 *Ibid.* at p. 142.

Article 113(2): Whoever commits any of the crimes mentioned in this Chapter may concurrently be sentenced to confiscation of property.[8]

Article 163(1): Where an employee of a company or enterprise who, taking advantage of his position, demands money or property from another person or illegally accepts another person's money or property in return for the benefits he seeks for such person, if the amount involved is relatively large, he shall be sentenced to fixed-term imprisonment of no more than five years or criminal detention; if the amount is huge, he shall be sentenced to fixed-term imprisonment of not less than five years and may also be sentenced to confiscation of property.[9]

Confiscation of property in all these three articles is supplementary to other principal forms of punishments. While Article 239(1) makes confiscation of property a mandatory supplementary penalty, the other two are discretionary. Even within Article 239(1), in the first sentence the mandatory supplementary penalty is either a fine or confiscation of property, while in the second sentence confiscation of property is the only mandatory supplementary penalty. Since the second sentence of Article 239(1) describes a graver situation than that in the first one, one might infer that the 1997 Criminal Law treats confiscation as being a more severe supplementary penalty than a fine. For confiscation under these three example articles, the Chinese judiciary has already developed standards in their application.

On 13 December 2000, the Supreme Court promulgated the Regulations of the Supreme People's Court on Several Questions Concerning the Application of Property-Oriented Penalty (hereinafter *2000 Regulations*).[10] This document is a legally binding judicial interpretation. It explains the penalty of confiscation of property and answers the following two questions: first, how to impose confiscation of property as a supplementary punishment, and secondly, how to execute the penalty of confiscation of property.[11]

These two questions are closely related and their respective answers are

---

8   *Ibid.* at pp. 49–55: 'This Chapter' refers to Chapter I of Part Two of the 1997 Criminal Law, being Arts 102–113 on crimes endangering national security.

9   *Ibid.* at p. 85.

10   See *Criminal Judicial Interpretation, supra* at pp. 156–157.

11   These two questions in the chapter are not raised by local courts but generalized by the present author specifically for confiscation, but sometimes judicial interpretations answer questions proposed by local courts, see for example the *Reply to the Higher People's Court of Sinkiang Uygur Autonomous Region on Whether Hearings Shall Be Held for the Confiscation of Property and the Legal Issues Relating to the Forfeiture in the Case of Medicinal Deals* (hereinafter *2004 Reply*). Also, scope of the *2000 Regulations of the Supreme Court on Several Questions Concerning the Application of Property-Oriented Penalty* (hereinafter *2000 Regulations*) is not limited to this penalty but include several important matters on the penalty of fine as well.

interwoven in the judicial interpretation. Article 1 of the *2000 Regulations* stipulates the following:

> For the crime which shall be concurrently imposed confiscation of property or fine under the criminal law, the criminal shall be sentenced to property-oriented penalty correspondingly by the people's court while being sentenced to the principal penalty; for the crime which may be concurrently imposed confiscation of property or fine, the people's court shall decide whether to apply the property-oriented penalty according to the concrete conditions of the case and the accused's property as well.[12]

This article is a rule of application for the three example articles mentioned above, but it only distinguishes the mandatory and optional supplementary penalties and gives no guidance in deciding between fine and confiscation of property as provided for in the first sentence of Article 239(1). The question is whether there are any preferences or guidelines in choosing between a fine or confiscation of property when an article of the 1997 Criminal Law provides that either shall be imposed. The *2000 Regulations* does not help in this matter so it shall be subject to the judge's discretion. From a literal meaning of a provision such as Article 239(1), it is almost certain that the court should not impose both penalties for the same offence. However, it may happen that both fine and confiscation of property are imposed concurrently if the defendant's conduct violated two or more articles of the 1997 Criminal Law, thus resulting in the commission of two or more offences. If for offence A the offender is imposed a fine and offence B confiscation of property, are there any considerations in executing such penalties? Article 3(2) of the *2000 Regulations* makes clear that 'the fines and confiscation of property concurrently imposed on a criminal for his plural crimes committed shall be executed together. However, in case that confiscation of full property is concurrently imposed, only confiscation of property shall be executed.'[13]

As has been introduced at the beginning of this part, for the status of supplementary punishment, the second paragraph of Article 34 in the 1997 Criminal Law provides that 'supplementary punishments may also be imposed independently'. So can confiscation of property be imposed on a criminal as his only penalty? Article 4 of the *2000 Regulations* lists situations where the court may impose a fine as an independent penalty but this is not so with confiscation of property. Therefore it can be inferred that, since there is no article in the 1997

---

[12]   See this document and its English translation on www.lawinfochina.com, accessed 30 December 2007. Other laws and cases cited in this chapter, unless otherwise acknowledged, are also found on this database; however, accessing some documents in this database requires a paid subscription.

[13]   *Ibid.* the English translation is slightly modified by the present authors.

Criminal Law imposing confiscation of property as an independent penalty and for this penalty there is also no similar provision to Article 4 of the *2000 Regulations*, under the current system confiscation of property can only be applied as a supplementary penalty in Chinese criminal law.

There is one more important article on the execution of penalties. Article 220 of the 1996 Criminal Procedure Law of the People's Republic of China (hereinafter 1996 Criminal Procedure Law) provides that:

> all judgments on confiscation of property, whether imposed as a supplementary punishment or *independently*, shall be executed by the People's Courts; when necessary, the People's Courts may execute such judgments jointly with the public security organs.[14] [emphasis added]

This article seems to be at variance with the 1997 Criminal Law, which does not appear to provide for confiscation of property as an independent and exclusive penalty. This contradiction results from an inconsistency within the 1997 Criminal Law. As discussed above, although its Article 34 provides that supplementary penalties may be imposed independently, there is no specific provision for applying confiscation of property as a supplementary penalty in that manner. When the 1996 Criminal Procedure Law was promulgated the criminal code then in force was still the 1979 Criminal Law of the People's Republic of China (hereinafter 1979 Criminal Law), which had an article allowing confiscation of property to be the exclusive penalty.[15] So when the 1996 Criminal Procedure Law was promulgated it was consistent with the criminal code at the time, but soon became contradictory when the 1997 Criminal Law came into force. The 1979 Criminal Law will be discussed later in this part when the application and history of the penalty is analysed.

Application of Confiscation of Property

The types of offences to which confiscation of property applies can be found in written statutes and in judicial policy and practice.

---

14   Online version at http://www.lawinfochina.com/law/display.asp?db=1 &id=347&keyword=criminal procedure, accessed 3 January 2008. Also see *Criminal Procedure Law of the People's Republic of China* (1998), Beijing, China: China Procuratorial Press, at pp. 103–104.

15   See 1979 Criminal Law of the People's Republic of China (hereinafter 1979 Criminal Law), Art. 120, first paragraph, which provides that '[W]hoever, for the purpose of profit, counterfeit or resell ration coupons, if the circumstances are serious, shall be sentenced to fixed-term imprisonment of not more than three years or criminal detention, or he may concurrently or exclusively be sentenced to a fine or confiscation of property. …': online version available at http://www.lawinfochina.com/law/display. asp?db=1&id=3&keyword=criminal law, accessed 18 January 2008.

Distribution of confiscation of property in the 1997 Criminal Law
The previous part discussed three legal provisions with confiscation of property as a penalty for specific crimes. Recalling Article 113(2), it is different from Article 163(1) in that the former provides that confiscation is an additional discretionary supplementary penalty for all crimes under the same chapter, while the latter provides that confiscation is the only discretionary supplementary penalty for crimes under that article.

Article 113(2) is in Chapter I of Part Two of the 1997 Criminal Law. The title of this chapter is 'Crimes Endangering National Security' and it contains Articles 102 to 113. It is understandable that for crimes endangering national security, confiscation of property may always be imposed as the supplementary penalty. The reason for such legislation might be to deprive the offender his or her financial competence to commit similar crimes in the future. Also, as a feature of China's legal system, the connection between crimes endangering national security with confiscation of property has its origin in the criminal law before 1997. The 1979 Criminal Law had a chapter called 'Crimes of Counter-Revolution', and the last article in that chapter had confiscation of property as the discretionary supplementary penalty to each offence therein.[16] In setting penalties for crimes endangering national security, being the updated version of 'Crimes of Counter-Revolution', the legislature inherited this tradition.

Coming to Article 163(1), although it is an example of an individual article and crime, it is not singular within its chapter. Chapter III of Part Two of the 1997 Criminal Law is entitled 'Crimes Disrupting the Order of the Socialist Market Economy'. This chapter has eight sections and 92 articles (Articles 140 to 231), and the titles of each section of this chapter reveal that they are all profit-making crimes: (1) producing and marketing fake or substandard commodities; (2) smuggling; (3) disrupting the order of administration of companies and enterprises; (4) disrupting the order of financial administration; (5) financial fraud; (6) jeopardizing administration of tax collection; (7) infringing on intellectual property rights; and (8) disrupting market order. Many articles in this chapter have confiscation of property as a penalty. The logic behind such legislation is to punish a criminal by depriving him of his assets which, although may not always be successfully proven to have been obtained through crimes, is commonly regarded as having been accumulated illegitimately. It is also vital and sensible to deprive offenders of such crimes the financial competence to commit similar crimes in the future – obviously it would be difficult to engage in such crimes without any capital.

---

[16]   See 1979 Criminal Law, Arts 90–104.

Some scholars have conducted research on distribution of the penalty among different offences and the conclusion is that among all 10 categories of crimes in Part Two, 'Specific Provisions', of the 1997 Criminal Law, all crimes endangering national security have confiscation of property as a penalty (by virtue of Article 113(1)); the second highest ratio is with offences of property violation in Chapter V (such as robbery and theft) 41.7 per cent; and for economic crimes in Chapter III, articles with confiscation of property constitute around 38.5 per cent of all the offences in that chapter. For an overall figure, confiscation of property is attached to 70 out of 418 offences in the 1997 Criminal Law.[17]

Another way of analysing the distribution of this penalty is that it is imposed for felonies rather than misdemeanours. Although there is no such distinction under Chinese criminal law, academics normally view offences carrying an imprisonment term of more than three years as felonies. Under the 1997 Criminal Law, confiscation of property only applies to crimes with principal penalties of imprisonment of five years or above.[18]

Policies and trends in judicial practice

The above analysis is based on the 1997 Criminal Law alone, and as far as complementary laws and interpretations are concerned, the 1996 Criminal Procedure Law and the *2000 Regulations* mentioned earlier are still general provisions on several technical problems but not reflections of the tendency in judicial practice. The Supreme Court has given even more detailed instructions in the last several years on different subject matters, in which the application of confiscation of property has been mentioned with special emphasis.

In May 2003 the Supreme Court addressed to all Higher Courts in China the Circular on Further Strengthening the Trial Work to Provide Powerful Judicial Safeguard for the Rectification and Regulation of the Market Economic Order, in which paragraph 3 provides that:

> … Thirdly, the application of fine or confiscation of property shall be rigidified, where the law *provides* concurrent imposition of fine or confiscation of property, such penalty *shall* be imposed firmly; where the law provides that fine or confiscation of property *may* be imposed, such penalty *shall* be also imposed *as a general principle*[19] [emphasis added].

---

[17]   See Huang Ziqiang and Wang Chengxiang (2003), 'Comments and Analysis on Legislation Objects of the Penalty Confiscation of Property', in (2003) **5** *Guangxi Social Sciences* (hereinafter Comments and Analysis on Confiscation), at pp. 101–103. The number of total crimes and that of crimes with confiscation of property are counted by authors of the article, and is distinct from the number of articles. The number of articles with the penalty is 58.

[18]   *Ibid.*

[19]   See www.lawinfochina.com, accessed 30 December 2007.

The above emphasis is not without any purpose: like confiscation of property in 'crimes disrupting the order of the socialist market economy' this guideline is specially targeting profit-making crimes, which is also the purpose with some of its later interpretations.

In September 2004 the Supreme Court addressed to all Higher Courts the Circular on Further Strengthening the Judicial Protection of Intellectual Property Rights, and the second paragraph states the following:

> Where any law provides that a fine or confiscation of property *shall* be imposed in addition to a principal punishment, such fine or confiscation of property *must* be imposed; where any law provides that a fine or confiscation of property *may* be imposed in addition to a principal punishment, such fine or confiscation of property *shall generally* be imposed ...[20] [emphasis added].

It is apparent from the provision that except on whether to impose confiscation of property in discretionary clauses this circular does not add anything new to the 1997 Criminal Law but only emphasizes the implementation of the penal code and the Supreme Court's earlier *2000 Regulations*.

Not all judicial interpretations follow a harsh attitude towards implementation of the penalty. In January 2006 the Supreme Court announced the Interpretation on Some Issues Concerning the Specific Application of Law in the Trial of Criminal Cases Involving Minors, and its Article 15 provides the following:

> In case a minor criminal commits a crime for which the confiscation of property or fine *shall* be concurrently imposed as prescribed by the Criminal Law, he *shall* be imposed on the corresponding property-related penalty; in case a minor criminal commits a crime for which the confiscation of property or fine *may* be concurrently imposed as prescribed by the Criminal Law, he *shall not* be imposed on the corresponding property-related penalty *as a general rule*[21] [emphasis added].

Despite this different interpretation, it is reasonable to believe that the policy on minor offenders is not the turning point from a reinforced attitude to the application of confiscation of property, but only one exception given the special circumstances of minor offenders. Provisions on confiscation of property in the criminal code and those in interpretations on economic crimes reflect the mainstream of legislative and judicial attitudes. From these above specific instructions over the years, guidelines of the Supreme Court on the application of confiscation of property are quite consistent with the purpose of this penalty: it is a penalty to punish and redress profit-making crimes but not

---

20 See www.lawinfochina.com, accessed 30 December 2007.
21 See www.lawinfochina.com, accessed 30 December 2007.

to impoverish all criminals regardless of their practical economic status. Rather, the Supreme Court is quite aware of the potential adverse effects of the penalty and thus advises lower courts that it not to be used on offenders who were under the age of 18 when they committed those offences. Also, it can be seen that the interpretations are always consistent with the literal provision of the criminal code. For provisions with a mandatory penalty clause, no matter for economic crimes or for minor offenders, the sentence shall always be mandatory in these judicial interpretations. The interpretations give instructions on how to apply discretionary clauses and these instructions are still, as with the original clauses in the penal code, not mandatory in its wording.

Moreover, if a comparison is made on the current system on confiscation of property with previous ones, one may find that the application of the penalty by the criminal code and by the Supreme Court are also in line with the general trend of China's criminal law reform as shaped by social demands. The historical development of confiscation and relevant debates will be further discussed in detail below.

Evolution of Confiscation of Property and its Impact

History of confiscation of property

The discussion thus far has only been concerned with confiscation under the 1997 Criminal Law, but like many other areas of law, confiscation of property has a very long history. In fact, confiscation appeared in China in the Warring Period (476 BC to 221 BC) and has lasted through the dynasties until today.[22] Therefore, it is not a feature or result of legal systems in socialist or communist countries.

The 1979 Criminal Law had 15 articles with confiscation of property as a penalty, among which 14 were single individual offences and one article applied it to offences in a whole chapter. The scope of the penalty is far less than the current figure of 58 articles, but then again there were only 192 articles in the 1979 Criminal Law, compared with 452 in the 1997 Criminal Law.[23] This expansion in the criminal code was mainly the result of further codification of offences and modernization of the code, but there is an increase in the ratio of confiscation of property to total number of offences in the 1997 Criminal Law. Despite the above, crimes with confiscation of property as the penalty in both the 1979 Criminal Law and the 1997 Criminal Law are similar, such as the earlier 'crimes of counter-revolution' instead of the modern

---

[22]   See Chen Xingliang (2006), *General Comments on the Application of the Criminal Law*, Beijing, China: Renmin University Press (hereinafter *General Comments on Criminal Law*), at p. 193.

[23]   See Comments and Analysis on Confiscation, *supra* at p. 102.

'crimes endangering national security', the earlier offences of 'undermining the socialist economic order' instead of the modern version of 'crimes disrupting the order of the socialist market economy', and crimes of property violation has remained the same.

Debate on the penalty

Some scholars have noted several defects of confiscation of property and proposed repeal of this supplementary penalty.[24] These criticisms are based on considerations to promote the modernization of the Chinese criminal law. It is argued that general confiscation of an offender's property is contrary to the principle of ensuring proportionality between the crime and the punishment and contrary to the objective of rehabilitation in a system of criminal punishment. These criticisms must be understood against the broader historical and social context that sees Chinese criminal law moving towards German and Japanese criminal law theories and away from its original Soviet Union origins.[25]

Despite the vocal academic criticisms, there is no indication that either the current code or judicial practice is moving towards such repeal or suspension of the practice. Compared with the former laws, confiscation has now gained a stronger presence in the statutory code and in a series of judicial interpretations. It is now regarded as a very important method of combating economic crimes, although it is hard to evaluate its deterrent effect as is the case with many other penalties. Due to its deep-rooted traditions in socialism or communism and even paternalism ideals, its repeal is certainly far from being top of the agenda of criminal law reform.

Confiscation of Illegal Property in Criminal Proceedings

The law

In addition to being a penalty 'confiscation' also appears in an article of the 1997 Criminal Law with a different legal nature. This is Article 64 in Chapter IV, 'The Concrete Application of Punishments', of Part One of the statutory code, which provides the following:

> Article 64: All money and property illegally obtained by a criminal shall be recovered, or compensation shall be ordered; the lawful property of the victim shall be returned without delay; and contrabands and possessions of the criminal that are used in the commission of the crime shall be *confiscated*. All the *confiscated* money and property and *fines* shall be turned over to the State treasury, and no one may misappropriate or privately dispose of them[26] [emphasis added].

---

24   See *General Comments on Criminal Law, supra* at p. 202.
25   *Ibid.*
26   See *Criminal Law of PRC, supra* at p. 32.

Article 64 provides for the confiscation of contrabands and possessions of the criminal that are used in the commission of the crime. It also goes to provide generally that confiscated money and property must be turned over to the State treasury. This general direction would apply to all confiscated property including property used in the commission of the crime and property ordered confiscated as a penalty by the court. One infers the generality of this direction by virtue of the reference to fines in general within the same clause.

The difference between the nature of Article 59 and that of the first reference to 'confiscated' in Article 64 is obvious. Article 59 refers to a penalty having the purpose of punishing the criminal by depriving his ownership of his previously legal and thus legitimate property (or at least the property that cannot be proven to be illegal), but confiscation of contrabands and possessions of the criminal that are used in the commission of the crime is not a type of criminal punishment: contrabands and crime tools are inherently illegal and thus shall always be subject to confiscation regardless of any sentence. Furthering this major difference in legal nature, the condition of application for Article 59 and that for Article 64 is also distinct, according to the general principle of criminal law of *nulla poena sine lege* (meaning 'no penalty without a law') and its corresponding provision in Article 3 of the 1997 Criminal Law, a penalty can only apply when the law has such provision and the criminal has been convicted and sentenced through legal procedures.[27]

Confiscation of property is not an available penalty for all crimes in the 1997 Criminal Law, rather, it can only be imposed on criminals of specific crimes for which confiscation of property is expressly stipulated by the law as a penalty. In contrast, confiscation of contrabands and crime tools apply to all criminals so long as the contrabands and crime tools exist.[28] In other words, the penalty of confiscation of property is imposed by specific sentence in the judgment according to specific provisions of the criminal law dealing with the crime in question, but confiscation of contrabands and possessions for the use of crimes is always imposed with Article 64 as the legal basis. This confiscation of contrabands and crime-related property and its relevance to penalties will be analysed here by the following case.

---

[27] *Ibid.* at p. 8: see also 1997 Criminal Law, Art. 3, which provides that '[F]or acts that are explicitly defined as criminal acts in law, the offenders shall be convicted and punished in accordance; otherwise, they shall not be convicted or punished'. This is generally agreed to be consistent with the criminal law principle *nulla poena sine lege* and as a major achievement of the 1997 Criminal Law than its predecessors, although procedural guarantees of this principle are still insufficient in the Chinese criminal procedure law.

[28] There are occasions that even the suspect is relieved of criminal responsibility because of lapse of prosecution period, but his illegal gains were still confiscated: see for example, *People's Procuratorate of Jingkou District, Zhenjiang, Jiangsu Province v. Sun Aiqin,* Zhenjiang Intermediate People's Court, 25 September 2002.

An exemplary criminal case on confiscation of illegal assets
The legal system in Mainland China is not a common law system, and so the above articles in the statute are the main sources and the basis for confiscation of property. In the Chinese legal system, decided cases do not have binding effect on subsequent cases but can serve as examples on how the written legal rules are applied in judicial practice. The case of *People's Procuratorate of Jingkou District, Zhenjiang, Jiangsu Province v. Sun Aiqin*, Zhenjiang Intermediate People's Court, 25 September 2002 (hereinafter *Sun Aiqin*), serves as a good example for differentiating Article 64 from Article 59.

Sun Aiqin was concerned with events that took place in June 1994 when Sun, the defendant, was an employee in the Zhenjiang Supply and Marketing Cooperative Real Estate Development Company in Zhenjiang city. On 15 November 2001 the Procuratorate lodged a prosecution to the Jingkou District Court against Sun, for the offences of accepting bribes, and accepting bribes in the identity of a company employee, and the District Court convicted him on both charges. Sun appealed to the Zhenjiang Intermediate People's Court (hereinafter Zhenjiang Intermediate Court) and the Zhenjiang Intermediate Court thought that Sun's conduct did not fall within the two crimes convicted by the Jingkou District Court but had constituted the crime of introducing bribes, which, according to the 1979 Criminal Law (criminal code then in force when Sun's alleged criminal activities took place), shall be sentenced to fixed-term imprisonment of no more than five years or criminal detention and that the RMB 50 000 he received from introducing bribes was illegal proceeds. However, according to Article 76 of the 1979 Criminal Law (or relevant provisions in the 1997 Criminal Law), the crimes with the statutory maximum punishment being fixed-term imprisonment of less than five years shall not be subject to prosecution after the lapse of five years. Sun committed the crime of introducing bribes in June 1994 and had not been detained until 21 June 2001. During this period from 1994 to 2001, no compulsory measure was taken on Sun, nor did he commit any new crime, therefore the five years' limitation on prosecution regarding the offence of introducing bribes had passed, and according to the law Sun could not shoulder criminal liability any longer. The Zhenjiang Intermediate Court thus ruled that (1) the conviction judgment of the court of first instance be reversed, (2) Sun be acquitted, but (3) Sun's illegal proceeds of RMB 50 000 would still be confiscated.

Confiscation in this appellate judgment was obviously not a penalty as the defendant was acquitted. The Zhenjiang Intermediate Court did not invoke Article 64 in its judgment, although this seems to be the most likely legal basis. This conclusion does not entirely rule out other possible legal basis, especially considering whether the court had the right to apply criminal law measures to an acquitted person and why it did not invoke Article 64. This case is also an illustration of what common law systems would call the application of a civil forfeiture power under Mainland Chinese law. In the following part, another important branch of law relevant to the system of confiscation will be discussed.

CONFISCATION OF ILLEGAL GAINS IN ADMINISTRATIVE LAW

Unlike in criminal law, confiscation in administrative law only possesses one nature, being an administrative punishment. Compared with criminal law, the administrative punishment system is not as strict and so may entrench itself into national laws, administrative regulations, local laws and regulations. This loose legal structure and the resulting proliferation of confiscation have posed problems to both the legislature and the judiciary.

The Starting Point

Unlike the criminal law system, there is no uniform administrative law code similar to the 1997 Criminal Law. Administrative laws in Mainland China are composed of laws passed by the National People's Congress or its Standing Committee, administrative regulations passed by the central government, and local regulations passed by regional People's Congresses.[29] Also, legislative and judicial interpretations are of binding effect on the court. Among these documents of different hierarchies, subjects and application areas, the Law of the People's Republic of China on Administrative Penalty as promulgated in March 1996 (hereinafter 1996 Administrative Penalty Law) is the major legal source on confiscation of illegal gains. This statute has eight chapters and 188 articles. Article 8 sets out seven kinds of administrative punishments:

(1)   disciplinary warning;
(2)   fine;
(3)   confiscation of illegal gains or confiscation of unlawful property or things of value;

---

[29]   See generally the Law on Legislation of the People's Republic of China, promulgated on 15 March 2000, and Art. 2 therein. Administrative regulations are passed by the State Council – the central government of China; local regulations are passed by the regional people's congress of a province, autonomous region or municipality. Besides these categories of legal sources, there are two types of subsidiary legal sources: administrative rules passed by branches of the central government, such as the Ministry of Commerce, and local rules passed by local governments. Examples of the subsidiary legal sources will be raised below.

(4) ordering for suspension of production or business;

(5) temporary suspension or rescission of permit or temporary suspension or rescission of licence;

(6) administrative detention; and

(7) others as prescribed by laws and administrative penalty may be created by law.[30]

The above seven categories of punishments escalate from warning to detention, to the last non-exhaustive category of penalties that may be provided or created by law. In this sequence confiscation of illegal gains or of unlawful property or things of value seems to be of moderate and varying severity, which can carry with it both advantages and disadvantages. The 1996 Administrative Penalty Law is cautious about restricting people's freedom. Article 9 provides that 'administrative penalty involving restrictions of freedom of person shall only be created by law', which means only by those statutes passed by the National People's Congress or its Standing Committee will suffice. In fact, the statute states that administrative regulations may create all types of administrative penalties except detention, and local regulations may impose all types of administrative penalties except detention and rescission of business licences.[31] Although this 1996 Administrative Penalty Law appears at first glance to restrict severe administrative penalties, these articles in fact further enlarge the power of administrative bodies by authorizing legislative powers on punishments of less severity. Further, it is not easy to compare severity of administrative punishments. Although administrative detention appears to be more severe than a fine, it would be impossible to compare the severity of one day's detention to a fine of RMB10 million. Therefore, confiscation of illegal gains is not necessarily less severe than that of detention, but according to the 1996 Administrative Penalty Law only the latter is expressly restricted.

The 1996 Administrative Penalty Law also sets out a series of procedural guarantees in imposing penalties, among which the first paragraph of Article 42 provides the following:

> An administrative organ, before making a decision on administrative penalty that involves ordering for suspension of production or business, rescission of business permit or license or imposition of a comparatively large amount of fine, shall notify the party that he has the right to request a hearing; if the party requests a hearing,

---

[30] See http://www.lawinfochina.com/law/display.asp?db=1&id=1148& keyword= administrative penalty, accessed 2 January 2008.

[31] See 1996 Administrative Penalty Law, Arts 10 and 11.

the administrative organ shall arrange for the hearing. The party shall not bear the expense for the hearing arranged by the administrative organ. ...[32]

Although this article does not expressly refer to confiscation of illegal gains or property, in September 2004 the Supreme Court in its Reply to the Higher People's Court of Sinkiang Uygur Autonomous Region on Whether Hearings Shall Be Held for the Confiscation of Property and the Legal Issues Relating to the Forfeiture in the Case of Medicinal Deals (hereinafter *2004 Reply*) decided in its paragraph 1 the following:

> Where the people's court is convinced, after trial, that an administrative organ fails to notify the parties involved of the right to request a hearing or fails to hold a hearing pursuant to the provisions before making an administrative punishment decision on the forfeiture of property of *a relatively large amount*, it shall, according to the relevant provisions as prescribed in the Administrative Punishment Law, affirm that the aforesaid administrative punishment decisions is against the statutory procedures [emphasis added].

The *2004 Reply* further explained what 'a relatively large amount' is: for administrative departments directly under the central government, it shall be determined by ministries and commissions of the State Council, and for any other administrative departments, it shall be determined by the local governments. This determination power should be interpreted as a kind of legislative power for all types of cases under their respective jurisdiction rather than a set of random decisions in individual cases. So, generally speaking, the monetary threshold that determines one's entitlement to a hearing before administrative forfeiture is pre-set by individual administrative organs in charge. This practice has its advantages: the ministry in charge is the most appropriate body to handle the branch of social affairs in question and the local government is most aware of the economic situation in that region. The problem is how to avoid a legislative vacuum or inconsistency as legislation is determined by many different local and central government bodies. The risk of misunderstandings or contradictions is higher than that with uniform national laws which are applied across the board. This problem also appears in the case discussed below.

---

[32]   The original Chinese text had '*et cetra* such administrative penalties' immediately after 'a comparative large amount of fine', which is missing from the English translation. This addition may include confiscation of illegal gains, so the *2004 Reply* does not add anything new to the Article or expand its scope; it just interprets this 'etc.' as including confiscation of illegal gains.

Types of Delegated Legislation

As seen in the *2004 Reply* that when setting what 'a relatively large amount' is, both the local governments and branches of the central government are entitled to legislate within their domain. However, the legislative power of administrative organs in fact goes into every subject the government deals with, and there are generally four types of legal sources concerned: administrative regulations (the central government), administrative rules (branches of the central government), local regulations (local People's Congresses) or local rules (local governments), and in each there is something relevant to confiscation.

Administrative regulations

Article 23 of the 2006 Organic Administration Regulation of Public Security Organs passed by the State Council provides that 'the public security organs shall, in accordance with the legal provisions of the state, fully turn in all fines, confiscation income and administrative charge income to the State treasury'.

Administrative rules

Article 5 of the 2007 Measures for Administrative Penalties against Illegal Acts Concerning Work Safety passed by the State Administration of Work Safety has listed confiscation of illegal proceeds and confiscation of coal products that are illegally mined and the relevant mining equipment as an administrative penalty. This specified category of items for confiscation is not inconsistent with the 1996 Administrative Penalty Law.

Local regulations

Article 23 of the 2005 Regulation of Liaoning Province on the Administrative Enforcement of Law passed by the Standing Committee of the People's Congress of Liaoning Province provides that 'an administrative enforcement authority shall take such administrative compulsory measures as sealing up, seizing or freezing properties of the parties involved pursuant to the laws and administrative regulation'.[33] It also prohibits any administrative enforcement officer 'illegally charging, withholding, expending, secretly dividing or appropriating any of the confiscated property' or 'illegally using the detained properties or making the detained properties seriously destroyed or lost due to bad management'.[34]

---

[33]   See www.lawinfochina.com, accessed 14 January 2008.
[34]   See *2005 Regulation of Liaoning Province on the Administrative Enforcement of Law,* Arts 43(5) and 43(7).

Local rules

Article 3 of the Interim Measures of Anhui Province for the Administration of Non-tax Government Revenues passed as an order by the People's Government of Anhui Province has listed confiscation revenues as one category of its non-tax revenues.

An Exemplary Case on Confiscation of Illegal Gains in Administrative Law

The multiplicity of legislative powers on confiscation of illegal gains is a problem which is likely to be of concern to the judiciary. The appellate case of *Paktanle Company v. Xiamen Customs* in the Higher People's Court of Fujian Province, decided 14 October 2005 (hereinafter *Paktanle*), is a case in which judgments of both levels deliberated on the choice of applicable laws on confiscation.

Paktanle Company, the appellant, sued Xiamen Customs for the latter's administrative penalty decision on 27 October 2004 to confiscate Paktanle's illegal gains of RMB44 978 766 and impose a fine of RMB10 million. The factual ground for the punishment was that the Paktanle Company had knowingly provided unloading and warehousing services for smuggled oil, and the legal ground was Article 6(2) of the 1987 Detailed Rules for the Implementation of Administration and Penalties of the Customs Law of the People's Republic of China passed by the General Administration of Customs as a set of administrative rules (hereinafter *1987 Detailed Rules*). Article 6(2) provided that:

> Persons who knew about the smuggling but did not report it to the authorities and facilitated the smugglers shall be punished by confiscating their illegal gains as a result of the smuggling plus a fine of not more than two times the amount of their illegal gains. In case no illegal gains are involved, a fine up to RMB 5,000 shall be imposed.[35]

The purpose of the *1987 Detailed Rules* was to implement the underlying statute of the 1987 Customs Law of the People's Republic of China (hereinafter 1987 Customs Law). The 1987 Customs Law was amended in 2000 by the NPCSC. On 1 November 2004, the *1987 Detailed Rules* was itself repealed by the new Regulations on Implementation of Administrative Penalties by the Customs promulgated by the State Council as administrative regulations (hereinafter *2004 Regulations*).

---

[35]   Available at http://www.lawinfochina.com/law/display.asp?db=1&id=714& keyword=customs%20lawm, accessed 17 January 2008.

The appellant argued that there were at least two flaws with the Xiamen Customs' decision: that it had no legal basis to make the orders as the 1987 Customs Law was amended in 2000 and since the amendment its implementing rules (the *1987 Detailed Rules*) ceased to be effective, and that the calculation of the illegal gains was wrong in the following manner. The Xiamen Customs calculated the 'illegal gains' of RMB44 978 766 by simply deducting the tax paid to the State of RMB3 006 505 by the Paktanle Company, from the total gain of US$5 797 142.97 from its business, which was equivalent to RMB47 985 271. The Paktanle Company argued the workers' wages of RMB26 809 123, warehousing equipment depreciation and other necessary expenditures should also have been deducted, and after these deductions, its income was merely RMB18 169 643.

The Intermediate People's Court of Xiamen City (hereinafter Xiamen Intermediate Court), the court of first instance, explained that the amended 1987 Customs Law did not automatically repeal the administrative regulations, being the *1987 Detailed Rules*, based on its pre-amendment predecessor, the original 1987 Customs Law. As long as articles in the administrative regulations, being the *1987 Detailed Rules*, do not contradict with the amended 1987 Customs Law, the former were still in force until formal repeal by the legislative body. Since the *1987 Detailed Rules* had not been repealed until 1 November 2004 when the *2004 Regulations* came into force, it was a proper legal basis for administrative decisions on 27 October 2004 before the repeal. As to the deduction of wages and cost, the Xiamen Intermediate Court in its brief analysis rejected the claim on the basis that the amount gained through illegal activities (and indirectly the expenses incurred to enable the activities) was directly connected thereto and thus constituted illegal gains.

The Higher People's Court of Fujian Province (hereinafter Fujian Higher Court), the appellate court, affirmed the judgment of the Xiamen Intermediate Court, but its reasoning was slightly different. On the legal basis ground, the Higher Court compared all relevant laws on smuggling, and it found that at the time of making the administrative decision there were three relevant laws in force: the *1987 Detailed Rules*, the 1987 Customs Law as amended in 2000 and the 1997 Criminal Law. The Fujian Higher Court reasoned that administrative penalties of confiscation and fine are already modest punishments because they are administrative punishments in nature, and only applicable after criminal liability has been excluded. Therefore, it was applicable law to this case.

In the appellate proceedings, the Paktanle Company invoked three legal documents on how to calculate illegal gains. The first document was a judicial interpretation of the Supreme Court on how to apply laws in criminal cases on illegal publication, the second was an announcement by the State Administration for Industry and Commerce on calculating illegal gains in illegal speculation, and the third document was a reply by the General Administration of Customs to the letter of the Legal Affairs Division of the State Council to answer the latter's request for opinions on illegal gains. In all these three documents the illegal gains were calculated only as the net profit. The Fujian Higher Court opined that the first two documents were only applicable to their specific subject matter, but not to smuggling matters, and as to the reply by the General Administration of Customs, as it was not a formally promulgated law, regulation or order, it could not be relied on in administrative case hearings in the court. The appeal claim was therefore without legal basis and could not be established.

The calculation of illegal gains in this case is crucial as it involved a vast sum of money, and the difference between two methods of calculation was more than RMB20 million. Even unfair confiscation of one million Renminbi is more than enough to bankrupt a company. With no intention to challenge the authority of the court, the present authors are of the opinion that on the point of calculating illegal gains this judgment is unfair to the appellant, although the court did not apply any law wrongly. There might be special purposes behind the judgment, but legally speaking the unfairness is the result of a legal vacuum and the lack of legal rules on maintaining consistency in judicial practice in cases where such legal vacuum arises.

CO-ORDINATION AND CO-OPERATION IN THE DOMESTIC AND INTERNATIONAL CONTEXTS

Domestic Co-ordination Among Branches of Law

As introduced in the first two parts, criminal law and administrative law are the two main areas of law relevant to confiscation. Some writers think there are three types of confiscation in China: criminal, administrative and civil.[36] Other branches of law have sporadic provisions referring to confiscation, being either a criminal penalty under Article 59 or a judicial measure under Article 64 of the 1997 Criminal Law, or being an administrative punishment. For instance, the first paragraph of Article 134 of the 1986 General Principles of the Civil Law of the People's Republic of China (hereinafter 1986 Civil Law) stipulates ten methods of bearing civil liabilities in Chinese civil law: '(1) cessation of infringements; (2) removal of obstacles; (3) elimination of

---

[36]   See Jia Luan (2007), 'A Brief Introduction to Confiscation System in Australia and China', in 2007 *Supervision in China*, **9** (hereinafter A Brief Introduction to Confiscation), at pp. 62–63.

dangers; (4) return of property; (5) restoration of original condition; (6) repair, reworking or replacement; (7) compensation for losses; (8) payment of breach of contract damages; (9) elimination of ill effects and rehabilitation of reputation; and (10) extension of apology'. The third paragraph of Article 134 then provides that 'when hearing civil cases, a people's court, ... may... confiscate the property used in carrying out illegal activities and the illegal income obtained therefrom. ...' This is a provision in the civil code, but even by this article, confiscation is not a civil law measure, and the problem was raised in the case of *Starbucks Corporation and Shanghai President Coffee Corporation v. Shanghai Starbucks Café Company Limited and Shanghai Starbucks Café Limited, Nanjing Road Branch* in the Higher People's Court of Shanghai Municipality, decided 20 December 2006 (hereinafter *Starbucks*).

Starbucks was a trademark dispute case. The plaintiff, a company incorporated in the United States, registered the trademark in China on 28 December 1999, as commonly known as 'the Starbucks Coffee', while the defendant registered the Chinese translation of 'Starbucks' on 20 October 1999 and had used very similar symbols in its business which allowed it to take advantage of the plaintiff's trademark. In this civil case the plaintiff lodged in the Shanghai No. 2 Intermediate People's Court (hereinafter Shanghai Intermediate Court) against the defendant several modes of civil liability, including stopping the defendant from infringing the right to the exclusive use of the trademark (subparagraph (1) of Article 134(1)), published apology in newspapers (subparagraph (10) of Article 134(1)), eliminating the negative influence (subparagraph (9) of Article 134(1)), compensation of around RMB1 060 000 (subparagraph (7) of Article 134(1)) and confiscation and destruction of the defendant's existing infringing articles (Article 134(3)). The Shanghai Intermediate Court ruled on 31 December 2005 that the defendant shall bear all these types of liability (although the Court only upheld around half of the compensation amount requested by the plaintiff) except confiscation of infringing articles, as confiscation was not a type of liability under civil law. The plaintiff was satisfied with the ruling, but the defendant appealed to the Higher People's Court of Shanghai, which affirmed the ruling one year later.[37]

It might not be that important that the infringing articles were not confiscated, because stopping the defendant from infringing the right to exclusive use of the trademark already meant that anything that bears the trademark could not be used any longer. Had the plaintiff insisted on the confiscation, the question of co-ordination of confiscation as between the different branches of

---

37 Available at www.lawinfochina.com, accessed 14 January 2008.

law would have arisen. In regards to this question, there are at least two important aspects in need of further coherence in the legal system: one is definitional and the other concerns implementation.

Co-ordination for definitional purposes

In the current legal system, several terms are used to refer to the legal relationship of taking the property from the person: confiscation, seizure and recovery. It might not be that important to invent new terms if the law can use these correctly.

Confiscation in both criminal law and administrative law is based on normative judgment. In criminal law the penalty is based on normative judgment of the person – whether the suspect is guilty or not, and the judicial measure is based on normative judgment of the property – whether it is illegal gains or not. It is obvious that in terms of normative judgment the separation of property from person is not unknown to the Chinese legal system, as evidenced by *Sun Aiqin*, although there is no such formal rule as civil *in rem* confiscation in this system.[38]

In administrative law, confiscation is also a punishment based on the normative judgment of the property and sometimes on the nature of the person's conduct. In *Paktanle*, the running cost of the company was not spared from confiscation because it was directly connected to the smuggling operation.

Seizure is mainly of a temporary nature as the measure prior to the final normative judgment on the person, property or conduct. Sometimes seizure is also used as a final measure, but still without normative judgment on the person. In the 2003 Administrative Measures of the People's Bank of China for the Seizure and Authentication of Counterfeit Currency the seizure of counterfeit currency is compulsory regardless of whether its holder is aware of their falsity.

Both confiscation and seizure describe a vertical relationship in that once the judgment or decision is made the person whose property is confiscated or seized would always have to obey the order, while recovery, compensation and restitution are terms applying between persons of equal status, or a horizontal relationship. In such relationships, to realize or enforce recovery and restitution the claimant has to apply for it to a State organ, the court or the government.

---

[38]   See Financial Action Task Force (FATF) (2007), *First Mutual Evaluation Report on Anti-Money Laundering and Combating the Financing of Terrorism on People's Republic of China*, available at http://www.fatf-gafi.org/dataoecd/33/11/39148196.pdf, accessed 23 January 2008, at p. 36.

If this terminology is followed and kept consistent among all branches of law, any type of measures using the term 'confiscation' shall refer to those in vertical relationships. Following this conclusion, the confiscation power in Article 134 (3) of the 1986 Civil Law can be re-examined to see why the court may refuse to order this measure. This confiscation power carries with it several conditions: (1) it is to be exercised by the court and cannot be an administrative punishment; (2) it shall be exercised within the context of a civil case and cannot be a penalty or criminal law measure; (3) it is not provided as a type of civil liability between parties of equal status before the law and thus is not ordered by the court to balance or redress rights and liabilities between such parties; (4) it carries with it a normative judgment as directed to illegal properties or illegal gains and therefore has to be a kind of punishment expressing the negative attitude of the legislature.

When these somewhat contradictory conditions are considered together, one begins to see why the Shanghai Intermediate Court refrained to exercise this power despite its express provision in the law. This does not mean properties infringing the patent law will always be exempt from confiscation. Whether to or how to confiscate shall be determined by looking into the illegal nature of a certain conduct. Suppose the plaintiff in *Starbucks* had insisted the infringing articles be confiscated and destroyed, then if it considered the defendant's conduct had violated administrative laws and regulations, it could have submitted the confiscation petition to the government organ in charge, and if the plaintiff believed the conduct was as grave as to amount to a crime, it could have reported the case as a victim in a criminal law case.

Co-ordination for implementation

In *Starbucks*, the reason the courts did not confiscate illegal property of the defendant was that confiscation was not a mode of civil liability. By invoking this reason the court rejected forms of punishment other than civil liabilities on the defendant, even though Article 134(3) has authorized the court to confiscate illegal properties in civil cases. Since Article 134(3) is only a permissive clause it is up to the court to decide whether to so order. However, there are occasions where the court cannot reject or evade making such an order. As introduced in the first part, in the 1997 Criminal Law, confiscation of property as a penalty must be executed after the criminal has paid his compensation to the victim and debts to the creditor, or in situations under Articles 201–205 of the 1997 Criminal Law, be executed after the criminal has paid the evaded or defrauded tax. Such provisions are still inadequate for implementation purposes, and provisions on technical and procedural arrangements are still needed for the implementation of both confiscation of property and the power in Article 134(3), especially in regards to problems such as the priorities in implementation, organs in charge, redress measures and procedures for false or unfair confiscation, etc.

International Co-operation and Human Rights Implications

For the time being, confiscation of property is not among the most debated topic in Chinese criminal law. However, one area in which confiscation of property could generate much debate is anti-corruption. China has ratified the United Nations Convention against Corruption[39] and for the purpose of benefiting from this convention, it is important that the Chinese legal system on confiscation meet the requirements of international co-operation. Decision-makers around the world have introduced such changes and developments in other countries; in particular the Australian Proceeds of Crime Act 2002 attracted the attention of the anti-corruption division of the Chinese Communist Party.[40]

One recently published article introduced the Australian legislation and compared it with the Chinese legal system on confiscation generally.[41] This article also explained that the term 'civil' in civil forfeiture laws in common law countries is not the equivalent to 'civil' in civil law relationships in civil law countries; rather, it is an emphasis on property rather than that of the equality in status of parties in civil law countries.

In order to benefit from international treaties and the legislative experiences of other countries, it is essential that China meets international standards, particularly in respect of the protection of property rights in the current administrative punishment system. In its preamble the UN Convention against Corruption acknowledges fundamental principles of due process of law in criminal proceedings and in civil or administrative proceedings to adjudicate property rights. Article 13 of the PRC Constitution (promulgated in 1982 and the most recent amendment made in 2004) provides that 'the lawful private property of citizens may not be encroached upon'.[42] The newly promulgated Property Law of the PRC in 2007 provides more extensively for the protection of private property.[43] This law which was subjected to substantial debate before its promulgation and has since attracted much international attention is

---

[39]   See generally and the text in English at http://www.unodc.org/unodc/en/treaties/CAC/index.html, accessed 23 January 2008.

[40]   See A Brief Introduction to Confiscation, *supra*; see also Chapter 5 of this book for the general law and practice on confiscation in Australia.

[41]   *Ibid.*

[42]   See http://www.lawinfochina.com/law/display.asp?db=1&id=3437& keyword= constitution, accessed 2 April 2008.

[43]   See http://www.lawinfochina.com/law/display.asp?db=1&id=5920& keyword= property, accessed 2 April 2008.

of particular significance for a country still officially adhering to communist doctrines. These fundamental laws appear as a contradiction to the very wide power and discretion of government in administrative confiscation. It is still too soon to tell what if any limiting effect the Property Law of 2007 will have on confiscation powers generally.

CONCLUSION

The problems discussed here are more with the legal system generally in China rather than with the confiscation system alone, and these are inevitable in building a legal system. Although for trained lawyers this should not prevent them from finding and applying the correct rules, more is demanded of their professional instincts to beware of the problems and to try to improve on the coherence and the justice of the system.

10. Civil forfeiture for Hong Kong: issues and prospects

Simon N.M. Young*

INTRODUCTION

While under British rule, Hong Kong enacted confiscation laws to ensure that those who committed serious offences would not be allowed to enjoy the fruits of their criminal wrongdoing. The laws were passed in two separate legislative exercises beginning in 1989, when the proceeds of drug trafficking were targeted, and followed in 1994, when serious crimes more generally were targeted. Both laws enabled law enforcement and prosecutors to obtain judicial orders to restrain and confiscate assets as part of a criminal case. These criminal confiscation laws were based on those which then existed in the United Kingdom. The motivations for these laws, however, were specific to the problems with dangerous drugs, triad societies, and organized criminal activities that afflicted Hong Kong at the time.[1]

In the first decade of being a special administrative region of China, Hong Kong has seen very little development in its laws and policies governing the confiscation of criminal assets. With the exceptions of mutual legal assistance legislation enacted in 1997 and anti-terrorist financing laws enacted in 2002–2004, Hong Kong has fallen behind most advanced societies in devel-

---

   * The work described in this chapter was fully supported by a grant from the Central Policy Unit of the Government of the Hong Kong Special Administrative Region and the Research Grants Council of the Hong Kong Special Administrative Region (hereinafter HKSAR), China (Project No. HKU 7023-PPR-20051). I would like to thank Jennifer Stone, with whom I co-authored an earlier discussion paper the contents of which are partially reflected in this chapter, Cheng Yulin, Kung Shun Fong and Jonathan Ah-weng for their research assistance.
   [1] See Fight Crime Committee (hereinafter FCC) (1986), A Discussion Document on Options for Changes in the *Law and in the Administration of the Law to Counter the Triad Problem*, Hong Kong: FCC Secretariat; see also Secretary for Security (Aug 1991), *Explanatory Notes on the Organized Crime Bill*, Hong Kong: Government Printer, at pp. 1–13; see also *Hong Kong Hansard*, 12 July 1989, 12 October 1994, at pp. 122–143; see also Simon Ip Sik-on (1994), 'Organised and Serious Crimes Bill Becomes Law', *Hong Kong Lawyer*, November 1994, at p. 25.

oping new laws and effective strategies to interdict crime-tainted property.[2] This chapter reviews the current state of confiscation laws and policies in Hong Kong. It also considers the case for reforming the status quo and assesses the prospects of introducing a new civil forfeiture regime.

CURRENT LAWS AND POLICIES GOVERNING THE CONFISCATION OF CRIME-TAINTED PROPERTY IN HONG KONG

Since 1989, Hong Kong has had a criminal confiscation system for drug trafficking proceeds, and in 1994 a similar system was adopted for the proceeds of organized and serious crimes. A separate provision exists for confiscating the unexplained wealth of government officials. There are also a host of provisions for forfeiting contraband and other crime specific property. With the exception of drug trafficking related cash found at the border and terrorist property, there is no general provision for the civil forfeiture of property. In regards to instruments of crime, there is a limited general power to forfeit property connected with offences and in the possession of the police. The following is a brief discussion of these and other provisions making up the existing regime governing the forfeiture of crime-tainted property.

International Obligations Binding on Hong Kong

There is an international law basis for forfeiture and confiscation laws. Multilateral treaties and United Nations (hereinafter UN) resolutions have called for measures to attack crime-tainted property. Such measures are considered essential to combating international money laundering, terrorism and other transnational organized crime.

The 1988 UN Convention Against the Illicit Traffic in Narcotic Drugs and Psychotropic Substances (hereinafter 1988 Narcotics Convention), required States Parties to adopt measures enabling the restraint, seizure and confiscation of proceeds and instruments of drug trafficking.[3] Similar provisions were also adopted in the 1999 International Convention for the Suppression of the

---

    [2]   The process of enacting anti-terrorism laws in Hong Kong is discussed in Simon N.M. Young, 'Enacting Security Laws in Hong Kong', in Victor V. Ramraj, Michael Hor and Kent Roach (eds) (2005), *Global Anti-Terrorism Law and Policy*, Cambridge, UK: Cambridge University Press, at pp. 368–395 (hereinafter Enacting Security Laws in Hong Kong).

    [3]   Vienna, 20 December 1988, (1989) 28 ILM 493 (entered into force 11 November 1990) (hereinafter 1988 Narcotics Convention): see Art. 5.

Financing of Terrorism,[4] the 2000 UN Convention Against Transnational
Organized Crime,[5] the 2001 UN Security Council Resolution 1373 concerning terrorist financing and the 2003 UN Convention Against Corruption (hereinafter the 2003 Corruption Convention).[6] China is a party to all of these
treaties and has extended their application to Hong Kong.[7] Both China and
Hong Kong have also taken steps to implement the requirements of the 2001
UN Security Council Resolution 1373.

In addition, the Financial Action Task Force (hereinafter FATF)'s 40
Recommendations to counter money laundering echo these obligations. In
particular, Recommendation 3 mandates the adoption of measures similar to
those seen in the relevant treaties to enable the confiscation of proceeds of
crime and instrumentalities used in or intended for use in the commission of
an offence.[8] Hong Kong has been a FATF member since 1991 and was a
founding member of the Asia/Pacific Group on Money Laundering (hereinafter APG) in 1997. It held the FATF presidency in 2001–2002, and in late
2007, the FATF and APG jointly conducted a mutual evaluation of Hong
Kong, the third FATF evaluation of Hong Kong.[9]

Proceeds of Drug Trafficking and Other Serious Crimes

The Drug Trafficking (Recovery of Proceeds) Ordinance (Cap. 405) (hereinafter DTROPO) and the Organized and Serious Crimes Ordinance (Cap.
455) (hereinafter OSCO) were enacted in 1989 and 1994 respectively.
Although both were amended significantly in 1995 (and to a lesser degree
in 1999 and 2002), they are still based very much on the previous English
criminal confiscation laws that were enacted in the late 1980s and early

---

4   New York, 9 December 1999, (2000) 39 ILM 270 (entered into force 10 April
2002) (hereinafter 1999 Terrorism Financing Convention).
5   New York, 15 November 2000, GA Resolution 55/25 (entered into force 29
September 2003) (hereinafter 2000 Organized Crime Convention).
6   New York, 31 October 2003, GA Resolution 58/422 (entered into force 14
December 2005) (hereinafter 2003 Corruption Convention).
7   The following treaties have applied to Hong Kong from the respective dates
stated: the 1988 Narcotics Convention since 15 May 1997, the 1999 Terrorism
Financing Convention since 19 April 2006, the 2000 Organized Crime Convention
since 27 September 2006 and the 2003 Corruption Convention since 13 January 2006.
8   See Financial Action Task Force on Money Laundering, *The Forty
Recommendations*, 20 June 2003 (incorporating the amendments of 22 October 2004),
which can be found at www.fatf-gafi.org (hereinafter *40 Recommendations*).
9   The FATF's final report was published in July 2008, see Financial Action Task
Force (2008), *Third Mutual Evaluation Report, Anti-money Laundering and
Combating the Financing of Terrorism, Hong Kong, China*, 11 July 2008, Paris:
FATF/OECD (hereinafter FATF 2008 Report).

1990s.[10] Both are notorious for being extremely technical and complex even for lawyers and judges.

Courts in both the United Kingdom and Hong Kong have repeatedly described the measures enacted in these laws as being 'draconian' and intentionally so, particularly because of the impact which an *ex parte* restraint order can have on a suspect and his family members,[11] the statutory presumptions as to how long and how much a person has benefited from criminal activity,[12] and the inflexibility of the law to give effect to third party interests in property.[13]

Scope and application of DTROPO and OSCO

The DTROPO applies when a person is convicted of a 'drug trafficking offence' specifically enumerated in schedule 1 to DTROPO. The list of offences in Schedule 1 includes various drug offences in the Dangerous Drugs Ordinance (Cap. 134) and the money laundering offence in section 25 of DTROPO. OSCO applies when a person is convicted of a 'specified offence' listed in its Schedules 1 or 2. While Schedules 1 and 2 capture many serious common law and statutory offences, they do not include all indictable offences. For example, tax evasion is not a specified offence in the OSCO.

Although many offences are not listed in schedules 1 and 2 of OSCO, it is still possible to capture the proceeds of such offences through the vehicle of the money laundering offences in DTROPO and OSCO, which are both listed in the schedules to the two ordinances.[14] If one 'deals' with the proceeds of any indictable offence, such as tax evasion, with the requisite *mens rea*, one commits the offence of money laundering, and thus one's proceeds of that indictable offence can come within the scope of the confiscation provisions in OSCO.[15] The money laundering offence is an indirect way of extending the scope of DTROPO and OSCO.

---

[10] See the following: Drug Trafficking Offences Act 1986; Criminal Justice Act 1988, Part VI; Criminal Justice (International Co-operation) Act 1990; Criminal Justice Act 1993; Drug Trafficking Act 1994; Proceeds of Crime Act 1995.

[11] See *Re "C"* [1990] 1 HKLR 127 (HC).

[12] See the following: *HKSAR v. Shing Siu Ming & Others* [2000] 3 HKC 83 (CFI); *In the matter of an application under s 3 of the Drug Trafficking (Recovery of Proceeds) Ordinance Chapter 405, Law of Hong Kong, The Queen and Ko Chi Yuen* [1993] HKEC 166 (HC); *R v. Dickens* (1990) 91 Cr App R 164, at p. 167 (CA); *R v. Ian Smith* (1989) 11 Cr App R (S) 290, at p. 294 (CA).

[13] See *HKSAR v. Lung Wai Hung* [1998] 4 HKC 161 (CA).

[14] The money laundering offence is found in s. 25 of both the Drug Trafficking (Recovery of Proceeds) Ordinance (Cap. 405) (hereinafter DTROPO) and Organized and Serious Crimes Ordinance (Cap. 455) (hereinafter OSCO).

[15] The *actus reus* element of 'dealing' is defined broadly in s. 2(1) of both

The DTROPO and OSCO also have a far reach in terms of place and time. Both ordinances apply to property situated outside of Hong Kong[16] and to offences committed prior to the coming into force of both ordinances.[17] Enforcement against property abroad must of course take place through established channels of international cooperation and mutual legal assistance.[18]

Financial investigation powers

There are special investigative powers given to law enforcement in DTROPO, OSCO and Dangerous Drugs Ordinance (Cap. 134) to assist in the gathering of financial intelligence and other evidence. These powers generally require court authorization from the superior court, the Court of First Instance (hereinafter CFI). There are powers that require individuals to answer questions, produce relevant documents, and allow the investigating officers access to information. These powers are controversial as they abrogate the common law right to silence, although safeguards were included to restrict the use of the compelled information.[19] There are also powers to authorize entry and search of premises and seizure of relevant evidence. The purposes for which the information obtained by these powers may be used or disclosed are specifically limited.

Where a restraint or charging order has been made, there are powers that require the holders of such property to provide information to assist in determining the value of the property. Immunity from legal liability is conferred on those who are required to make such disclosures.

Another useful source of financial information can come from the Joint Financial Intelligence Unit (hereinafter JFIU), which is jointly run by the Hong Kong Police Force and Hong Kong Customs and Excise Department. The Independent Commission Against Corruption (hereinafter ICAC), however, is not part of the JFIU. The JFIU was setup in 1989 to receive reports of suspicious financial activity made pursuant to obligations under DTROPO and OSCO. All persons have a duty to make a report to the JFIU if they know

---

DTROPO and OSCO. The *mens rea* element is also broad as it includes both knowledge and 'having reasonable grounds to believe', which has been interpreted as being an objective standard: see the following: *HKSAR v. Ma Zhujiang and Another* [2007] HKEC 1528 (CA); *HKSAR v. Yam Ho Keung* [2002] HKLRD (Yrbk) 277 (CA); *HKSAR v. Shing Siu Ming and Others* [1999] 2 HKC 818 (CA).

[16]   See DTROPO, s. 2(3); see also OSCO, s. 2(4).

[17]   See DTROPO, s. 2(4); see also OSCO, s. 2(5); see also *Re Law Kin Man* [1994] 2 HKC 118 (HC).

[18]   See for example, the Mutual Legal Assistance in Criminal Matters Ordinance (Cap. 525) (hereinafter MLA Ordinance).

[19]   See concerns expressed at the time, 'Right to Silence Infringed by Crimes Bill?', *Hong Kong Lawyer*, November 1994, at pp. 6–7.

or suspect that any property is the proceeds of drug trafficking or any indictable offence.[20]

Confiscation where the suspect/accused has died or absconded
Both DTROPO and OSCO were amended in 1995 to enable confiscation where the suspect/accused died or absconded before conviction or sentencing. The scheme has been criticized for presenting interpretative difficulties:

> It is clear that amendments made in 1995 were designed to adapt the provisions for the case where the defendant had died or absconded, but the end product does not achieve this objective very well, if at all. I hasten to say that this may not be the fault of the draftsman. I know how pressures from legislators and unwelcome contributions to the drafting process during the legislative process can sometimes destroy a carefully crafted legislative structure.[21]

The following prerequisite conditions under OSCO must be satisfied before confiscation is possible:[22] (a) proceedings for one or more specified offences have been instituted against a person;[23] (b) the proceedings have not been concluded because the person has either died or absconded; (c) the person *could* have been convicted in respect of the offence(s); and (d) the person has benefited from the specified offence of which he could have been convicted. Where the person is alleged to have absconded, three further conditions must be satisfied: (a) six months have elapsed from the date on which the person absconded; (b) reasonable steps have been taken to ascertain the person's whereabouts or, if he is known to be outside Hong Kong, reasonable steps have been taken to obtain the return of the person to Hong Kong;[24] and (c) adequate notice of the proceedings has been given.

It is unclear whether the person's death or absconding must occur *after* proceedings have been instituted and before they have concluded. It would seem odd that a court would allow criminal proceedings to be instituted against a person known to be deceased. As well the word 'abscond' typically

---

[20]   See s. 25A of both DTROPO and OSCO.

[21]   See *In the Matter of the Drug Trafficking (Recovery of Proceeds) Ordinance, Chapter 405, The Attorney General (Applicant) and Lee Chau Ping (First Respondent) and Tam Wai Hung (Second Respondent)* [1997] HKEC 654 (SC) (hereinafter *In the Matter of DTROPO*), per Findlay J.

[22]   See OSCO, s. 8.; see also DTROPO, s. 3 for a similar provision.

[23]   Generally, proceedings are instituted when a warrant or summons has been issued for the person, when the person has been arrested and released on bail or refused bail, charged with an offence, or when an indictment has been preferred: see OSCO, s. 2(15); see also DTROPO, s. 2(11).

[24]   A special rule applies if the person is known to be in custody abroad, see OSCO, s. 8(3)(c)(i)(B)(bb); see also DTROPO, s. 3(2)(c).

signifies wilfully keeping oneself outside the reach of the authorities and not simply an inability on the part of the authorities to locate the person in question. However the legislature probably decided against this narrow meaning of absconded when it specifically provided that a person will be treated as having absconded for any reason and whether or not, before absconding, the person had been in custody or released on bail.[25] Certainly the policy of the law would favour the application of the scheme regardless of when the death or absconding takes place.[26]

The scheme was extensively considered and explained by Deputy Judge Lugar-Mawson (as he then was) in the case of *Secretary for Justice v. Lee Chau Ping and Another*.[27] Briefly, the case held that the standard of proof to satisfy the court that the person could have been convicted was the balance of probabilities, that proof of this requirement did not require evidence and could be done by way of the statutory statement filed by the prosecution, that the hearsay rule did not apply in these proceedings, and that third parties did not have standing in the confiscation hearing, although they could be heard later when proceedings were taken to appoint a receiver to assist in the enforcement of the confiscation order.[28] The enforcement mechanism of imposing a default term of imprisonment does not apply to confiscation orders made under this scheme.

It is unknown how many confiscation orders have been made under the 'died or absconded' scheme. Judging from the number of reported cases, the total number is expected to be very low.[29] Despite the wide breadth of the scheme, the number of hurdles which must be surpassed before confiscation is possible prevents it from becoming an efficient and effective mechanism for attacking profit-motivated crime. It cannot be described as an *in rem* civil forfeiture power because there is still considerable attention paid to the proof of a substantive offence committed by a certain individual, albeit with more relaxed evidential and procedural standards than that required in a traditional criminal prosecution.

---

25   See OSCO, s. 2(1); see also DTROPO, s. 2(1).

26   The broad interpretation of absconding has been accepted by at least one court, see *Secretary for Justice v. Lee Cheung Wah* [2001] HKEC 682 (CFI) (hereinafter *Lee Cheung Wah*).

27   See *Secretary for Justice v. Lee Chau Ping and Another* [2000] 1 HKLRD 49 (CFI) (hereinafter *Lee Chau Ping*).

28   *Ibid.*

29   Only four reported cases were found, see the following: *Lee Chau Ping, ibid.*; *Lee Cheung Wah*; *Secretary for Justice v. Chow Sui Kwong* [1999] 2 HKC 118 (CFI); *In the matter of DTROPO*. The most recent case is known to have occurred in March 2005 when HK$15 million was confiscated and paid. There has yet to be any appellate consideration of the scheme.

Restraint and charging orders

Both DTROPO and OSCO provide powers for the restraint or charge of property in order to preserve it for purposes of satisfying a confiscation order, if and when it is made.[30] A restraint order prohibits specified persons from dealing with the property under restraint. An item of property under restraint may also be seized by an authorized officer for the purpose of preventing realizable property from being removed from Hong Kong. A charging order imposes a charge on the property for securing the payment of money to the government in an amount equivalent to the value of the property (and, after a confiscation order has been made, in an amount not exceeding the amount payable under the confiscation order). Charging orders are applied to the beneficial interest held by the accused in land in Hong Kong or in securities.[31]

These orders against a person's property are made by the CFI after proceedings for a 'drug trafficking offence' or 'specified offence' have been instituted and the judge is satisfied that there is reasonable cause to believe that the person has benefited from the relevant offence. The orders are broad as they apply to all the realizable property of the accused (being property which may be used to realize a confiscation order) and not only property traceable to the relevant offence. In other words, property obtained from legitimate sources can still be subject to restraint on the basis that if later a confiscation order is made against the person the property could be used to satisfy the amount of the confiscation order.

Once a restraint order is made, the court can appoint an interim receiver to take possession of realizable property, manage it and sell it if warranted.[32] Private accounting firms have typically been appointed as interim and final receivers. There is no special government department in Hong Kong that manages restrained and confiscated assets. Charging orders are enforceable in the same way as equitable charges.

Accessing restrained or charged property pending confiscation

The Rules of the High Court provide for exceptions to be made to restraint and charging orders for purposes of paying reasonable living or legal expenses of the defendant.[33] Little guidance, however, is provided in these rules on how the discretion should be exercised. These provisions, in theory, recognize and

---

[30] See OSCO, ss 15 and 16; see also DTROPO, ss 10 and 11.

[31] See OSCO, Sch. 3; see also DTROPO, Sch. 2.

[32] See Michael Blanchflower (2004), 'Restraint and Confiscation of Proceeds of Crime' paper, presented at the Archbold Hong Kong Criminal Law Conference 2004, Hong Kong, November 2004, at p. 9.

[33] See Rules of the High Court (Cap. 4A), Order 115, Rule 4; see also *HKSAR v. Cheng Wai Keung and Others* [2003] HKCFI 329 (CFI).

attempt to mitigate the often harsh consequences of preservation orders on the presumed innocent defendant and his or her family members. They also serve to protect the defendant's constitutional right to legal representation and assistance.

It is necessary to examine the practice of prosecutors and courts in granting exceptions and to assess whether these theoretical goals are being achieved. If the practice has been too restrictive, it may mean that individuals have had to go to trial without counsel of choice or legal representation at all, which has human rights implications. Further, innocent family members may have had to suffer financially for long periods of time while the case makes its way through the courts. On the other hand, if the courts are too generous in granting exceptions, it could leave nothing or next to nothing left for confiscation. Such practices have been criticised as 'judicial laundering' of proceeds of crime with the legitimised property ending up usually in the hands of lawyers. The release of restrained property to pay legal fees means that the defendant continues to profit from his crime unless the scheme has a way to claw back this benefit upon conviction.

Applications for interim release of preserved property always present a dilemma for the accused awaiting trial. Putting forward one's best case for release typically requires full disclosure of relevant financial matters. Thus, it has been held that '[i]f a court were to conclude that [a defendant] has not made full disclosure in this regard then, very often, [the defendant] would be unable to satisfy that court he has no other assets to fund his living and legal expenses, and it is unlikely any release of assets or any substantial release of assets would be allowed'.[34] However, such disclosures may in some cases (such as money laundering cases) effectively require the accused to disclose his defence or provide incriminating evidence which the prosecution can use at trial. Even if such disclosures are inadmissible at trial, it still provides a fruitful opportunity for the prosecution and investigating officers to obtain derivative evidence which they might never have discovered had the accused not made the application for release. Thus, unless there are adequate procedural safeguards to such disclosures, making an application to access restrained or charged property may in fact be a double-edged sword.[35]

---

[34] See *In the Matter of Choi Kong & Wong Lai Hung*, unreported judgment, HCMP2801/2002, 4 December 2002, per Deputy Judge McMahon, at para. 23; see also *Secretary for Justice v. CKS and Another (No. 2)* [2001] 1 HKC 611 (CFI).

[35] See the Canadian Criminal Code, s. 462.34 for an interesting procedure which involves the exclusion of the prosecution for part of the proceeding. The procedure has been adopted in the Bahamas: see Money Laundering (Proceeds of Crime) Act 1996, s. 11. Singapore adopted almost the same provision in their Terrorism (Suppression of Financing) Act 2002, s. 19, but without the clause excluding the prosecution from the hearing.

The response in Hong Kong to this dilemma has been to insert a clause in the restraint order which prohibits the prosecution from making use of any disclosures made by the defendant in compliance with the order.[36] As for the argument based on the possible unfairness arising from the derivative use of the disclosed information, courts have found on the facts of the cases before them any fruitful derivative use to be only speculative.[37] One court citing English authority has also noted that a court has a discretion, 'if there be good reason, to allow expenses of a respondent to be paid out of restrained assets even though it is not satisfied full disclosure has been made'.[38]

Confiscation process
After conviction, the prosecution may apply as part of sentencing in the CFI or District Court for a confiscation order to be made *in personam* against the offender and not against any particular property. Confiscation orders may not be made by a magistrate. If the judge is satisfied that the offender had bene-fited from drug trafficking or a specified offence, he or she *must* order confis-cation; the only remaining issue is the quantum to be confiscated. A person will have 'benefited' from a relevant offence by having received any payment or other reward in connection with the commission of the offence.[39] The judge must also impose a default term of imprisonment which is to be served if the confiscation order is not satisfied. The length of the term of imprisonment will depend on the amount of the confiscation order and can be as long as 10 years if the amount of the order exceeds HK$10 million.

Under OSCO, the prosecution may also request that the judge determine if the specified offence of which the person has been convicted is an 'organized crime' which is loosely defined as a Schedule 1 offence connected with the activities of a triad society or committed by two or more persons in a manner involving substantial planning and organization.[40] If the judge finds that the accused has been convicted of an 'organized crime', the scope of offences from which to value the accused's proceeds of crime is widened, and statutory presumptions concerning the extent to which the accused has benefited from organized crime apply.

---

[36] See *Department of Justice v. Yeung Chun Pong and Others* [2004] HKEC 440 at paras. 20–25 (CFI);

[37] See *ibid.* at paras. 35–36; see also *Re Susanto Kam and Another* [2003] 1 HKLRD 612 at para. 18 (CFI).

[38] See *Re Susanto Kam and Another, ibid.*, at para. 14.

[39] See OSCO, s. 2(8); DTROPO, s. 3(4).

[40] See OSCO, s. 2(1). Under DTROPO, all drug trafficking offences are treated in the same manner as organized crime offences.

The prosecution need only prove the preconditions to confiscation on a balance of probabilities.[41] The legislation contemplates that most confiscation orders can be made without hearing oral evidence. It provides that the prosecution will file a statement (not made under oath or affirmation) setting out the facts to support an application for confiscation.[42] The statement of facts is treated as conclusive except those facts which the accused expressly does not accept. The accused is also expected to submit a statement on the amount that might be realized at the time the confiscation order is made. Those facts which are accepted by the prosecution may be treated as conclusive. A hearing resolves any disputed facts.

Third parties

The sentencing court has no discretion to reduce the amount of a confiscation order to benefit third parties because once all the preconditions are satisfied the confiscation order is mandatory. Thus, third party interests are not normally considered at the confiscation stage. The Court of Appeal has noted the possible unfairness this inflexibility can have for both offenders and third parties.[43]

After the confiscation order is imposed, if the convicted person does not pay, a second proceeding must be initiated to recover property from the offender for the purposes of satisfying the confiscation order. In this proceeding, third parties with an interest in the property to be realized will have an opportunity to be heard. This is the only opportunity for third parties to have their interests recognized.

Both Ordinances allow for applications to the CFI for compensation to property holders where a proceeding has been wrongfully initiated.[44] However, the threshold test for obtaining compensation is high as it requires proof of 'some serious default' on the part of law enforcement or the prosecution.[45]

Determining the confiscation order

The amount to be recovered in the confiscation order is the value of the accused's proceeds of any specified offence.[46] The definition of 'proceeds' is

---

41   See OSCO, s. 8(8B); see also DTROPO, s. 3(12).
42   See OSCO, s. 10; see also DTROPO, s. 5.
43   See *HKSAR v. Lung Wai Hung* [1999] 1 HKLRD 598, at p. 606 (CA).
44   See OSCO, s. 29(1); see also DTROPO, s. 27(1).
45   See OSCO, s. 29(2); see also DTROPO, s. 27(2).
46   A person's proceeds of an offence include: (i) any payments or other rewards received by him at any time in connection with the commission of that offence; (ii) any property derived or realised, directly or indirectly, by him from any of the payments or other rewards; and (iii) any pecuniary advantage obtained in connection with the commission of that offence: see OSCO, s. 2(6)(a); see also DTROPO, s. 4(1)(a).

very broad as it includes not only movable and immovable property but also 'pecuniary advantages'.[47] The House of Lords has held that a pecuniary advantage includes the duty which ought to have been paid on goods entering the country even if the shipped goods were destroyed before reaching land.[48] Under these confiscation schemes, it is feasible to have a broad definition of proceeds because the order ultimately made is an *in personam* order (similar to a fine) for the value of the proceeds.

But if the amount that might be realized at the time the confiscation order is made is less than the amount of the accused's proceeds then the recoverable amount is only the amount that might be realized.[49] This rule mitigates the harshness of the confiscation order by reducing the accused's liability to the sum which he is currently able to pay by virtue of his owned and controlled property and gifts.

In all cases under OSCO, the value of the accused's proceeds of a specified offence must be at least HK$100 000 before a confiscation order will be made.[50] The judge has the power to reduce the confiscation order amount to take into consideration any fines and other penalties which may be or have been imposed on the accused.[51]

A statutory presumption aids the prosecution in the quantification process by presuming that property transferred to the offender in the past six years is his or her proceeds of crime. The presumption applies in all cases under the DTROPO and, in respect of the OSCO, only in those cases where the accused has been convicted of an 'organized crime'. The presumption insofar as it applies to drug trafficking offences has survived constitutional challenge both in Hong Kong and the United Kingdom.[52]

Enforcing the confiscation order

To facilitate enforcement, the judge in making the confiscation order must also impose a default term of imprisonment, ranging from 12 months to 10 years, which the offender will serve if he or she fails to pay the order within a specified time.

The judge has discretion to fix the exact length of the imprisonment term in accordance with the maximum period prescribed for certain amounts

---

47   See DTROPO, s. 4(1); see also OSCO, s. 2(6)-(7).
48   See *R v. Smith (David)* [2002] 1 Cr App R 35 (HL).
49   See OSCO, s. 11(3); see also DTROPO, s. 6(3).
50   See OSCO, s. 8(4). No similar provision exists in the DTROPO.
51   See OSCO, s. 8(7)(b); see also DTROPO, s. 3(6)(b).
52   See the following: *R v. Ko Chi-yuen* [1994] 2 HKCLR 66 (CA); *R v. Benjafield; R v. Rezvi* [2003] 1 AC 1099 (HL); *HM Advocate v. McIntosh (Sentencing)* [2003] 1 AC 1078 (PC). See also *Phillips v. United Kingdom* [2001] ECHR 437.

ordered confiscated. The term ordered must be served on top of any other term of imprisonment for which the offender has been sentenced in respect of the offence(s) for which he has been convicted. This applies also in the District Court even if the total term of imprisonment is more than seven years, the usual upper-limit on the sentencing jurisdiction of a District Court judge. The confiscation order is treated as a fine for purposes of enforcement. The court should not ordinarily fix a period of more than six months to pay the confiscation order unless special circumstances justify it doing so.

Where it is known that realizable property exists and the accused has not paid his confiscation order, the prosecutor can apply to the CFI for the appointment of a receiver.[53] The receiver may be empowered to enforce any charge imposed by a charging order, and to take possession of property and sell it. The legislation provides for a detailed scheme of how sums collected by the receiver should be applied. Here the court may return property to legitimate third parties. Ultimately, any sums remaining are paid into the government's general revenue.[54] No special fund exists to collect and distribute the pool of confiscated property.

International cooperation
Where the proceeds of crime have taken flight and crossed borders to elude detection, cooperative measures that require one country to assist another in investigating, restraining, forfeiting and returning the proceeds of crime become engaged. These measures are found in several multilateral treaties and also in bilateral mutual legal assistance agreements. Relevant multilateral treaties binding on Hong Kong include the four UN conventions mentioned earlier concerned respectively with narcotic drugs, organized crime, terrorism financing and corruption. These treaties provide international cooperation mechanisms which are binding on all parties, unless the party has entered an applicable reservation.

Bilateral mutual legal assistance agreements are another important means by which international cooperation occurs. As at 18 June 2008, Hong Kong had entered into such agreements in criminal matters with 25 countries.[55] These agreements allow for, among other things, the taking of evidence, search and seizure, the production of materials, and cooperation in the restraint and confiscation of proceeds of crime.

The Mutual Legal Assistance in Criminal Matters Ordinance (Cap. 525) (hereinafter MLA Ordinance) permits the sharing of assets internationally with

---

53   See OSCO, s. 17; see also DTROPO, s. 12.
54   See OSCO, s. 18(7); see also DTROPO, s. 13(7).
55   Eighteen in force; the remaining seven with Finland, Germany, Ireland, Indonesia, Italy, Japan and Sri Lanka are not yet in force.

'prescribed places'. These are places with which Hong Kong has bilateral or multilateral agreements in existence and which have been made the subject of a section 4 order applying those arrangements to Hong Kong. Section 10 of Schedule 2 to this ordinance provides for the proceeds of realization to be paid to the Registrar of the High Court and held for five years pending any application by the government of a prescribed place for sharing. In order to better facilitate mandatory requirements for sharing at the international level now found in some multilateral conventions (for example the 2003 Corruption Convention, Article 57(3)(a)), section 4 orders implement such obligations domestically.

While the Department of Justice's Commercial Crime/Corruption Sub-division specializes in handling the restraint and confiscation of crime proceeds under DTROPO and OSCO in the domestic context, international asset recovery is handled by the Mutual Legal Assistance Unit in the International Law Division.[56]

Sections 28 and 29 of DTROPO provide for external confiscation orders (being those from another jurisdiction) to be registered and enforced in Hong Kong. The Drug Trafficking (Recovery of Proceeds) (Designated Countries and Territories) Order (Cap. 405A) (hereinafter DTROP Order) is the subsidiary legislation that allows external confiscations orders from designated countries to be enforced in Hong Kong as if it was a domestic confiscation order.[57] Schedule 1 to DTROP Order contains a list of designated countries, which would include countries party to the 1988 Narcotics Convention.

By contrast, OSCO does not provide for a separate international cooperation mechanism. Instead, the MLA Ordinance and Order 115A of the Rules of the High Court (Cap. 4A) provide for the enforcement of external confiscation orders in respect of serious crime cases, including those concerned with drug trafficking. The definition of 'external confiscation order' expressly includes civil forfeiture orders even though Hong Kong does not have a domestic civil forfeiture system.[58]

---

56   See Administration, 'Freezing of Assets under Existing Legislation', paper for the Legislative Council Panel on Security, LC Paper No. CB(2)1640/01-02(01), February 2002 (hereinafter Freezing of Assets under Existing Legislation): available online at www.legco.gov.hk; see also Hong Kong Department of Justice (2006), *Hong Kong Department of Justice 2006 Report*, Hong Kong: Department of Justice, p. 36.

57   Note that there is an overlap between ss 28 and 29 of the DTROPO and ss 27 and 28 of the MLA Ordinance. The provisions of the latter are broad enough to include drug cases, and MLA Ordinance, s. 36 provides for consequential amendment of the DTROPO by repealing ss 28 and 29, the relevant rules under Order 115, and the subsidiary legislation in Cap. 405A. The repeal provisions have yet to come into operation.

58   See s. 2 of the MLA Ordinance.

Proceeds of Bribery and Corruption

The Prevention of Bribery Ordinance (Cap. 201) (hereinafter PBO) allows the ICAC to obtain *ex parte* restraining orders from the CFI against all of the property of a suspected person.[59] The power is far-reaching as it freezes all property of the suspect whether tainted or not, and whether held by the suspect or a third party. The person who is the subject of a restraint order can apply to the CFI to vary or revoke the restraint order.[60] As with DTROPO and OSCO restraint orders, the court has discretion to impose such conditions or exemptions as it thinks fit to allow individuals to access the restrained property pending forfeiture. Oddly, when the suspect is convicted, the PBO does not provide for the forfeiture or confiscation of the restrained property. For this purpose, the prosecution must rely upon the provisions in OSCO, and even here confiscation only extends to convictions under sections 4(1), 4(2), 5(1), 5(2), 6(1), 6(2), 9(1) and 9(2) of the PBO.[61] While the PBO confers a confiscation power, it is only for the limited purpose of forfeiting the assets of a government servant who has been convicted of the possessing unexplained property offence under section 10(1)(b) of the PBO.[62]

There are, however, mandatory restitution orders that apply where the accused is convicted of a corruption or bribery offence.[63] A person convicted of an offence 'shall be ordered to pay to such person or public body and in such manner as the court directs, the amount or value of any advantage received by him, or such part thereof as the court may specify'.[64] The restitution order may be enforced in the same manner as a civil judgment of the High Court.[65] In private sector cases, the only role of law enforcement and/or the prosecution is to inform the principal of the making of the order; it is then for the principal to decide whether to enforce it. In public sector corruption cases the principal will include the government, which will usually take action to enforce the civil order. But in private sector cases the principal may not necessarily follow through with enforcement action.

---

[59]   See Prevention of Bribery Ordinance (Cap. 201), s. 14C.
[60]   *Ibid.* s. 14D.
[61]   It was only in December 2007 that sections 4(2), 5(2), 6(2) and 9(1) were added in order to meet international obligations, see Organized and Serious Crimes Ordinance (Amendment of Schedule 2) Order 2007, L.N. 228 & 229 of 2007.
[62]   *Ibid.* s. 12AA.
[63]   *Ibid.* s. 12.
[64]   *Ibid.* s. 12(1).
[65]   *Ibid.* s. 12(4).

Restitution Orders

Restitution of property ordered pursuant to section 84 of the Criminal Procedure Ordinance (Cap. 221) (hereinafter CPO) or section 30 of the Theft Ordinance (Cap. 210) (in respect of stolen goods) is another way to ensure that offenders do not continue to enjoy their ill-gotten gains.[66] The orders allow the court to do justice to victims directly by ordering the return of property. In cases involving public corruption or bribery, the government is a recognized victim for purposes of ordering restitution.

The discretionary power in the CPO, which is subject to the provisions of the Pawnbrokers Ordinance (Cap. 166), applies only after a person has been convicted of an indictable offence and only to 'property found in his possession, or in the possession of any other person for him'. The identifiable property is ordered to be delivered 'to the person who appears to the court or magistrate to be entitled thereto' even if that person is the offender.[67] Neither provision, however, confers a forfeiture power on the court.

Civil Forfeiture of Drug Money Entering or Leaving Hong Kong

Part IVA of the DTROPO was added in 1995 to allow for seizure and forfeiture of money (not less than HK$125 000) being imported into or exported from Hong Kong which is the proceeds of or is intended for use in drug trafficking. The power is an example of a civil forfeiture provision as it expressly provides that forfeiture is possible upon proving these elements on a balance of probabilities irrespective of whether criminal proceedings are brought against any person. Case law has confirmed that the more liberal hearsay rules governing civil proceedings apply to forfeiture proceedings brought under Part IVA.[68]

No similar scheme, however, exists in OSCO. Thus, for example, if cash from a human trafficking operation was intercepted at the border, the Hong Kong authorities would only be able to forfeit this property if either it successfully prosecuted someone for the substantive offence or received an external confiscation order from a foreign jurisdiction.

---

[66] Magistrates may also order restitution for indictable offences triable summarily, see Magistrates Ordinance (Cap. 227), s. 93(c).

[67] See Criminal Procedure Ordinance (Cap. 221) (hereinafter CPO), s. 84(2), but such return must be consistent 'with the interests of justice and with the safe custody or otherwise of the person so charged'.

[68] See *Secretary for Justice v. Lin Xin Nian* [2001] 2 HKLRD 851 (CA) and similarly, civil hearsay rules apply to cases where the accused has absconded: see *Lee Chau Ping*.

The seizure, detention and forfeiture powers under Part IVA are available to the police and customs department. Given that only HK$1.9 million in total has been forfeited from 1995 to 2006, this is a power that is little used and very little if any has been forfeited in recent years.

Terrorist Property and United Nations Sanctions

Another civil forfeiture provision is found in the United Nations (Anti-Terrorism Measures) Ordinance (Cap. 575) (hereinafter UNATMO), which was passed in July 2002, and amended in July 2004.[69] This law provides for the freezing and forfeiture of 'terrorist property' which is defined as the property of a terrorist or terrorist associate or any funds used or intended to be used to finance or assist the commission of a terrorist act. The UNATMO was enacted to bring Hong Kong in line with the UN Security Council resolutions concerning terrorism and terrorist financing after the '9-11' terrorist attack in the United States. But it is of some concern that even as of the end of 2008 the freezing and forfeiture provisions in the UNATMO have yet to come into operation.

As with DTROPO and OSCO, UNATMO allows for applications for compensation where a person or property has been improperly specified under the specification scheme in the legislation. However, the threshold test for obtaining compensation in UNATMO (being showing 'some default' by the police or prosecution) is lower than that in the other two ordinances.

There are a number of subsidiary pieces of legislation under the United Nations Sanctions Ordinance (Cap. 537), which implement UN Security Council resolutions into Hong Kong law. Many of these implement embargoes imposed in conflict zones and generally allow for the preservation of certain types of property found pursuant to a search warrant or other authorization. Broad powers to order the production of any documents or other evidence are also set out.

Property in the Possession of the Police and Connected with an Offence

Section 102 of CPO provides a scheme for disposing of property which comes into the possession of the police or customs department in the course of its investigations. The section covers the following three classes of property:

(a) any property *has come into the possession of* a court, the police or the Customs and Excise Service *in connection with any offence*;

---

69   The history of this law is described in Enacting Security Laws in Hong Kong, *supra.*

   (b)   it appears to a court that an *offence has been committed in respect of any property* in the possession of the court, the police or the Customs and Excise Service; or

   (c)   it appears to a court that *any property in the possession of* the court, the police or the Customs and Excise Service *has been used in the commission of an offence*[70] [emphasis added].

A conviction is not a prerequisite to the application of section 102 but it must be established that an offence has been committed or appears to have been committed, whether in Hong Kong or abroad.[71] Generally, the judge or magistrate may either order the property to be delivered to the person entitled to the property or order the forfeiture of the property.[72] As a discretionary power, the court has the ability to recognize and give effect to legitimate third party interests.[73]

There are two significant limitations to the operation of section 102. First, it does not apply to 'immovable property or any aircraft, motor vehicle or ship'.[74] Thus a flat used solely for cultivating marijuana or a boat used solely for trafficking persons for prostitution would not be forfeitable under this section.

Secondly, if another ordinance provides for the forfeiture of the particular property or class of property in question, the provisions of this other ordinance 'shall prevail' over section 102.[75] One case has highlighted a possible lacuna arising from this limitation. In *Attorney General v. Yeung Lui*, the prosecution sought the forfeiture of an unlawfully obtained Argentinean passport under section 46A of the Immigration Ordinance (Cap. 115) which allowed for such forfeiture, but only in respect of offences under section 38 of the Immigration Ordinance or section 90 of the CPO.[76] The accused had been convicted of an offence under section 42 of the Immigration Ordinance and thus the forfeiture power in section 46A was inapplicable. At the same time, there could be no forfeiture under section 102 of CPO because section 46A was found in *obiter*

---

   [70]   See CPO, s. 102(1).

   [71]   See *Leung Yuen v. The Queen* [1975] HKLR 516 (AJ).

   [72]   This roughly captures the general idea but the actual legislative language is more technical: see CPO, s. 102(2).

   [73]   The discretionary decision to forfeit is reviewable but was not disturbed in *HKSAR v. Fung Lin Cheong* [2003] HKEC 572 (CFI). Contrast with *HKSAR v. Poon To Kun* [2004] HKEC 1494 (CFI)), where the judge exercised his discretion against forfeiture.

   [74]   See CPO, s. 102(7). See also *HKSAR v. Chan Kwok Choi* [2004] 1 HKLRD A9 (CA), a case in which the court incorrectly used s. 102 to forfeit the offender's car which was parked at the scene of the burglary.

   [75]   See CPO, s. 102(6).

   [76]   See *Attorney General v. Yeung Lui* [1989] HKLY 248 (HC).

to be a prevailing provision. This clearly could not have been the intended effect of the exclusionary clause in section 102(6).

There is another anomaly in respect of the ability of aggrieved third parties to appeal or otherwise challenge a forfeiture order made under section 102. The circumstances in *Multi-Solid Ltd v. Secretary for Justice* vividly illustrate this problem.[77] The applicant company was the victim from whom the convicted robbers had stolen HK$2 million worth of diamonds. The police had recovered HK$143 000 which was proceeds from the sale of the diamonds. After trial and on application from the prosecutor, the court summarily forfeited these proceeds without seeking to hear from the victim company. The Court of Appeal held that it was wrong for the prosecutor to have made the application and that the court should have on its own motion ordered the return of the proceeds to the victim company. Nevertheless, the court had to dismiss the appeal by the company because there was no right of appeal for third parties.[78]

Vehicles and Property Taken into Custody by Police

Section 57 of the Police Force Ordinance (Cap. 232) provides that where any person having charge of a 'vehicle, boat, horse or any other animal or thing' comes into police custody under this Ordinance, it is lawful for the police to take charge of the property and to deposit it safely as security. This is in the event that the individual is convicted and the property (or proceeds from its sale) is needed to satisfy a penalty owing (for example, a fine) and/or for any costs incurred in the storage of the property. It is necessary under section 57(2) to seek a magistrate's order to sell the property. This appears to be tantamount to conviction-based forfeiture.

Offence or Context Specific Forfeiture Provisions

Scattered amongst different ordinances, there are a number of forfeiture provisions for specific types of property found or used in certain contexts. The powers target property ranging from those of very specific social concern to property used in serious organized crime. Many of the powers target contraband, that is property for which it is an offence to possess.

The case of *In the Matter of Causeway Bay Police Station R.B. No. X6649 of 1986* illustrates the possible unfairness that mandatory forfeiture powers

---

77   [1997] HKLY 295 (CA).
78   Persons convicted may however appeal a s. 102 order pursuant to CPO, s. 83G, see *HKSAR v. Chai Man-Fong* [1998] 2531 HKCU 1 (CA).

can sometimes have on third party interests.[79] In this case, the court denied an application to have a pleasure vessel returned to the registered owners. The police seized the vessel after finding that it was being used for illegal gambling. It was undisputed, however, that the owners were unaware of the illegal activities which were being orchestrated by the boat-keeper. Nevertheless, as the forfeiture power under section 26 of the Gambling Ordinance (Cap. 148) was mandatory, the court had no alternative but to forfeit the vessel.

Some of the criminal law related forfeiture powers are described and highlighted briefly here. Section 38B of the Dangerous Drugs Ordinance (Cap. 134) allows the Commissioner for Customs and Excise to arrest and detain a ship for 48 hours if he has 'reasonable cause to suspect' that an excessive quantity of dangerous drugs is on board. After the 48-hour period, a magistrate must grant an order for its continued detention, at which time the proceedings must also be transferred to the CFI. Section 55 of this Ordinance also allows for the forfeiture of dangerous drugs brought into Hong Kong for any unlawful purpose or without proper documentation.

Perhaps the most significant provision of this Ordinance is section 56, which allows a court to order any money or 'thing' used in the commission of any offence in the Ordinance or a drug trafficking offence under DTROPO, whether or not any person has been convicted of that offence, to be forfeited to the government. Specifically excluded properties include premises, a ship exceeding 250 gross tonnes, an aircraft or a train. Vehicles are not excluded.

The Crimes Ordinance (Cap. 200) has disparate provisions throughout providing for forfeiture. Under section 106(2)–(4), a magistrate may order the forfeiture of counterfeit items if he or she is satisfied that it is in the public interest. Section 106(4) allows for an interested third party (such as the owner of the item) to make submissions as to why the thing should not be forfeited; in such a case, forfeiture cannot be ordered until those submissions are heard.

Forged items can also be ordered forfeited at section 78(2) by a magistrate if it is in the public interest to do so. Section 78(3) also allows for the broader forfeiture of 'any object which [the magistrate] is satisfied relates to the commission of the offence' where there is a conviction for any offence under Part IX of the Ordinance on forgery and related offences. Again, forfeiture under this provision cannot be ordered unless an opportunity has been given to any interested claimant to show cause why the order should not be made.

Under section 10(3) of the Crimes Ordinance, where a person is convicted of an offence in respect of seditious publications, the publication may be ordered forfeited from the convicted person or anyone else who is believed to

---

79   [1987] HKEC 8 (SC).

possess it. Unmarked plastic explosives possessed by a person unlawfully are administratively forfeited (that is without the necessity of a court order) at section 58E. Vessels used as vice establishments or for prostitution offences are liable to forfeiture at sections 153D–H and 153N, whether or not the owner or another person (such as a tenant) is convicted of the related offences. Section 153(2) allows a court to order the forfeiture of any other property (not being immovable) that the court has reasonable grounds to believe was used in the commission of such offences as well.

The Gambling Ordinance (Cap. 148) defines gambling broadly, to include 'gaming, betting and bookmaking'. It provides at section 26 for a court to order the forfeiture of any money, gambling equipment or other property (but not immovable property) if it is satisfied that it was used in the commission of unlawful gambling. This is so whether or not anyone has been convicted of an offence under this Ordinance.

The Customs and Excise Service Ordinance (Cap. 342) contains a number of provisions allowing for the search and inspection of suspected property. In addition, section 17 grants a power to Customs and Excise officers to enforce a large number of other ordinances referred to in Schedule 2 to this Ordinance. Schedule 2 includes DTROPO and OSCO as well as several other ordinances dealing with controlled substances. The effect is that Customs and Excise officers acquire powers to seize and detain property under these associated laws.

Closure Orders for Vice Establishments

It is possible under the Crimes Ordinance (Cap. 200) to obtain a closure order in respect of a premise used for prostitution. Under section 153A, where a person has been convicted of an offence related to running a vice establishment or using a premise for the purpose of prostitution, a magistrate may order those premises (other than a vessel) to be closed. Under section 153B, such closure orders are usually made for six months. Under section 153C, *bona fide* purchasers and mortgagees may apply to the court for the closure order to be rescinded. Although the premises are not forfeited to government, closure orders are an alternative crime control tool for addressing a dwelling-based enterprise crime.[80]

Private Law Civil Remedies

In the absence of general civil forfeiture laws, the government (and more

---

[80]   See, for example, Joshua But (2006), 'Yuen Long love hotels closed by police', *South China Morning Post*, 10 June 2006.

oftentimes the victims) can bring a traditional civil suit to recover the proceeds of crime. While such proceedings by government are rare, they nevertheless have been brought when the criminal justice system has been ineffective or otherwise inapplicable, for example where the defendant has fled the jurisdiction before charges are brought and extradition is no longer possible. Civil courts have been creative in recognizing equitable remedies to ensure that criminals are disgorged of their crime proceeds. Nevertheless, while legal doctrine may be favourable, a case that follows existing civil procedures can be met with considerable delays and complexities given that such proceedings must be *in personam* (rather than *in rem*) in nature and do not cater well to the transnational nature of money laundering and organized crime. In addition, the existing civil process offers few if any remedies against the instruments of crime unless they are traceable to the profits of crime.

Consider the well-known case of *Attorney General for Hong Kong v. Reid*.[81] Warwick Reid, a New Zealand national working in Hong Kong as an acting Deputy Director of Public Prosecutions, was convicted of taking bribes to influence and cover up cases. Reid was ordered to pay restitution (presumably under section 12(1) of the PBO as discussed above) following conviction, but he never did. The Attorney General brought a subsequent civil case in New Zealand, seeking to recover Reid's properties in that country, which had been purchased with the bribe money and had increased substantially in value. Denied at the New Zealand Court of Appeal, the Attorney General appealed to the Privy Council, which held that any benefit a fiduciary receives during the course of his duties is held in trust for his principal. Through this principle of equity, the property was ultimately recovered after five years of litigation in three different jurisdictions.[82]

It is interesting to consider what would happen in such a case now. Since 1999, Hong Kong has had a mutual legal assistance agreement with New Zealand in criminal matters, which now permits enforcement of external confiscation orders. Once confiscated in New Zealand, the property could be repatriated to Hong Kong subject to any agreement on the sharing of the proceeds with New Zealand. But it is unclear whether the arrangement permits

---

[81] [1994] 1 AC 324 (PC).

[82] Following his release from prison, Reid was subsequently charged in relation to payments received for false affidavit testimony in an unrelated criminal appeal of Mr. Ch'ng Poh in Hong Kong. An extradition request was made to New Zealand in 1996. Reid pleaded guilty to offences in New Zealand relating to the same offence (the affidavit was signed and the payments were received in New Zealand), and he was convicted. As a result, the New Zealand authorities were able to claw back the payments made to him under their own domestic proceeds of crime legislation.

mutual enforcement of restitution orders.[83] The Agreement with New Zealand refers to orders 'forfeiting' or 'confiscating' property. The definition of a Hong Kong confiscation order in section 2 of the MLA Ordinance refers to a 'confiscation' and 'forfeiture' order, although it may be broad enough to capture the purpose for which the restitution order is also made.

The existing confiscation regime may, therefore, be able to accommodate cases like *Reid* in large part because the offender was successfully prosecuted in Hong Kong. But what if the offender absconded from the jurisdiction and could not be extradited back to Hong Kong? Having absconded, it may be possible to bring a 'dead or absconded' confiscation proceeding under OSCO, but as discussed above there are numerous hurdles to obtaining confiscation under this method. The alternative option is to bring a traditional civil action. This was the situation in the Hon Sum case which finally came to a conclusion in 2006 with a HK$140 million settlement with the family of the late Hon Sum.[84] This case involved a three decade odyssey to try to bring Hon Sum to justice and to recover his ill-gotten bribery proceeds. Hon Sum was a police sergeant who in the 1960s was known to have amassed a sizeable wealth from the systematic taking of bribes. He retired from the police force in 1971 and went to live in Canada. It is reported that he evaded extradition from Canada by fleeing to Taiwan where he eventually died in 1999. The Department of Justice filed a writ in 2000 against the estate of Hon Sum to try to recover property in Hong Kong and abroad on the equitable principles set down in the *Reid* case. After six years, the government announced in May 2006 that an out-of-court settlement had been reached with the family of Hon. This case is a good example of how inefficient and potentially ineffective the use of the traditional civil process can be for recovering the proceeds of serious crime.

The Mareva injunction is a recognized *in personam* order to freeze assets pending the outcome of a civil action. While it is possible to obtain Mareva injunctions for worldwide assets, obtaining such orders will typically involve substantial costs and can lead to protracted litigation at home and abroad.[85] These impediments to obtaining worldwide Mareva injunctions are a further limitation of the traditional civil process. At present, rather than resorting to a Mareva injunction, the government is more likely to use mutual legal assistance arrangements to freeze overseas property which it hopes to have confiscated.

---

[83]   See Mutual Legal Assistance in Criminal Matters (New Zealand) Order (Cap. 525D).

[84]   See Patsy Moy and Benjamin Wong (eds) (2006), 'Family Settles in ICAC's Bid for Officer's Millions', *South China Morning Post*, 30 May 2006; 'When Bad Cops and Bribes Ruled Streets', *The Standard*, 1 June 2006.

[85]   See Stephen Gee (2004), *Commercial Injunctions*, 5th edn, London, UK: Sweet & Maxwell, pp. 362–3.

THE CASE FOR REFORM

There exists a strong case for reforming the current laws and practices targeting crime-tainted property in Hong Kong. A review of performance indicators in respect of DTROPO and OSCO by the Hong Kong Police Force and Customs and Excise Department reveals diminishing performance in recent years and low levels of enforcement against proceeds of crime. Existing laws have had little impact in eliminating or reducing money laundering and other forms of profit-motivated criminal activity in Hong Kong. The prevalence of organized crime groups, particularly triad societies, and profit-motivated criminal activity is of such a level to justify the introduction of new laws and practices targeting the property element in crime.

Performance Indicators Raise Concerns

On the JFIU website, statistics are available on the number of persons convicted of money laundering, the value of assets restrained, the amount ordered to be confiscated and the amount recovered and paid to government over the past four years.[86] For example, in the year 2006, it is reported that 90 persons were convicted of money laundering (up from 68 in 2003), HK\$327.4 million worth of assets was restrained (three times the amount in 2003), HK\$4.4 million was ordered confiscated (substantially more compared to the HK\$0 ordered confiscated in 2003), and HK\$49.7 million was paid to government (almost five times more than the amount in 2003). By these figures, one might be left with the impression that government performance in restraining and confiscating proceeds of crime had improved substantially from 2003–2006 and that overall performance was good. However, these figures alone do not disclose the full picture.

Other performance indicators show that law enforcement action against proceeds of crime has fallen in recent years, and the overall amount of enforcement is generally low when compared to the number of prosecutions in the District Court and High Court. This criticism was echoed in the FATF's 2008 evaluation report.[87]

In the eight years period from 2000 to 2007, the average annual number of combined DTROPO and OSCO restraint and confiscations orders obtained was 8.25 and 4.25 respectively.[88] These figures were significantly down from those in the initial eight years period of enforcement, from 1990 to 1997, when

---

[86] See Joint Financial Intelligence Unit (hereinafter JFIU) website, www.jfiu.gov.hk, accessed 17 December 2007.

[87] See FATF 2008 Report, *supra* p. 44, para. 209.

[88] Based on data provided by JFIU in January 2008.

the annual average number of restraint and confiscation orders was 18.5 and 9.0 respectively. The number of restraint and confiscation orders obtained in recent years is quite low when compared to the average number of prosecutions brought each year in the High Court (231 indictments) and District Court (1282 charge sheets).[89] While it is not expected that every prosecution will result in a proceeds of crime investigation, it is of some concern when the proportion of restraint cases makes up only half a per cent of the total volume of prosecutions brought in the two levels of court. Given the prevalence of profit-motivated crime in Hong Kong (which is discussed below), the inference that the existing criminal confiscation laws are currently under-enforced is a strong one.

Another performance indicator suggesting limited enforcement is the time taken to proceed from restraint to confiscation and to payment of the confiscation order by the offender. Based on available data detailing the history and progress of 55 cases from 1998 to 2007, it was found that on average it takes approximately 22 months to obtain a confiscation order from the court after property has been frozen by a restraint order.[90] It takes a further four months before the confiscation order is paid (either fully or partially) by the offender. Overall, the average time it takes from restraint until some payment of the confiscation order is made is just over two years (26 months).

These are significant periods of time when compared to the average time for a criminal case to proceed through the speedy courts of Hong Kong. The average time for a case to proceed from when the indictment is filed to trial by jury in the High Court is 6.2 months.[91] The average time from filing the charge sheet to trial in the District Court is only 2.9 months.[92] This delay in enforcement is indicative of inefficiencies in the processes for pursuing proceeds of crime, some of which are systemic to a conviction-based confiscation system.

The accumulated sums restrained, confiscated and paid to government also give an indication of performance. Even in ideal conditions, disparities in these three sums are inevitable given the preventative purpose served by restraint orders, the impossibility of a 100 per cent conviction rate and fluctuations in asset value over time. However gross disparities may reflect an excessive (and possibly unjustified) amount of property being restrained, the

---

[89]   See data available in Appendix III of the *Yearly Review of the Prosecutions Division* from 2000 to 2006, published by the Department of Justice, Hong Kong.

[90]   This analysis is based on data provided by the Prosecutions Division, Department of Justice, in December 2007 and by JFIU in January 2008.

[91]   Based on data for the period from 1999 to 2006 (up to the end of September) found in table 6 of the *Hong Kong Judiciary Annual Report* from 2000 to 2006.

[92]   Based on data for the period from 1999 to 2006 (up to the end of September) found in table 8 of the *Hong Kong Judiciary Annual Report* from 2000 to 2006.

inherent weaknesses of a conviction-based system and inefficiencies in realizing confiscation orders.

Taking into consideration the time normally required to process a case through to confiscation and payment, a comparison of the three sums reveals that the accumulated total value of property restrained at the end of 2005 was HK$2.05 billion, while the accumulated total amount ordered confiscated was only HK$241.39 million (at the end of 2007) and the accumulated total amount paid to government was only HK$124.54 million (at the end of 2007).[93] This translates to a confiscation rate of 12 per cent of the value of restrained assets and a payment rate of 6 per cent of the value of restrained assets and 52 per cent of the value of confiscated assets. Bearing in mind that restraint is not a prerequisite to confiscation, these disparities are of some concern.

In a paper for the Legislative Council (hereinafter LegCo) Panel on Security, the policy coordinator on asset recovery for the Department of Justice gave several reasons for these disparities foremost of which was the limitations of a conviction-based confiscation system where on average 15 per cent of defendants tried were acquitted in the period 1999 to 2002.[94] Other reasons given was the access to restrained property for payment of reasonable living and legal expenses, the return of property to victims and the falling prices of real property after 1997 resulting in lower valuations of the same real property at the time of confiscation and payment.[95]

The civil forfeiture power under DTROPO to seize and restrain cash involved in drug trafficking found entering or leaving Hong Kong has only yielded a modest amount of forfeited property (about HK$1.9 million) since its introduction in 1995.[96] This data is consistent with the trend of decreased enforcement against drug trafficking under DTROPO and increased enforcement against organized and serious crimes under OSCO. Given this trend, the obvious question that arises is why there has yet to be legislative extension of this power to offences beyond drug trafficking in order to provide law enforcement with a further tool to curtail the profits of organized crime generally.

A further indicator raises some concerns in the area of international enforcement. While countries have sent over their restraint and confiscation

---

[93] Based on data provided by JFIU in January 2008.
[94] See Prosecutions Division, Department of Justice (2003), 'Fighting money laundering and terrorist financing activities within the rule of law: A prosecutorial perspective', paper for the Legislative Counsel Panel on Security, LC Paper No CB(2)2366/02-03(01), pp. 4–5 (hereinafter Fighting Money Laundering).
[95] *Ibid.*
[96] Based on data current to end of May 2006 provided by JFIU in September 2006.

orders for enforcement in Hong Kong, the numbers have generally been low. From 2000 to 2006, a total of 17 overseas restraint orders and 16 overseas confiscation orders were filed and registered in Hong Kong.[97] The vast majority of these orders come from a civil forfeiture system, typically from the United States and Australia, and thus it could be said that for many years Hong Kong has been enforcing the civil forfeiture laws of other countries. These low figures do not raise concerns on their own as they largely reflect the extent of measures taken by other countries. Of more concern is the extent of international enforcement by Hong Kong authorities in trying to repatriate assets which have been transferred abroad. Since 1990, there has only been one case of an outgoing restraint order being filed in a jurisdiction outside of Hong Kong. In this case which concerned alleged fraud proceeds in a Swiss bank account no money was ever recovered in the end as the individual was ultimately acquitted in Hong Kong.[98] This low performance in international enforcement reflects the absence of any policy to trace and target proceeds of crime beyond the four corners of the Hong Kong Special Administrative Region.

Prevalence of Profit-motivated Criminal Activity in Hong Kong

While crime in Hong Kong is comparatively low, the vulnerability of Hong Kong to money laundering and the level of profit-motivated crime in recent years support the need for more effective measures that target the property element in crime.

The 2007 annual country report by the US Department of State describes Hong Kong's vulnerability in this way:

> Hong Kong is a major international financial center. Its low taxes and simplified tax system, sophisticated banking system, the availability of secretarial services and shell company formation agents, and the absence of currency and exchange controls, facilitate financial activity but also make Hong Kong vulnerable to money laundering. The primary sources of laundered funds are tax evasion, fraud, illegal gambling and bookmaking, and intellectual property rights violations. Laundering channels include Hong Kong's banking system, and its legitimate and underground remittance and money transfer networks.[99]

---

[97] Data provided by the International Law Division, Department of Justice, in September 2006 and by JFIU in December 2007.

[98] See mention of case in Freezing of Assets under Existing Legislation, *supra*.

[99] Bureau of International Narcotics and Law Enforcement Affairs (2007), 'International Narcotics Control Strategy Report 2007: Country Reports: Hong Kong', www.state.gov/p/inl/rls/nrcrpt/2007/vol2/html/80887.htm, accessed December 2007.

Another reason for its vulnerability is the huge volume of persons and goods entering and leaving Hong Kong each day. As reported by the Customs and Excise Department, Hong Kong has one of the busiest airports and container ports in the world.[100] Each day about 361 scheduled flights, 36 343 passengers and 3414 tonnes of imported cargo arrive at the airport.[101] On average each day, nearly 200 000 people arrive from Mainland China by land, and a further 4261 passengers enter Hong Kong by through-trains.[102] In 2005, 39 140 ocean vessels and 192 680 river vessels arrived in Hong Kong, and 9.67 million passengers arrived from the Mainland and Macau by sea and by helicopters.[103]

Law enforcement in Hong Kong has seen an increased amount of money laundering activity in recent years. The annual number of investigated money laundering cases by the Hong Kong Police Force and Customs and Excise Department increased from 401 cases in 1997 to 715 cases in 2005.[104] The number of persons prosecuted and convicted for money laundering under OSCO also increased significantly from 1997 to 2005.[105] The number of suspicious transactions reported to JFIU tripled in this same period.[106] Every money laundering prosecution is a potential asset confiscation case. Yet the total number of restraint and confiscation orders obtained for all applicable offences lags well behind the number of persons convicted of money laundering alone.[107]

---

[100]   See Customs & Excise Department (2006), 'Hong Kong: The Facts', published by the Information Services Department, HKSAR Government, 2006, available online at www.customs.gov.hk (hereinafter Customs Facts).

[101]   *Ibid.*

[102]   *Ibid.*

[103]   *Ibid.*

[104]   The numbers of investigated money laundering cases from 1997 to 2005 are as follows: 401, 621, 866, 625, 607, 687, 972, 1 071, and 715. Data provided by JFIU in August 2006.

[105]   The numbers of persons prosecuted from 1997 to 2005 are as follows: 22, 28, 28, 32, 41, 86, 114, 90 and 107. The numbers of persons convicted from 1997 to 2005 are as follows: 10, 13, 18, 28, 29, 42, 72, 51 and 73. See Security Bureau (September 2006), 'Organized and Serious Crimes Ordinance: Report on Implementation (1997–2005)', paper for Legislative Council Panel on Security, Annex C, LC Paper No. CB(2)3020/05-06(01) (hereinafter OSCO Report on Implementation).

[106]   The numbers of suspicious transactions reported to JFIU from 1997 to 2005 are as follows: 4227, 5570, 5804, 6104, 6484, 10 871, 11 678, 14 029 and 13 505. See OSCO Report on Implementation, *ibid.*

[107]   From 1997 to 2005, the average number of persons convicted of money laundering under OSCO was 31. However, in the same period, the average number of restraint and confiscations orders obtained under the OSCO was 6.6 and 2.1 respectively. See OSCO Report on Implementation, *ibid.*; data provided by JFIU in August 2006.

Money laundering is closely related to other forms of organized criminal activity. Hong Kong's Secretary for Justice noted this connection at a meeting of Asian prosecutors in 2007:

> As we review anti-crime strategies, it is salutary to consider how organized criminal groups conduct themselves. Quite clearly, they need finance. They need people willing to commit the offences. They have to obtain equipment and transportation. They need to convert the products of crime into money or other usable assets. They have to find people and places willing to store proceeds. They also, and this is of particular concern, need to neutralise law enforcement by using technical skills, corruption, or legal techniques to frustrate investigations and prosecutions.[108]

The existence and activities of Chinese triad societies in Hong Kong are well documented.[109] They were in Hong Kong before 1842 and continue to be a dominant force behind organized criminal activity in the territory.[110] Professor Yiu wrote in 1999 that Hong Kong triads 'are known to have been long involved in the illegal business of drugs, gambling, prostitution, loan sharking, debt collecting, and smuggling'.[111] In his study of the business and economic ambition of triads, he found that Hong Kong triads are not centrally controlled but are 'loose cartels consisting of numerous autonomous gangs which adopt a similar organisational structure and rituals to bind their members together'.[112] David Hodson has made the point that not all organized crime in Hong Kong is triad-related and that such crime can also be traced to youth gangs, street gangs, other criminal gangs, enterprise criminals (for example corruption and delinquent professionals) and multi-crime syndicates.[113]

---

[108]   See Wong Yan Lung (2007), speech published in *The Fourth China-ASEAN Prosecutors-General Conference Commemorative Edition*, Macau: The Public Prosecutions Office of Macao Special Administrative Region, pp. 36, 38.

[109]   See Kong Chu Yiu (2000), *The Triads as Business*, London: Routledge (hereinafter *Triads as Business*); see also James J. McKenna, Jr (1997), 'Organized Crime in the Former Royal Colony of Hong Kong' in Patrick J. Ryan and George E. Rush (eds) (1997), *Understanding Organized Crime in Global Perspective: A Reader*, California, US: Sage Publications, pp. 205–213.

[110]   See *Triads as Business, ibid.* p. 1. For more recent literature, see Rod Broadhurst (ed), *Bridging the GAP: A Global Alliance Perspective on Transnational Organised Crime*, Hong Kong: Hong Kong Police Force (hereinafter *Bridging the GAP*), at pp. 246–273 (Part V: Triads and Chinese Criminal Groups); see also Kong Chu Yiu (2007), 'Hong Kong Gangs', in James O. Finckenauer and Ko-Lin Chin (eds) (2007), *Asian Transnational Organized Crime*, New York, US: Nova Science Publishers, pp. 87–95.

[111]   See *Triads as Business, ibid.* p. xi.

[112]   *Ibid.* at p. 135.

[113]   See David M. Hodson (2002), 'Triads in Business: "To Get Rich is Glorious"', in *Bridging the GAP, supra,* pp. 258–259.

The levels of reported crime in Hong Kong can provide some indication of the performance of asset confiscation laws and the potential need for reform. While the crime rate in Hong Kong fell in the period 1990 to 2000, the rate was stable from 2000 to 2007.[114] It is unlikely the decrease in the 1990s was attributable to the impact of confiscation laws which only began to apply against serious offences generally in 1995. Professor Broadhurst has noted a number of other factors that explain Hong Kong's low crime rate, highlighting changing demographics, particularly the proportion of high-risk young males in the population, as being a crucial factor.[115]

Of more relevant interest is the prevalence of profit-motivated crime in Hong Kong. From police statistics on reported crime, profit-motivated crime makes up approximately 70 per cent of all crimes reported.[116] The number of reported profit-motivated crimes has increased from 1999 to 2006.[117] The total number of corruption reports made to ICAC has fluctuated in recent years but the average number reported each year from 2000 to 2006 is much greater than that reported in the 1980s and 1990s.[118]

---

[114] Crime rate is defined by the Hong Kong Police Force as the number of reported crimes per population of 100 000. From 1990 to 2000, the rate peaked in 1990 at 1548 and bottomed out in 1997 at 1036. From 2000 to 2006, the rate peaked in 2003 at 1299 and bottomed out at 1086 in 2001. See Security Bureau (November 1999), 'State of Crime and Detection Rate', paper for the Legislative Council Panel on Security, at Annex, CB(2)532/99-00(03); 'Chart 1: Overall Crime, 1996–2006', paper for the Legislative Council Panel on Security, LC Paper No. CB(2)910/06-07(01).

[115] See Rod Broadhurst (2005), 'Crime Trends in Hong Kong, 1978–1998', in R. J. Estes (2005), *Social Development in Hong Kong: the Unfinished Agenda*, Oxford, UK: Oxford University Press, at pp. 185, 190–192.

[116] 'Profit-motivated crime' is not a term used by the Hong Kong police but is employed here to capture a group of offences which by their nature are generally committed for profit or other monetary gain. Based on available police data, this group includes certain categories of reported offences including violent crimes against property (excluding arson), burglary and theft, fraud and forgery, keeping vice establishments, procuring/controlling of prostitution, serious narcotics offences, aiding and abetting of illegal immigrants, unlawful society offences, money lending, serious gambling offences and going equipped for stealing. See *Hong Kong Police Review*, editions from 1999 to 2006, Apps 6 and 7 (2006), which are available online at www.police.gov.hk (hereinafter *Hong Kong Police Review 1999–2006*).

[117] The numbers of reported profit-motivated crimes from 1999 to 2006 are as follows: 51 889, 53 634, 51 945, 54 671, 64 262, 56 995, 52 343 and 54 991. See *Hong Kong Police Review 1999–2006, ibid.*

[118] The average annual number of corruption reports from 1980 to 1989 was 2333, from 1990 to 1999 was 2967 and from 2000 to 2006 was 4045. However the number of persons prosecuted for corruption in recent years has fallen from 608 in 2000 to 341 in 2006. See ICAC (2006), 'Number of Corruption Reports Received (excluding election-related reports)', table of data available from the ICAC website at www.icac.org.hk; ICAC, *2006 Annual Report*, Hong Kong, App. 9.

Hong Kong has a particular problem with commercial and consumer fraud. It makes up about 10 per cent of all reported profit-motivated crimes, making it the second most frequent category of such crimes, next to burglary and theft offences at 76 per cent.[119] Victimization surveys also show a significant problem with consumer fraud. In a study released in 2006, it was found that 21.7 per cent of all respondents had been a victim of consumer fraud in Hong Kong.[120] This is much higher than the rate of victimization in other countries and the United Nations International Crime Victim Survey average rate of 7.7 per cent.[121] Reports of syndicated or serious commercial frauds have been on the decrease since 2002, but the average annual total reported loss of HK$1.6 billion from 2002 to 2006 is still a matter of concern.[122] In 2005, 157 persons were prosecuted for commercial crimes, and of those prosecuted 128 were convicted, again a number that far exceeds the average annual number of restraint and confiscation orders obtained.[123]

From the analysis thus far, it is possible to draw the following conclusions: Hong Kong is particularly vulnerable to local and trans-border money laundering; statistics show that money laundering continues to be a problem in Hong Kong; triad societies and other organized crime groups continue to have a strong presence; the existing asset confiscation laws have had little impact in deterring profit-motivated criminal activity; and the prevalence of such criminal activity within and passing through Hong Kong is currently at such a level to justify the need for more effective measures to prevent and interdict such activities.

Inadequacies of the current regime
The current legal regime is not conducive to the expeditious, efficient and

[119]   Calculated from data found in *Hong Kong Police Review 1999–2006*, *supra*.
[120]   See R. Broadhurst, J. Bacon-Shone and K.W. Lee (2006), 'United Nations International Crime Victim Surveys Hong Kong 2006', powerpoint presentation slides dated 6 October 2006, slide 32 (hereinafter UNICVS 2006). Report to be published on the International Crime Victims Survey website: http://rechten.uvt.nl/icvs/.
[121]   For example, the rate in Finland is 10 per cent, Japan 2.3 per cent, Australia 8.8 per cent, US 11.4 per cent, Canada 7.5 per cent and Poland 12.8 per cent. The only reported country which had a higher rate was Cambodia at 34 per cent. See UNICVS 2006, *ibid.* at slide 33.
[122]   The numbers of reported complaints from 2002 to 2006 are as follows: 101, 83, 69, 62 and 62. See the following: FCC (2003), *2003 FCC Report No. 23*, Hong Kong: FCC Secretariat, at para. 4.3; FCC (2004), *2004 FCC Report No. 24*, Hong Kong: FCC Secretariat, at para. 4.3; see also FCC (2005), *2005 FCC Report No. 25*, Hong Kong: FCC Secretariat, at para. 5.3; see also FCC (2006), *2006 FCC Report No. 26*, Hong Kong: FCC Secretariat, at para. 6.3.
[123]   See 'Report on Follow-up Action by Police', paper for Legislative Council Panel on Security Meeting on 24 January 2006, LC Paper No. CB(2) 1687/05-06(01).

effective interdiction of proceeds and instruments of crime. Rather, its scattered and complex state renders it inaccessible to most persons. Its many shortcomings and anomalies are reasons in themselves for undertaking a comprehensive and comparative review of the legal regime. The administrative regime does not fair much better. For years, inadequate resources have limited the extent to which the aims of the legislation have been realized.

Inaccessibility of the law

The current law governing the restraint and confiscation of crime tainted property is scattered across many ordinances which were enacted at different times and often for different purposes. The scattered state of the law makes understanding and accessibility of the law difficult not only for the ordinary person and law enforcement personnel but also for lawyers and judges. Having four separate ordinances (DTROPO, OSCO, UNATMO, and PBO) for interdicting proceeds of crime is repetitive and contributes to possible confusion. The ordinances reflect differences in standards and procedures without evident policy justifications for the differences. The confiscation schemes in DTROPO and OSCO are extremely technical and complicated, and unnecessarily so when one considers the simpler and highly effective legislative schemes of other jurisdictions.[124]

When the law is so complex, the perception arises that proceeds of crime work should be left for a small group of experts or specialist personnel. But leaving the work to only a small team of people has obvious implications for the level of enforcement that can be achieved. It also means that the team will need to rely heavily on referrals and information from non-specialist personnel who may not be well informed on the law.

Gaps, loopholes and other anomalies

There are many gaps and anomalies in the existing legal regime. The confiscation schemes in DTROPO and OSCO do not apply at the magistrates level, which occasionally hears cases involving profit-motivated offences, such as theft, corruption and fraud, punishable up to two years' imprisonment. The list of offences to which the OSCO applies is limited and recent experience has shown how difficult it can be to have the legislature amend and add to the list of offences (see discussion below).[125] As mentioned already, there is no reason why the power in DTROPO to seize and forfeit drug trafficking proceeds at the borders should not be extended to other forms of property and to the scheduled

---

[124] Note in particular the schemes in the United States, Canada, South Africa and Ireland as explained in Chapters 2, 6, 4 and 3 respectively in this book.
[125] This criticism was also echoed in the FATF's 2008 report, see FATF 2008 Report, *supra*, p. 44, para. 210.

list of offences in OSCO. The FATF's 2008 evaluation report also highlighted the limiting effect of having the HK$100 000 threshold for OSCO confiscations.[126]

The existing law does not allow for the forfeiture of 'facilitating property' in the broad sense as understood in other jurisdictions particularly the United States. While disparate provisions exist for forfeiting contraband and property directly used in the commission of an offence, there is a reluctance to extend forfeiture to property (such as residential premises) that facilitate the criminal enterprise even though it may also serve other innocent purposes. The existing limitations in section 102 of CPO preclude it from being a general provision against facilitating property.

Existing laws also fail to give proper attention to legitimate third party interests. Mandatory forfeiture or confiscation provisions give the courts no leeway to grant relief to third parties, including victims of crime. For such individuals, relief will only be afforded at the discretion of the executive either before or after the court's order. Discretionary forfeiture powers allow the court some leeway but without clear statutory criteria there is a risk that varying standards will be applied by courts in deciding whether to grant relief. An inconsistency has also arisen in the test for obtaining compensation; the requirement of showing 'serious default' in DTROPO and OSCO is higher than the standard of 'some default' in the UNATMO.

In respect of regional cooperation, DTROP Order lists 'China (except Hong Kong)' as a jurisdiction whose restraint and confiscation orders in respect of drug trafficking can be registered in Hong Kong. However, it is unclear whether this would allow for the recognition of orders from Macau and Taiwan. More problematic is that the MLA Ordinance, which provides for international cooperation in both OSCO and DTROPO cases, expressly does not apply to the Chinese mainland, thus leaving no possibility for formal regional cooperation in non-drug trafficking cases.[127]

Inefficient procedures

Experience has shown that the time required in Hong Kong to restrain and confiscate property and to realize a confiscation order is well beyond the time normally required to prosecute a person. There may be many reasons for the delay. Financial investigation is a specialized area of investigatory work that presents unique challenges and difficulties, particularly in a conviction-based system where it is necessary to trace the origins of assets to a particular person and offence. The complicated task of assessing the quantum of realizable

---

[126] Ibid.
[127] See MLA Ordinance, s. 3(1).

assets can be daunting for investigators untrained in accounting methods. Ensuring adequate and standard training in financial investigation and evidence-gathering in confiscation cases remains a major challenge. Adequate training of prosecutors is also required together with their strategic placement in advisory roles during investigations. Turnover and internal transfer of personnel can present obstacles in major cases.

Delay has also resulted from the current practice of waiting until a convicted person has exhausted his or her appeal rights before obtaining the confiscation order from the original trial court. If confiscation is supposed to be part of the sentencing process, a confiscation order being part of the sentence should be obtained as soon as possible after conviction. In the event that an appeal from conviction is successful, return of confiscated property (plus compensation if warranted) is an unproblematic consequence especially when compared to the more difficult problem of remedying unjustified incarceration time.

To some extent, inefficiencies will arise (and have arisen) simply due to human neglect and error. Such was likely the root cause of the failing in the case of *Secretary for Justice v. Yiu Chik Chuen* where the prosecution had waited almost two years after conviction to obtain the confiscation order.[128] In dismissing the proceedings for want of prosecution, the District Court judge noted the prosecutor's concession that the delay was inordinate, inexcusable and ultimately prejudicial to the offender.[129]

Inadequate resources

The delay which appears systemic in nature probably reflects the inadequate resources and low policy priority accorded to criminal asset confiscation over the years. As of March 2008, the Hong Kong Police Force had only 52 police officers in its Narcotic Bureau Financial Investigation Division dedicated to restraint and confiscation cases under DTROPO and OSCO. This represents less than 0.2 per cent of the total number of police officers (26 921 strong at the end of 2006).[130] While the Commercial Crime Bureau sometimes carries out restraint and confiscation work, it has no dedicated officers. The Customs and Excise Department has approximately 30 officers and civilians in this area, out of a total establishment size of 5611 as of October 2007.[131] There is little if any in-house forensic accounting and legal expertise in the two agencies.

---

[128] See *Secretary for Justice v. Yiu Chik Chuen* [2006] 1 HKC 507 (DC).
[129] *Ibid.* at para. 25.
[130] See *Hong Kong Police Review 2006*, App. 1.
[131] See Customs Facts, p. 1. Updated information provided by the Customs & Excise Department in February 2008.

The Prosecutions Division of the Department of Justice has had for some time a special section dedicated to restraint and confiscation consisting of only five prosecutors including the section head in a division of about 100 government counsel. For many years, the special section also carried out duties unrelated to asset confiscation, and it was only in 2007 that the section was relieved of such duties.

Without adequate resources to enforce the laws, no degree of law and policy reform will have an impact on enforcement and crime levels. The absence of in-house expertise to assist with the complexities of financial investigation will often require additional expenditure to retain such expertise. Without a special fund (such as one made up of the confiscated assets themselves) to cover such expenditures, the number of pursued restraint and confiscation cases is limited by the reality of budgetary constraints.

Room for Policy Development

There is a lack of policy development in the laws and practices targeting crime-tainted property in Hong Kong. Law reform in this area since 1989 and 1994 has been incremental and minor in scale. Little innovation is seen, and few ideas which have proven to be effective in other countries have been borrowed. For example, the idea of directing confiscated property to a special fund to help victims of crime and to further other criminal justice goals has been adopted by many countries and is suggested by the FATF but finds little mention in Hong Kong where such property continues to disappear into the general revenue.[132] Recent statements of policy initiatives by the Security Bureau and Department of Justice make no mention of strengthening or developing asset confiscation polices or practices.[133]

Law enforcement practices and strategies are also underdeveloped. The strategy of using integrated law enforcement units which sees agents from different enforcement agencies working together with legal, financial and accounting experts on individual cases has yet to be adopted in Hong Kong, even though it has been effectively employed for some time in other jurisdic-

---

[132]   The interpretive note to FATF Recommendation 38 provides that 'Countries should consider (a) Establishing an asset forfeiture fund in its respective country into which all or a portion of confiscated property will be deposited for law enforcement, health, education, or other appropriate purposes'.

[133]   See for example, Department of Justice (October 2007), '2007–08 Policy Initiatives of the Department of Justice', paper for the Legislative Council Panel on Administration of Justice and Legal Services, LC Paper No. CB(2)45/07-08(03); Security Bureau (October 2007), 'Policy Initiatives of Security Bureau', paper for Legislative Council Panel on Security, LC Paper No. CB(2)41/07-08(01) (hereinafter 2007 Policy Initiatives of Security Bureau).

tions such as Canada, Ireland and the United Kingdom.[134] No specific policy and practice manual exists to assist with the training and co-ordination of law enforcement efforts in this area. Data collection and analysis of performance is also at a very primitive stage. As mentioned earlier, there is no coherent policy to trace and repatriate proceeds of crime that have been transferred to other countries.

OBSTACLES TO ACHIEVING EFFECTIVE REFORM AND PROGRESS

Many of the obstacles to achieving effective reform and progress are political in nature. In Hong Kong's inchoate democratic system, the introduction of major policy initiatives is reserved for the Administration which needs to secure the support of a majority of the 60 legislators in LegCo if the initiative is to be enacted. Thus inertia or resistance at either the executive policy-making level or at the level of the legislature can set back a civil forfeiture proposal, irrespective of how much support it may have from law enforcement and prosecutors. The experience in 2003 of trying to enact national security legislation has shown how vocal and strong public opposition can be to the introduction of laws that impinge on the human rights of Hong Kong residents.[135]

Uncertain Political Will in the Executive Branch

At a meeting of the LegCo Panel on Security in June 2003, the possibility of introducing civil forfeiture laws was discussed in relation to Hong Kong's work in combating money laundering and terrorist financing.[136] The then

---

[134] In Canada, see the Integrated Proceeds of Crime Units, which are described on the website of the Royal Canadian Mounted Police, at www.rcmp-grc.gc.ca. For the position in Ireland, see Chapter 3 in this book. The United Kingdom now has the Serious Organised Crime Agency, see Chapters 7 and 8 in this book.

[135] See generally Enacting Security Laws in Hong Kong, *supra*; see also Hualing Fu, Carole J. Petersen and Simon N.M. Young (eds) (2005), *National Security and Fundamental Freedoms: Hong Kong's Article 23 Under Scrutiny,* Hong Kong: Hong Kong University Press (hereinafter Article 23 book).

[136] See LegCo Secretariat (2003), 'Panel on Security: Minutes of meeting held on Thursday, 5 June 2003', LC Paper No. CB(2)2676/02-03, 4-10 (hereinafter 5 June 2003 Minutes); see also Security Bureau (May 2003), 'Hong Kong's Work on Combating Money Laundering and Terrorist Financing', paper for the Legislative Council Panel on Security, LC Paper No. CB(2)2247/02-03(03), at para. 28; see also Fighting Money Laundering, *supra* at para. 10.

Commissioner for Narcotics stated that consideration was being given to introducing civil forfeiture as a result of developments in other developed economies such as the United States, the United Kingdom and Australia and because of recommendations by experts from the International Monetary Fund and World Bank.[137] At the meeting, legislators asked questions about but did not show any resistance or negativity to the idea.[138] Since this time, however, the topic of civil forfeiture has not been mentioned again in either the records of the LegCo or the public policy statements of the Security Bureau. The government's current resolve and commitment to introduce civil forfeiture is unclear.

In its 2007/08 statement of policy initiatives, the Security Bureau stated that 'Hong Kong is committed to maintaining a robust regime to combat money laundering and terrorist financing'.[139] It stated the initiative of '[p]utting into effect, through legislation and other means, the recommendations of the Financial Action Task Force on Money Laundering to further enhance our anti-money laundering and counter-terrorist financing regime', a reference to the FATF evaluation that was conducted at the end of 2007.[140] No specific mention was made of civil forfeiture or asset confiscation.

There is a potential problem with invoking FATF reviews to lend greater legitimacy to a major programme of reform that includes civil forfeiture. None of the 40 FATF recommendations require the introduction of a civil forfeiture system. The Introduction to the 40 Recommendations states that the FATF 'recognises that countries have diverse legal and financial systems and so all cannot take identical measures to achieve the common objective, especially over matters of detail. The Recommendations therefore set minimum standards for action for countries to implement the detail according to their particular circumstances and constitutional framework.'[141] This explains why Recommendation 3 only goes as far as stating that countries

> *may consider adopting* measures that allow such proceeds or instrumentalities to be confiscated without requiring a criminal conviction, or which requires an offender to demonstrate the lawful origin of the property alleged to be liable to confiscation, *to the extent that such a requirement is consistent with the principles of their domestic law*[142] [emphasis added].

---

137 See 5 June 2003 Minutes, *ibid.* p. 5.
138 *Ibid.*
139 See 2007 Policy Initiatives of Security Bureau, *supra*, p. 5.
140 *Ibid.*
141 See *40 Recommendations*, *supra* at introduction, 3rd paragraph.
142 *Ibid,* at p. 2, para. 3.

While the FATF's 2008 evaluation of Hong Kong was critical of the low numbers of restraint and confiscation orders obtained in recent years, the report did not recommend the adoption of a full civil forfeiture regime, even though it noted that the scope for civil forfeiture under the existing law was 'greatly limited in terms of the circumstances including predicate offences, that trigger forfeiture and the property that may be forfeit'[143].

Possible Resistance in the Legislature

It is difficult to read what the legislative response would be to proposals to introduce civil forfeiture to Hong Kong. Adding to the uncertainty is the September 2008 elections that put in office a new crop of legislators for another four-year term.

At least two groups of legislators are likely to have concerns. The pan-democratic legislators will have concerns with any legislation that tends to encroach on fundamental rights and freedoms. The pro-business legislators, particularly those elected from functional constituencies, will be concerned with any new anti-money laundering measure that may impose new costs or impediments to conducting business in Hong Kong. Indeed it was the combined concerns of these two groups that frustrated law enforcement efforts to try to introduce new money laundering criminal offences in 2001–2002. The proposal would have created new offences with lower standards of *mens rea*, but was ultimately dropped to make way for the passage of the remaining parts of the bill.[144] In 2003, the vocal concerns of legislators and members of the community also led to the demise of proposed national security legislation, which have yet to be reintroduced.[145]

More recently, however, some legislators have expressed disappointment with the effectiveness of asset confiscation laws. For example, James To, a long-time member of the Democratic Party and chairman/deputy chairman of the LegCo Panel on Security, stated the following in response to the Chief Executive's 2006 Policy Address:

> I have been talking about the Organized and Serious Crimes Ordinance *ad nauseam*. I have said time and again in recent years that since the passage of the Organized

---

[143]   See FATF 2008 Report, *supra*, p. 42, para. 203 and p. 223. It only recommended that three anomalies and limitations in the existing law be rectified and that the enhanced focus on confiscation that began in 2007 continue.

[144]   See LegCo Secretariat (28 June 2002), 'Paper for the House Committee meeting on 28 June 2002: Report of the Bills Committee on Drug Trafficking and Organized Crimes (Amendment) Bill 2000', LC Paper No CB(2)2417/01-02.

[145]   See mention of this earlier in this chapter; also, see Enacting Security Laws in Hong Kong, *supra*; Article 23 book, *supra*.

and Serious Crimes Ordinance nearly 10 years ago, the public have been eagerly expecting the authorities to invoke the most powerful provisions of the legislation. And, in fact, the Government did give us very great hope at the time of passing the legislation. According to the Government, the passage and enforcement of the legislation will enable it to effectively dismantle some triad societies and crime syndicates. However, after 10 years of implementation, we still cannot see any great effect. (If the legislation is not powerful enough, should the Government come back to us for further discussions?).[146]

In June 2006, a committee of legislators studying a bill to amend betting and gambling laws sought an explanation from government on why only HK$2.5 million out of an aggregate amount of HK$2.5 billion of gambling proceeds had been confiscated since 1998.[147] Ultimately a letter was sent by the Home Affairs Bureau to the Security Bureau conveying the legislators' view that consideration be given to whether amendments to OSCO were required to counter money-laundering activities more effectively.[148]

But despite these statements in favour of more effective enforcement against proceeds of crime, it took the government and legislators 17 months to effect two straightforward changes by subsidiary legislation that were intended to bring Hong Kong in compliance with its international obligations under the 2003 Corruption Convention. The changes were simply to add several existing corruption offences to the list of scheduled offences in OSCO and to make the MLA Ordinance applicable vis-à-vis other States Parties to the Convention. Although the Convention came into force for China and Hong Kong in February 2006, the matter of implementation was first discussed in the Panel on Security in July 2006 and later from June to November 2007 in a subcommittee convened to consider the proposed subsidiary legislation before the proposal was finally approved in December 2007.[149]

---

[146]   See *Hong Kong Hansard*, 25 October 2006, p. 866.

[147]   See 'Follow-up action arising from the meeting on 8 June 2006', paper for the Bills Committee on Betting Duty (Amendment) Bill 2006, June 2006, LC Paper No. CB(2)2343/05-06(01).

[148]   See Letter of Jenny Yip for Secretary for Home Affairs to Appollonia Liu, principal assistant secretary in the Security Bureau, dated 15 June 2006, LC Paper No. CB(2)2433/05-06(02).

[149]   See Security Bureau (June 2006), 'Legislation to Implement the United Nations Convention Against Corruption in Hong Kong and Related Matters', paper for the Panel on Security, LC Paper No. CB(2) 2577/05-06(03); see also LegCo Secretariat (November 2007), 'Report of the Subcommittee on Subsidiary Legislation to Implement the Obligations under the United Nations Convention Against Corruption', paper for the House Committee meeting on 16 November 2007, LC Paper No. CB(2)336/07-08; see also Organized and Serious Crimes Ordinance (Amendment of Schedule 2) Order 2007, L.N. 229 of 2007; see also Mutual Legal Assistance in Criminal Matters (Corruption) Order, L.N. 231 of 2007.

Human Rights Considerations

Hong Kong has a very robust framework for the constitutional protection of fundamental human rights and freedoms.[150] Unlike other constitutions, Hong Kong's Basic Law also protects 'the right of individuals and legal persons to the acquisition, use, disposal and inheritance of property and their right to compensation for lawful deprivation of their property'.[151]

Since the enactment of the Hong Kong Bill of Rights Ordinance (Cap. 383) in 1991, Hong Kong confiscation and money laundering laws have stood up well against challenges based on human rights.[152] This is consistent with the international trend that sees most human rights challenges against criminal and civil forfeiture laws failing.[153]

A civil forfeiture system in Hong Kong could attract four kinds of challenges. First of all, there would be the familiar challenge that a civil forfeiture proceeding involved the determination of a criminal charge, and thus all of the usual protections for criminal defendants in Article 11 of the Hong Kong Bill of Rights would apply.[154] The second kind of challenge would be from innocent property owners who claim an interest in the targeted property. If the law imposes too much of a burden on the claimant to prove either their legitimate interest or the innocent character of the property, it might be argued that their right to property or right to a fair hearing have been infringed.

Thirdly, claimants, whether innocent or not, whose property has been restrained might argue that they no longer have the means to retain counsel to defend against the civil forfeiture action. Thus they would argue that their right to the effective assistance of counsel of choice has been infringed. Lastly, claimants who are also the subject of a criminal investigation may raise self-incrimination complaints if their participation, compelled or otherwise, in the

---

[150] See generally 'Chapter 19: Human Rights', in *Archbold Hong Kong 2009*, Hong Kong: Sweet & Maxwell Asia, pp. 1057–1141; see also Albert H.Y. Chen (2006), 'Constitutional Adjudication in Post-1997 Hong Kong', *Pacific Rim Law & Policy Journal*, **15**, 627.

[151] See Basic Law, art. 105.

[152] See *R v. Ko Chi-yuen* (HC); see also *Attorney General v. Lee Kwong-kut* [1993] AC 951 (PC).

[153] See for example the relevant discussion of challenges in Chapters 3 to 7 of this book.

[154] The leading authority on this issue is *Koon Wing Yee v. Insider Dealing Tribunal* [2008] 3 HKLRD 372 (CFA). While the court did not determine the question of whether forfeiture or confiscation was a criminal proceeding under the Bill of Rights, it did note the case of *Air Canada v. United Kingdom* (1995) 20 EHRR 150 (ECHR) which held that the forfeiture of a plane carrying drugs was civil and not criminal in character.

civil proceeding realizes incriminating evidence that could be used against them in the criminal proceeding.

None of these challenges are new, having been tried in one form or another in other jurisdictions. None of them are necessarily prohibitive to reform. Ultimately it will be an issue of whether there exist sufficient safeguards in the proposals to ensure fairness and/or a reasonable restriction on rights. For example appropriate allocation of legal and evidential burdens of proof, allowing access to restrained property or some modified form of legal aid, and legal prohibitions on the use of compelled information are examples of safeguards that could help to address the concerns underlying these challenges. Laws aside, there will also need to be safeguards adopted in law enforcement practices to ensure that rights are not infringed in the administration and application of the law.

Issues in Regional Cooperation

Even with a strengthened asset confiscation system in Hong Kong, there remains the concern that criminals will transfer and hide their ill-gotten gains in overseas jurisdictions. This raises the issue of international and regional cooperation. By entering into bilateral agreements and becoming a party to relevant multilateral treaties, Hong Kong has mutual legal assistance obligations in respect of proceeds of crime with a large number of countries. Such agreements and treaties form the basis for clear and transparent procedures and cooperative efforts typically involving both the judicial and executive branches of government.

By contrast, with one exception, Hong Kong has no formal arrangements for extradition or mutual legal assistance in criminal matters with Mainland China, Macau or Taiwan.[155] This is an issue of some concern given the large numbers of persons travelling to and from these four jurisdictions daily. To complicate matters, the legal systems of the four jurisdictions are fundamentally different, and the principle of 'one country two systems' ensures that the differences continue.

Nevertheless, limited *ad hoc* cooperation, typically in the exchange of information and intelligence, has occurred. But *ad hoc* co-operation is susceptible to criticisms for being non-transparent and extra-legal in nature. It is also

---

[155]   Formal arrangements in other areas between Hong Kong and Macau and between Hong Kong and Mainland China can be found on the website of the Department of Justice at www.legislation.gov.hk/intracountry/eng/index.htm. Under Part VIII of the Evidence Ordinance (Cap. 8), it is possible to issue and execute letters of request to gather oral and documentary evidence on a court-to-court basis to Macau and the Mainland.

limited in scope. Given that the MLA Ordinance specifically excludes the 'provision or obtaining of assistance in criminal matters between Hong Kong and any other part of the People's Republic of China', no *ad hoc* co-operation will allow Hong Kong courts to recognize and enforce a restraint or confiscation order in respect of non-drug trafficking proceeds from these three jurisdictions.[156] As formal arrangements have already been achieved between Hong Kong, Macau and Mainland China in other areas of mutual legal assistance, it is not unimaginable for an agreement on the mutual recognition of restraint and confiscation orders to come into being in the near future.[157] An amendment to the MLA Ordinance could bring it in line with the DTROP Order to allow for the recognition of mainland Chinese restraint and confiscation orders in all types of serious crimes. But this would be co-operation in one direction without assurances that Hong Kong orders would receive the same treatment in the mainland.

OVERCOMING OBSTACLES AND THE WAY FORWARD

None of the obstacles to reform discussed in this chapter are insurmountable. In the absence of a clear recommendation from the FATF to adopt a civil forfeiture system, a case for reform has been independently made out in this chapter. For many years, enforcement performance has lagged far behind the need for enforcement in Hong Kong, particularly in respect of money laundering, triad and other organized crime groups and profit-motivated offending generally. Experience from other countries has shown that civil forfeiture laws can have an immediate, significant and positive impact on law enforcement performance indicators.[158]

The introduction of civil forfeiture laws must be accompanied with a heightened policy priority to asset confiscation together with the necessary resources to see that the objectives of such a policy can be fulfilled. In addition to law reform, there will need to be administrative reform that sees greater

---

[156] See MLA Ordinance, s. 3(1).

[157] For example, on 14 July 2006, Hong Kong and the Mainland signed an arrangement on reciprocal recognition and enforcement of judgments in civil and commercial matters by the courts of the Mainland and of Hong Kong pursuant to choice of court agreements between parties concerned. In May 2005, an arrangement between Hong Kong and Macau was signed concerning the transfer of sentenced persons. For the text of these arrangements, see the website of the Department of Justice at www.legislation.gov.hk/intracountry/eng/index.htm.

[158] See particularly the impact in the United States, Ireland, South Africa and Australia, as discussed in Chapters 2 to 5 of this book.

co-operation of law enforcement agencies and better integration with expert financial and legal advisers in investigating cases. Wide public consultation and sensitivity to human rights issues and safeguards will help to address the concerns and scepticism of legislators. For now Hong Kong has yet to realize the full potential and impact of asset confiscation laws and policies on organized criminal activity within its borders and beyond.

11. Civil confiscation of proceeds of crime: a view from Macau

Jorge A.F. Godinho

INTRODUCTION

Having noticed the title of this text, a reader familiar with the legal system of Macau in general,[1] and its criminal law in particular,[2] may wonder what its useful purpose is, and immediately remark that to consider civil confiscation or civil forfeiture of proceeds of crime in connection with the legal system of Macau is to write about something that simply does not exist. And such remark would of course be accurate.

This therefore could be an extremely short and laconic chapter, which would simply inform the reader that there is no such thing in the laws of the Macau SAR and that, furthermore, the issue is so unfamiliar to lawyers trained in the civil law tradition that most probably have never heard of it. It is highly likely that anyone questioning the legal professions and the legal academics of Macau as to what is their opinion regarding the issue of civil confiscation

---

[1]   For an overview, see J. Godinho (2007), *Macau business law and legal system*, Hong Kong: Lexis Nexis, chapter I; see also the writings of various authors in (2007), *Repertório do direito de Macau*, Macau: University of Macau.

[2]   The main source is the 1995 Penal Code (hereinafter Code), approved by Decree-Law no. 58/95/M, of 14 November, which entered into force 1 January 1996. The Code is clearly influenced by the German Penal Code (the Strafgesetzbuch of 1871, as amended, especially in 1975). However, the criminal law of Macau suffers from a certain degree of 'decodification', a lack of unity arising from the fact that various important matters remain outside of the Code. The matter of voluntary interruption of pregnancy (abortion) was kept out of the Code, and approved by Decree-Law 59/95/M, of 27 November. A number of other criminal law issues remain regulated outside of the Code as well, including the following: pornography-related offences (Law 10/78/M), drug offences (Decree-Law 5/91/M), offences in connection with organ transplants (Law 2/96/M), crimes against the economy and public health (Law 6/96/M), road traffic offences (Law 7/96/M), gaming crimes (Law 8/96/M), crimes related to horse and greyhound racing (Law 9/96/M), organized crime (Law 6/97/M), illegal immigration (Law 6/2004), money laundering (Law 2/2006) and terrorism (Law 3/2006).

would be greeted with a preliminary call for clarification regarding what exactly is the question all about. Still, this 'void', this non-existence, is itself a legitimate basis for enquiry. If indeed there is no civil confiscation in Macau, a number of questions may be posed.

The first is a straightforward enquiry as to why there is no civil confiscation in the laws of Macau. It may be already anticipated that, in view of the fact that part of the answer may have to do with a lack of compulsory provisions in the main international criminal law treaties in force in Macau, it would also be useful to try to appreciate why is it that civil confiscation has never been required by international law instruments. On this basis, and if there is no civil confiscation in Macau law, then it becomes necessary to ask what legal provisions on confiscation of proceeds of crime actually exist under current law. Finally, one needs to ask if there could be civil confiscation in Macau and, if it was to be introduced, what questions and tests would likely have to be faced.

WHY IS THERE NO CIVIL CONFISCATION IN MACAU?

It is relatively clear that civil confiscation has been expanding: a number of jurisdictions have in the last few years introduced laws in this regard and, in addition, others such as New Zealand are moving in the same direction. The Hong Kong Civil Forfeiture Project's Discussion Paper noted that 'since the mid-1990's, many countries have introduced civil forfeiture laws as a new means to eliminate and prevent organized and serious crime'.[3] The jurisdictions mentioned are (in chronologic order): United States (1970); Ireland (1996); South Africa (1998); United Kingdom (2002); Australia (2002); Ontario (2002), Manitoba (2004) and British Columbia (2006).[4]

In any case, it seems reasonable to assert that civil confiscation, despite having been adopted recently in a number of common law jurisdictions, still is a relatively rarified entity, which is not recognized in the vast majority of legal systems.

In particular, civil confiscation is currently not *required* by international law or by the law of the European Union (hereinafter EU), although the latter

---

[3]   See Simon N.M. Young and Jennifer Stone (August 2006), *Civil Forfeiture for Hong Kong? A Discussion Paper of the Hong Kong Civil Forfeiture Project*, Hong Kong: Centre for Comparative and Public Law, University of Hong Kong (hereinafter *Civil Forfeiture for HK*): online version available at http://papers.ssrn.com/sol3/papers.cfm?abstract_id=924724, accessed 21 December 2007, p. 1.

[4]   *Ibid.*

has recognized in passing its existence.[5] This lack of compulsory provisions differs strikingly from other patrimonial strategies of crime control, including the criminalization of the financing of terrorism, the criminalization of money laundering, criminal confiscation, Financial Action Task Force (hereinafter FATF) inspired detection mechanisms, and United Nations (hereinafter UN) and EU asset freezing – all of which have been pursued vigorously in the international arena by means of treaties and decisions of international organizations.

It appears that the issue of civil confiscation is related to the common law versus civil law divide, considering their different historical evolution. Although the practice of what can today be described as civil confiscation has a long history,[6] it occurs that civil confiscation remains today well known in

---

5   See Council of the European Union Framework Decision 2005/212/JHA of 24 February 2005, on Confiscation of Crime-Related Proceeds, Instrumentalities and Property, Official Journal L68 of 15 March 2005, at art. 3(4), which stated that '[M]ember States may use procedures other than criminal procedures to deprive the perpetrator of the property in question'. As the language makes it extremely clear, this is a permissive and not a mandatory provision.

6   Practices similar to what is today described as 'civil confiscation' have been reported since ancient Greece, where proceedings were conducted against animals and inanimate objects: see Paul Schiff Berman (1999), 'An anthropological approach to modern forfeiture law: the symbolic function of legal actions against objects', *Yale Journal of Law and the Humanities*, 1 (an interesting enquiry into the historical background of common law jurisdictions; the author explains pre-modern practices as providing meaning, a narrative that would reconstruct reality and provide a sense of community.) *In rem* procedures were frequent in the European Middle Ages; the *deodand* (from Latin *Deo dandum*: 'that which is to be given to God') can be mentioned. *Deodand* was an *in rem* procedure whereby inanimate objects or animals involved in the accidental death of a person were to be destroyed or forfeited to the Crown. There were very specific rules on which object (or part of it) was a *deodand*, which could depend on whether the object was moving or not; the most valuable cases were horses and carriages. The *deodand* had a religious origin and represented a symbolic 'purification' or expiation of an object which had breached the established order, and a manner for the community to channel the need for healing. Later, Blackstone characterized it as a superstitious practice of feudal origin. With the advent of modernity this type of procedure came to be seen mostly as irrational, given that objects are not capable of independent decision making and guilt. The later evolution saw *deodand* becoming a sort of punishment for crimes committed with negligence – see an historical account in *Calero-Toledo v. Pearson Yacht Leasing Co.*, 416 U.S. 663, at p. 681 n. 16 (1974) and in Chapter 2 of this book (many US cases make extensive references to the historical background) – and the appearance of norms on confiscation of dangerous objects. In UK, *deodand* was abolished in 1846, when its application to railway engines 'brought its irrational nature to public attention': see J. Baker (1979), *An introduction to English legal history*, London: Butterworths, at p. 322, and legislation on negligence was approved in its place; see also Steven Kessler (1998), 'Asset

the common law tradition. Instead, it is not part of the living memory of the civil law tradition, and only civil lawyers familiar with the common law tradition might be aware of it. This renders it, to the eyes of the average civil lawyer, as a hard to understand legal construct, much like the law of trusts. As in so many other legal matters, the decisive explanation arises probably from an historical evolution.

This in turn helps explain why civil confiscation has so far not been pursued at the international level. Being a tradition peculiar to common law legal systems, it does not have the critical mass that would allow its inclusion in international negotiations and treaties. The apparent lack of interest of civil law jurisdictions on this matter does provide a strong inertia that may prevent any sort of internationalization of civil confiscation in the foreseeable future.

CONFISCATION UNDER CURRENT MACAU LAW

If there is no civil confiscation in Macau law, then what means to fight criminality through the financial flank actually exist? There are essentially two sets of provisions. Confiscation is regulated in the legal system of Macau in the 1995 Penal Code (arts 101 and 103), which provides for 'traditional' confiscation, which depends upon concrete evidence of the unlawful source of the property liable to confiscation.[7] In addition, a special case of confiscation with reversal of the burden of proof is provided for in anti-corruption legislation.

1995 Penal Code

The seat of the general regulation on confiscation is the Code, which regulates separately the confiscation of *proceeds* of crime (art. 103) and of *instrumentalities* (art. 101).

Article 103
(Confiscation of things, rights or proceeds)
1. Any reward given or promised to the perpetrators of a tipified unlawful act, to be given to themselves or to a third party, shall be confiscated in favor of the Territory.

forfeiture: home and abroad', *ILSA Journal of International & Comparative Law*, **4**, 385, at 386; see also Scott Hauert (1994), 'An examination of the nature, scope, and extent of statutory civil forfeiture', *Dayton Law Review*, 162. Overall, it does appear that civil confiscation is not derived from the mediaeval *deodand*, and is a later development.

[7]   In addition, the legislation regarding drug trafficking does have legal provisions regarding confiscation of proceeds of crime, which do not deviate from the 'classic' model adopted by the Macau Penal Code, which requires evidence of the unlawful origin.

2. Without prejudice to the rights of the victim or of good faith third parties, the things, rights or proceeds that, by means of the tipified unlawful act, have been directly acquired by the perpetrators, by themselves or by a third party, shall also be confiscated in favor of the Territory.

3. The provisions of the previous paragraphs shall apply to the things or rights obtained by means of transactions or exchanges with the things or rights directly obtained by means of the tipified unlawful fact.

4. If the reward, the things, the rights or the proceeds mentioned in the previous paragraphs cannot be appropriated in kind, the confiscation shall be substituted by the payment of the respective value to the Territory.

As to the confiscation of instrumentalities, article 101 applies.

Article 101
(Confiscation of objects)
1. The objects that served or were intended to serve for the commission of a tipi-fied unlawful act, or that have been produced by it, shall also be confiscated in favor of the Territory, when, by their nature or by the circumstances of the case, they create a danger for the safety of persons or to public morals or order, or pose a seri-ous risk of being used for the commitment of further tipified unlawful acts.

2. The provisions of the previous paragraph shall apply even if no person can be prosecuted for the fact.

3. If the law does not provide for a specific destination for the objects that have been confiscated in accordance with the previous paragraphs, the judge may order their total or partial destruction, or order that they be placed out of circulation.

The basic criminal policy underlying these provisions is that crime prevention is a valid reason to take action against objects, involving restrictions to the right of private ownership – a fundamental right guaranteed by the Macau Basic Law. This covers two strands: the first relates to removing the profit incentive and to the obstruction of the financing of crime (art. 103); and the second relates to instrumentalities and dangerous objects (art. 101).

First, the justification for confiscation is related to patrimonial strategies of crime control: assets which are proceeds of crime, or which are intended to finance crime, ought to be confiscated irrespective of their potential danger. Article 103 of the Code applies to all cases not covered by special laws,[8] and requires the commission of an unlawful act under criminal law. Its exact legal nature is debated. Professor F. Dias states that it is analogous to a security measure, given that it does not require fault.[9] The applicable standard of

---

[8]   Art. 22(2) of Decree-Law 5/91/M, on drug cases, provides for the confisca-tion of all objects, rights, proceeds, or any assets which have been gained through the crime, or that came into the possession of the perpetrators, namely movables, airplanes, boats, vehicles, bank deposits or securities, without prejudice to the rights of good faith third parties.
[9]   See J. Figueiredo Dias (1993), *Direito penal português. Parte Geral. II. As*

evidence is the criminal one (beyond a reasonable doubt). Confiscation includes the replacement value of goods; if it is not possible to confiscate such, then value confiscation shall apply. The amount payable may be reduced if found to be excessive (art. 104(2) of the Code).

Secondly, a justification for confiscation may lie in the potential danger of the thing being forfeited. This strand, visible in article 101 of the Code, relates to what could perhaps be described as risk management: the objective is to provide a legal basis for removing *dangerous* objects and crime instruments from public circulation, irrespective of evidence of any specific crime.

Anti-corruption Legislation

In addition to the general rules just mentioned, Macau law also provides for a specific form of 'expanded' confiscation, in the context of anti-corruption laws, under article 28 of Law no. 11/2003, of 28 July 2003, which provides:

'Unjustified wealth'
1. Any persons under an obligation to make a declaration of assets in accordance with article 1 who, by themselves or by means of third parties, are found to be in the possession of patrimony or income which are abnormally higher than that which has been indicated in prior declarations, and who do not justify, in concrete terms, how and when such came to their possession or do not demonstrate their lawful origin, shall be punished with a penalty of imprisonment of up to three years and a fine of up to 360 days.
2. The patrimony or income the possession or origin of which has not been justified in accordance with the previous paragraph may be apprehended and confiscated for the Macau SAR, in a judicial decision of conviction.

In summary, civil servants who are found to have assets abnormally higher than those declared in their prior declarations of assets (which are compulsory for all civil servants), and who do not explain in detail when and how such assets were gained, or their lawful origin, shall be liable to *two different types* of consequences: the *first* is a penalty of imprisonment of up to three years' imprisonment and a fine, and the *second* is the confiscation of the assets the lawful origin of which has not been established, in court, by the civil servant.

It should be emphasized that the situation described by the law as a crime is neither a crime nor an omission. It is a mere status or observation that assets of unclear origin do exist. This, by itself, does not amount to an attack to any

---

consequências jurídicas do crime, Lisbon, Portugal: Aequitas e Editorial Notícias. Therefore, if a person who commits a fact which is described by the law as a crime, and obtains a profit from it, the respective proceeds should be disgorged even if the person cannot be held criminally responsible (for example, a minor).

legally protected interest, and represents purely a suspicion. For this reason, crimes of this nature have been described in Italy as crimes 'of mere suspicion' (*reato di mero sospetto*), or 'of position' (*di posizione*) or 'without action' (*senza condotta*).[10] It is clear that the crime is merely a scheme to overcome the difficulty in providing evidence of actual unlawful conduct in general and corruption in particular. The underlying presumption is that further crimes of corruption have been committed by the civil servant, from which proceeds have been obtained, and it is for the civil servant to rebut such presumption. Should the civil servant not take action in order to disprove the presumed unlawful origin of the assets, the court shall have no other option but to convict that person of this particular crime of having 'unjustified wealth'. This provision, in my view, is unconstitutional, given that it amounts to a breach of the presumption of innocence.

The presumption of innocence is firmly established in many legal systems, and certainly is a common constitutional tradition of the EU Member States. It is mentioned, with extremely similar language, in all major international human rights instruments: the UN International Covenant on Civil and Political Rights (hereinafter ICCPR),[11] the European Convention on Human Rights (hereinafter ECHR),[12] the American Declaration of the Rights and Duties of Man,[13] the African Charter on Human and Peoples' Rights,[14] the EU Charter of Fundamental Rights (hereinafter EUCFR),[15] the International Criminal Tribunal for Former Yugoslavia Statute[16] and the International

---

[10]   See Rosaria Calisti (2003), *Il sospetto di reato*, Milan, Italy: Giuffrè Editore, 25. For more details, see J. Godinho (2003), 'Brandos costumes? O confisco penal com base na inversão do ónus da prova (Lei n.° 5/2002, de 11 de Janeiro, artigos 1.° e 7.° a 12.°)' ['Benign customs? Criminal confiscation on the basis of a reversal of the burden of proof'], in *Liber Discipulorum para Jorge de Figueiredo Dias*, Coimbra, Portugal: Coimbra Editora, 1315.

[11]   See art. 14(2): '[e]veryone charged with a criminal offence shall have the right to be presumed innocent until proved guilty according to law'.

[12]   See art. 6(2): '[e]veryone charged with a criminal offence shall be presumed innocent until proved guilty according to law'.

[13]   See art. XXVI: '[e]very accused person is presumed to be innocent until proved guilty'.

[14]   See art. 7(1)(b): '[e]very individual shall have the right to have his cause heard. This comprises: ... (b) the right to be presumed innocent until proved guilty by a competent court or tribunal; ... .'

[15]   See art. 48(1): '[e]veryone who has been charged shall be presumed innocent until proved guilty according to law'; see also the Treaty establishing a Constitution, Official Journal of the European Union, C 310, Vol. 47, 16 December 2004 (hereinafter Constitutional Treaty), art. II-108(1).

[16]   See art. 21(3): '[t]he accused shall be presumed innocent until proved guilty according to the provisions of the present Statute'.

Criminal Tribunal for Rwanda Statute.[17] It is most clearly encapsulated in the Statute of the International Criminal Court.[18]

A reversal of the burden of proof for the purpose of confiscation – which exists namely in the legal system of the UK[19] – assumes explicitly, as a starting point, that the assets subject to confiscation have an unlawful origin, and does impose on the accused the onus to show evidence to the contrary.[20] This is based on a suspicion, which generates an unstated presumption of guilt. The facts on the basis of the presumption generate the suspicion that other crimes such as corruption may have been practised, but the issue is discussed in an

---

[17]	See art. 20(3): '[t]he accused shall be presumed innocent until proven guilty according to the provisions of the present Statute'.

[18]	See United Nations (17 July 1998), *Rome Statute of the International Criminal Court*, at art. 66, on the presumption of innocence:

1.	Everyone shall be presumed innocent until proved guilty before the Court in accordance with the applicable law.
2.	The onus is on the Prosecutor to prove the guilt of the accused.
3.	In order to convict the accused, the Court must be convinced of the guilt of the accused beyond reasonable doubt.

[19]	See Drug Trafficking Offences Act 1986, which introduced the so-called 'lifestyle provisions', currently regulated by the Proceeds of Crime Act 2002, s. 10, which states that four assumptions shall be made in case of criminal lifestyle, namely that any property transferred or held by the defendant at any time after a set date was obtained by him as a result of his general criminal conduct, and at the earliest time he appears to have held it. The assumptions are not to be made if shown to be incorrect, or if there is a serious risk of injustice.

[20]	That the problem is framed in this manner is, in itself, already a considerable change to standard criminal procedure concepts in those continental legal systems, such as Portugal and Macau, where it is said that in criminal proceedings, as a rule, there is no formal issue of burden of proof, but rather a need for evidence: see for example, J. Figueiredo Dias (1974), *Direito processual penal*, Coimbra, Portugal: Coimbra Editora, at 192 f. and 211 f.; see also G. Marques da Silva (1993), *Curso de processo penal*, vol. II, Lisbon, Portugal: Verbo Editorial, 1993, at 92 f. In criminal proceedings, if the defendant does not rebut the theses advanced by the accusation this does not imply that the judge should consider them without further ado as proven. The judge has an independent duty to investigate the facts. In this sense, there is no formal burden of proof. An objection to this has been raised: 'Figueiredo Dias states that continental criminal procedure law does not know the problem of *onus probationis*, because it is for the judge to establish the facts' and the 'distinction made by the Portuguese scholar is too theoretical'; see S. Trechsel (2005), *Human Rights in Criminal Proceedings*, Collected Courses of the Academy of European Law, Volume XI, European University Institute, Oxford, UK: Oxford University Press (hereinafter *HR in Criminal Proceedings*), at p. 167. However, this is unfounded and rests probably on a misapprehension: there is nothing theoretical about deriving or not deriving legal consequences from a lack of rebuttal by a defendant.

indirect manner, through the patrimonial flank – by showing the lawful origin of his assets, the accused is simultaneously rebutting the implied accusation made.

The presumption then becomes a sufficient condition for the application of a criminal sanction (confiscation). The reversal of the burden of proof for the purpose of 'expanded' confiscation of assets acquired in the past rests upon the assumption that criminal activity has been ongoing for a certain period of time and that the assets being confiscated were gained through the commission of such criminal offences. Confiscation may take place in the absence of any concrete judicial determination of the real origin of the assets. This therefore directly breaches the presumption of innocence in its most basic content, for the debate in court becomes the possible lawful origin of the assets, and not the unlawful origin of the assets. The latter is assumed as a matter of principle.

As a result of the presumption, the accused is confronted with a need to question an implied accusation of the practice of crimes; his inactivity works against him, and his right to silence is suppressed. Therefore, there is a direct and clear breach of the presumption of innocence of the accused, which, as seen, implies that it is not for the accused to carry evidence to the case – that onus resting with the accusation – and that his silence cannot operate against him. In addition, the principle *in dubio pro reo*, as a criterion for resolving *non liquet* cases, is also breached. As a result of a presumption of unlawful origin by which the judge must obey, doubts are resolved *pro Republica* and not *pro reo*.[21]

In this manner, it is clear that confiscation on the basis of a reversal of the burden of proof incurs a series of breaches of the principle of presumption of innocence: it assumes guilt and centres the debate on whether there is innocence, assigns the burden of proof to the accused, suppresses the right to silence and resolves *non liquet* cases against the accused.

---

[21]   The UK provisions have a 'safeguard clause' in that the assumptions may not be made if there 'would be a serious risk of injustice if the assumption were made': see Proceeds of Crime Act 2002, s. 10(6)(b). This provision is not a rule of evidence but a more general clause based on an overall assessment of the proceedings. This provision explicitly recognizes the potential for injustice and the draconian nature of the measure.

COULD THERE BE CIVIL CONFISCATION IN MACAU? THE CONSTITUTIONAL ISSUE: IS CIVIL CONFISCATION COMPATIBLE WITH FUNDAMENTAL RIGHTS?

The Primacy of the Fundamental Rights Debate

Consistency with fundamental rights enshrined in the Basic Law in Macau and in the ICCPR is likely to be the major issue faced by any proposals to introduce civil confiscation. It is clear that civil confiscation is a rather polemic issue; it is highly likely that any policy proposal in this regard should face questions of fundamental rights. There is a need to understand the restrictions brought by international law and constitutional law.

The need to respect fundamental rights is also a standard requirement for sound policy making, and a structural issue of the legal system, which is best appreciated from the point of view of legal theory. Luigi Ferrajoli has called attention to the fact that the validity of a norm depends not only upon the fact that it has been enacted in accordance with established procedures, but also upon its substantive conformity with constitutional positive standards; the question of constitutional conformity is still part of the assessment of validity, and is not merely a formal assessment.[22]

Framing the Debate

This question translates into an analysis of a range of fundamental rights that may be affected. For the purpose of this discussion, civil confiscation has two major features: it is a confiscation measure, that is, it is an interference with the right of private ownership, and it is conducted through a civil rather than criminal process.

The right of private ownership is a substantive rather than procedural issue. The legal protection of private property is considered as a fundamental right in market economies. Where private property is protected, arbitrary or unjustified deprivation of property is not tolerated, and any interference (either permanent or temporary) with the peaceful enjoyment of possessions is only allowed in justified circumstances. Confiscation, being by definition a permanent deprivation of property without compensation, clearly affects the property right; indeed, it severs it entirely.[23]

---

[22]   See L. Ferrajoli (1995), *Derecho y razón. Teoría del garantismo penal*, Madrid, Spain: Trotta publishing house: this being a Spanish translation of the original Italian edition published in 1989.

[23]   Being therefore a sort of 'death penalty' over the assets, although not really,

However, the protection of private property does not extend to the proceeds of crime: there is no right to keep such proceeds; on the contrary, they should be confiscated, so as to affirm the centuries old crime prevention principle (and moral rule) according to which 'crime should not pay'.

In Europe, this is expressly mentioned in article 17 of the EUCFR,[24] which states that '[e]veryone has the right to own, use, dispose of and bequeath his or her *lawfully acquired* possessions' [emphasis added], thereby making it clear that the right does not extend to unlawfully acquired property. The general legitimacy of confiscation of proceeds of crime, where the lawful origin has been clearly established, is therefore beyond discussion. Confiscation of proceeds of crime is a generally acceptable measure that may be resorted to in order to prevent and repress crime.

Civil confiscation does not modify these fundamental criminal policy goals: rather, it attempts to achieve them in a more expedited manner, by doing away with the need to demonstrate beyond a reasonable doubt that a crime has been committed, and by doing away with any link with a criminal process. Civil confiscation has the fundamental difference over criminal confiscation that, being a civil case litigated under civil procedure rules and standards of evidence, it does not need to observe established criminal law guarantees such as the presumption of innocence and the need to prove material facts beyond a reasonable doubt. It therefore emerges, in my view, that the procedural issue of the *presumption of innocence* is the fundamental point is this regard.

The Presumption of Innocence

Civil confiscation proceedings can be alleged to breach the presumption of innocence for the simple reason that the judicial debate is not conducted under a basic assumption or starting point according to which the assets are of lawful origin. Instead, it follows the neutral rules of civil law, which treat both parties equally. Once the plaintiff (for example, an asset confiscation agency) makes a civil claim for confiscation by showing probable cause, the onus is on the owner of the assets (normally the accused) to show evidence of their lawful origin, and his lack of action may result in confiscation. Therefore, civil confiscation may be seen as a circumvention of criminal law guarantees: by conducting confiscation proceedings under civil rather than criminal procedure rules, a rejection of the presumption of innocence seems to occur. It is no longer necessary to prove beyond a reasonable doubt that a crime has been committed and that a person has obtained benefits from such crime.

---

as it must be kept in mind that the assets do not in fact 'die' or disappear but rather pass to the hands of someone else.

[24]   See also art. II-77 of the Constitutional Treaty (not yet in force).

In the field of civil confiscation the punitive power of the state is at issue, rather than mere disputes among private entities. To equate private disputes between citizens (who by the very nature of private law must be regarded as being equal by civil procedure law) with the exercise of state powers to appropriate assets for crime prevention, is to cause a conflation of two matters which are and should remain separate. In criminal law matters the presumption of innocence and the need for proof beyond a reasonable doubt should be in place as a basic guarantee designed to ensure that confiscation is not applied to assets which were lawfully acquired.

The Presumption of Innocence and the ECHR

The trend, however, seems to be to consider that civil confiscation does not interfere with the presumption of innocence, for the reason that it does not involve a criminal charge. The test of what is a criminal charge may become the deciding factor.

It appears that the matter has never been directly addressed in connection with civil confiscation proceedings. In other cases, the European Court of Human Rights (hereinafter European Court HR) has put forth three criteria: the classification of the proceedings under national law, their essential nature and the type and severity of the penalty that the person may incur.[25]

As to the classification of the civil confiscation proceedings under national law, it is obviously civil and not criminal; however, the European Court HR has consistently held that the national classification should not be taken at face value and should be investigated further. However, in *Phillips v. UK*,[26] the European Court HR has held that for the presumption of innocence to be triggered, there must be an explicit 'criminal charge'. In this case, the application of the UK 'lifestyle provisions',[27] which reversed the burden of proof on the basis of certain 'assumptions', was at issue. The European Court HR considered that confiscation proceedings do not amount to a (new) criminal charge for the purpose of article 6(2) of ECHR, as the person is not being accused of new crimes; namely, there is no effect on the criminal record.[28] The assess-

---

[25]   See the following European Court of Human Rights (hereinafter European Court HR) cases: *Engel and others* (1976), judgment of 8 June 1976/23 November 1976, A Series, Vol. 22 (hereinafter *Engel*); *A.P., M.P. and T.P. v. Switzerland*, 29 August 1997, at para. 39; *Welch v. the United Kingdom*, 9 February 1995, Series A, no. 307-A, at paras 27-28; *Phillips v. UK*, Application No. 41087/98, 5 July 2001 (hereinafter *Phillips*), at para. 31. See also *HR in Criminal Proceedings, supra* at para. 16.

[26]   See *Phillips*.

[27]   See Drug Trafficking Act 1994, s. 4(3).

[28]   See *Phillips*, at paras 28–35; reiterated in *Crowther v. UK*, Application No. 53741/00, 1 February 2005, at para. 25.

ment of the confiscation order is described as a procedure 'analogous to the determination by a court of the amount of a fine or the length of a period of imprisonment to impose upon a properly convicted offender'.[29] Therefore, it does not fall within the scope of the presumption of innocence, because 'the right to be presumed innocent under Article 6(2) arises only in connection with the particular offence "charged"'.[30]

This then calls up the second criteria, the 'essential nature' of civil confiscation procedures. In my view, the claim that civil confiscation is not criminal in nature is wrong and rather formalistic, which fails to see what is substantially at issue in civil confiscation. It is very clear that civil confiscation is an action related to possible crimes, the commission of which is suspected but remains unclear for the precise reason that there is no evidence; if there was, normal criminal proceedings would have been instituted. It is, in this sense, an explicit accusation of the unlawful origin of the assets and an implicit accusation of the practice of crimes. Civil confiscation proceedings are based on a suspicion of the practice of crimes; without taking this suspicion into account, such proceedings would hardly make any sort of sense.

In essence, what is called 'civil confiscation' has mainly a procedural connotation, although it is by no means the decision of a private dispute. As stated by an author discussing the Irish model[31]:

> ... an agency operating under the Irish model would only be 'civil' in the senses that the standard of proof that would apply is the civil one, civil courts are used and that there would be no requirement of a criminal conviction before an order could be made. In every other respect this would be exercise of the power of the State against designated individuals in a way that has nothing in common with the resolution of disputes by means of civil law.

The accusation of the practice of crimes is, however, not formulated clearly and directly, but rather in an indirect and implied manner, through the

---

[29]   See *Phillips*, at para. 34.

[30]   *Ibid.* at para. 35. To reach this conclusion, the European Court HR used the three tests in *Engel* to decide what a criminal charge is. For a critique of this point, see S. Trechsel, *HR in Criminal Proceedings, supra* at 34. This was, in my opinion, the only conceivable 'escape route' from the extremely clear provision of art. 6(2) of the European Convention on Human Rights (hereinafter ECHR) on presumption of innocence. It seems rather difficult, to say the least, to argue that a reversal of the burden of proof does not amount to a presumption of guilt. The only possible way to set aside art. 6(2) of ECHR was to argue that the scope of the provision is not met and that is precisely what the court held.

[31]   See Peter Alldridge (2003), *Money Laundering Law. Forfeiture, Confiscation, Civil Recovery, Criminal Laundering and Taxation of the Proceeds of Crime*, Oxford, Portland, Oregon, US: Hart Publishing, at p. 232.

patrimonial flank. In proving the lawful origin of the assets, the accused is implicitly rebutting the indirect accusation of the commission of crimes. In rejecting as not convincing the justification presented, a court is implicitly accepting that crimes were committed, which have generated proceeds. It is therefore clear that civil confiscation involves an accusation and a criminal charge: an *implied* or *indirect* one. The European Court HR, by using a rather narrow[32] concept of what a 'criminal charge' is, has opened the door to legal techniques where no charge is openly formulated but where in no different terms an accusation is formulated.

Overall, the bill of conformity of civil confiscation with the ECHR may rest upon this distinction between an explicit or open criminal accusation, and other situations where there is no formal criminal charge. The decision in *Phillips* may turn out to be the decisive precedent regarding civil confiscation.

CONCLUSION

Civil confiscation is tied to legal tradition and legal history, which promotes its acceptability in legal systems where there is a degree of familiarity with its existence and operation. Civil confiscation is not reminiscent of irrational approaches that consist of suing objects rather than persons. In terms of comparative law, it exists only in common law jurisdictions, and for this reason it is not required by modern international law instruments.

So far, civil confiscation has not been considered to be incompatible with fundamental rights in general, and the presumption of innocence in particular. This is based on a narrow interpretation of the presumption of innocence, according to which it only comes into play where a criminal charge is openly formulated.

---

[32]   Defending that the presumption of innocence should apply to everyone, irrespective of involvement in criminal proceedings, see S. Trechsel, *HR in Criminal Proceedings*, *supra* at 154 f.

12. The current forfeiture regime in Taiwan

Lawrence L.C. Lee

INTRODUCTION

Asset forfeiture has been and remains a highly effective tool for taking the profit out of crime.[1] Crime related to obtaining monetary interests seems to be a necessary evil which cannot be eliminated. Once money becomes the aim for crime, the incentives for recidivism are strong. The most effective way to prevent such crimes is to cut off the temptations for such activities.

The goal of a forfeiture system is to sever the tie between crime and the motivation to commit crime. Another important goal is to transfer the criminal interests in property, such as a drug dealer's helicopter or fancy automobile, to benefit the governmental resources in fighting crime. The dual effects of a forfeiture regime will therefore cut off the criminal interest in property and preserve the beneficial outcome for the national authorities. This is one of the major reasons why most common law countries, such as the United States (US), have established a forfeiture regime.[2]

Taiwan's constitution ensures its citizens have the right of property.[3] The government cannot deprive citizens of property without monetary compensation or legal judicial process. Taiwan currently has a regime for judicial forfeiture (criminal forfeiture) and non-judicial forfeiture (detention by the

---

[1]   See Department of the Treasury (US) (April 2004), *Guide to Equitable Sharing for Foreign Countries and Federal, State, and Local Law Enforcement Agencies*, Washington DC, US: Executive Office for Asset Forfeiture: see online version at http://www.ustreas.gov/offices/enforcement/teoaf/guidelines/greenbook.pdf, accessed 16 January 2008.

[2]   For more on the US system of forfeiture, see Chapter 2 of this book.

[3]   See Constitution of the Republic of China, art. 15, which states that the 'right of existence, the right to work and the right of property shall be guaranteed to the people': English version available online at http://www.president.gov.tw/en/prog/news_release/document_content.php?id=1105498684&pre_id=1105498701&g_category_number=409&category_number_2=373&layer=on&sub_category=455, accessed 16 January 2008.

prosecutors in the investigative process and administrative confiscation), but it does not have a civil forfeiture regime.

In order to halt the motivation of criminal activities, Taiwan authorities have enacted the Criminal Law 1935 (hereinafter Criminal Law) and the Code of Criminal Procedure 1928 (hereinafter Code of Criminal Procedure) to forfeit proceeds derived from criminal activities or employed as tools during those criminal activities.

Administrative confiscation, which operates without legal judicial procedure, is no longer allowed in Taiwan's legal system, although it used to be allowed before 14 July 1987 when Taiwan abandoned martial law and increased its focus on human rights for the country. Nevertheless, for breach of duty under administrative law, an administrative agency can punish the offender with fines, confiscation and other types of administrative penalties, unless it is otherwise prescribed by other applicable laws.

Taiwan does not have a civil forfeiture law to forfeit property involved in non-criminal action or breach of administrative regulations. However, in order to prevent transfers of the criminal proceeds to third parties to avoid criminal forfeiture and to avoid problems arising from ambiguous legal regulations, Taiwan needs to enact civil forfeiture by adopting the US model.

This chapter discusses Taiwan's current forfeiture regime including judicial forfeiture and non-judicial forfeiture. It goes on to propose a reform blueprint for Taiwan to enact a civil forfeiture regime and related regulations.

FORFEITURE REGIME IN TAIWAN

Currently, Taiwan has judicial forfeiture (criminal forfeiture) and non-judicial forfeiture (including administrative forfeiture) but does not have a civil forfeiture regime.

In order to halt the motivation of criminal activities, Taiwan authorities enacted criminal laws and a code of criminal procedure for forfeiture of property derived from criminal activities or employed as tools during criminal activities.[4] In accordance with the spirit of Taiwan's Constitution, the legal sources of criminal forfeiture come from the Criminal Law, Code of Criminal Procedure and Judicial Yuan interpretations, which serve to protect the constitutional rights of the Taiwanese people.

Taiwan followed the international movement to combat money-laundering crimes by monitoring money flow and providing for forfeiture of money or

---

4   The Criminal Law and the Code of Criminal Procedure (hereinafter Code of Criminal Procedure) respectively.

any benefits derived from criminal activities. Taiwan enacted the Money Laundering Control Act (hereinafter MLCA) on 23 October 1996 and amended it in 2003 to forfeit criminally derived properties. After the '9-11' terrorists attack in the US, Taiwan began drafting anti-terrorism legislation in 2002.

Administrative confiscation was allowed before 14 July 1987, but as Taiwan abandoned martial law and became focused on the public's awareness of human rights, it was disallowed after that date. In other words, an administrative agency could no longer confiscate citizens' properties without a court order in Taiwan.

Taiwan does not have a civil forfeiture law to forfeit property involved in criminal activities without the defendant first committing a breach of administrative regulations or the authorities attaining a court order. However, in order to battle the increasing abuse and circulation of controlled substances and illegal material which are not connected to any criminal activities proven in court, Taiwan should consider enacting civil forfeiture laws to allow the authorities to forfeit such matters and proceeds derived from criminal activities during the investigative process.

Non-judicial Seizure, Detention and Forfeiture

According to the concept adopted by the United States, non-judicial forfeiture refers to administrative forfeiture, which is an *in rem* action that permits a federal seizure agency to detain and forfeit property without judicial involvement. Non-judicial forfeiture in Taiwan refers to the forfeiture of property which is not a part of sentencing, but rather during the criminal investigative process.

While investigating a criminal case, the prosecutor can seize a controlled substance or proceeds derived from criminal activities. Although Taiwan has storage facilities for seized items in a procuratorial organ, it is possible under article 140 of the Code of Criminal Procedure[5] for the prosecutor to command someone to guard seized goods which are not easily moved or protected, or to command the owner or another person who is suitable to safeguard them. In practice, however, due to negligence and lack of professionalism in the guarding process, the seized goods are often stolen, lost or even hidden secretly away from the authorities.

---

5   '... [A] person may be ordered to guard seized property which is inconvenient to transport or preserve, or the owner or other proper person may be ordered to preserve it. ...'

The investigation practice in Taiwan does not require establishment of a database of seized goods. There have been cases where seized property was ordered forfeited but the prosecutors were unable to locate them and thus resources were wasted in locating them. Even if they are found, they may be damaged from being in poor storage facilities.

Due to the lack of a database on the forfeited properties, it is also possible that where the same seized goods are closely connected to two cases, they may be destroyed upon the order given in the one case, and thus making them unavailable as evidence in the second case. Establishing a computer database of seized goods is essential for the proper running of the forfeiture system.

Taiwan does not have the same non-judicial forfeiture process as in the US. Taiwan police, in the investigation process, do not have the right to return the seized goods temporarily. According to the second paragraph of article 142 of the Code of Criminal Procedure,[6] the judge or the prosecutor can effect a temporary return of seized properties; however, questions have been raised about the possible arbitrariness of decisions to return property under this provision.

The Administrative Enforcement Agency of the Ministry of Justice in Taiwan can detain at the request of a particular authority but not forfeit properties in cases involving public law. While general administrative confiscation was abolished in 1987, limited administrative forfeiture exists in the context of customs regulation. In order to prevent the importation and smuggling of a controlled substance, animals or plants from abroad, the customs authority can confiscate those imported articles which violate customs regulations, whose process is enforced for public interest as an administrative control. Thus administrative forfeiture exists to enforce customs regulation, but not in regards to the enforcement of criminal regulations or civil torts law.

Judicial Forfeiture

Taiwan has a judicial forfeiture regime which includes only criminal forfeiture and not civil forfeiture. In Taiwan judicial practice, if a defendant makes a false statement related to evidence or commits perjury during the trial, the defendant is not liable to be prosecuted for the offences of destruction of evidence or perjury. This immunity not only affects the outcome of prosecutions, it also encourages the defendant to lie and makes it easier for him to hide ill-gotten gains. Therefore, to best deal with this issue, reference should be made to the approach taken in the US.[7]

---

6 '... [S]eized property may temporarily be returned to the owner, possessor or custodian if he asks for return of property and undertakes to preserve it.'

7   See *United States v. Carroll*, 346 F.3d 744 (7th cir. 2003).

In Taiwan judicial practice, the only way to forfeit the ill-gotten gains which have already been transferred to a third-party is by a decision of the court. In judicial practice, a procuratorial organ has no right to void a transfer of property to a third-party or to bring a charge to acquire the ill-gotten gains from an unfaithful third-party.

In Taiwanese law, forfeiture is a criminal punishment, but confiscation is an administrative disciplinary action, and they have different characteristics. According to Article 34 of the Criminal Law, forfeiture is an accessory punishment.[8] The regulations related to criminal forfeiture in the Criminal Law include Article 38, which regulates seized properties which are contraband, instruments used in the commission of or preparation for the commission of an offence, and proceeds acquired through the commission of an criminal offence.[9]

While contraband should be forfeited whether or not it belongs to the offender, the instrument used in and proceeds of criminal offences which belong to the offender should be forfeited unless there are other specified laws applicable.

Article 39 of the Criminal Law regulates independent forfeiture as part of sentencing, but forfeiture can be imposed independently. Taiwanese criminal procedure distinguishes between a person who is acquitted and a guilty person who has his punishment remitted. No forfeiture should be imposed where the person has been acquitted but independent forfeiture is permitted in respect of the person whose punishment has been remitted.

Article 40 of the Criminal Law regulates the timing of forfeiture. Unless there is another regulation applicable, forfeiture must be pronounced at the time of sentencing made by the court while contraband may be pronounced forfeited separately and later.

Article 84 of the Criminal Law regulates the statute of limitation as applicable to forfeiture. Article 84(I)(5) was amended, effective 1 July 2006, to the effect that the execution of punishment with detention, fine or forfeiture is barred if it is not executed within seven years, which before the amendment was three years.

Chapter 2 of Taiwan's Criminal Law as amended on 1 July 2006, provided that where the benefits received through the commission of an offence which should be forfeited but cannot be forfeited whether in whole or in part, the law allowed the authorities to collect the value of such benefit from the offender's other property.

---

8 See Criminal Law, art. 34 which states that accessory punishments are of the following kinds: deprivation of citizen's rights and forfeiture.
9 See Criminal Law, art. 38.

Some examples of specific provisions that provide for express confiscation are summarized below:

(1) Article 120 of the Criminal Law states that a public official or an arbitrator who demands, agrees to accept or accepts a bribe or other improper benefit for an official act shall be punished with imprisonment for not more than seven years, and in addition, a fine of not more than NT$5000 may be imposed, or proceeds should be forfeited.
(2) Article 122 of the Criminal Law states that benefits received by a public official or an arbitrator who demands, agrees to accept, or accepts a bribe or other improper benefit for a breach of his official duties or a person who offers, promises or gives a bribe or other improper benefit to a public official or an arbitrator for breach of his official duties, shall be confiscated.
(3) Article 131 of the Criminal Law states that benefits received from a public official directly or indirectly from a function under his control or supervision shall be confiscated; if the whole or a part of such benefit cannot be confiscated, the value thereof shall be collected from the offender.
(4) Article 143 of the Criminal Law states that a benefit received by a qualified voter who demands, agrees to accept or accepts a bribe or other improper benefit for refraining from exercising his right to vote or for exercising such right in a particular manner shall be confiscated; if the whole or a part of such benefit cannot be confiscated, the value thereof shall be collected from the offender.

The last two provisions are examples of a way to make the offender accountable for the benefits of proceeds of crime which cannot be located by the time of trial.

In Taiwan's criminal law, property that may be an instrument and evidence of a crime can be forfeited even if the offender is not the owner of such property. The following are some examples:

(1) Article 200 of the Criminal Law states that a counterfeit or altered currently used coin, paper currency, or banknote, currently used coin of reduced weight, or material specified in Article 199 of the Criminal Law shall be confiscated whether or not it belongs to the offender.[10]

---

[10] Criminal Law, art. 199 states that a person who manufactures, delivers or receives an instrument or material with intent that it be used to counterfeit or alter a currently used coin, paper currency or banknote or that it be used to reduce the weight of a currently used coin shall be punished with imprisonment for not more than five years; in addition thereto, a fine of not more than 1000 yuan may be imposed.

(2) Article 205 of the Criminal Law states that a counterfeit or altered security, postal or revenue stamp, or a financial instrument or materials specified in Article 204 of the Criminal Law shall be confiscated whether or not it belongs to the offender.[11]

(3) Article 209 of the Criminal Law states that a weight or measure not in conformity with the legal standard shall be confiscated whether or not it belongs to the offender.

(4) Article 219 of the Criminal Law states that a forged seal, impression of a seal or signature shall be confiscated whether or not it belongs to the offender.

(5) Article 235 of the Criminal Law states that obscene writings, pictures or objects shall be confiscated, whether or not it belongs to the offender.[12]

(6) Article 265 of the Criminal Law states that if an offence is committed, the opium, morphine, cocaine, heroin, one of their compounds, their seeds or an instrument specially used to smoke opium shall be confiscated whether or not it belongs to the offender.

(7) Article 266 of the Criminal Law states that gambling apparatus at the site or a thing of value found at the gambling table or place for exchange of gambling tokens shall be confiscated whether or not it belongs to the offender.

(8) Article 315 of the Criminal Law states that the taping, pictures or records of private dialogue and conduct without the consent of the individual concerned and the taping, recording or photographic equipment should be confiscated, whether or not the items belong to the offender.

Moreover, Judicial Yuan's Interpretation No. 45 made on 23 October 1954, explains that forfeiture is not necessarily connected to a primary sentence.[13] Further, the standard of proof is different from those in criminal and civil

---

[11] Criminal Law, art. 204 states that a person who manufactures, delivers, or receives an instrument or material with intent that it be used to counterfeit or alter a valuable security or postal or revenue stamp shall be punished with imprisonment for not more than two years; in addition thereto, a fine of not more than 5000 yuan may be imposed.

[12] Criminal Law, art. 235 states that a person who distributes, sells, publicly displays or by other means shows to another person obscene writings, pictures or other objects shall be punished with imprisonment for not more than one year, detention; in lieu thereof, or in addition thereto, a fine of not more than 3000 yuan may be imposed.

[13] When probation (ie suspension) of a primary sentence is ordered, the normal rule is that the probation extends also to subordinate sentences. However, this Interpretation makes clear that confiscation, although a subordinate sentence in nature, is not connected to the primary sentence for purposes of applying this normal rule when probation of a primary sentence has been ordered.

proceedings. The responsibility of raising evidence is the key to forfeiting ill-gotten gains.

The plea bargain process in the Code of Criminal Procedure has no rule about the forfeiture of third-party property. If Taiwan decides to follow the judicial practice of the US,[14] Taiwan can enact laws to forfeit the property which has already been transferred to a third-party. Moreover, the third-party in the plea bargain process will retain a lawyer and sign a document which can be publicly reviewed after signatures by the lawyer, the third-party, and the prosecutor. Therefore, the whole process is not only to safeguard the rights of third-party over such properties but also prevents abuse of process by the prosecutor.

In Taiwan, defendants have tried to argue that expenditures should be deducted from the amount to be forfeited. Deduction here should be understood as a capital expenditure. However, the important question is by what standards are such capital expenditures to be measured. Another difficulty is that the costs to the defendant are usually used for criminal purposes. Since the costs were incurred to further the crime, it should all be forfeited or detained. The essential character of forfeiture is that it is a part of punishment. Any deduction allowed in forfeiture is the same as stating that some part of the defendant's offence is legal. To forfeit the gross income from crime is not injustice. Taiwan should refer to the judicial practice of the US for guidance and expand the basis of forfeiture. As the third-party in the plea bargain process must be represented by a lawyer, the rights of a third-party should be completely protected.

Limited Civil Forfeiture

In Taiwan, only controlled substances and specific instruments of crime provided for in statute are subject to forfeiture without the need for a conviction. Taiwan does not have a general civil forfeiture regime which allows an action brought in court against property. Thus, a defendant who has not been prosecuted or has had charges withdrawn will not have to face forfeiture action by the government.

The owners of seized property can plea to the court for the temporary release of those seized items. But after the temporary release of those properties to the defendant, it is often the case that the defendant will damage or lose the seized properties. Due to the frequency of such occurrences, Taiwanese courts and prosecutors often are not willing to temporarily release such items. Again, Taiwan should consult the US judicial practice of applying proper

---

14   See *Christunas v. United States*, 61 F. Supp. 2d 642 (E.D. Mich. 1999).

protection to those items temporarily released. This can alleviate the burden on the government and enhance enforcement.

CREATING ADMINISTRATIVE FORFEITURE PROCEDURE AND A CIVIL FORFEITURE (NON-CONTENTIOUS) PROCEDURE

Administrative Forfeiture Procedure

Administrative forfeiture procedure should belong to judicial forfeiture. Administrative forfeiture procedure in Taiwan means forfeiture by an administrative court's judgment. The reason for the US to accept administrative forfeiture without judicial order is the concern that the forfeiture could be frustrated by long delays to trial and a verdict in a criminal trial.

From the perspective of social security and protection for plaintiffs and victims, the criminal trial process is too slow to be effective. Administrative forfeiture still can be reviewed by the courts, and the property rights of people will be sufficiently protected. Given the efficiency of meeting administrative needs, administrative forfeiture is likely to be economical and speedy. Taiwan should adopt an administrative forfeiture procedure.

Civil Forfeiture (Non-contentious) Procedure

Taiwan does not have a non-contentious procedure for forfeiting criminal property. The only way to forfeit the ill-gotten gains which has been transferred to a third-party is through the decision made by the court. In judicial practice, a procuratorial organ has no right to proceed with a charge to recover the ill-gotten gains from such a third-party. This is a loophole which can be addressed by adopting the civil forfeiture system applied in the US.

EXPAND THE RANGE OF FORFEITABLE PROPERTY

In Taiwan, the forfeiture in proceeds occurs at the same time as the judgment is given on sentence. Before the judgment, the property can be restrained or seized using the enforcement powers of the prosecutor. But the restraint or seizure is not possible if the property has been transferred to a third-party and cannot be traced. This is a serious inadequacy in the law. Once the property is transferred to a third-party, it could become an obstacle for a prosecutor to investigate.

In the criminal forfeiture procedures in the US, it is possible to go after untraceable proceeds of crime through the doctrine of substituted property which allows forfeiture of offender's legitimate property as substitute for the tainted property which cannot be located anymore. This idea exists to some extent in Taiwan laws which allow collection of untraceable proceeds from the offender but it would be worthwhile to have a general provision which allows for actual forfeiture of substituted property.

REVISE THE EVIDENTIAL AND PROCEDURAL RULES FOR FORFEITURE

Burden of Proof

According to the Code of Criminal Procedure, the prosecutor's responsibilities of raising evidence to prove the elements of the crime are the same with the elements of forfeiture. In doing so, the standard of proof by the prosecution is proof beyond reasonable doubt. This high standard of proof can cause delays in gathering sufficient evidence for the prosecution, and as a result the defendant will usually have enough time to transfer away their property safely and completely.

In the US, however, the burden of proof is on the defendant or applicant to demonstrate their innocent interest in the property. The shift of the burden of proof from the prosecutor to the defendant would make forfeiture more efficient in Taiwan.

Right of Silence

As mentioned already, a defendant cannot be prosecuted for perjury if he lies while testifying at this trial. The enjoyment of such an immunity together with the right of silence means that the chances of recovering proceeds of crime will depend heavily on the work of the investigative agencies. If the defendant is a money-laundering organization, for instance laundering money in cross-border activities with a bank in a developing country, the investigation could fail due to the lack of international co-operation. In order to improve enforcement, Taiwan should revise the scope of offences regarding destruction of evidence and perjury by an accused at his trial.

REVENUE GAINED FROM FORFEITURE IN A CRIMINAL INVESTIGATION

The revenue gained from forfeiture ought not to become part of the national financial resource, and therefore should be excluded from the national treasury. Instead, it should be shared by the relevant administrative agencies. Apart from the common properties, technology nowadays is changing fast, and along with various real properties, they are often used in innovative ways to commit crime, and they can become serious obstacles to investigative actions.

The forfeited properties and funds can be reinvested into the investigation agency and provide a useful source of income by removing the financial strain on the national resources. Furthermore, in taking the seized property to an investigation agency for use in official business, the investigation staff at all levels can see their achievements in reality and this serves as encouragement to their work, and the benefits of a strong investigation staff will be shared with the society as a whole.

However, if the seized property eventually belongs to the national treasury department, the investigation staff will not experience the fruits of their own efforts, and in solely relying on the national financial budget which is often short, the investigation of crime can be hindered critically by lack of proper funding or equipment, and in turn society as a whole will suffer.

CONCLUSION

There are numerous rules about forfeiture in the Criminal Code and the other affiliated regulations (see for example Article 33-1 of the Statute for Narcotics Hazard Control 1955). However, these rules do not detail how forfeiture should be determined and ordered. The responsibilities of raising evidence, the rules of evidence, even the rules for subpoenas are found in the Code of Criminal Procedure.

With reference to the experience of the US, Taiwan should strengthen the system of forfeiture in order to more effectively strip criminals of their ill-gotten gains and thus reduce the crime rate. Strengthening the skills of investigators is not enough for crime prevention, as the government currently does not support crime investigation sufficiently in financial terms.

In order to block fully the motivation to commit most crimes, Taiwan should introduce administrative forfeiture and civil forfeiture legal frameworks. With the increasing amount of transnational criminal activity, Taiwan should expand the range of forfeitable property.

In order to facilitate the process of the forfeiture procedure, Taiwan should revise the evidence rules for forfeiture procedures. The enlargement of international cooperation and facilitation of criminal investigations will force Taiwan to enact a programme for sharing confiscated property.[15]

---

[15]   See Money Laundering Control Act, art. 12-1, which states that:

The Ministry of Justice may distribute the confiscated property or property interests in whole or in part to a foreign government, foreign institution or international organization which enters a treaty or agreement in accordance with Article 14 of this Act to assist our government in confiscating the property or property interests obtained by an offender from his or her commission of a crime or crimes.

The Executive Yuan shall promulgate regulations for management, distribution and use of the property or property interests mentioned in the preceding two paragraphs.

Index